fluffy

Published by Jonathan Cape 2007
First published by Cabanon Press 2003–5

2 4 6 8 10 9 7 5 3

Copyright © Simone Lia 2003, 2004, 2005

Simone Lia has asserted her right under the Copyright,
Designs and Patents Act 1988 to be identified as the author
of this work

First published in one volume Great Britain in 2007
by Jonathan Cape
Random House, 20 Vauxhall Bridge Road,
London SW1V 2SA

The Random House Group Limited Reg. No. 954009
www.randomhouse.co.uk

A CIP catalogue record for this book is available
from the British Library

ISBN 9780224080484

Printed and bound in China by C&C Offset Printing Co., Ltd.

Part 1

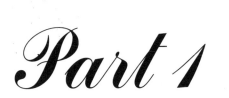

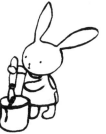

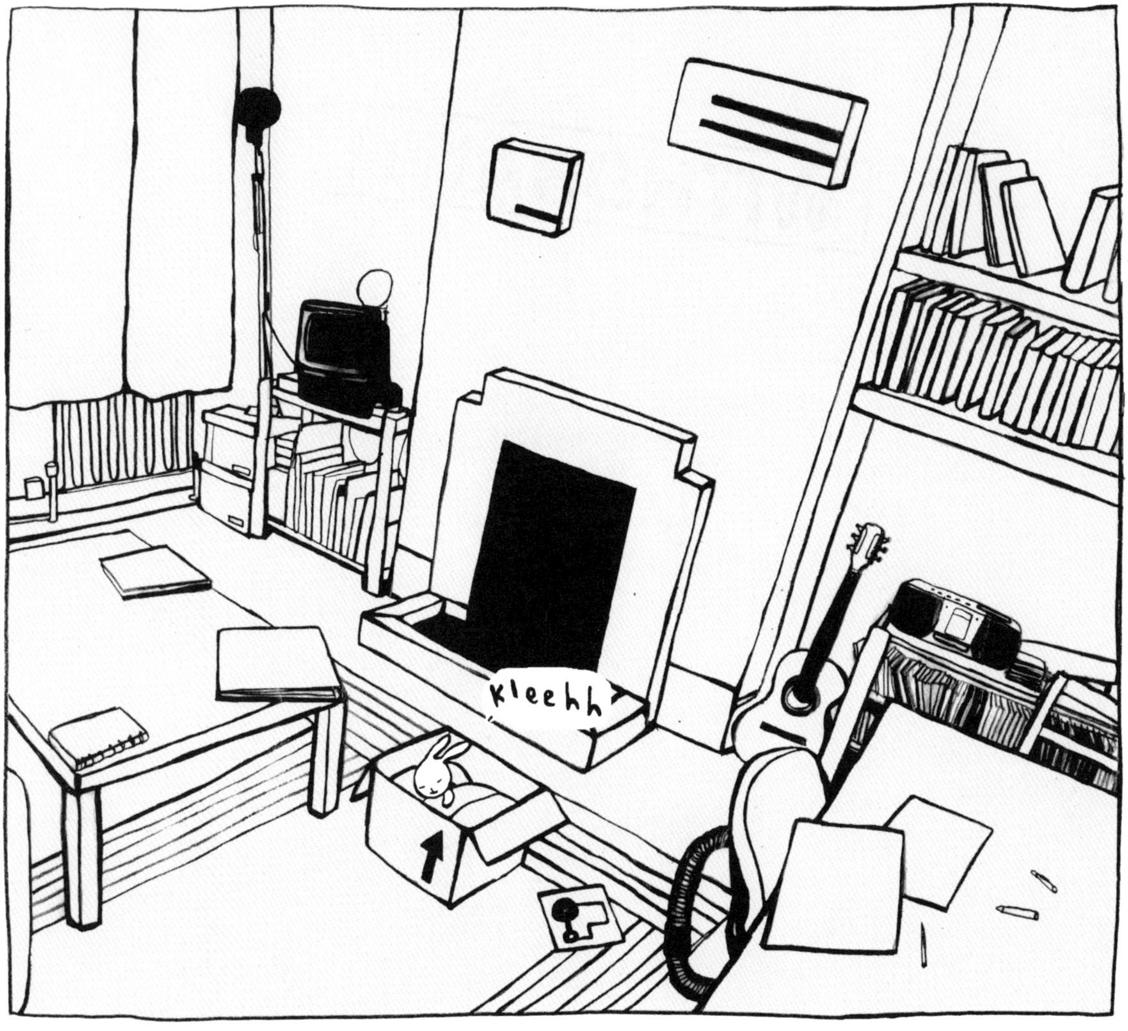
kleehh

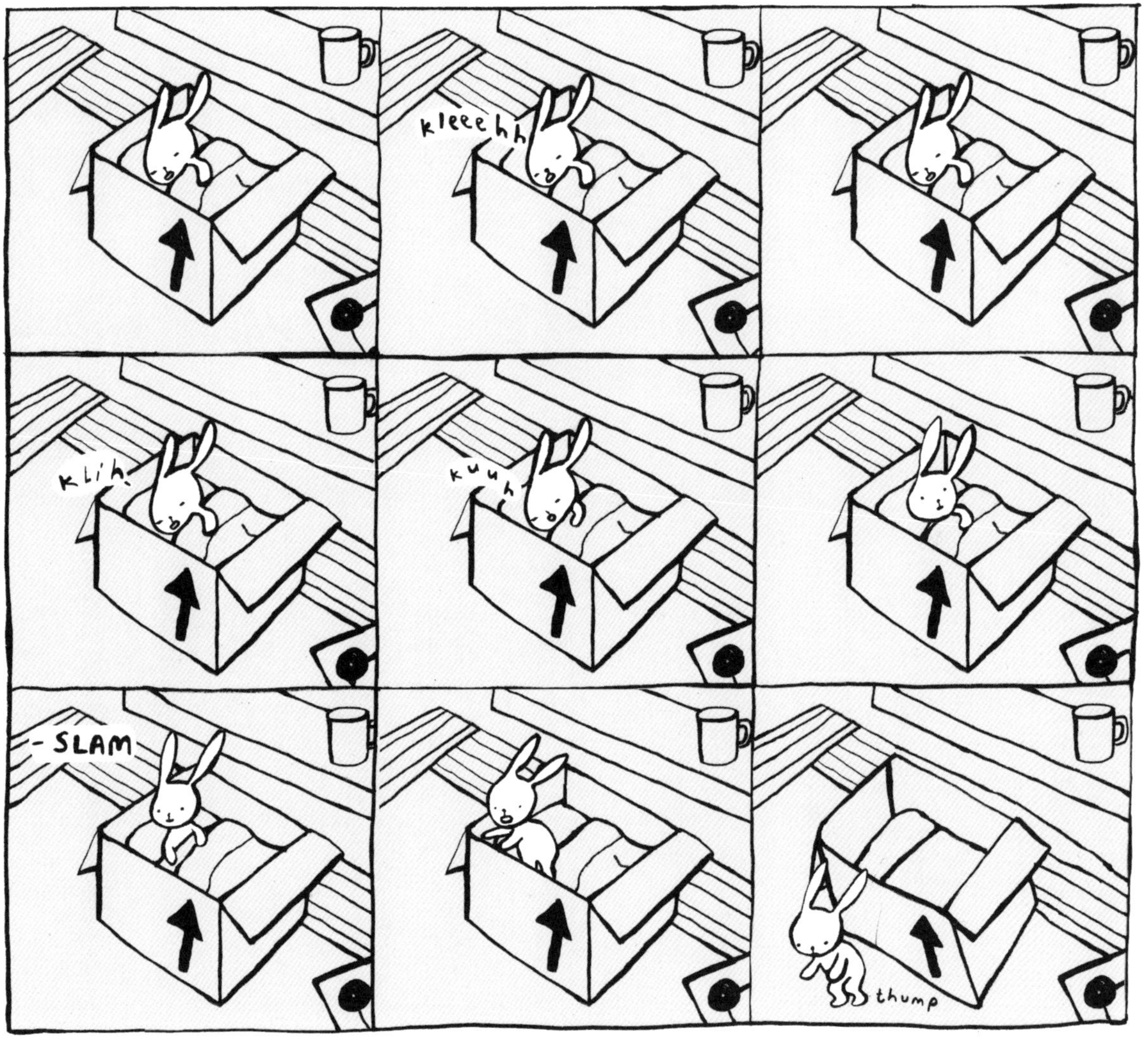
kleeehh
klih
kuuh
-SLAM
thump

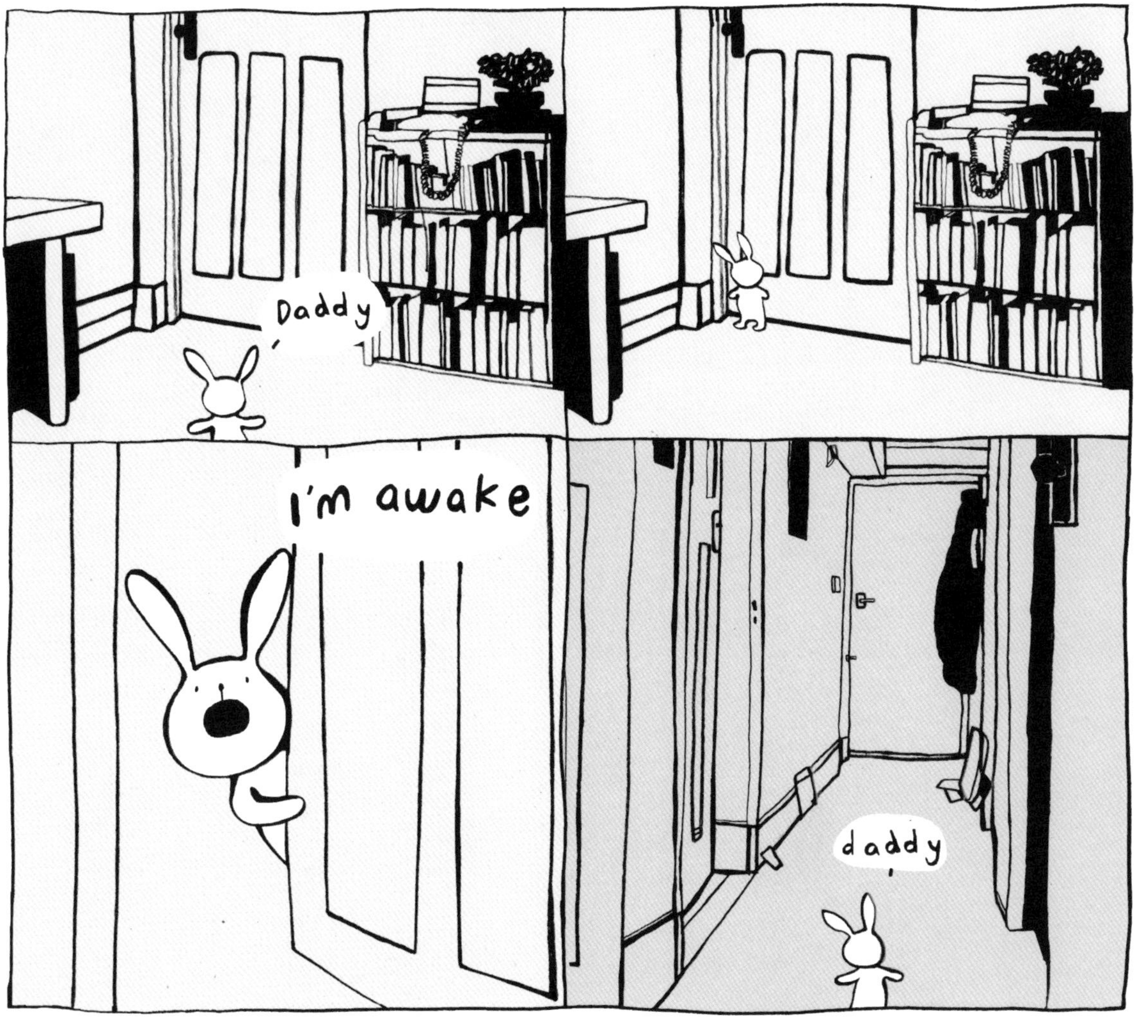
Daddy
I'm awake
daddy

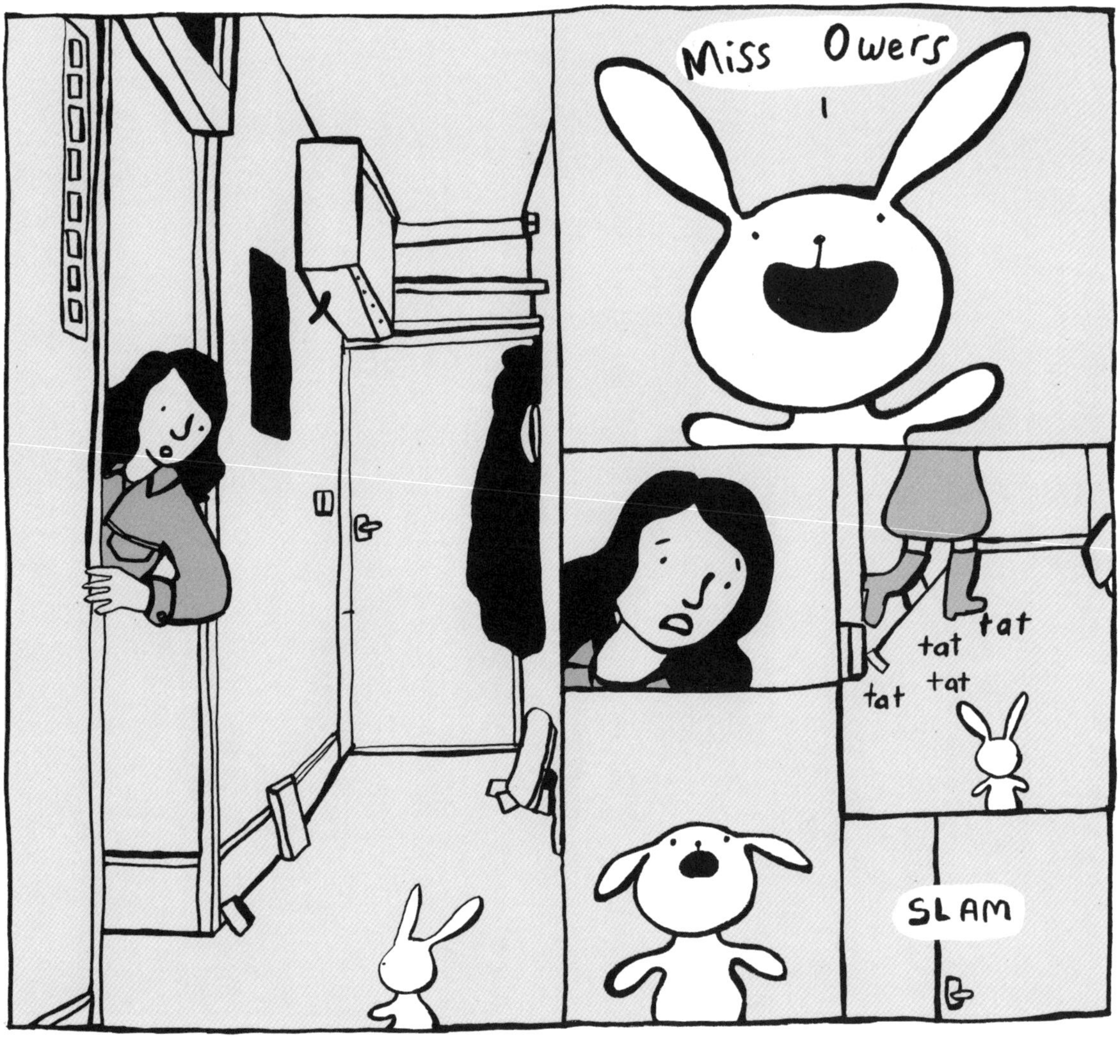
Miss Owers
!
tat
tat
tat
tat
tat
SLAM

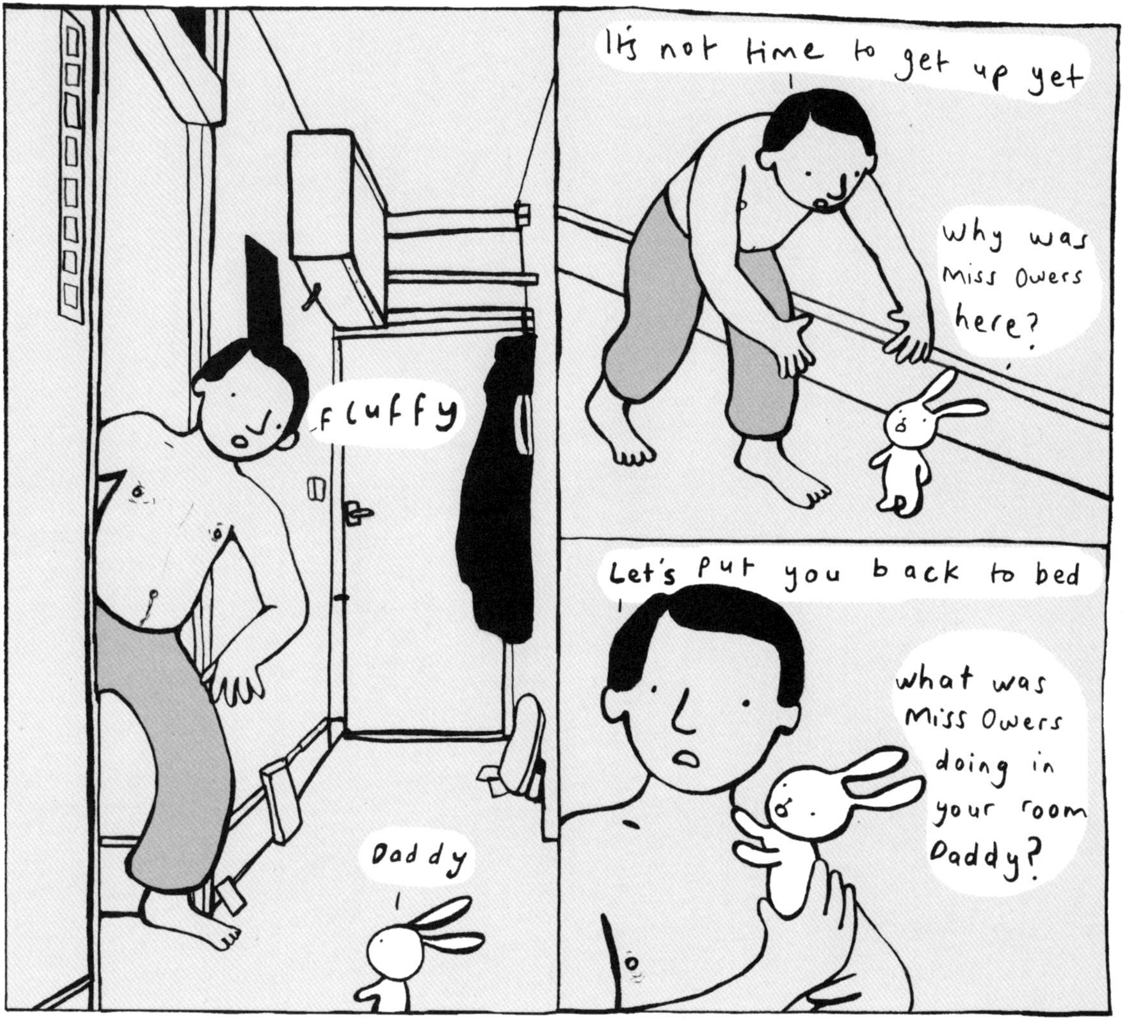
fluffy
Daddy
It's not time to get up yet
Why was Miss Owers here?
Let's put you back to bed
what was Miss Owers doing in your room Daddy?

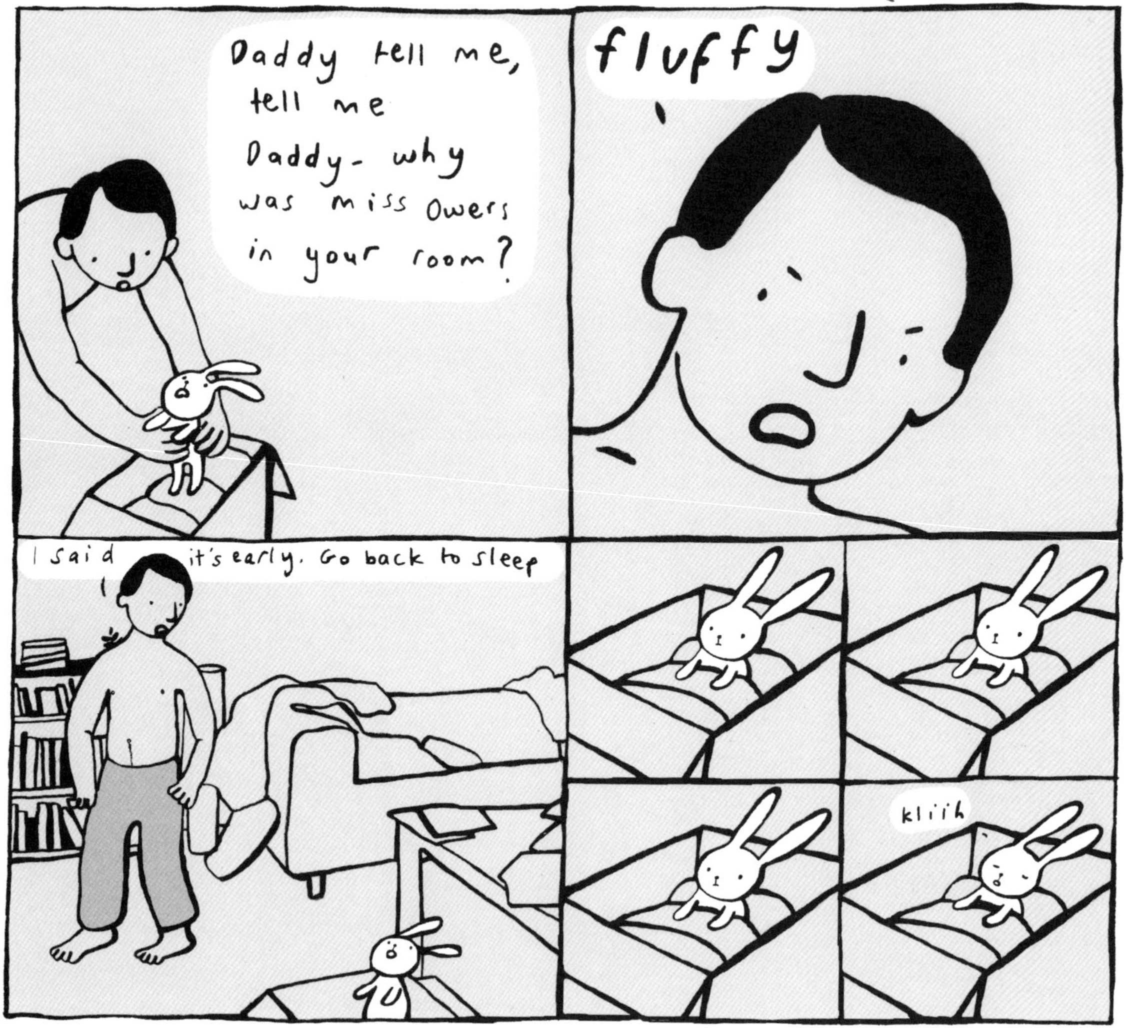
Daddy tell me, tell me Daddy- why was miss Owers in your room?
fluffy
I said it's early. Go back to sleep
kliih

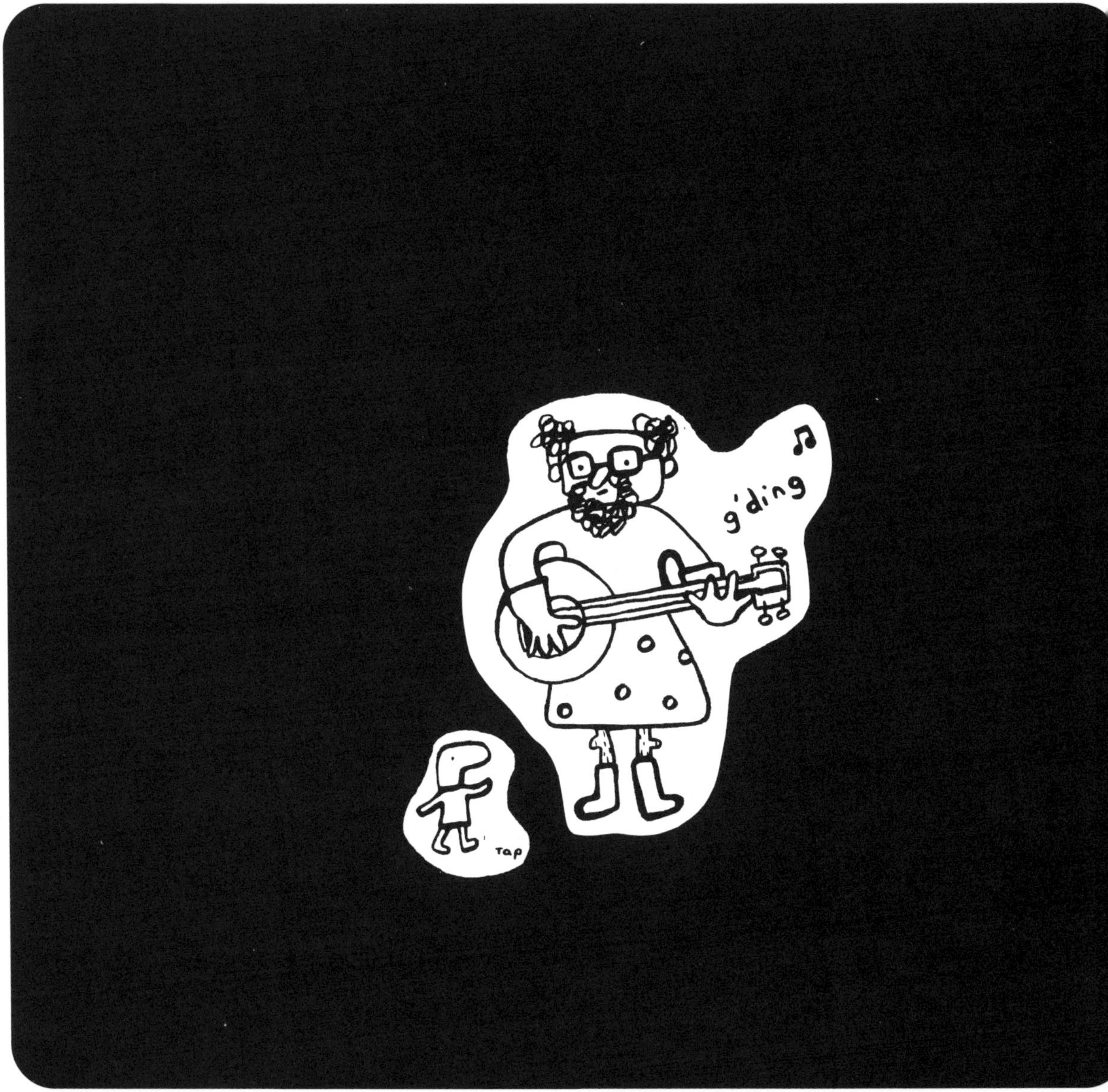
g'ding
tap

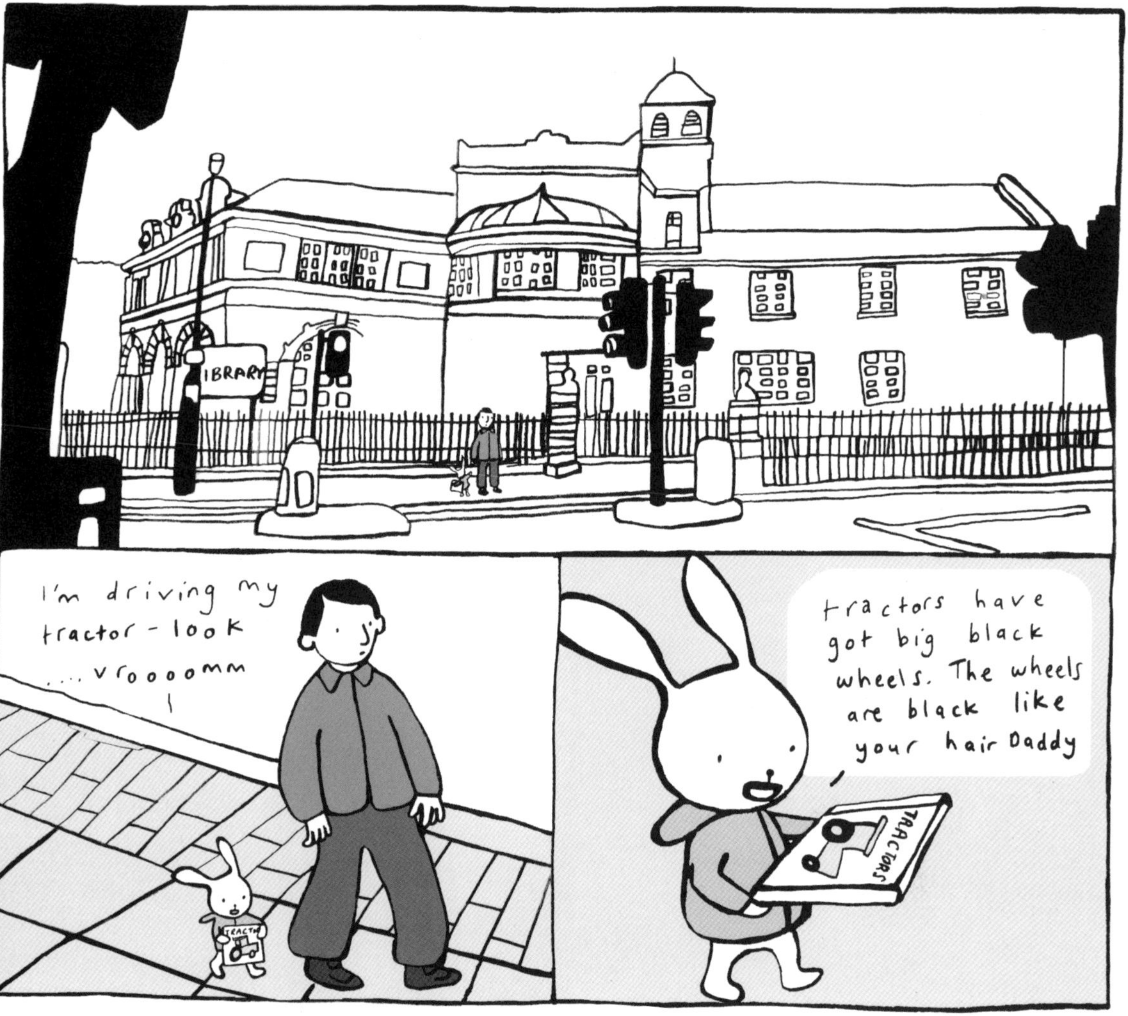

LIBRARY
I'm driving my tractor - look ....vroooomm
TRACTORS
tractors have got big black wheels. The wheels are black like your hair Daddy
TRACTORS

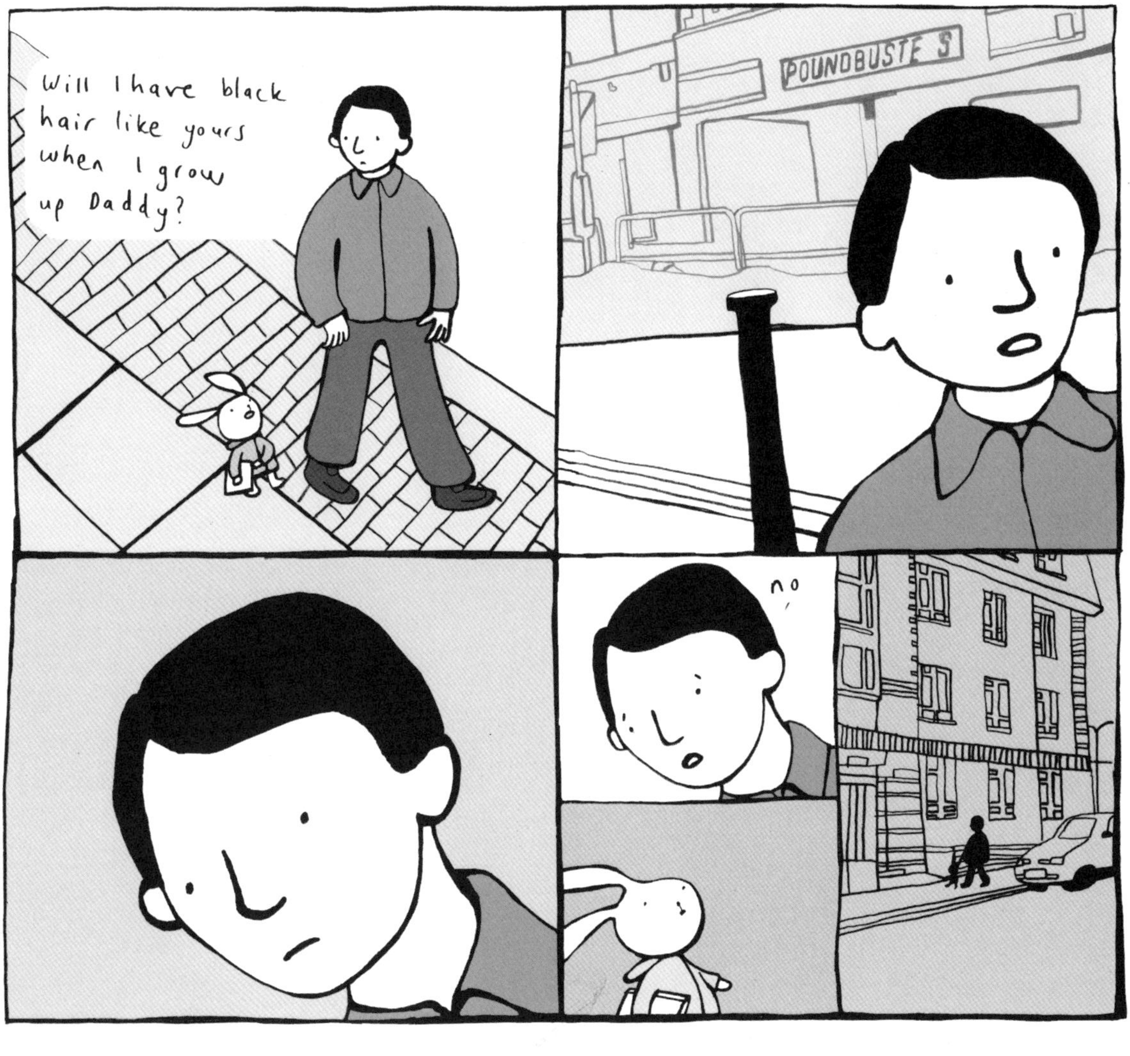
Will I have black hair like yours when I grow up Daddy?
POUNDBUSTE S
no

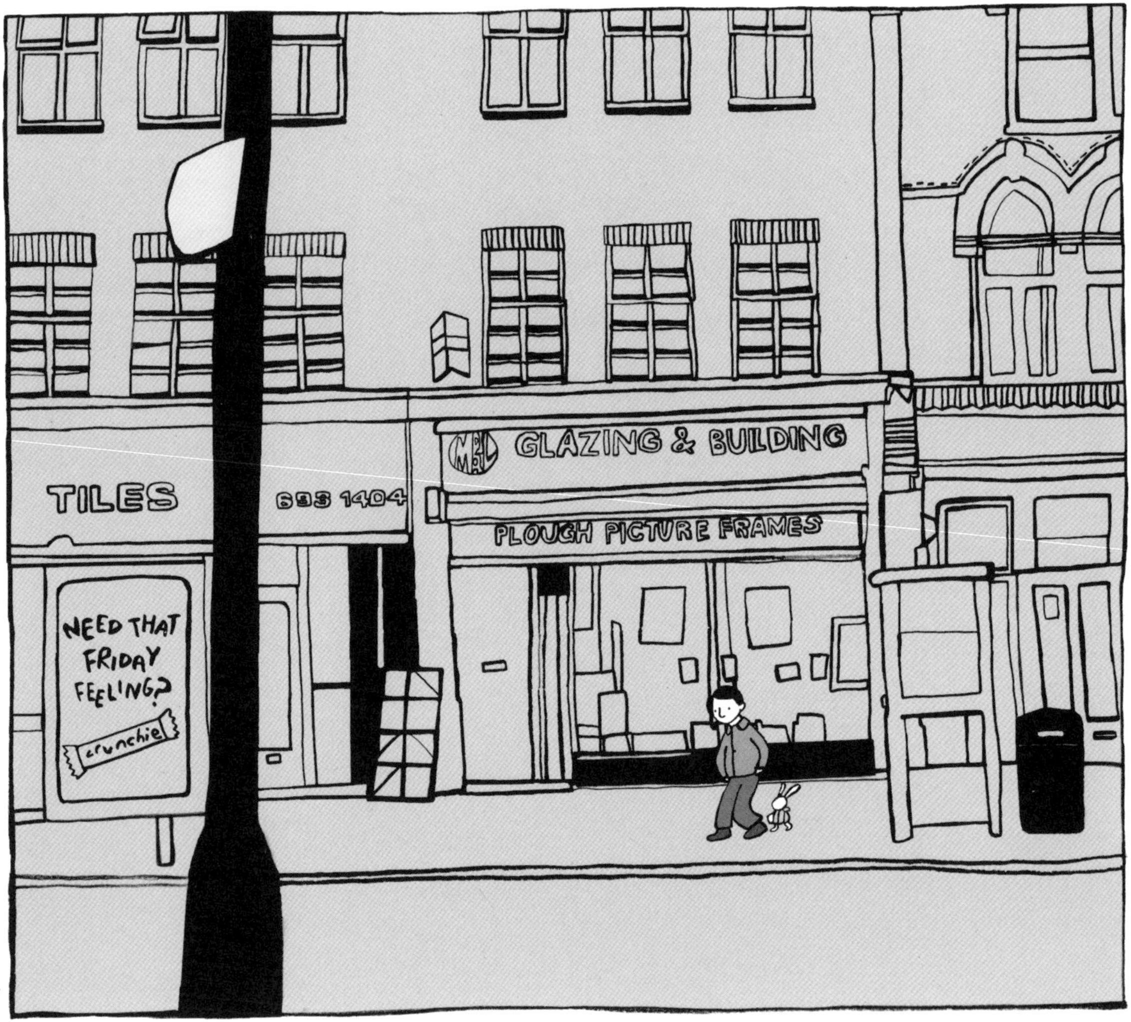
GLAZING & BUILDING
TILES
693 1404
PLOUGH PICTURE FRAMES
NEED THAT FRIDAY FEELING?
crunchie

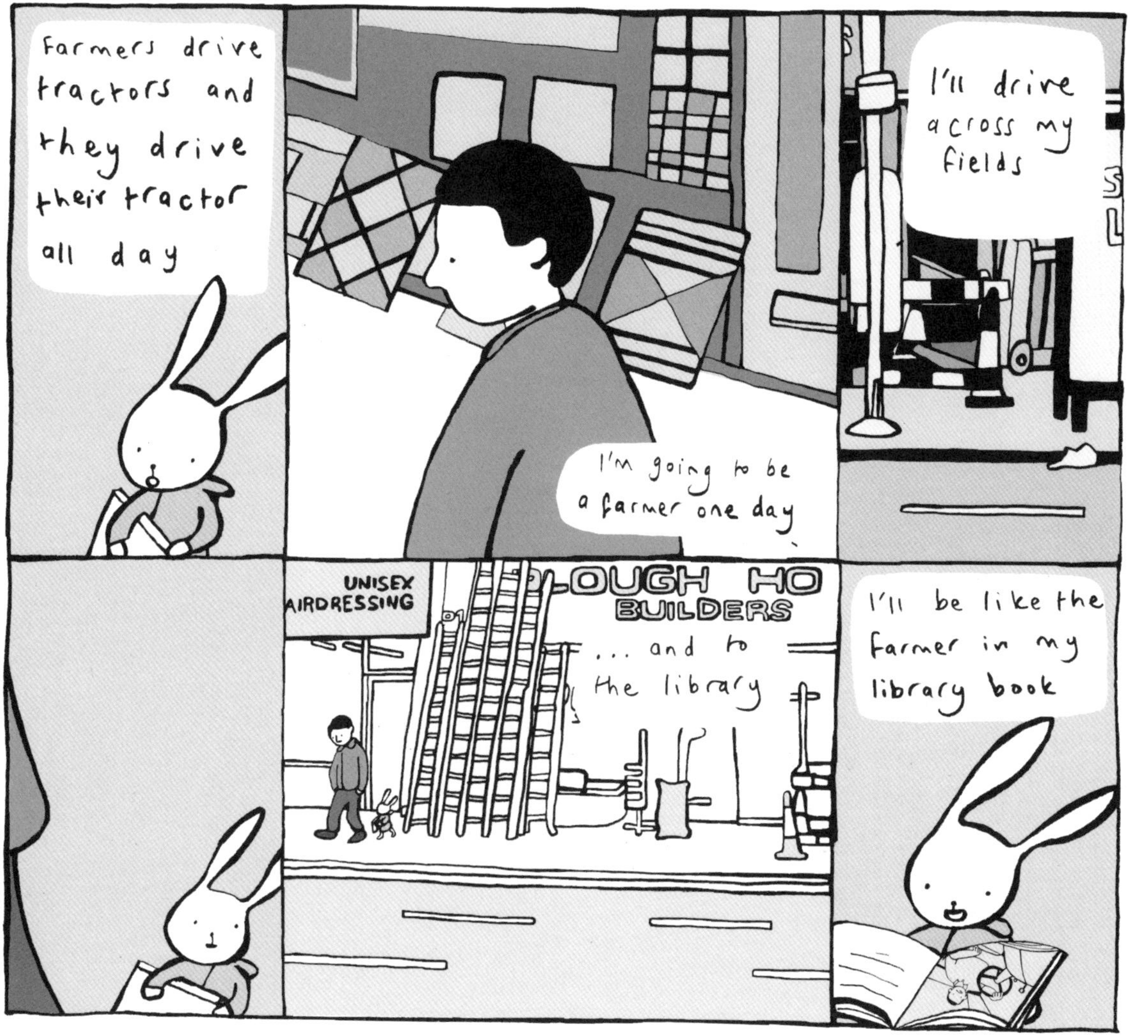
Farmers drive tractors and they drive their tractor all day
I'm going to be a farmer one day
I'll drive across my fields
UNISEX AIRDRESSING
LOUGH HO BUILDERS
... and to the library
I'll be like the farmer in my library book

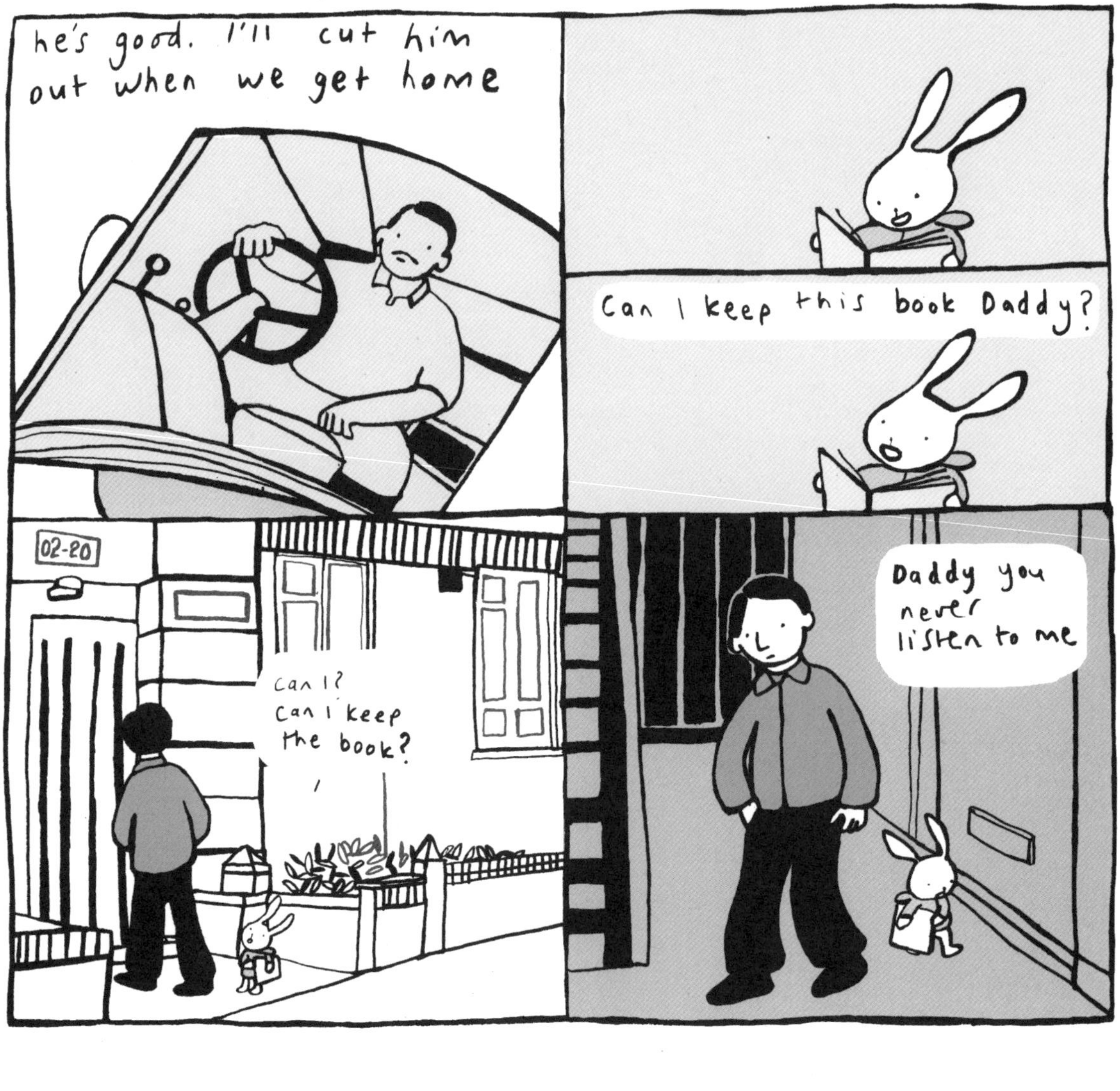
he's good. I'll cut him out when we get home
Can I keep this book Daddy?
02-20
Can I? Can I keep the book?
Daddy you never listen to me

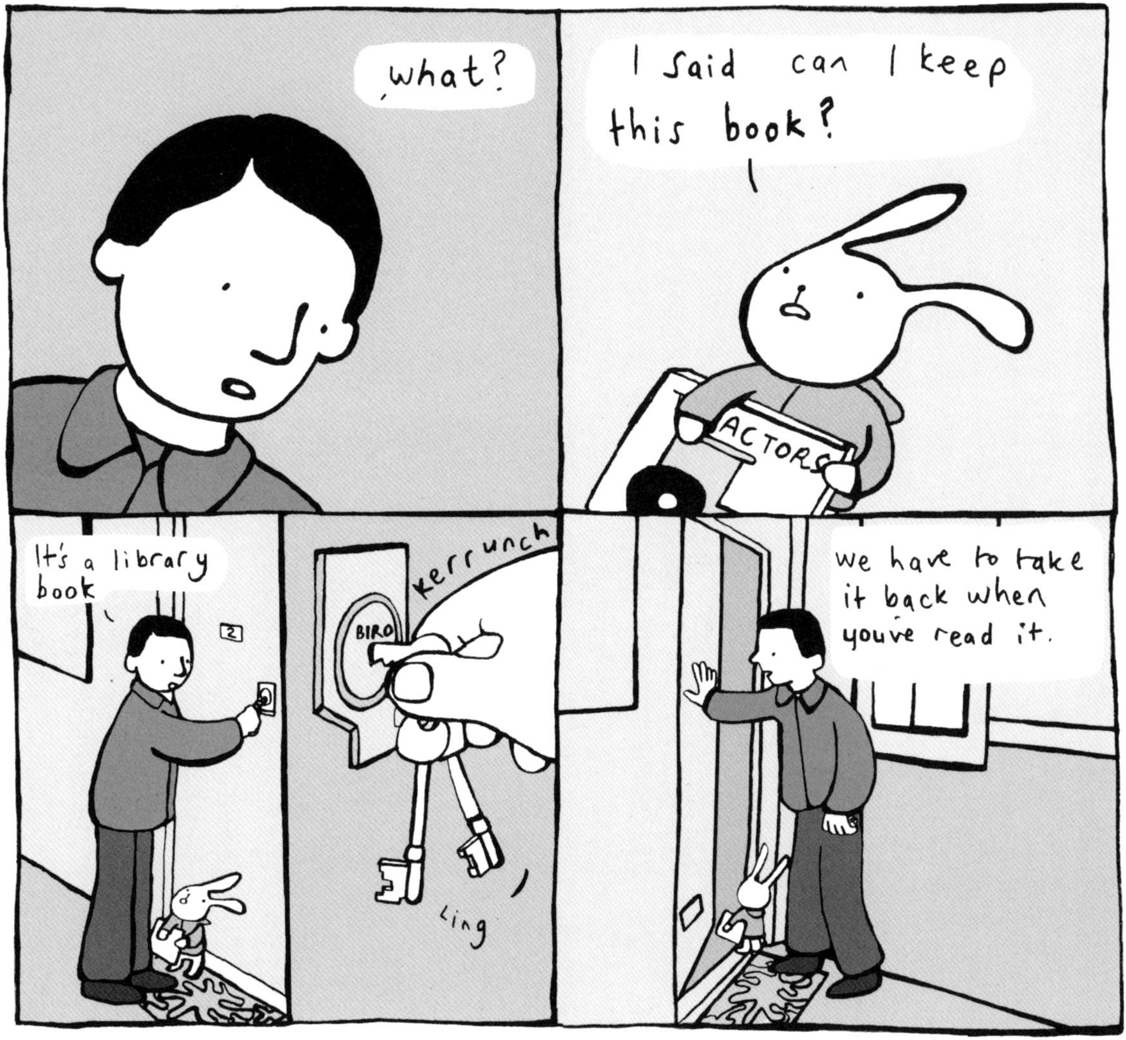
what?
I said can I keep this book?
ACTORS
It's a library book
2
BIRO
kerrrunch
Ling
we have to take it back when you've read it.

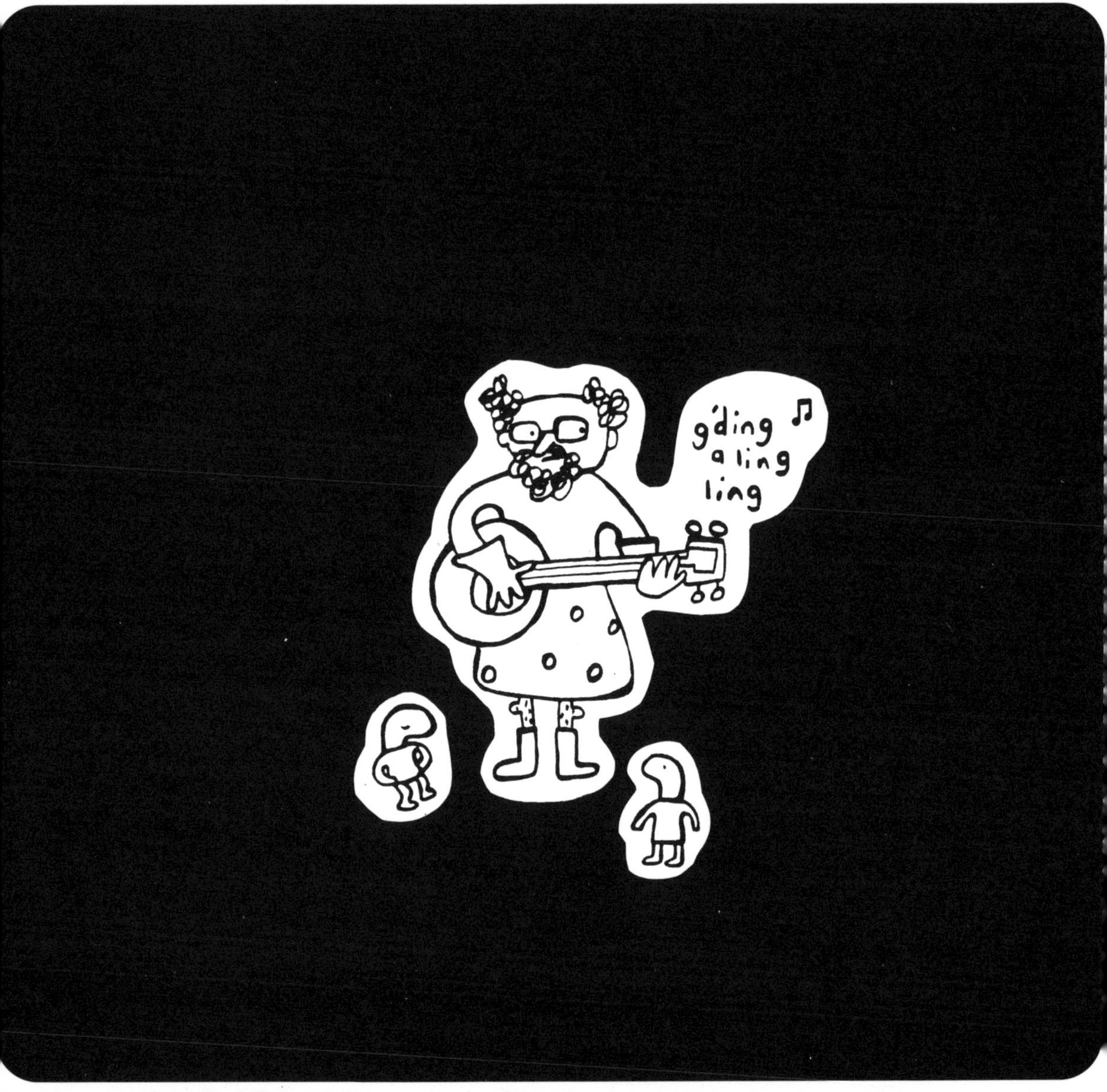
g'ding a ling ling ♫

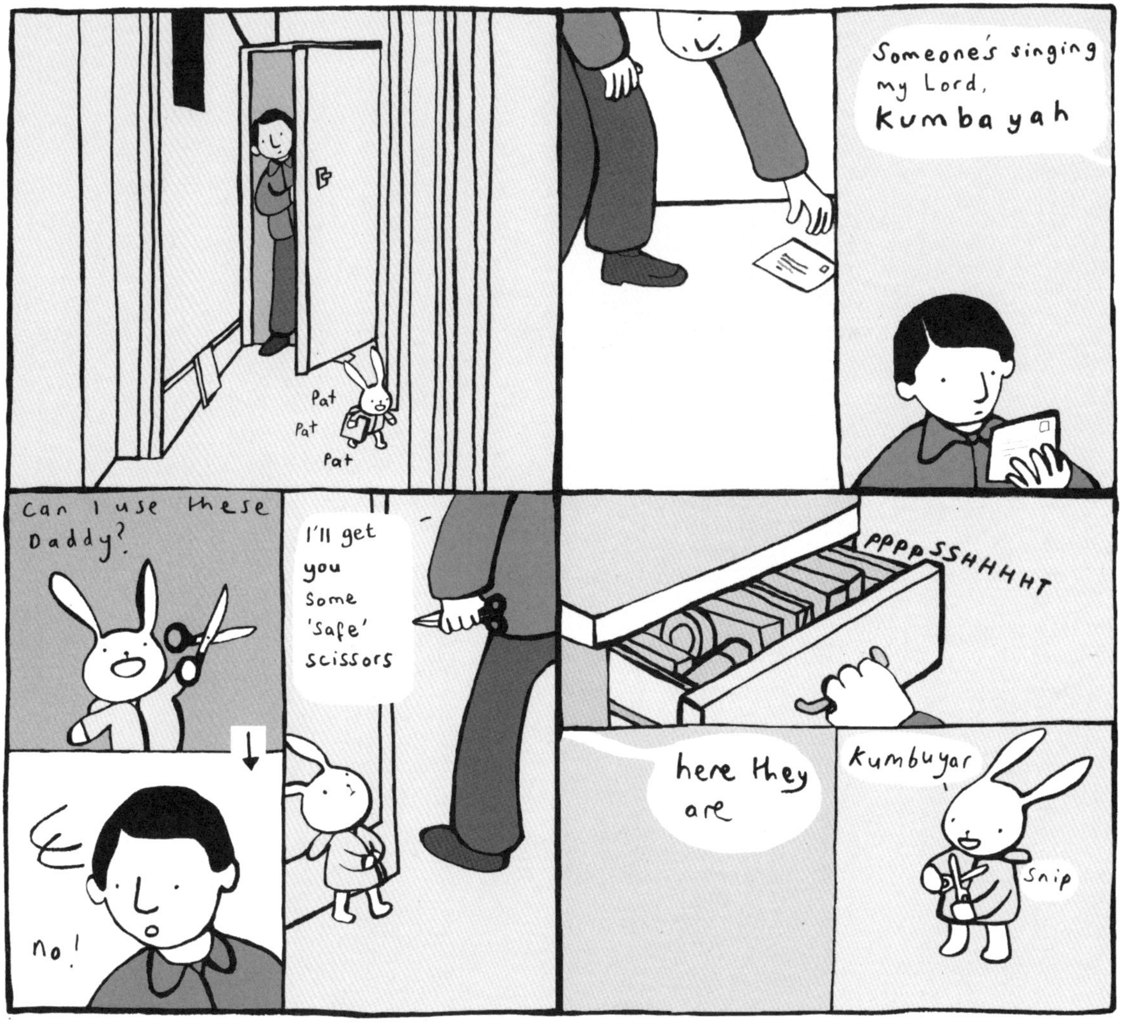
Pat
Pat
Pat
Someone's singing my Lord, Kumbayah
Can I use these Daddy?
no!
I'll get you some 'safe' scissors
PPPPSSHHHHT
here they are
Kumbuyar
Snip

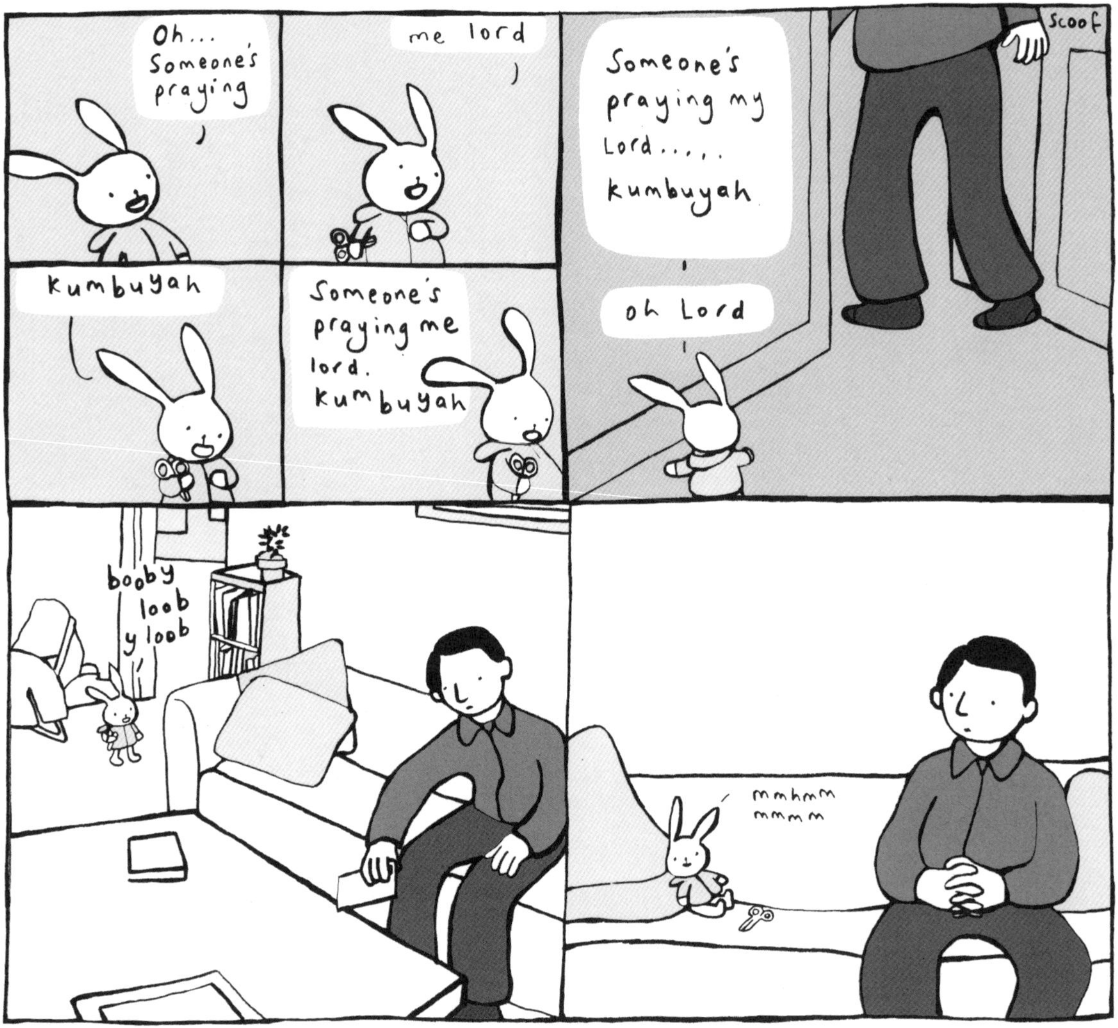
Oh...
Someone's praying
me lord
kumbuyah
Someone's praying me lord. kumbuyah
Someone's praying my Lord..... kumbuyah
oh Lord
scoof
booby loob y loob
mmhmm mmmm

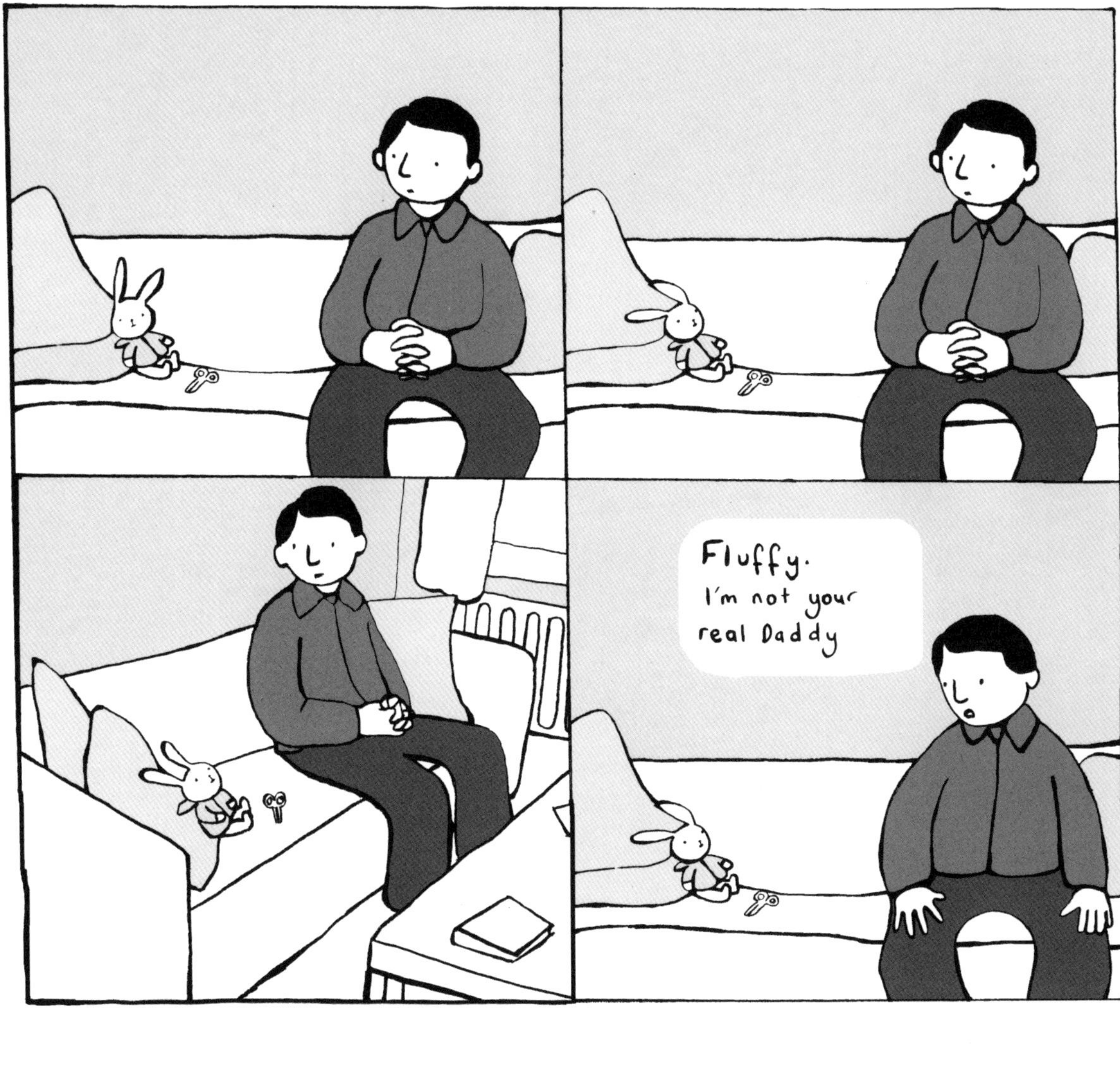
Fluffy.
I'm not your real Daddy

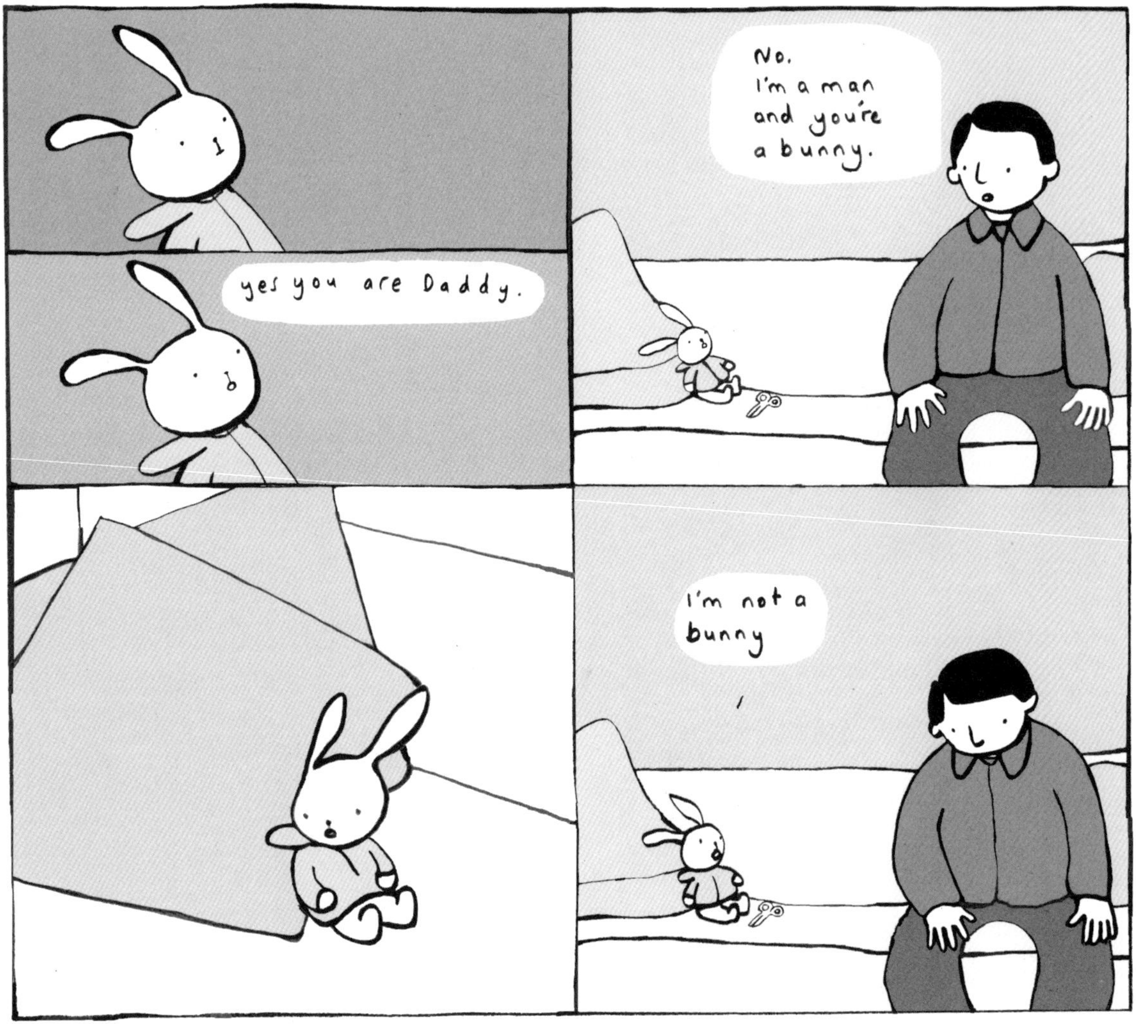
yes you are Daddy.
No. I'm a man and you're a bunny.
I'm not a bunny

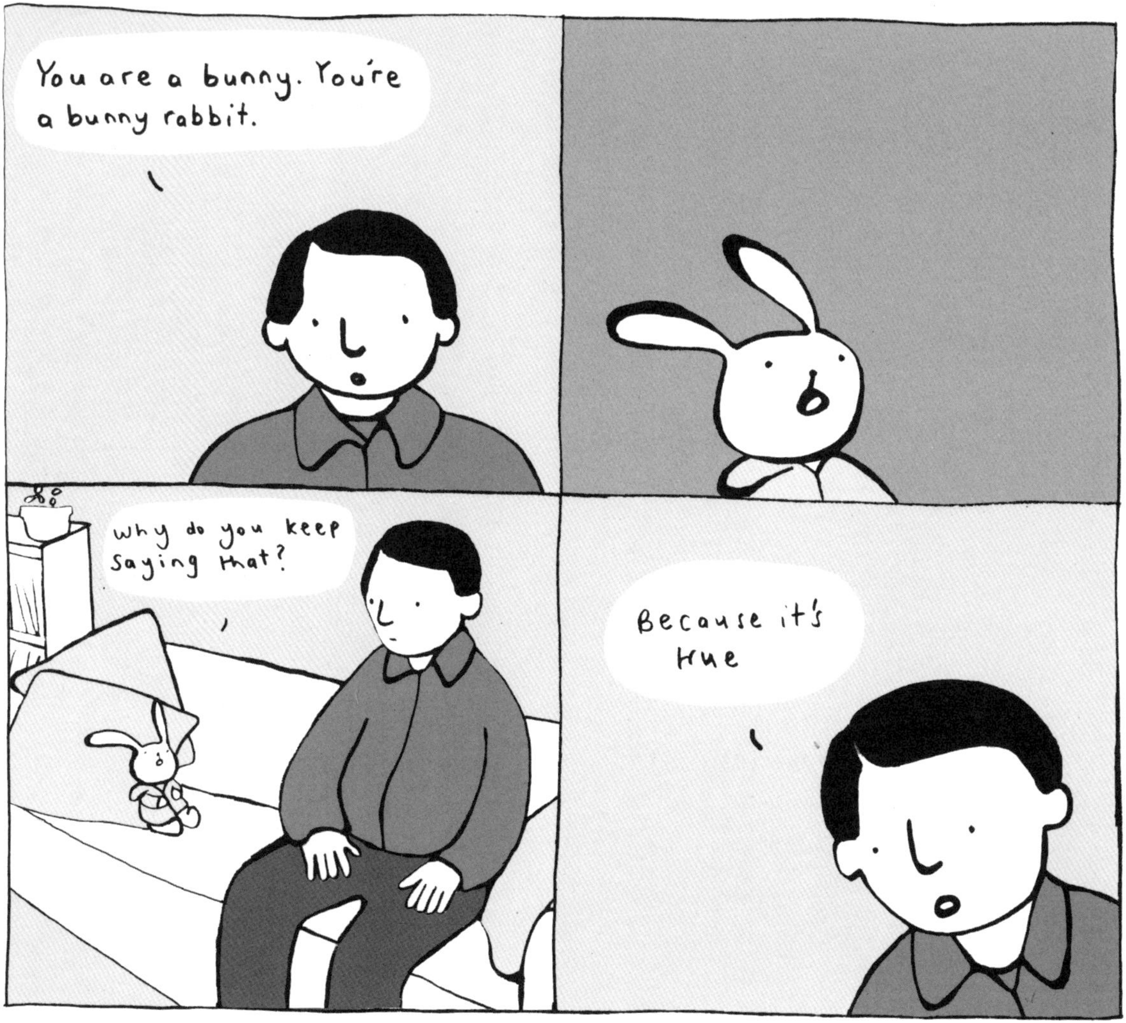
You are a bunny. You're a bunny rabbit.
why do you keep saying that?
Because it's true

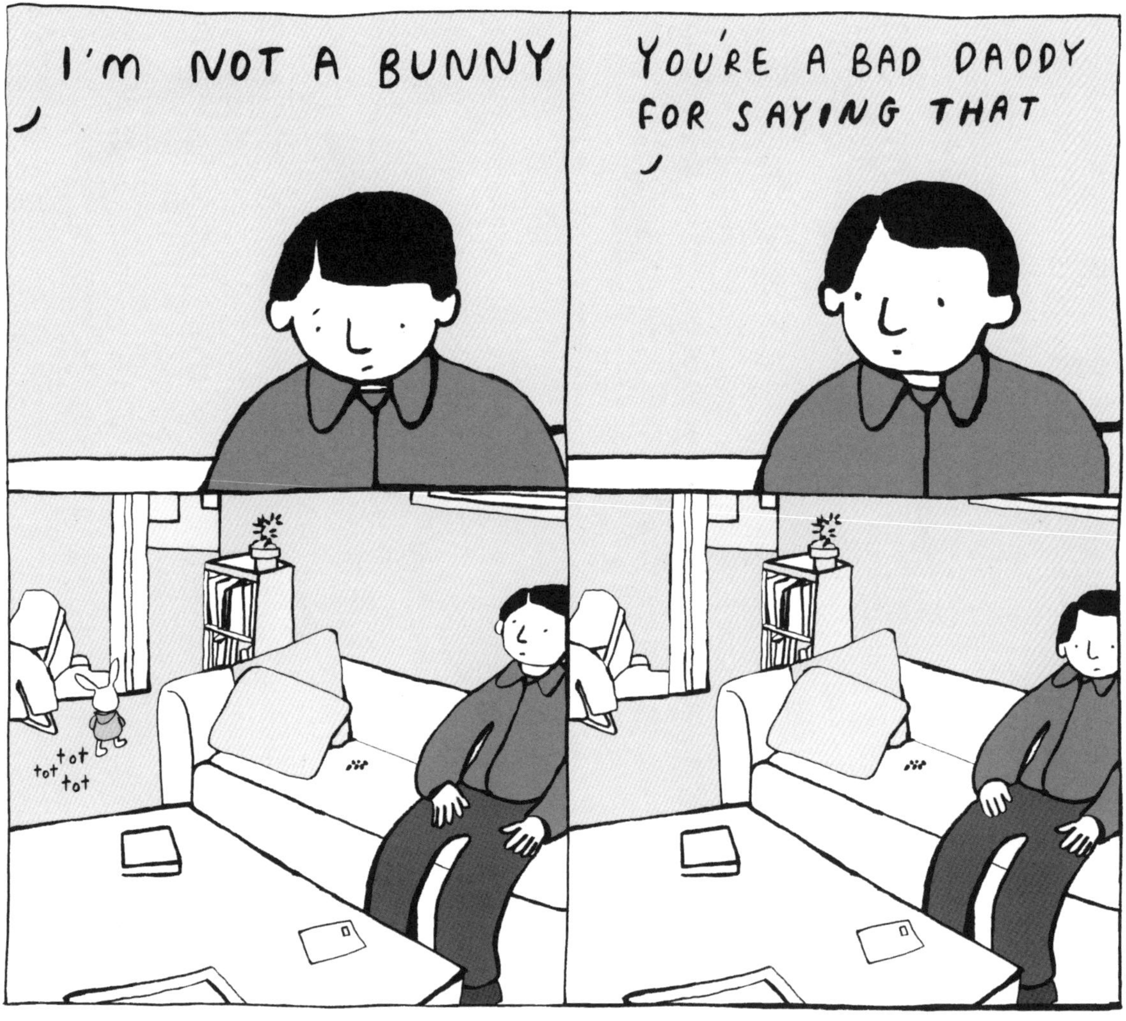
I'M NOT A BUNNY
YOU'RE A BAD DADDY FOR SAYING THAT
tot tot tot tot

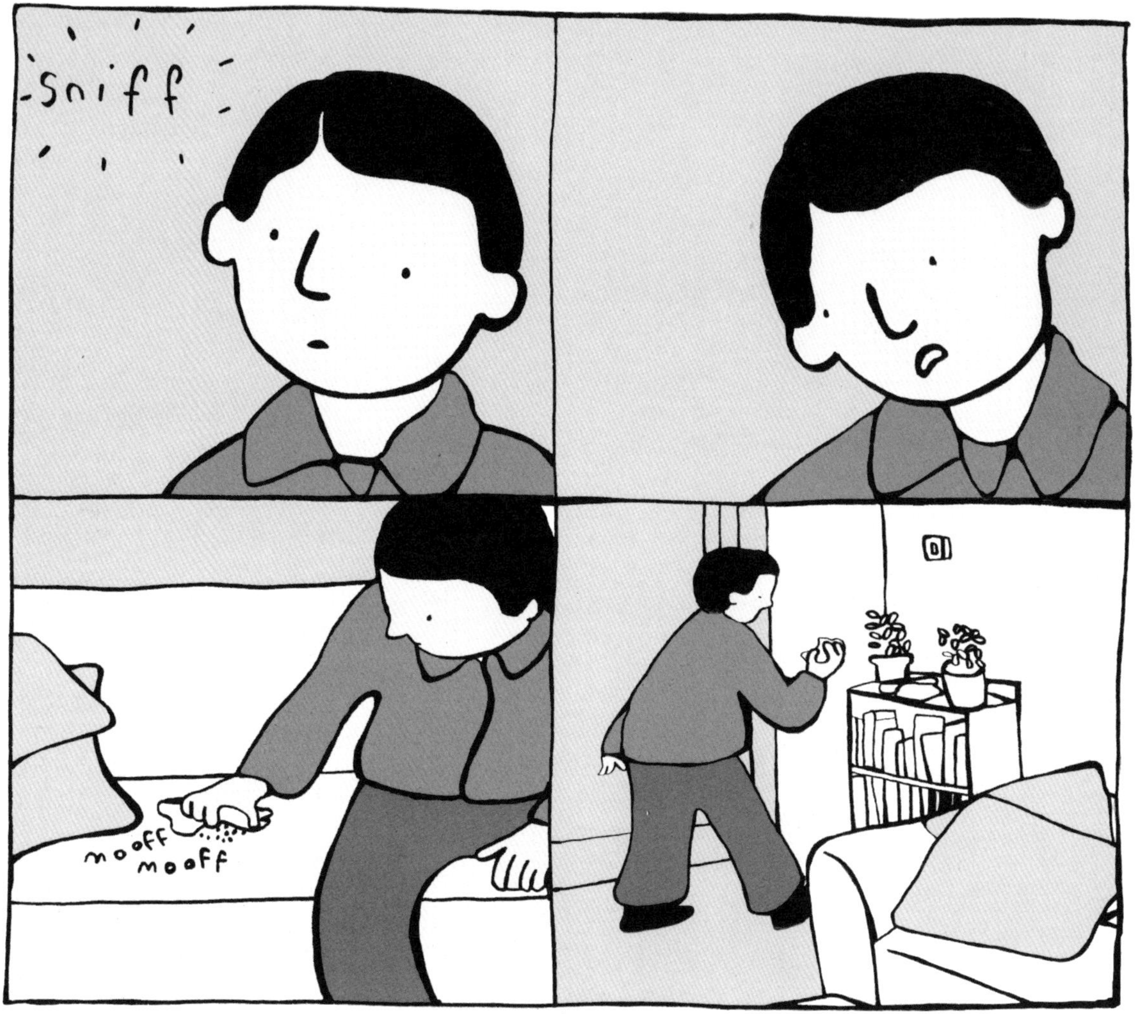
sniff
mooff
mooff

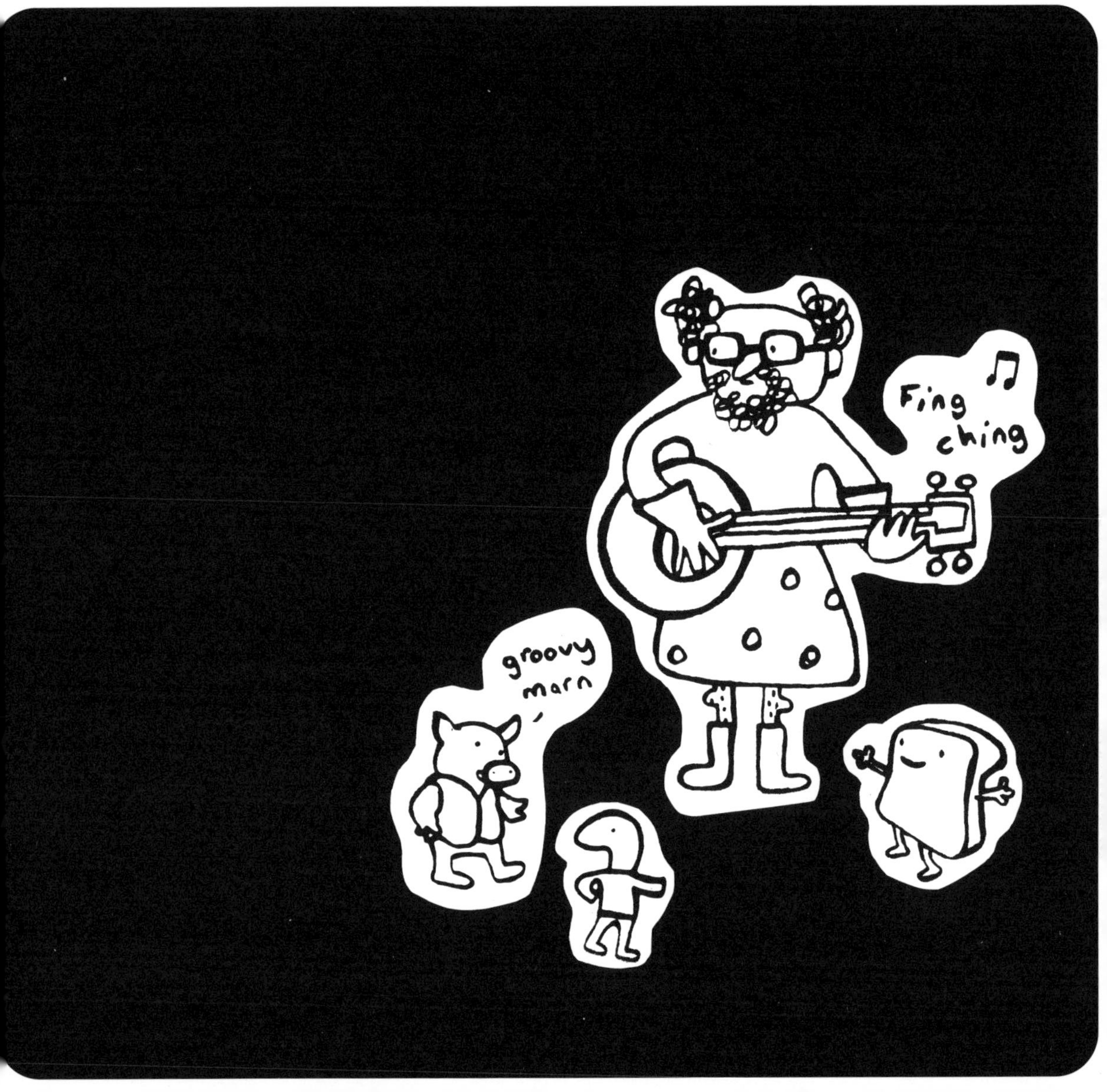

Fing ching
groovy marn

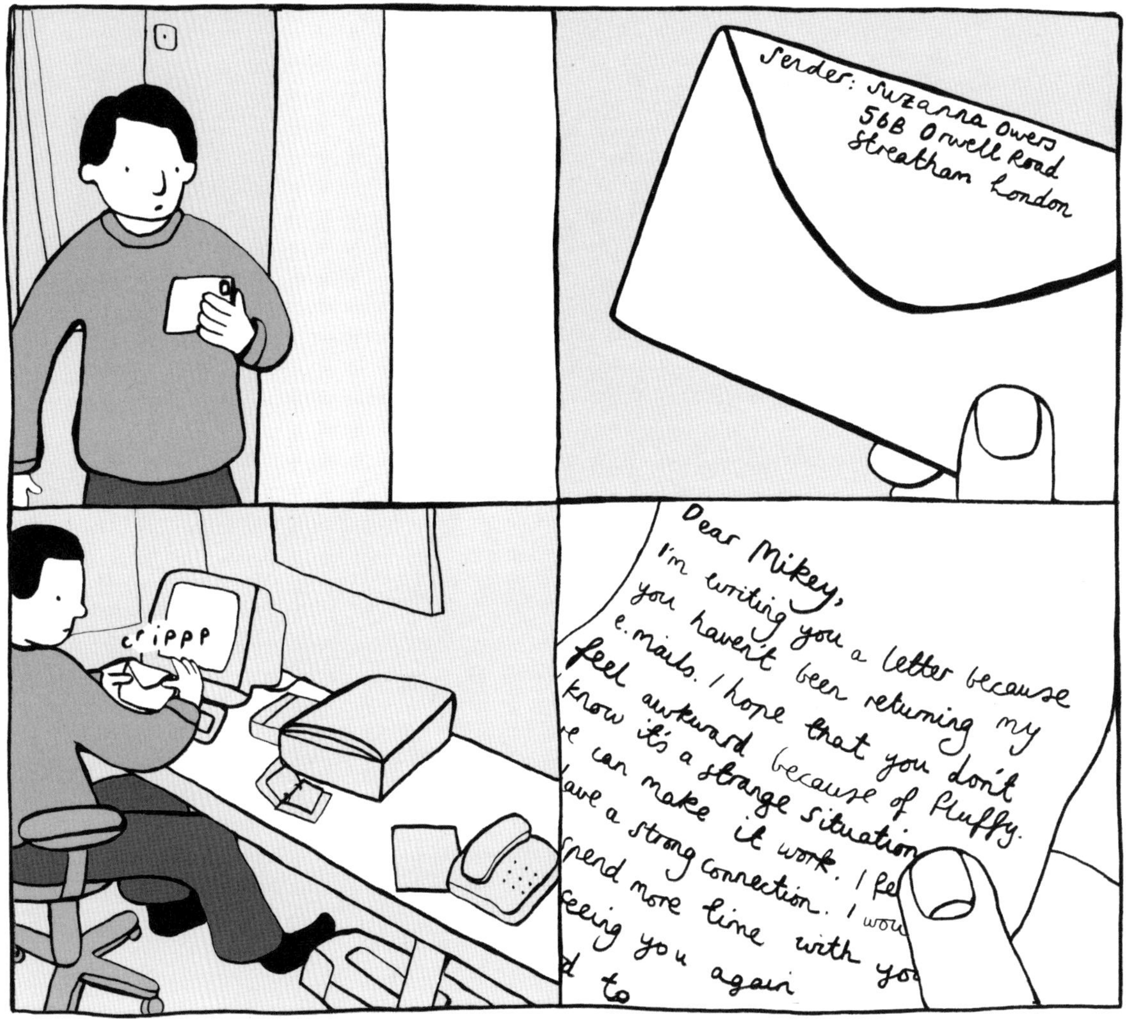
Sender: Suzanna Owens
56B Orwell Road
Streatham London
crippp
Dear Mikey,
I'm writing you a letter because
you haven't been returning my
e.mails. I hope that you don't
feel awkward because of Fluffy.
know it's a strange situation
e can make it work. I fe
ave a strong connection. I wou
pend more time with yo
eeing you again
d to

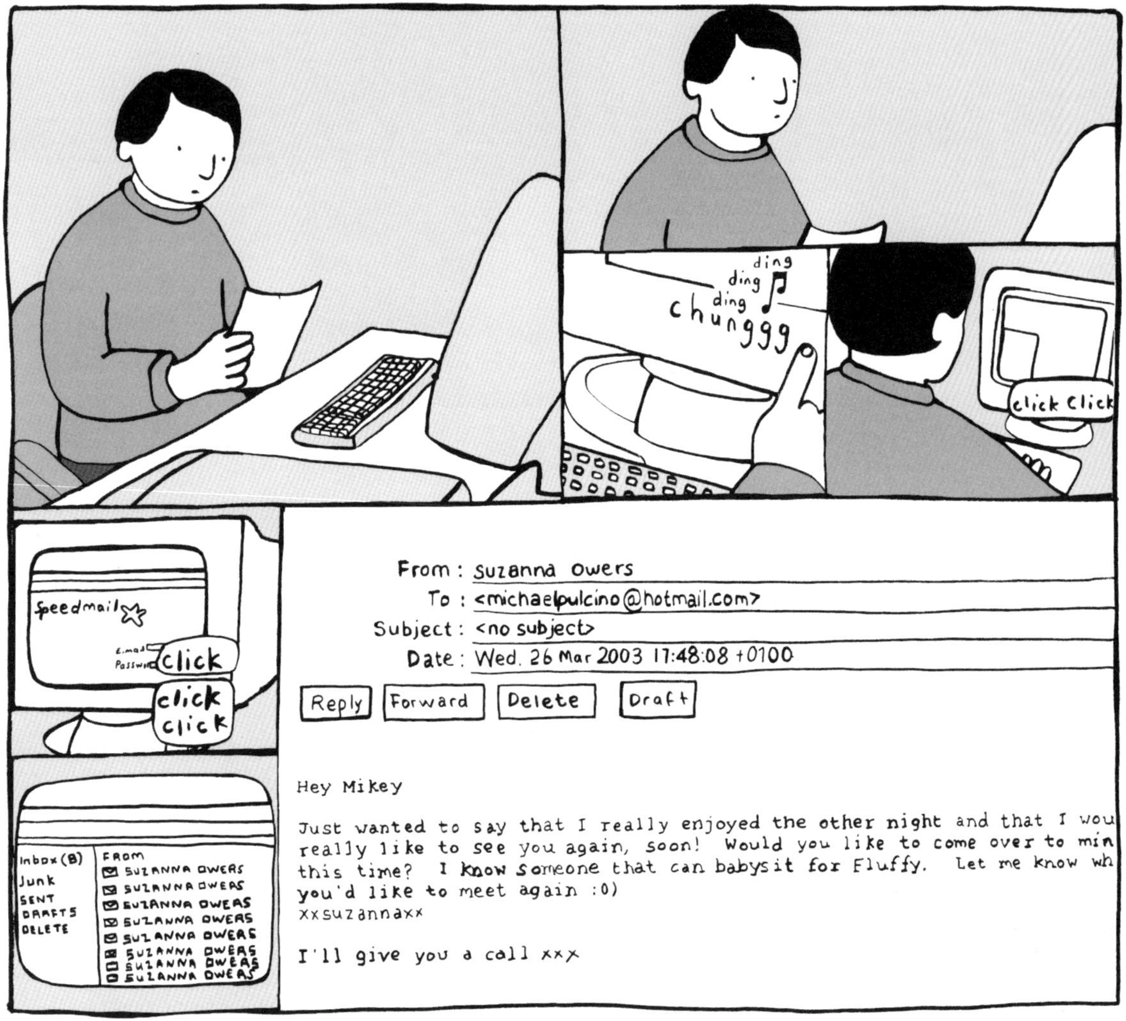

ding
ding
ding
chungggg
click click
speedmail
click
click
click
Inbox (8)
Junk
SENT
DRAFTS
DELETE
FROM
SUZANNA OWERS
SUZANNA OWERS
SUZANNA OWERS
SUZANNA OWERS
SUZANNA OWERS
SUZANNA OWERS
SUZANNA OWERS
SUZANNA OWERS
From : suzanna owers
To : <michaelpulcino@hotmail.com>
Subject : <no subject>
Date : Wed. 26 Mar 2003 17:48:08 +0100
Reply
Forward
Delete
Draft
Hey Mikey
Just wanted to say that I really enjoyed the other night and that I wou
really like to see you again, soon! Would you like to come over to min
this time? I know someone that can babysit for Fluffy. Let me know wh
you'd like to meet again :0)
xxsuzannaxx
I'll give you a call xxx

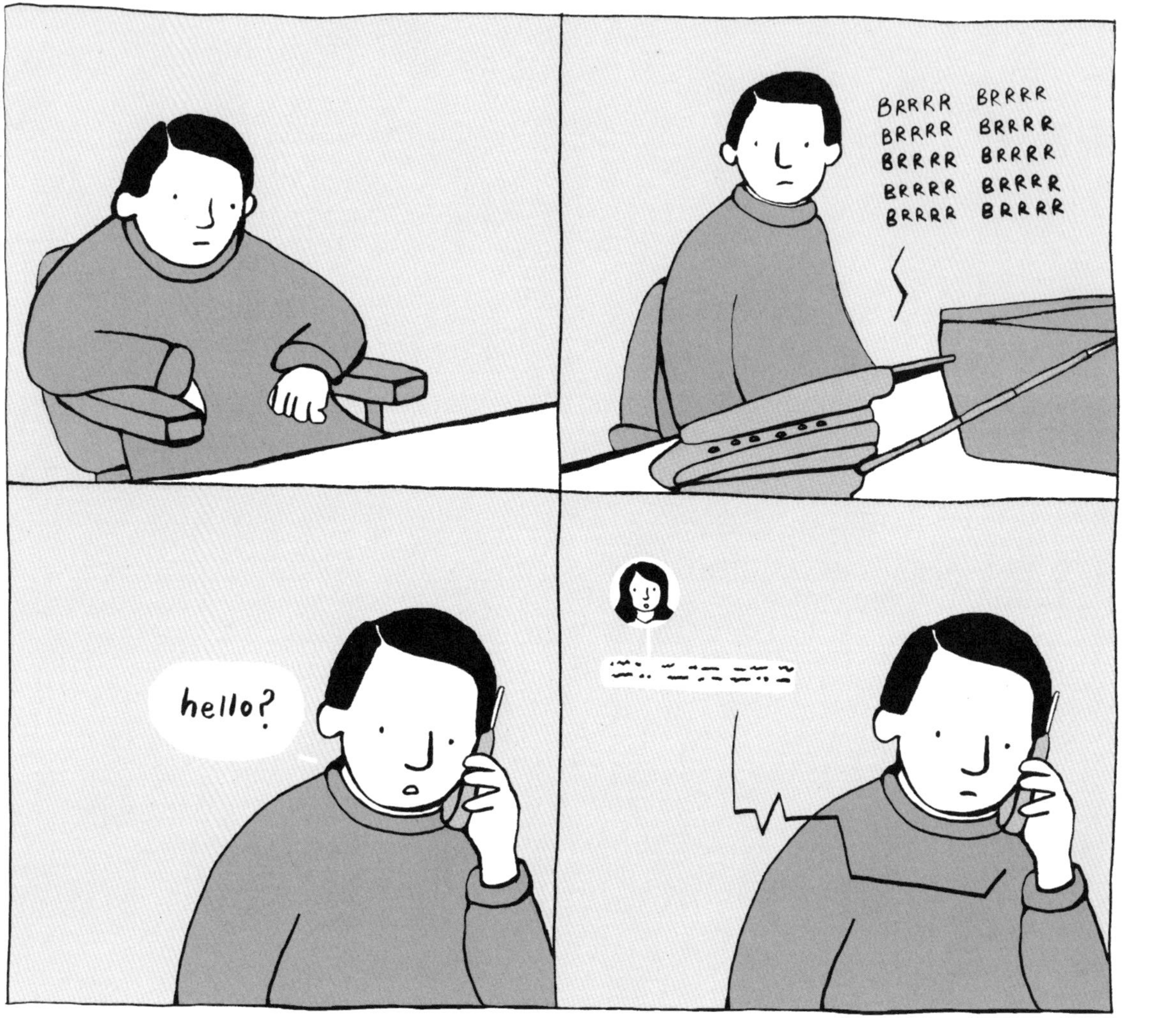
BRRRR BRRRR
BRRRR BRRRR
BRRRR BRRRR
BRRRR BRRRR
BRRRR BRRRR
hello?

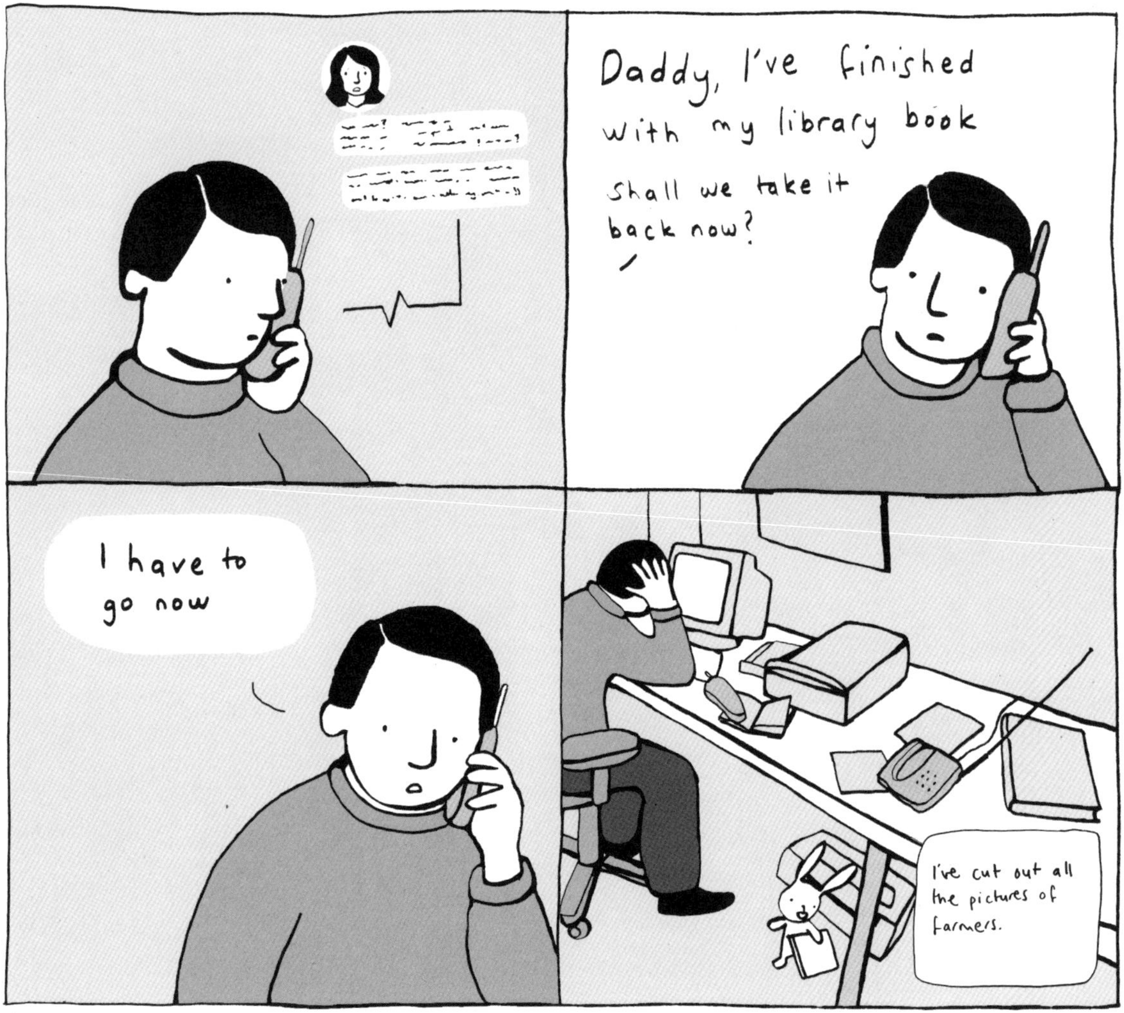
Daddy, I've finished with my library book
Shall we take it back now?
I have to go now
I've cut out all the pictures of farmers.

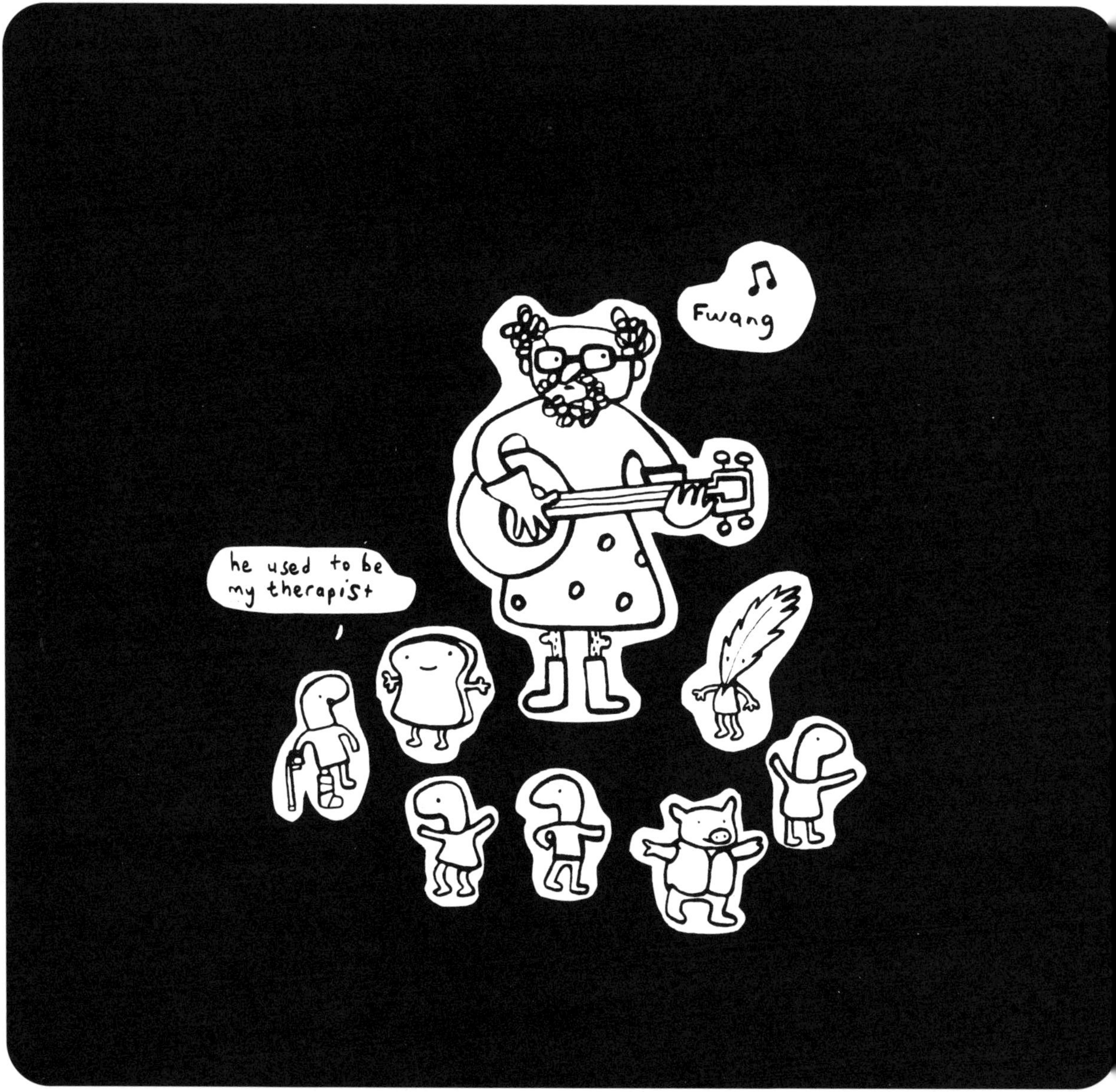
he used to be my therapist
Fwang

Some days later

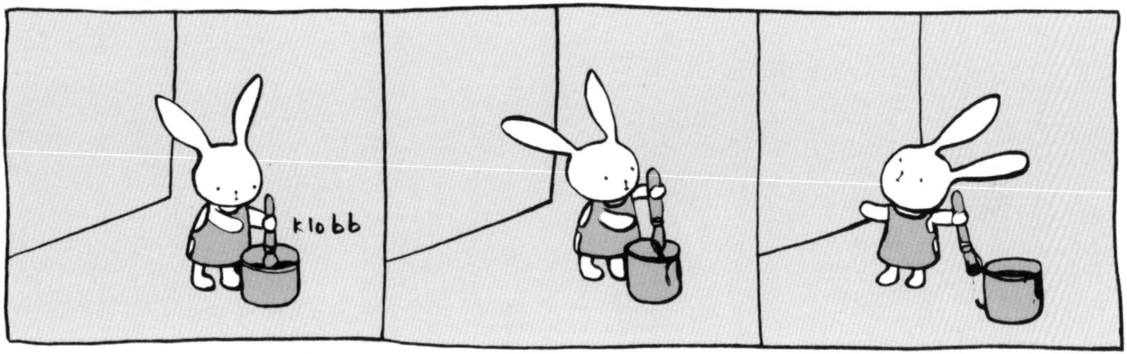
klobb

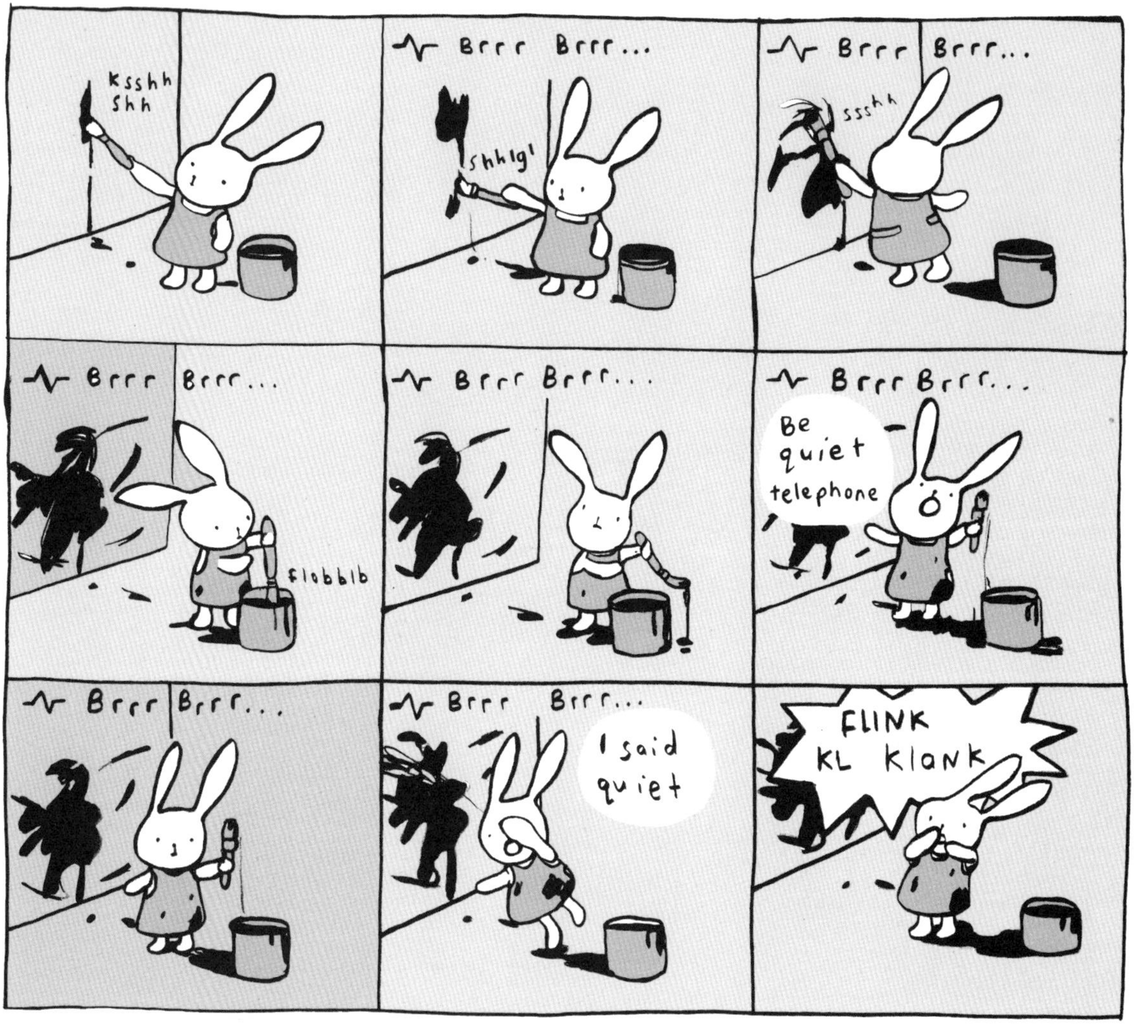
ksshh
shh
Brrr Brrr...
shhlg'
Brrr Brrr...
ssshh
Brrr Brrr...
flobblb
Brrr Brrr...
Brrr Brrr...
Be quiet telephone
Brrr Brrr...
Brrr Brrr...
I said quiet
FLINK
KL Klank

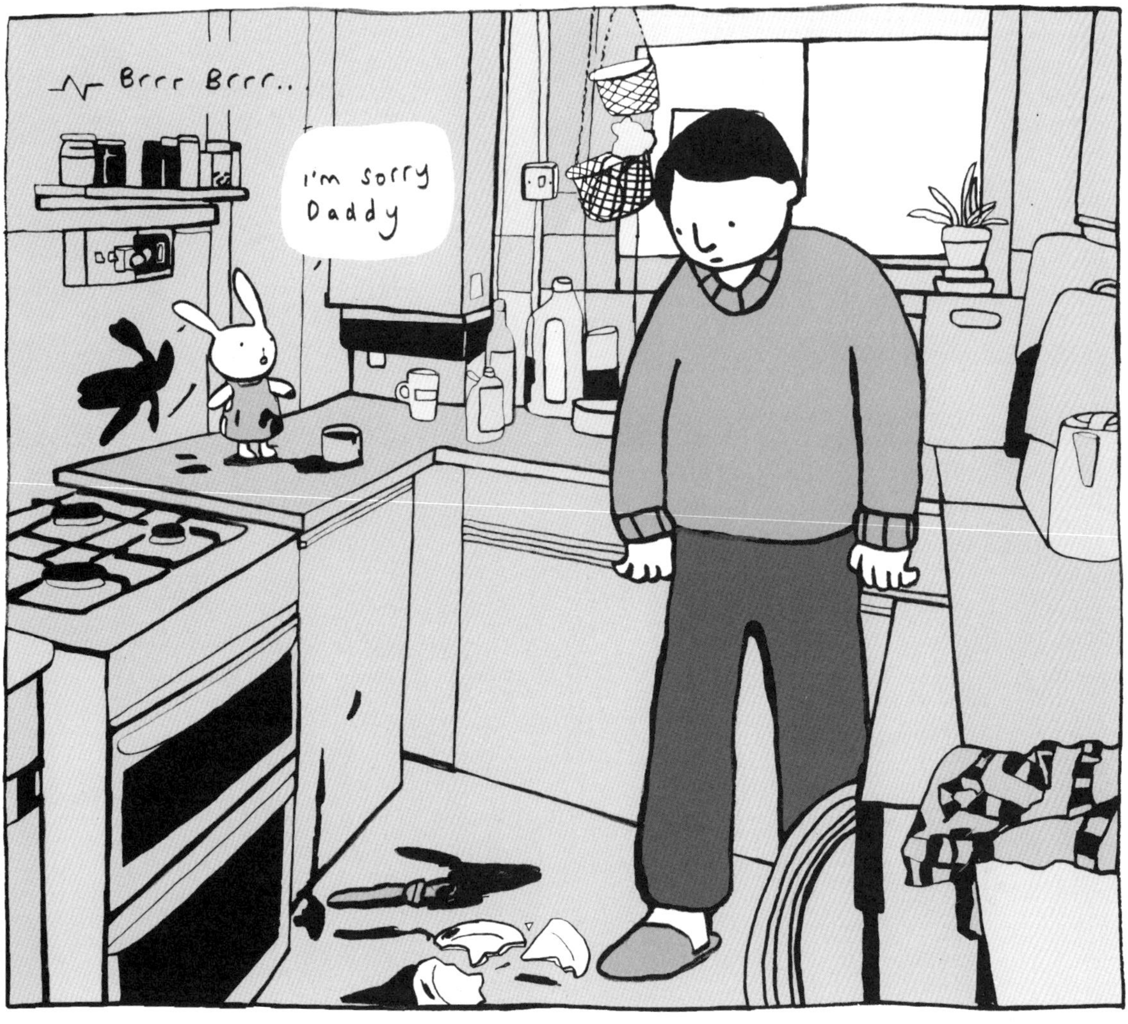
Brrr Brrr..
I'm sorry Daddy

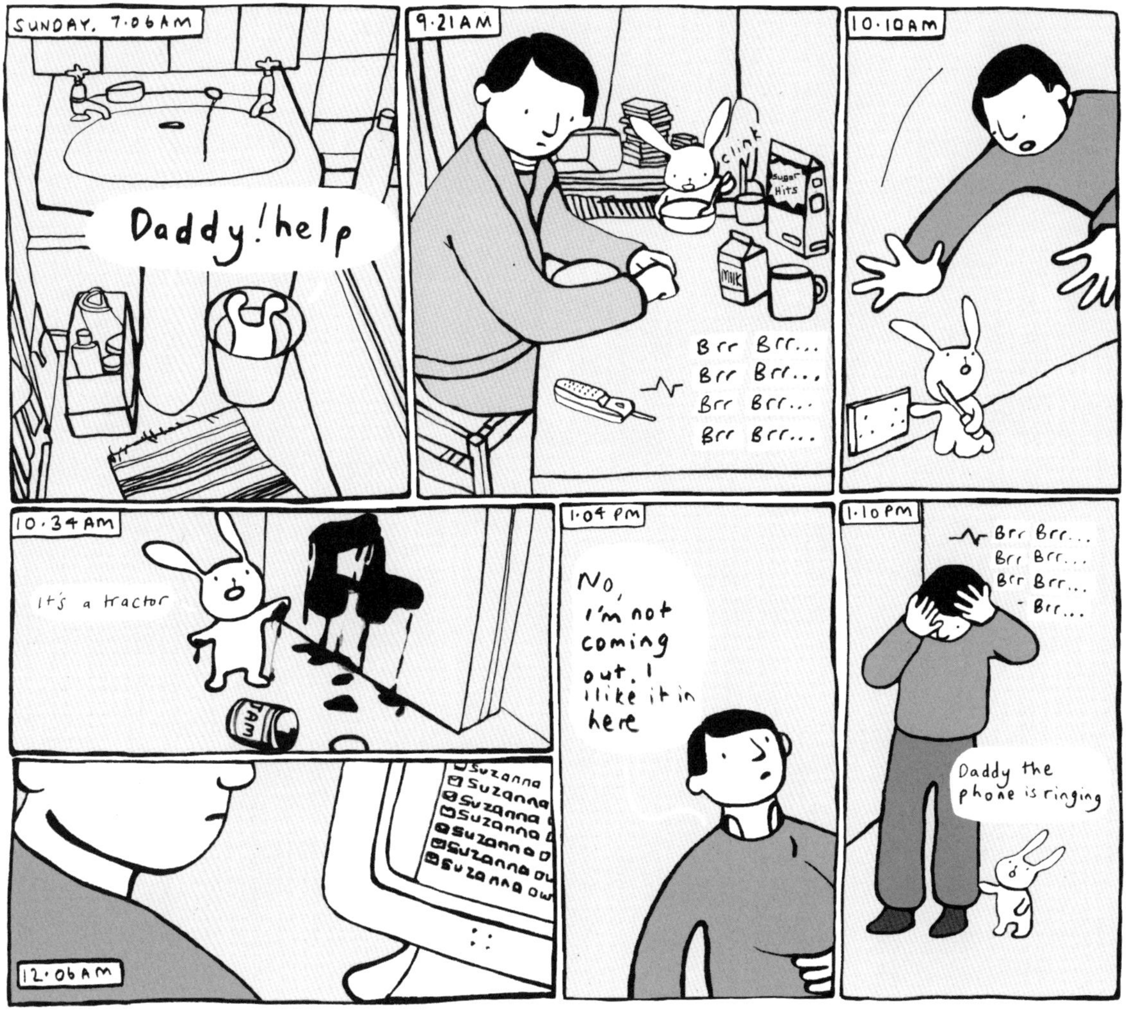
SUNDAY, 7·06AM
Daddy! help
9·21AM
clink
Sugar Hits
MILK
Brr Brr...
Brr Brr...
Brr Brr...
Brr Brr...
10·10AM
10·34AM
It's a tractor
JAM
1·04 PM
No, I'm not coming out. I like it in here
1·10PM
Brr Brr...
Brr Brr...
Brr Brr...
Brr...
Daddy the phone is ringing
12·06AM

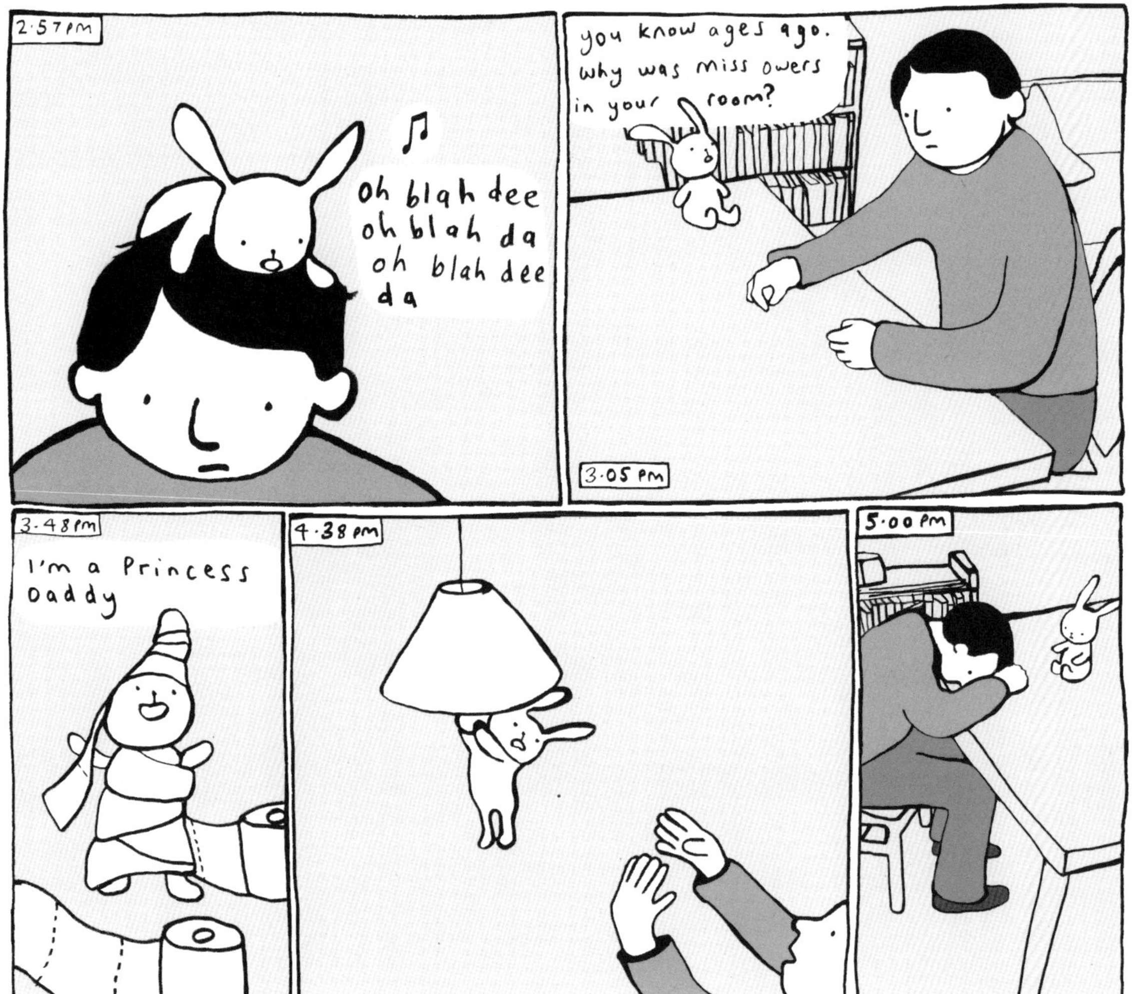
2·57PM
♪
oh blah dee
oh blah da
oh blah dee
da
you know ages ago.
why was miss owers
in your room?
3·05 PM
3·48PM
I'm a Princess
Daddy
4·38 pm
5·00 PM

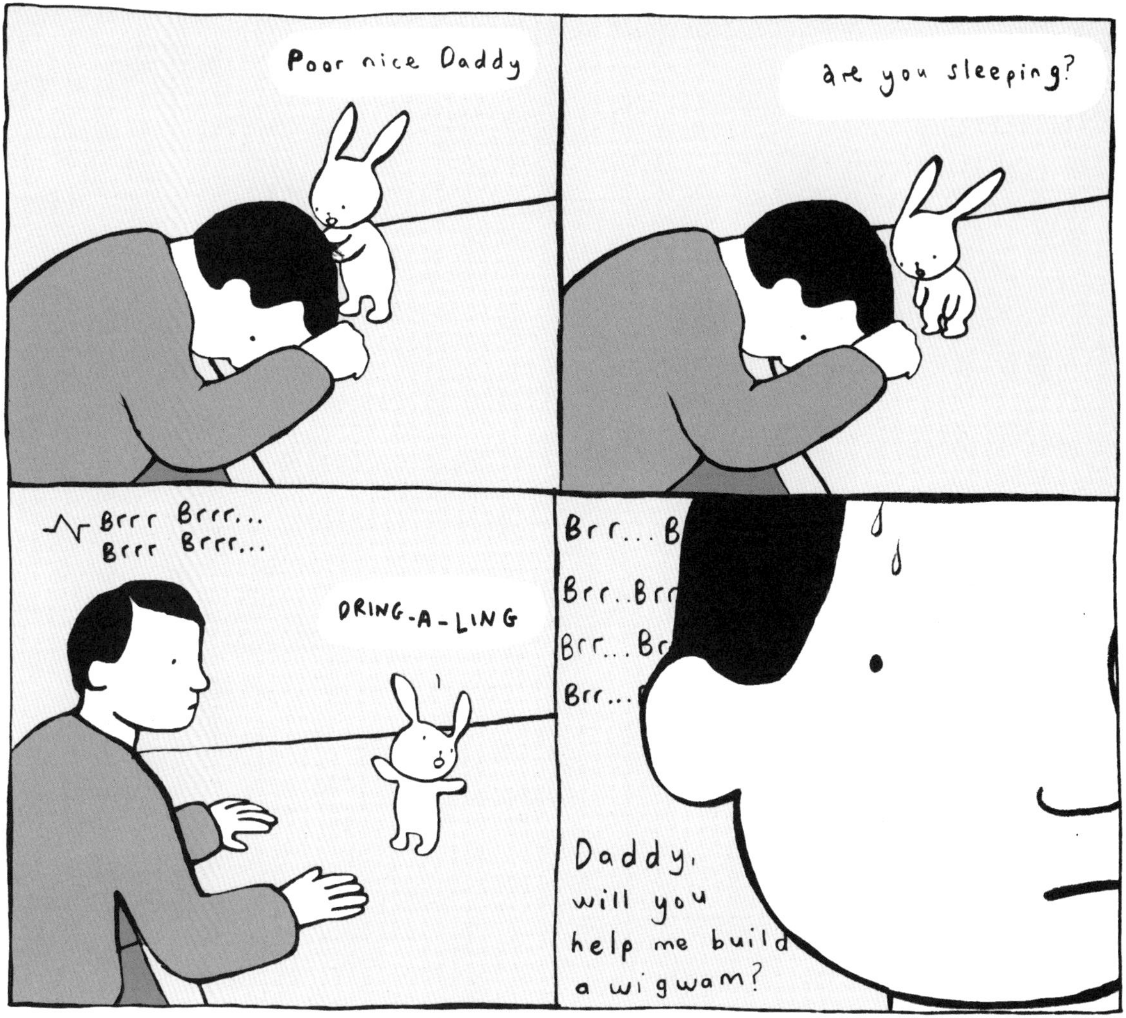
Poor nice Daddy
are you sleeping?
Brrr Brrr...
Brrr Brrr...
DRING-A-LING
Brr... B
Brr..Brr
Brr... Br
Brr...
Daddy,
will you
help me build
a wigwam?

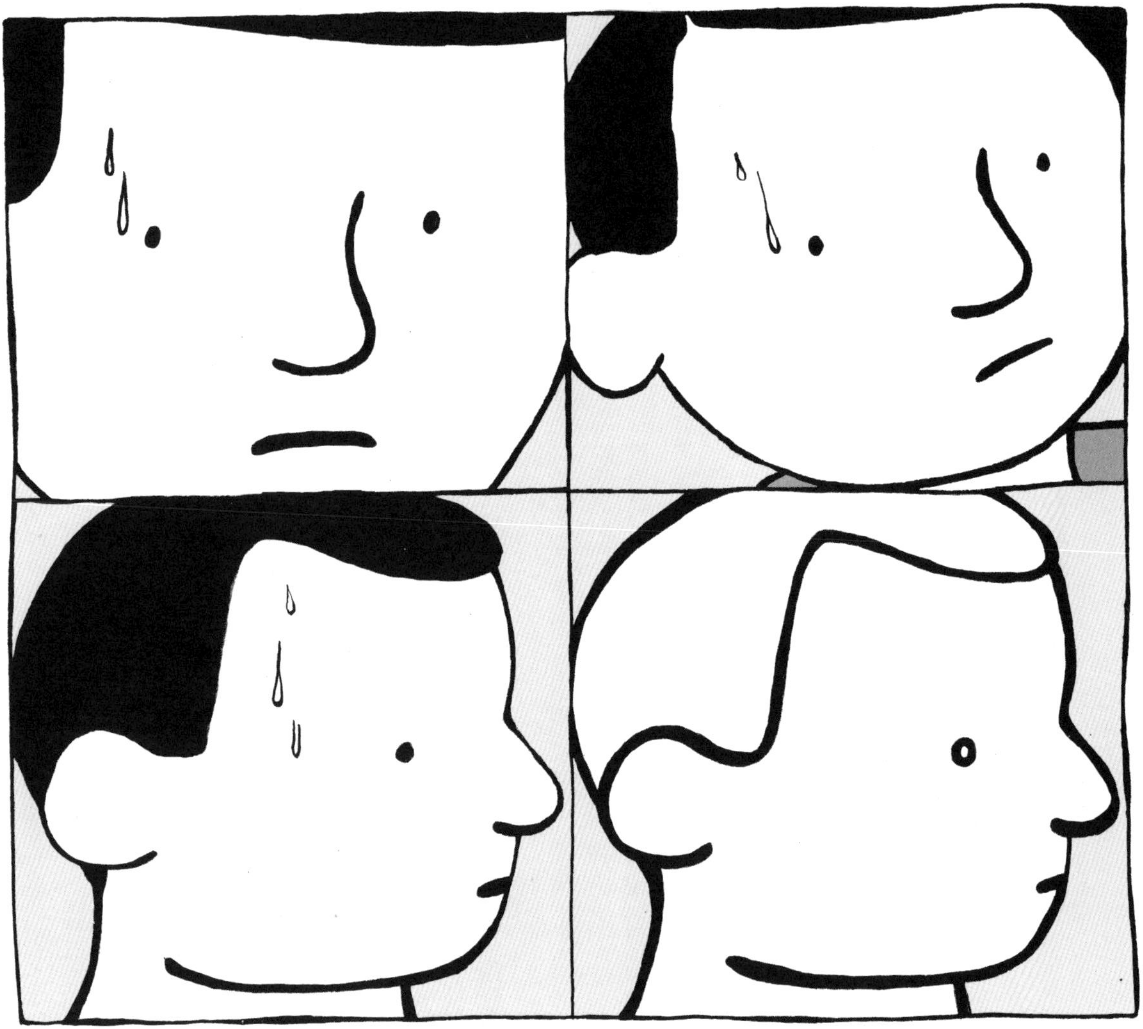

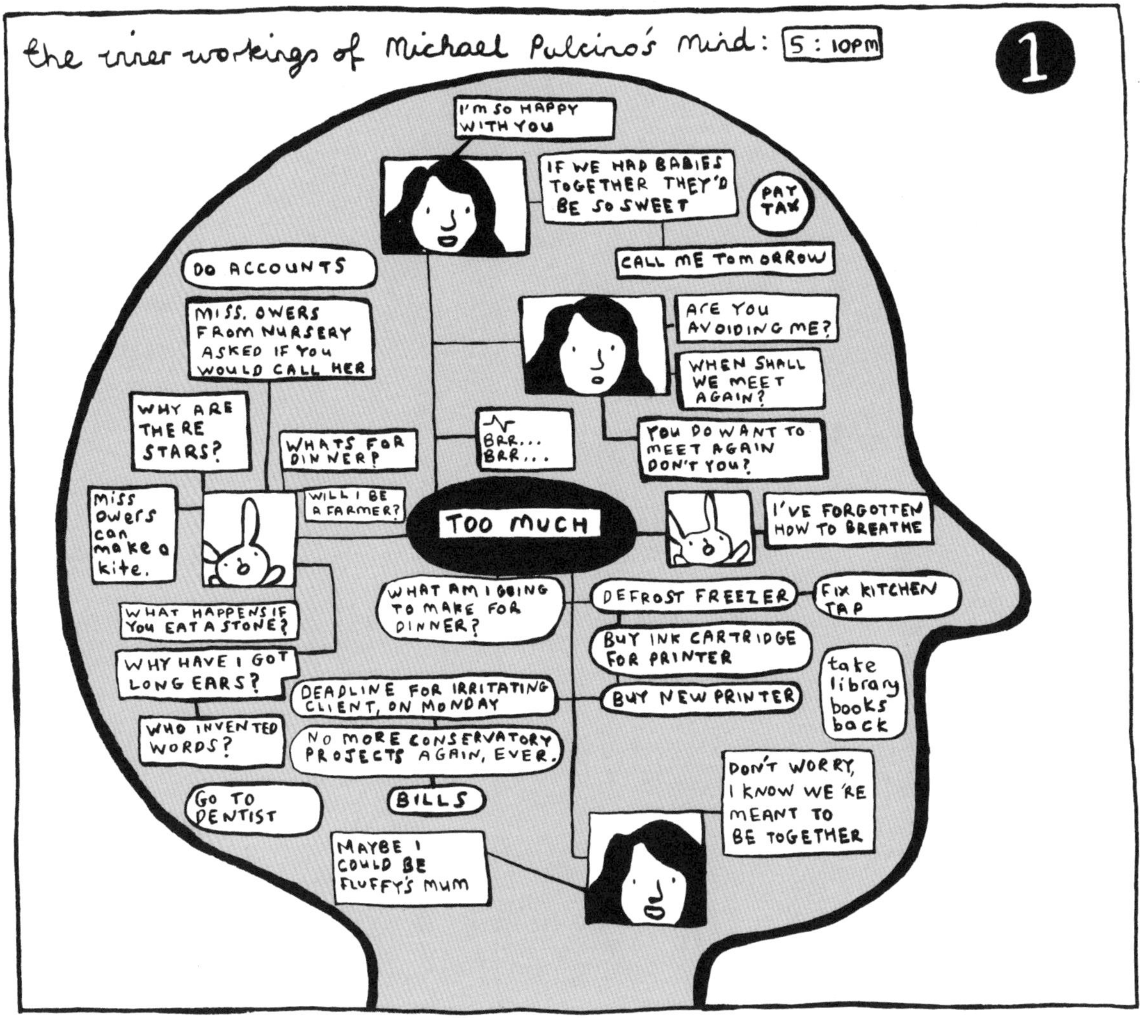
the inner workings of Michael Pulcino's mind: 5:10PM
1
I'M SO HAPPY WITH YOU
IF WE HAD BABIES TOGETHER THEY'D BE SO SWEET
PAY TAX
CALL ME TOMORROW
DO ACCOUNTS
MISS. OWERS FROM NURSERY ASKED IF YOU WOULD CALL HER
ARE YOU AVOIDING ME?
WHEN SHALL WE MEET AGAIN?
YOU DO WANT TO MEET AGAIN DON'T YOU?
WHY ARE THERE STARS?
WHATS FOR DINNER?
BRR... BRR...
Miss owers can make a kite.
WILL I BE A FARMER?
TOO MUCH
I'VE FORGOTTEN HOW TO BREATHE
WHAT AM I GOING TO MAKE FOR DINNER?
DEFROST FREEZER
FIX KITCHEN TAP
WHAT HAPPENS IF YOU EAT A STONE?
BUY INK CARTRIDGE FOR PRINTER
WHY HAVE I GOT LONG EARS?
take library books back
DEADLINE FOR IRRITATING CLIENT, ON MONDAY
BUY NEW PRINTER
WHO INVENTED WORDS?
NO MORE CONSERVATORY PROJECTS AGAIN, EVER.
DON'T WORRY, I KNOW WE'RE MEANT TO BE TOGETHER
GO TO DENTIST
BILLS
MAYBE I COULD BE FLUFFY'S MUM

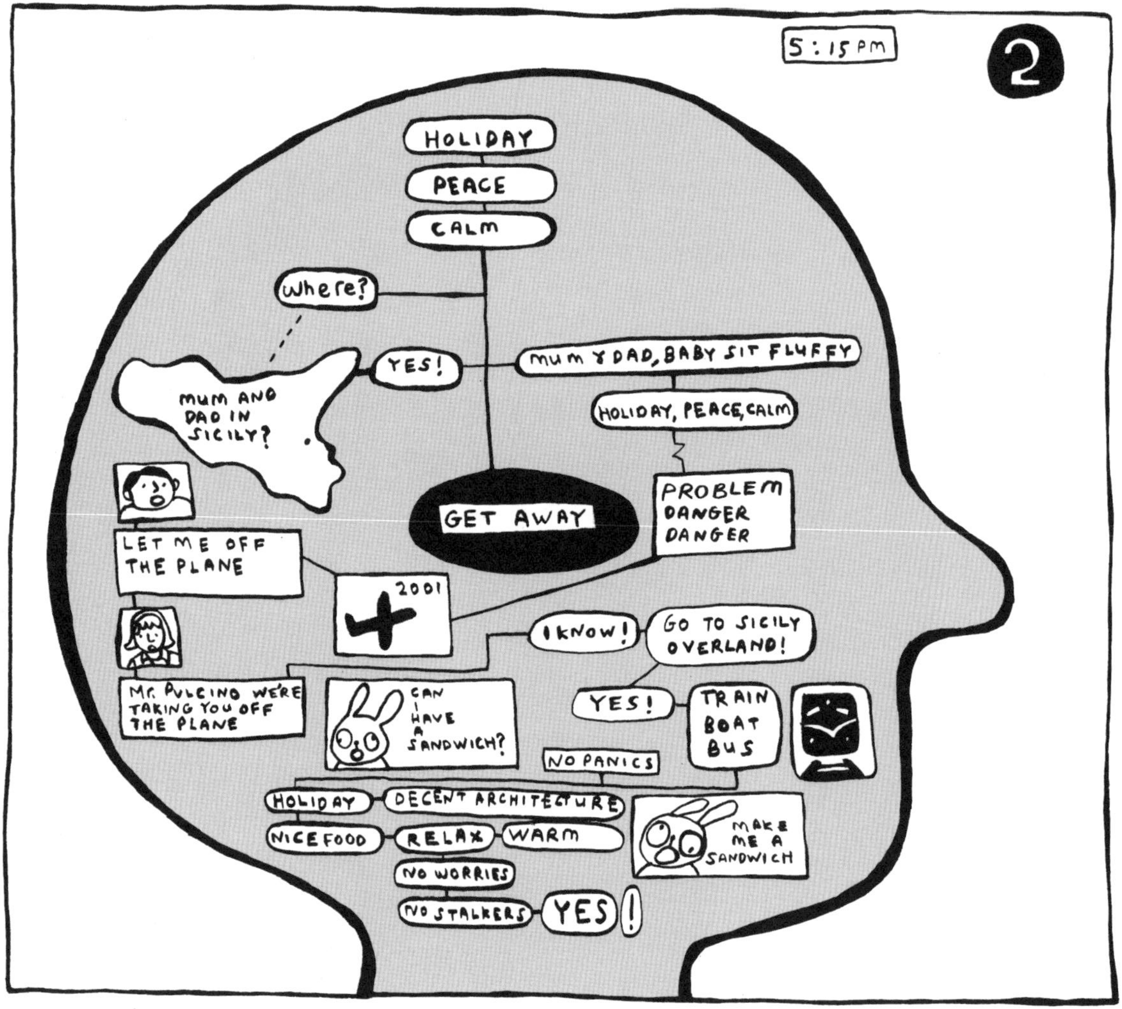
5:15 PM
2
HOLIDAY
PEACE
CALM
where?
YES!
MUM AND DAD IN SICILY?
MUM & DAD, BABY SIT FLUFFY
HOLIDAY, PEACE, CALM
PROBLEM DANGER DANGER
GET AWAY
LET ME OFF THE PLANE
2001
I KNOW!
GO TO SICILY OVERLAND!
MR. PULCINO WE'RE TAKING YOU OFF THE PLANE
CAN I HAVE A SANDWICH?
YES!
TRAIN BOAT BUS
NO PANICS
HOLIDAY
DECENT ARCHITECTURE
NICE FOOD
RELAX
WARM
MAKE ME A SANDWICH
NO WORRIES
NO STALKERS
YES!

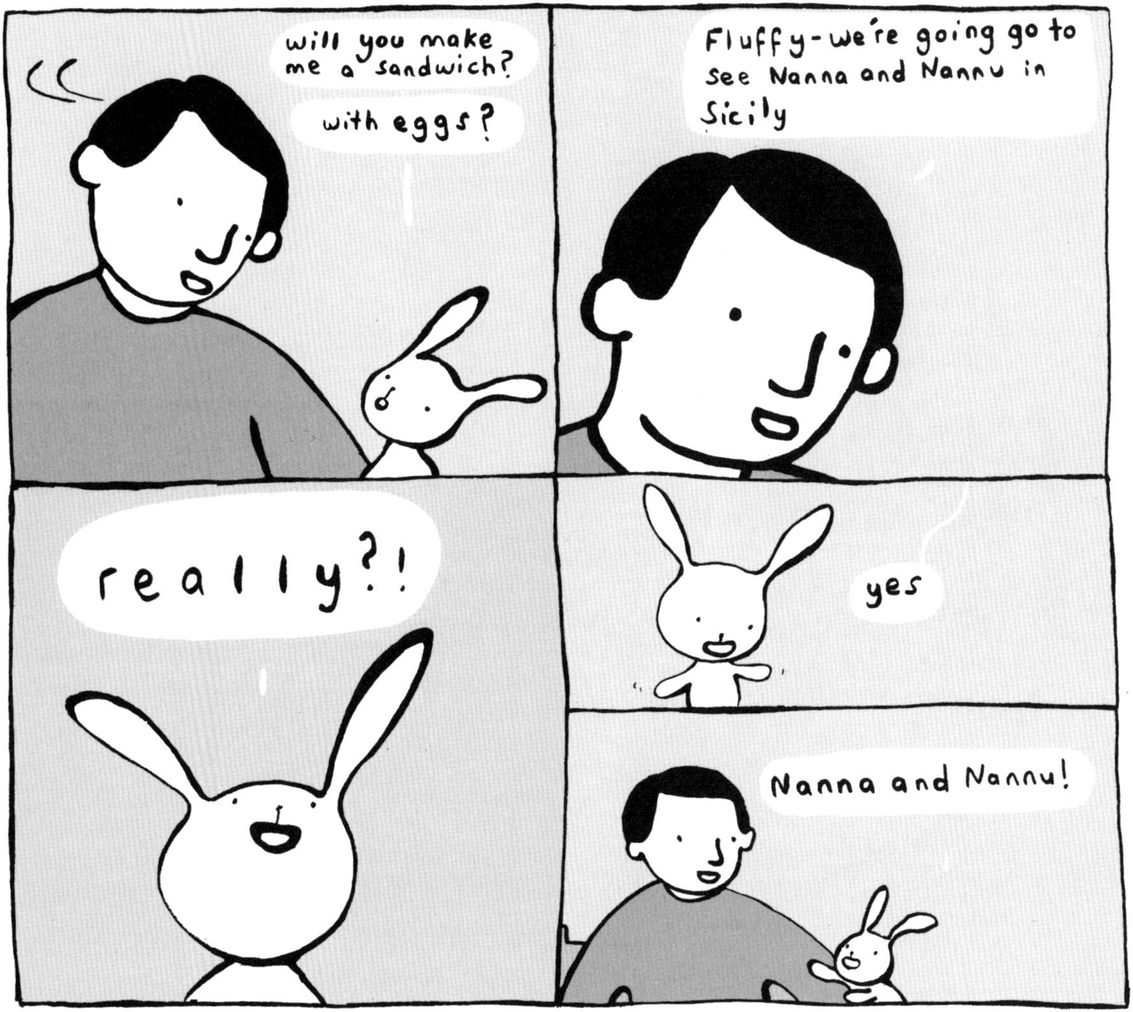
will you make me a sandwich?
with eggs?
Fluffy-we're going go to see Nanna and Nannu in Sicily
really?!
yes
Nanna and Nannu!

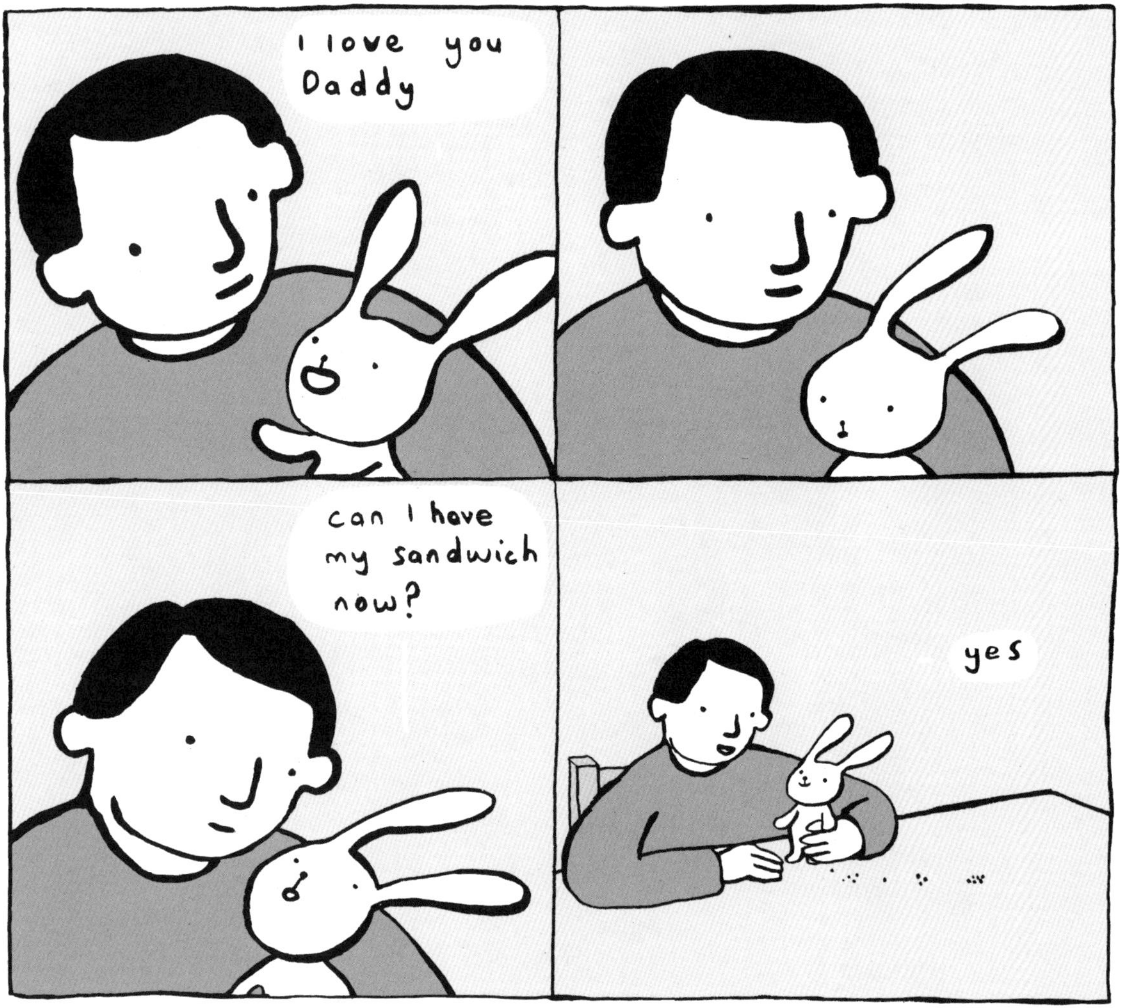
I love you Daddy
can I have my sandwich now?
yes

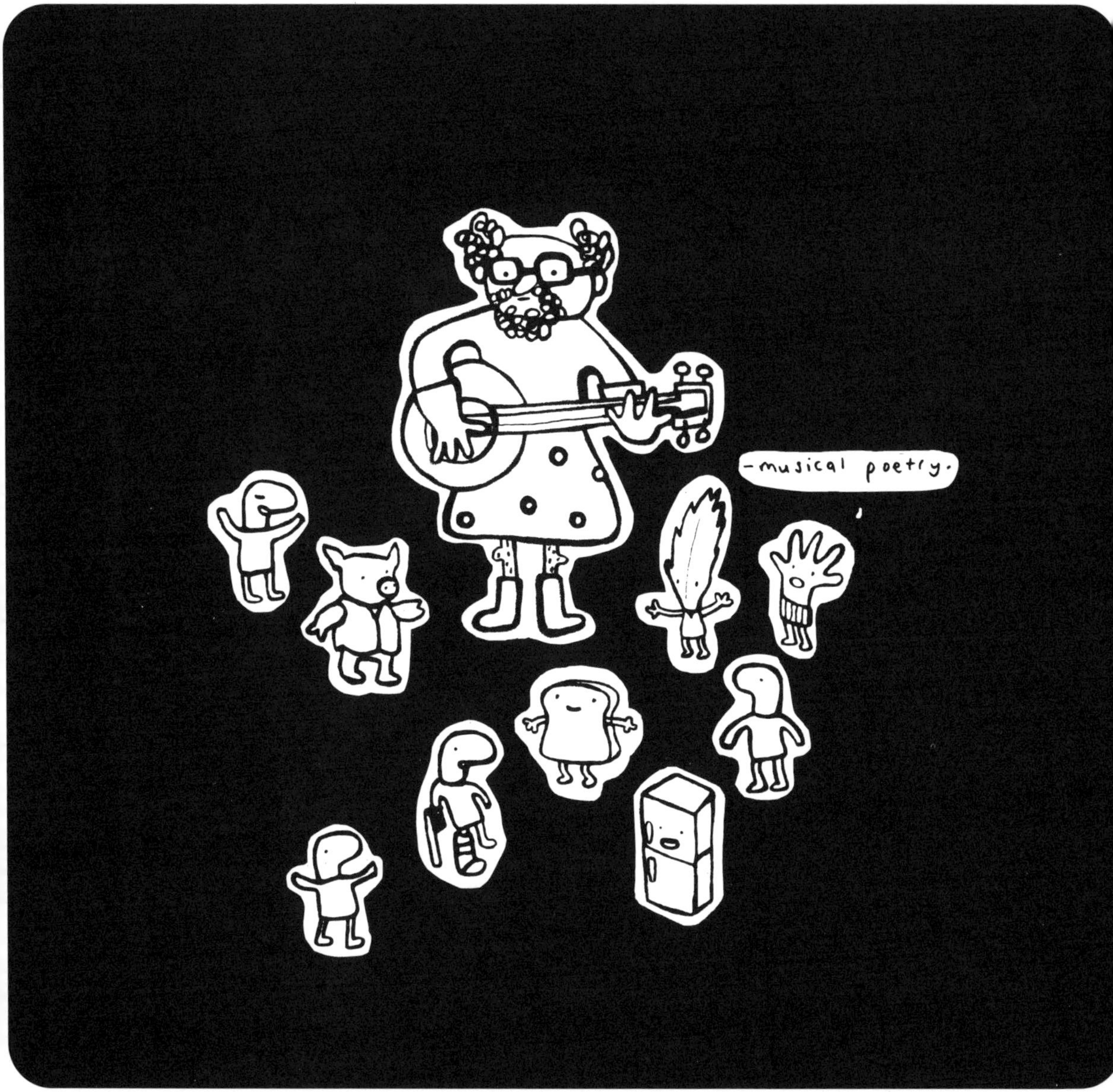
-musical poetry-

Part 2

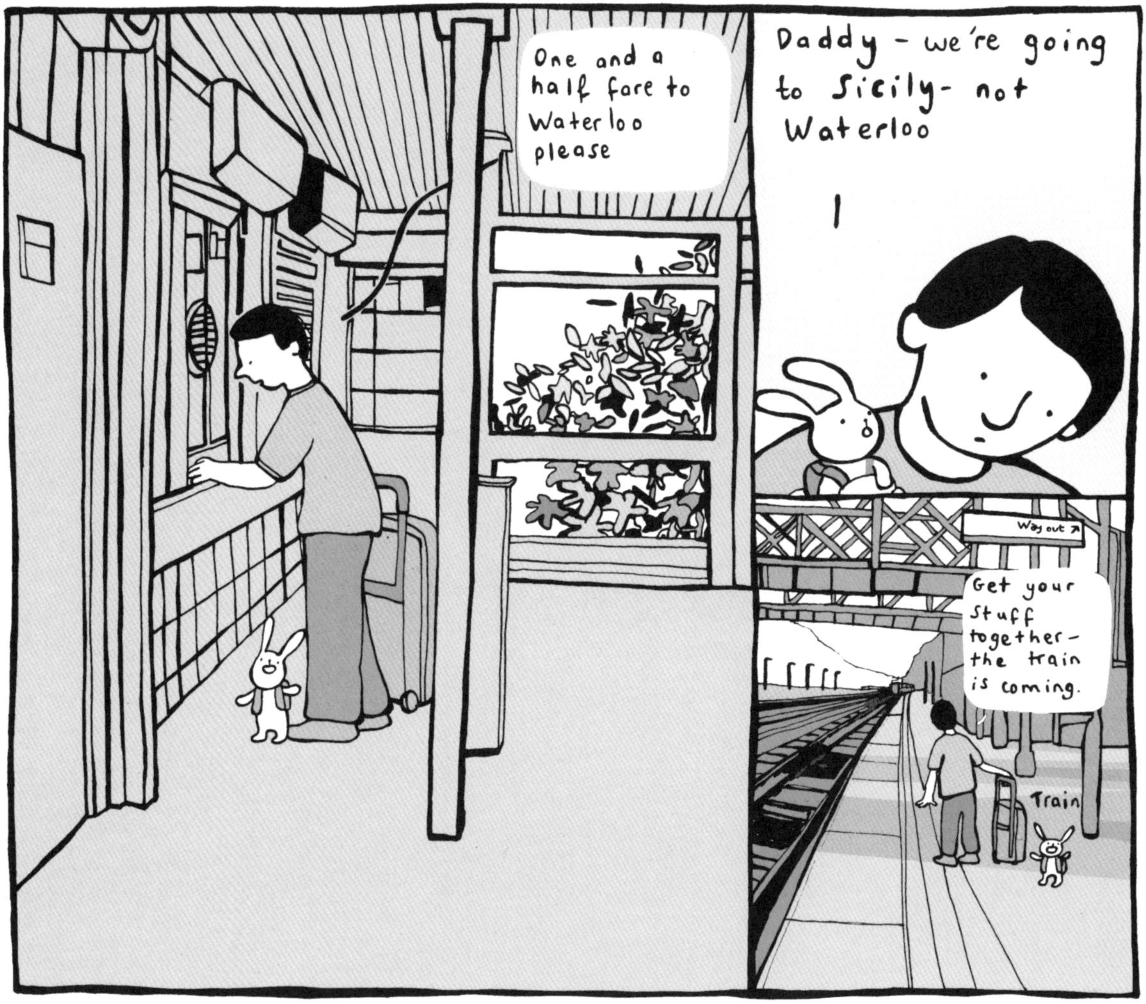
One and a half fare to Waterloo please
Daddy - we're going to Sicily - not Waterloo
Way out
Get your stuff together - the train is coming.
Train

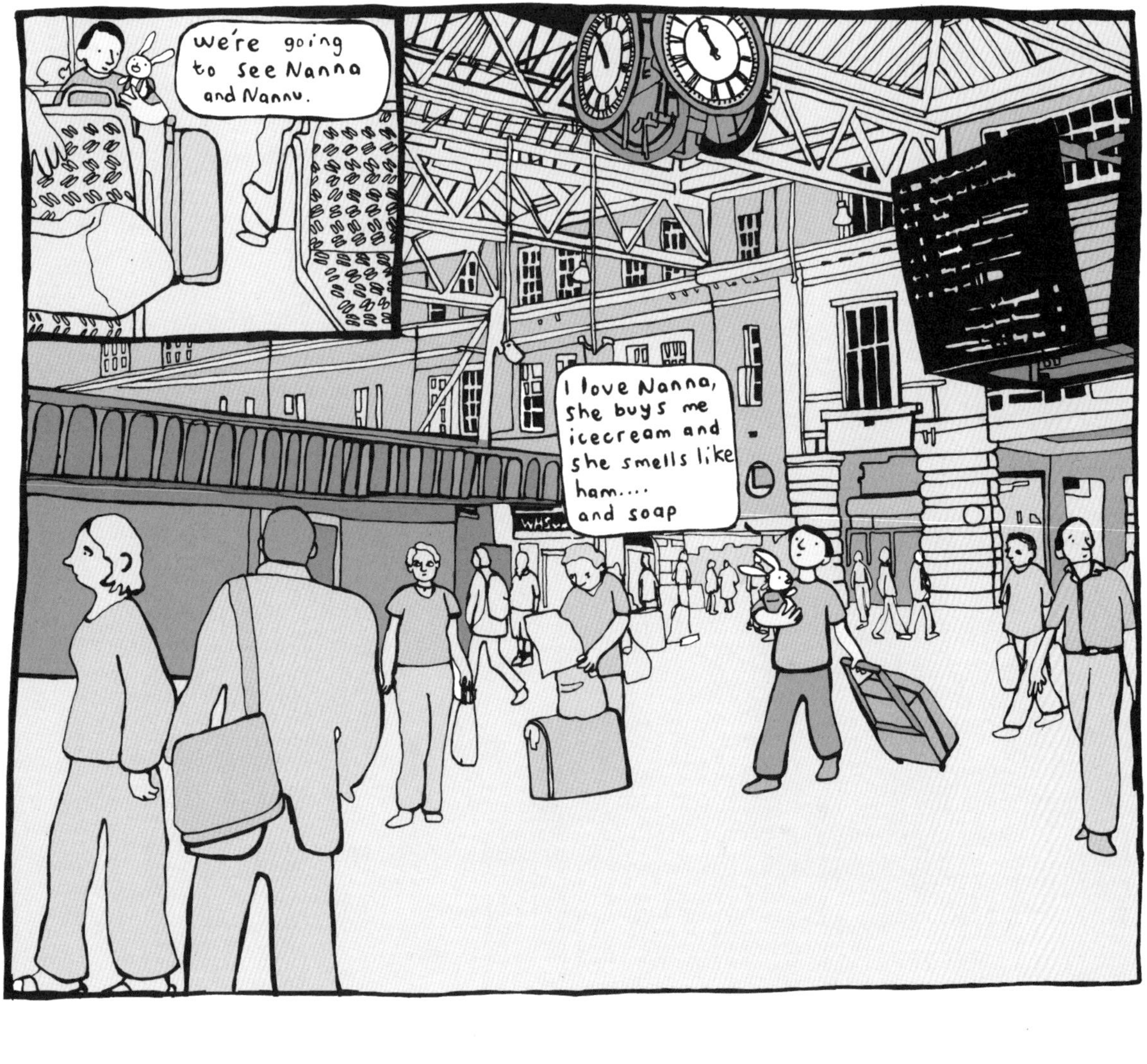
we're going to see Nanna and Nannu.
I love Nanna, she buys me icecream and she smells like ham.... and soap

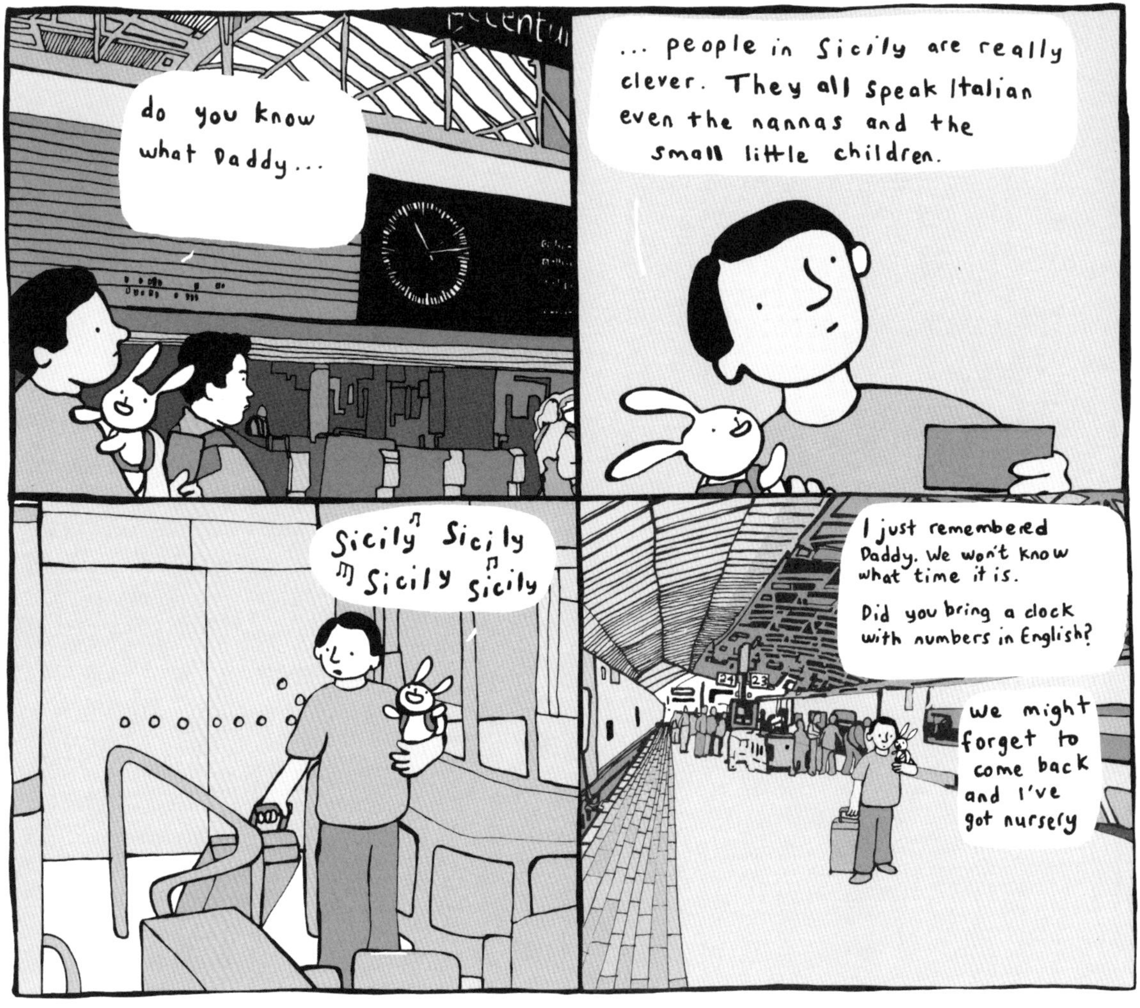
do you know what Daddy...
... people in Sicily are really clever. They all speak Italian even the nannas and the small little children.
Sicily Sicily Sicily Sicily
I just remembered Daddy. We won't know what time it is.
Did you bring a clock with numbers in English?
we might forget to come back and I've got nursery

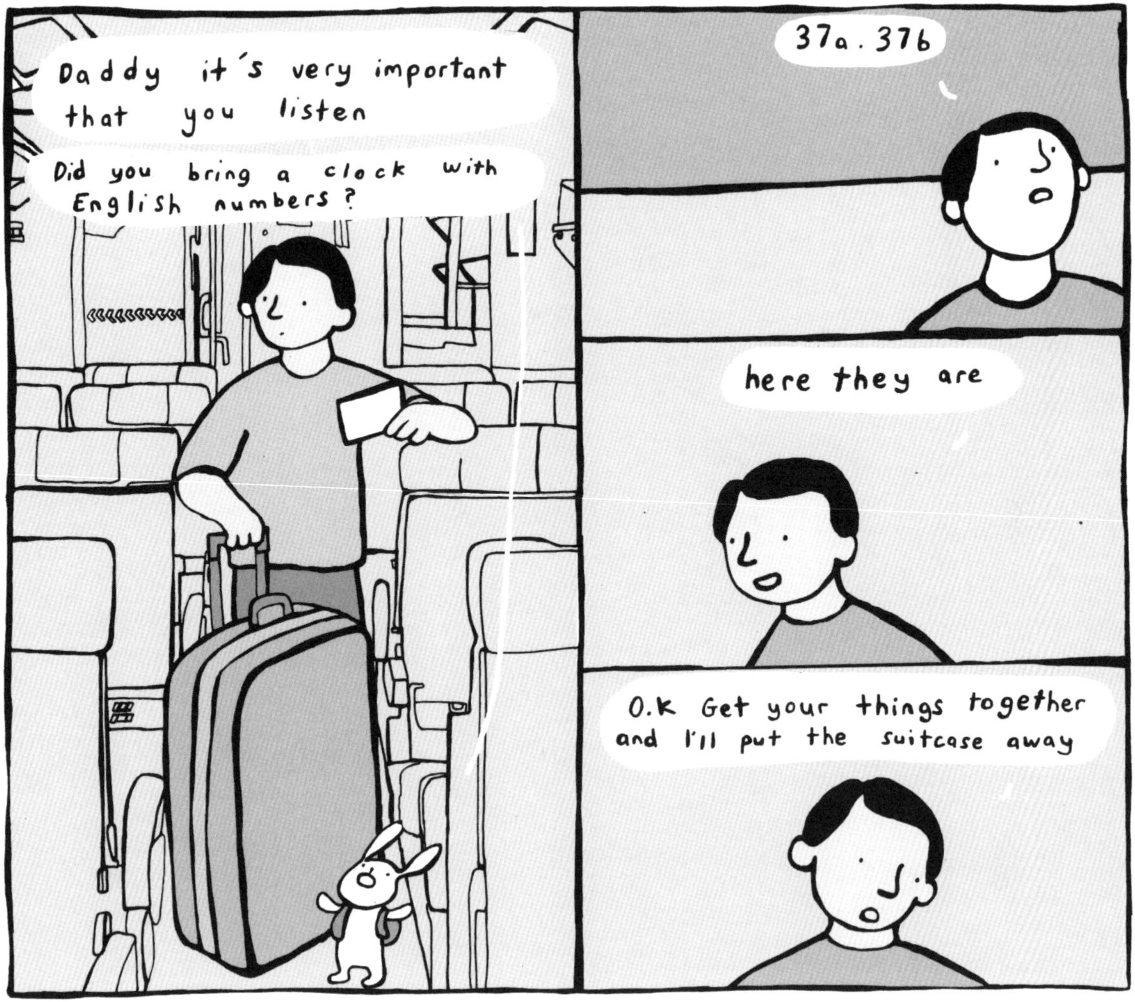
Daddy it´s very important that you listen
Did you bring a clock with English numbers?
37a. 37b
here they are
O.K Get your things together and I'll put the suitcase away

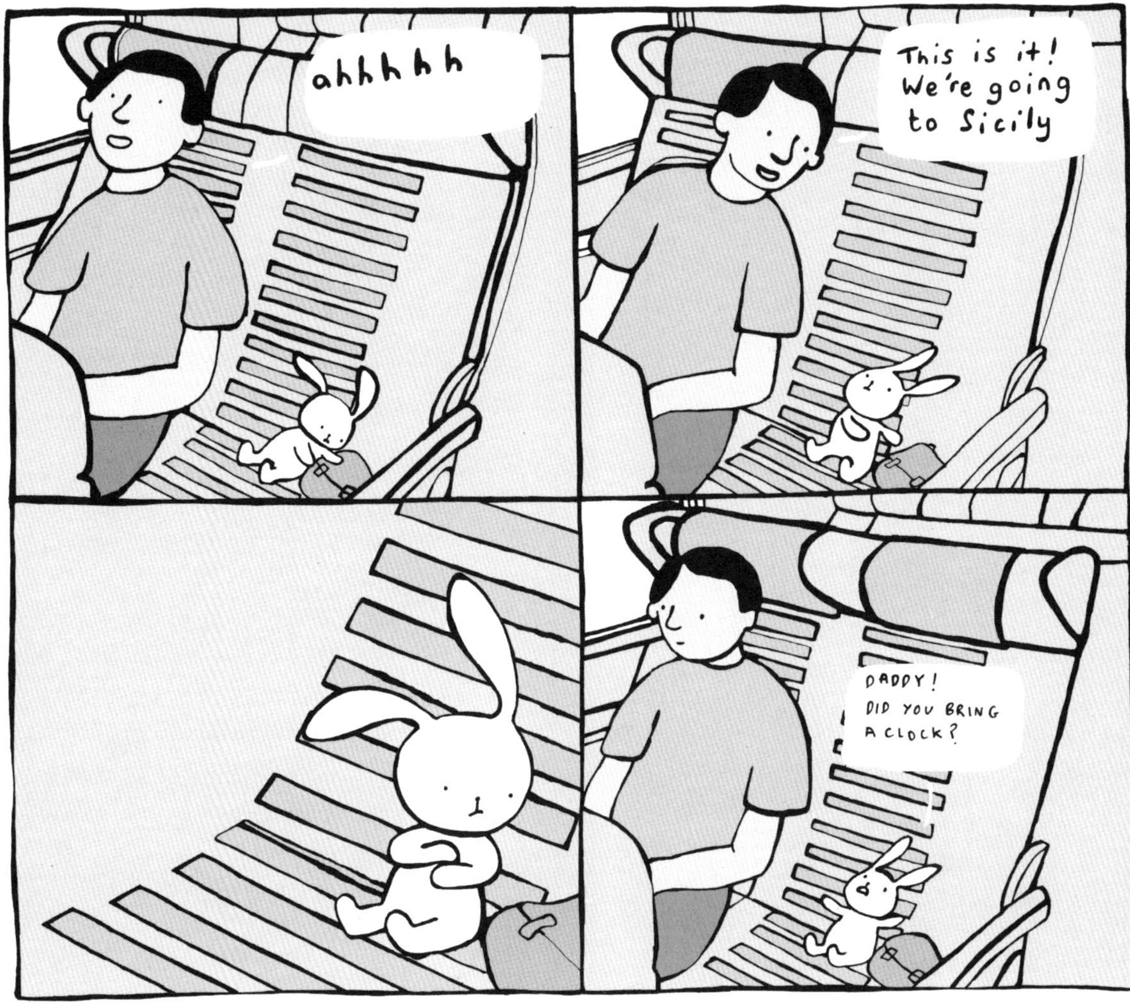
ahhhhh
This is it! We're going to Sicily
DADDY! DID YOU BRING A CLOCK?

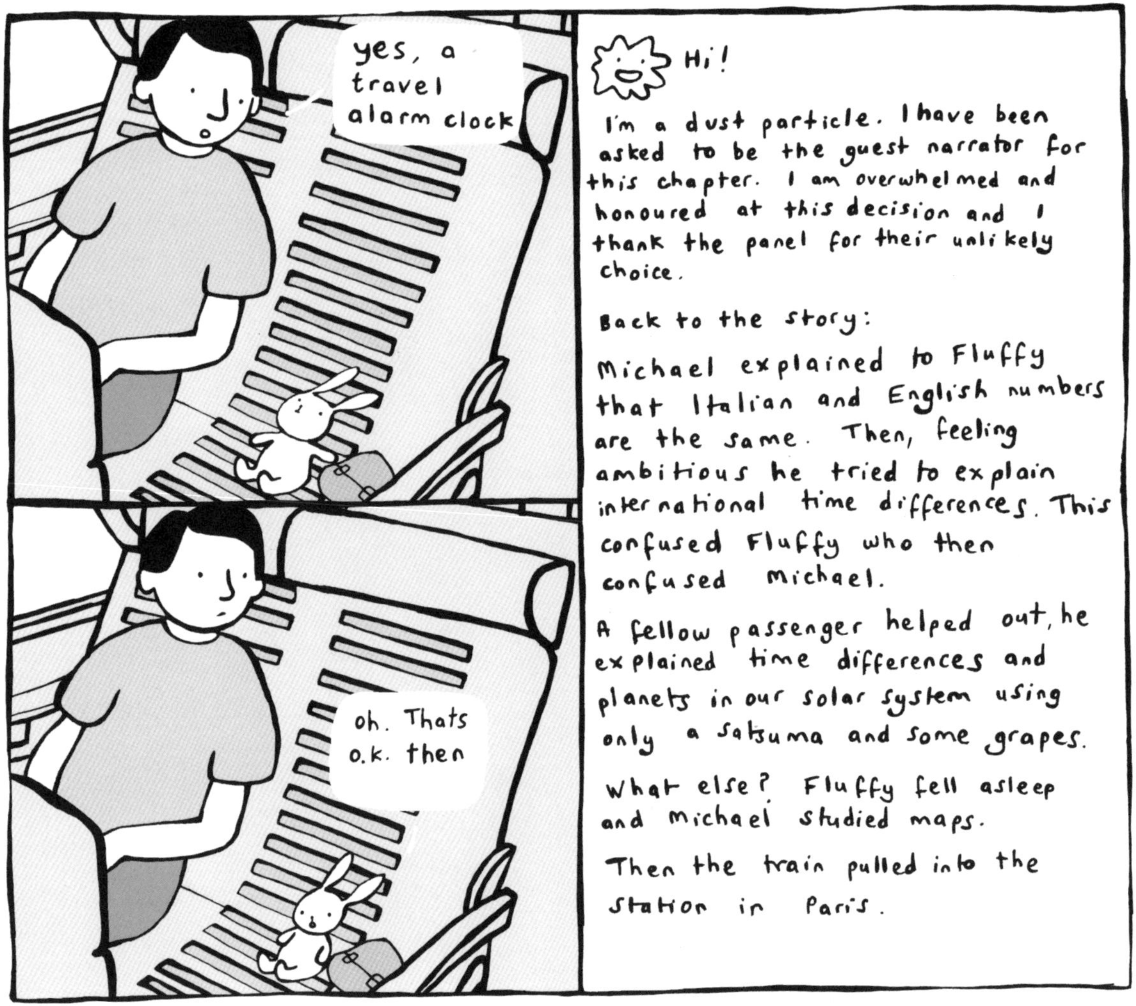
yes, a travel alarm clock
oh. Thats o.k. then
Hi!
I'm a dust particle. I have been asked to be the guest narrator for this chapter. I am overwhelmed and honoured at this decision and I thank the panel for their unlikely choice.
Back to the story:
Michael explained to Fluffy that Italian and English numbers are the same. Then, feeling ambitious he tried to explain international time differences. This confused Fluffy who then confused michael.
A fellow passenger helped out, he explained time differences and planets in our solar system using only a satsuma and some grapes.
What else? Fluffy fell asleep and michael studied maps.
Then the train pulled into the station in Paris.

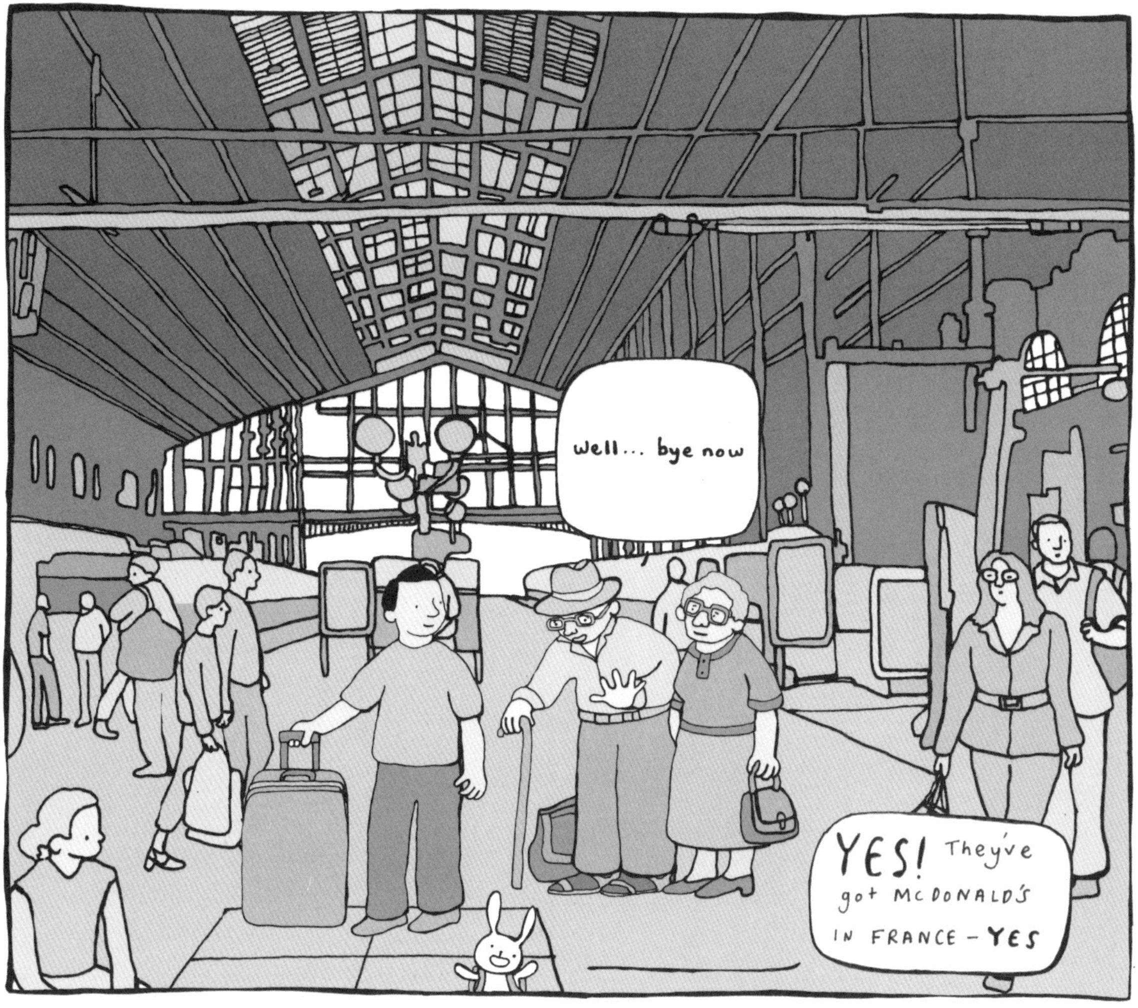
well... bye now
YES! They've got McDONALD'S IN FRANCE - YES

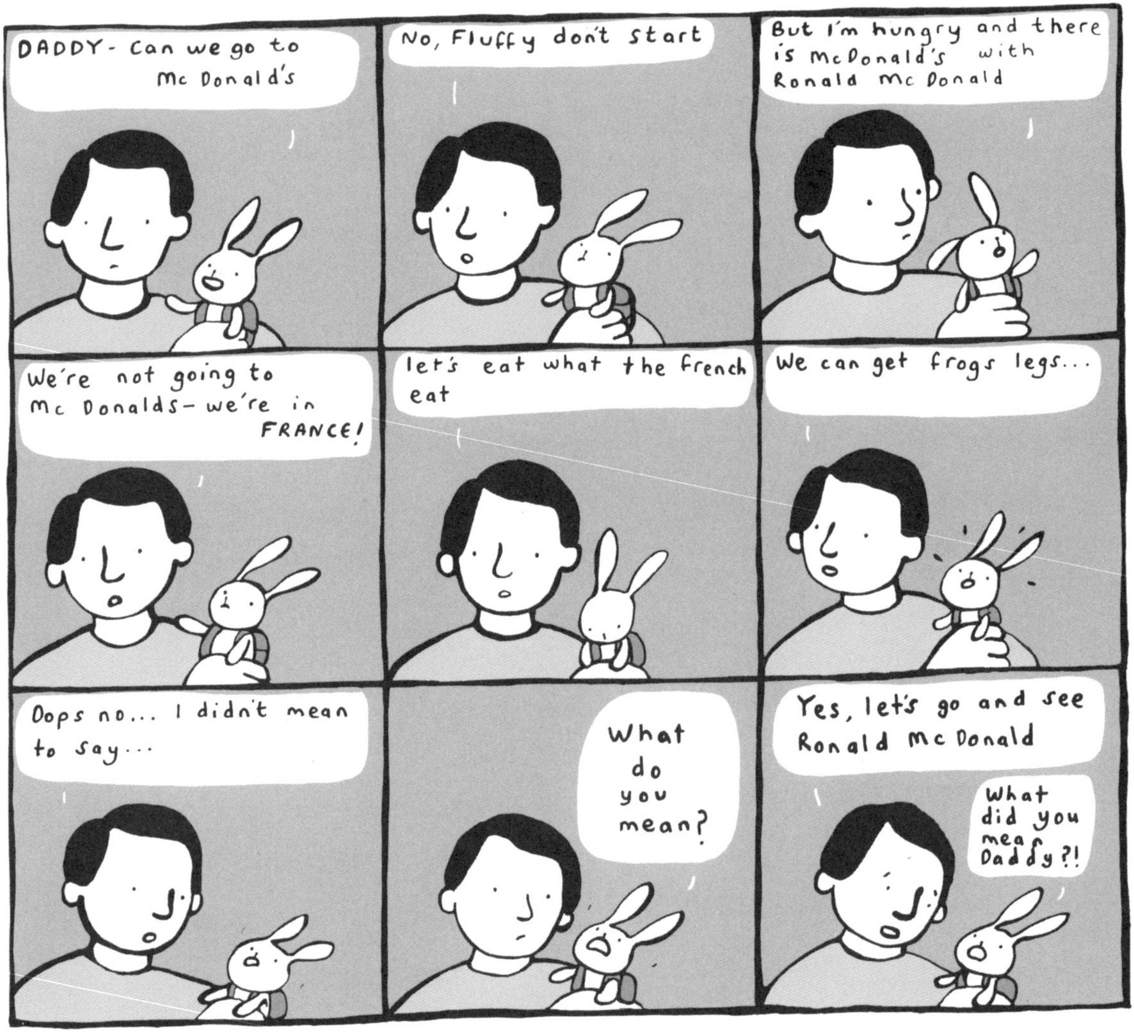
DADDY- Can we go to Mc Donald's
No, Fluffy don't start
But I'm hungry and there is McDonald's with Ronald Mc Donald
We're not going to Mc Donalds- we're in FRANCE!
let's eat what the french eat
We can get frogs legs...
Oops no... I didn't mean to say...
What do you mean?
Yes, let's go and see Ronald Mc Donald
What did you mean Daddy?!

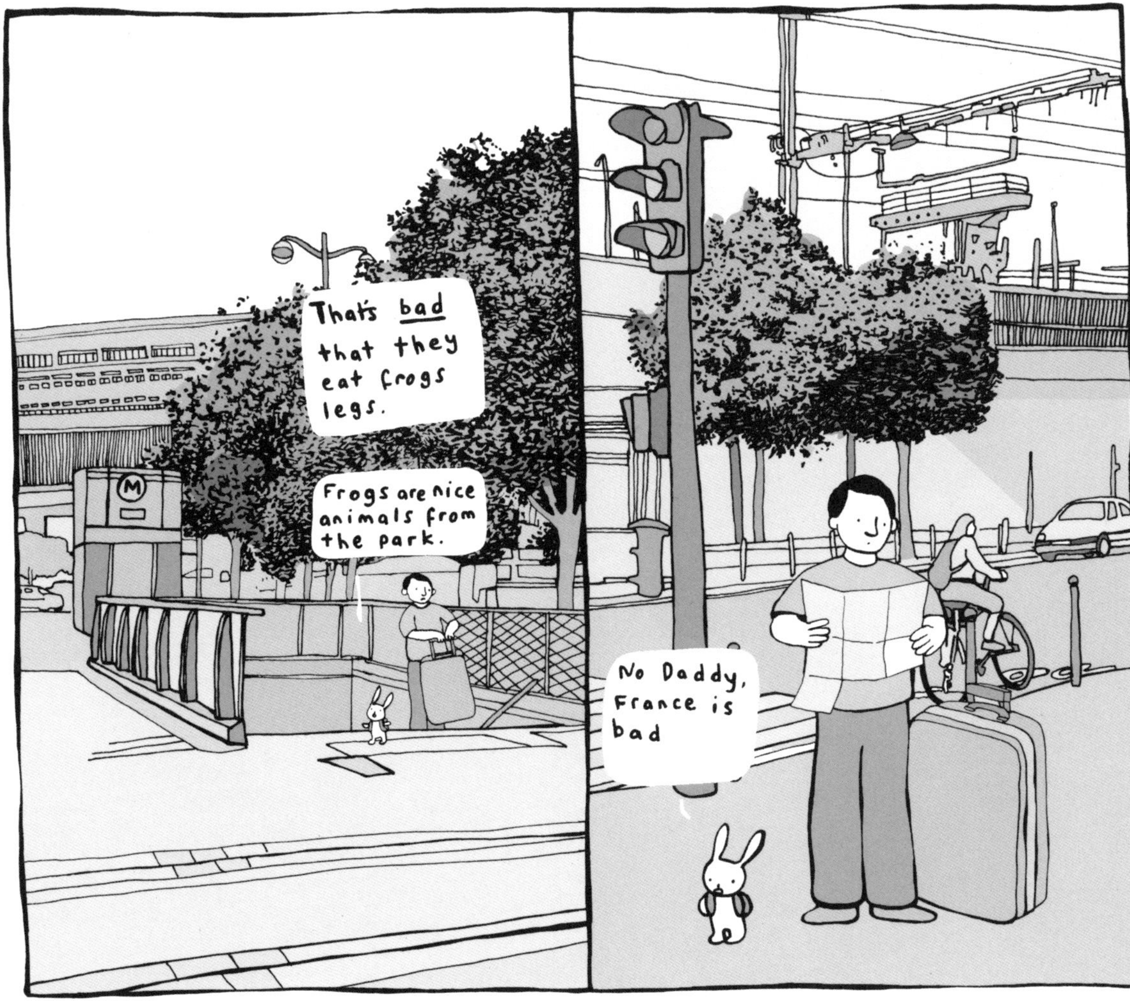
That's bad that they eat frogs legs.
Frogs are nice animals from the park.
No Daddy, France is bad

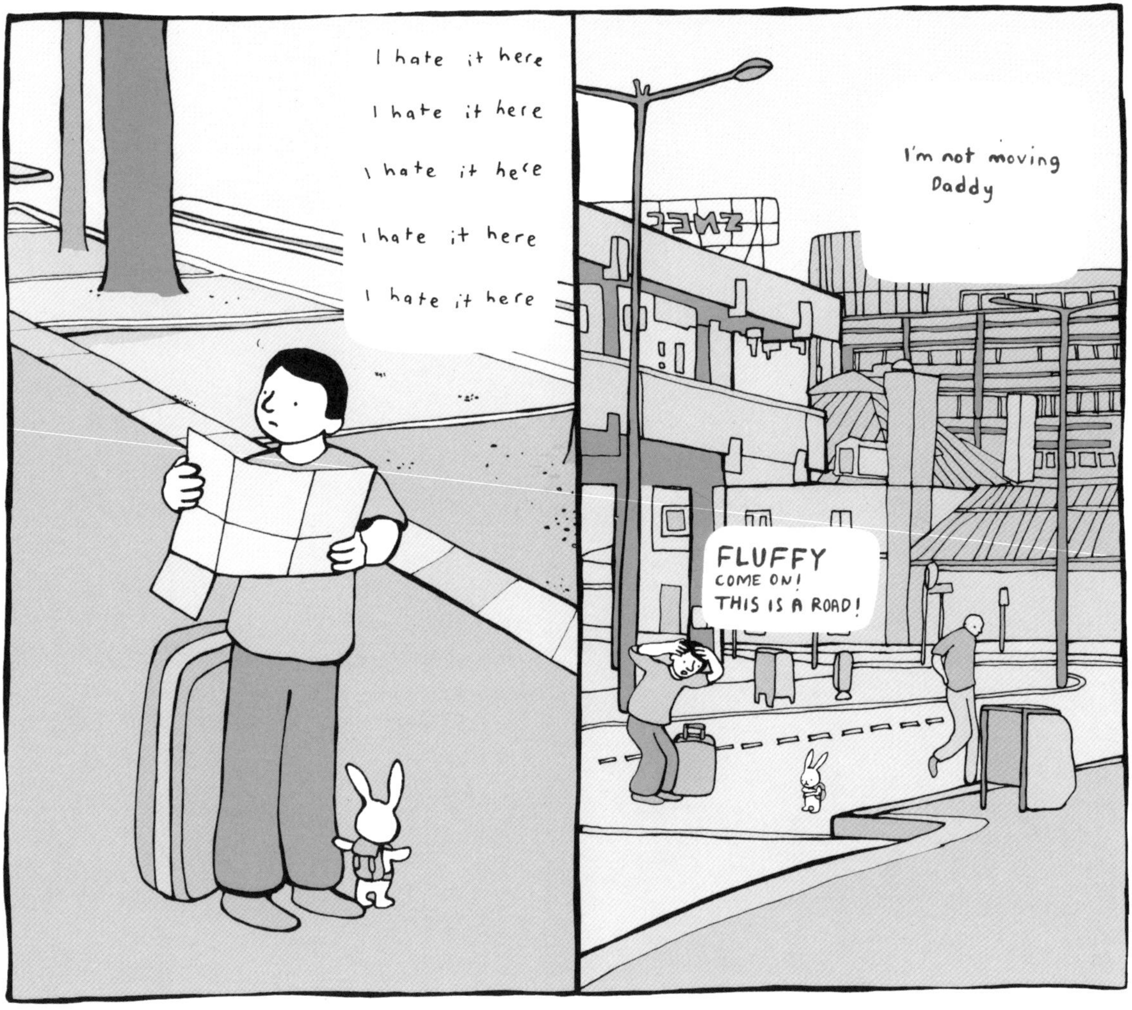
I hate it here
I hate it here
I hate it here
I hate it here
I hate it here
I'm not moving Daddy
FLUFFY COME ON! THIS IS A ROAD!

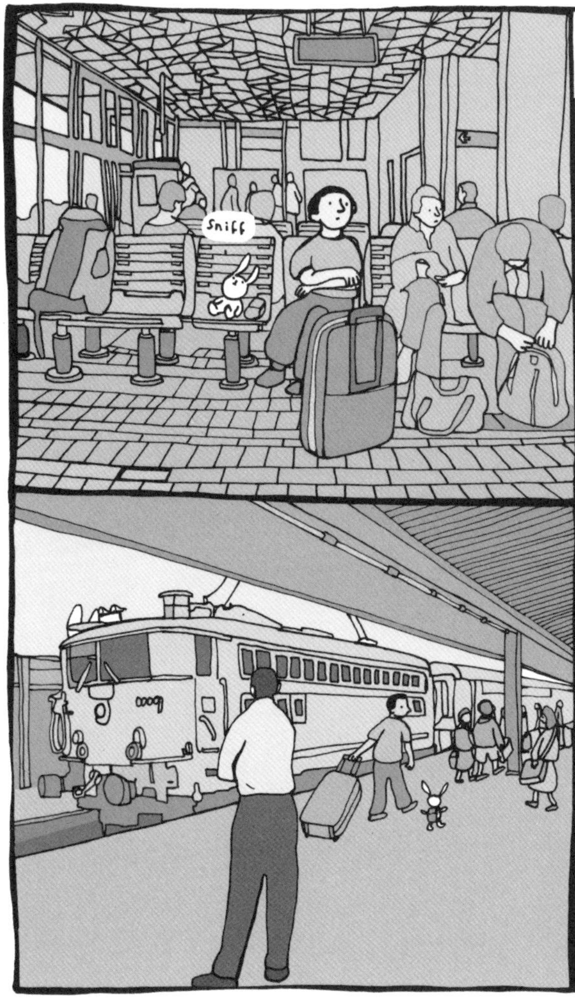
Sniff

Michael Pulcino and Fluffy boarded the Paris to Rome train at 5.30. Michael found their sleeper, put away his case and said hello to the other passengers.
Everyone was being simultaneously polite and annoyed with each other because the carriage was too small for six adults and a bunny.

As a dust particle I don't have that problem. There were millions of us particles in that carriage and we all got along famously – we were partying like it was 1999.

Here is a bit about the other people in the same carriage.

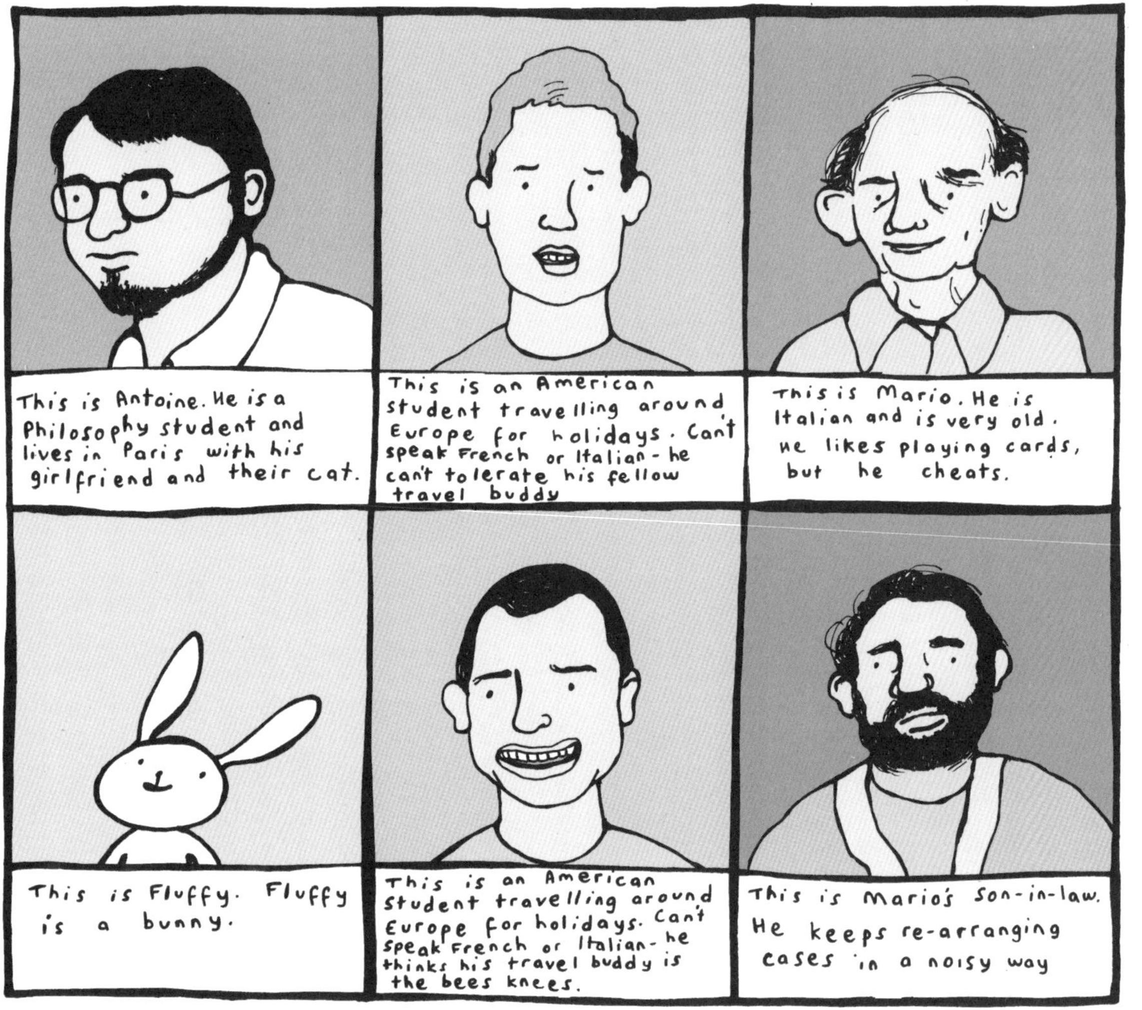
This is Antoine. He is a philosophy student and lives in Paris with his girlfriend and their cat.
This is an American student travelling around Europe for holidays. Can't speak French or Italian - he can't tolerate his fellow travel buddy
This is Mario. He is Italian and is very old. He likes playing cards, but he cheats.
This is Fluffy. Fluffy is a bunny.
This is an American student travelling around Europe for holidays. Can't speak French or Italian - he thinks his travel buddy is the bees knees.
This is Mario's son-in-law. He keeps re-arranging cases in a noisy way

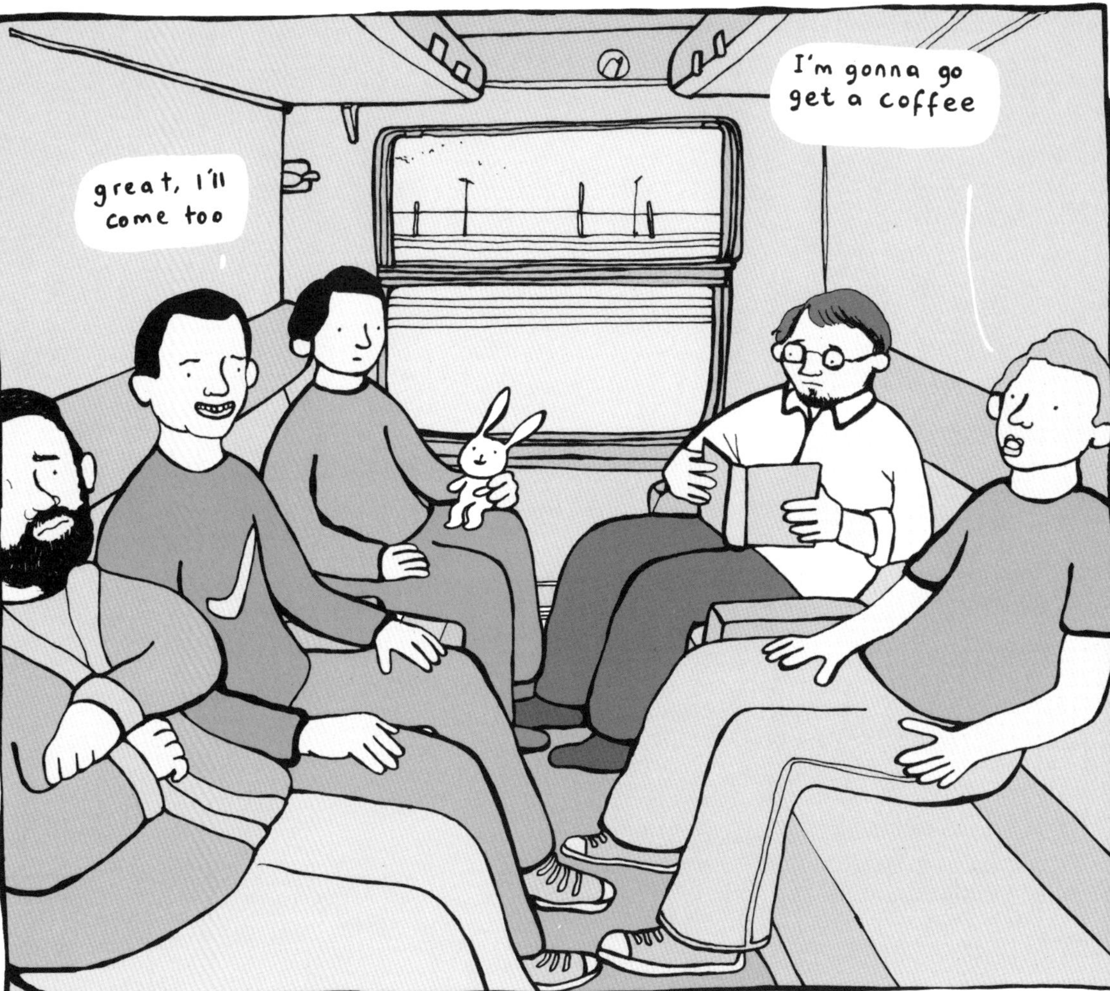
I'm gonna go get a coffee
great, I'll come too

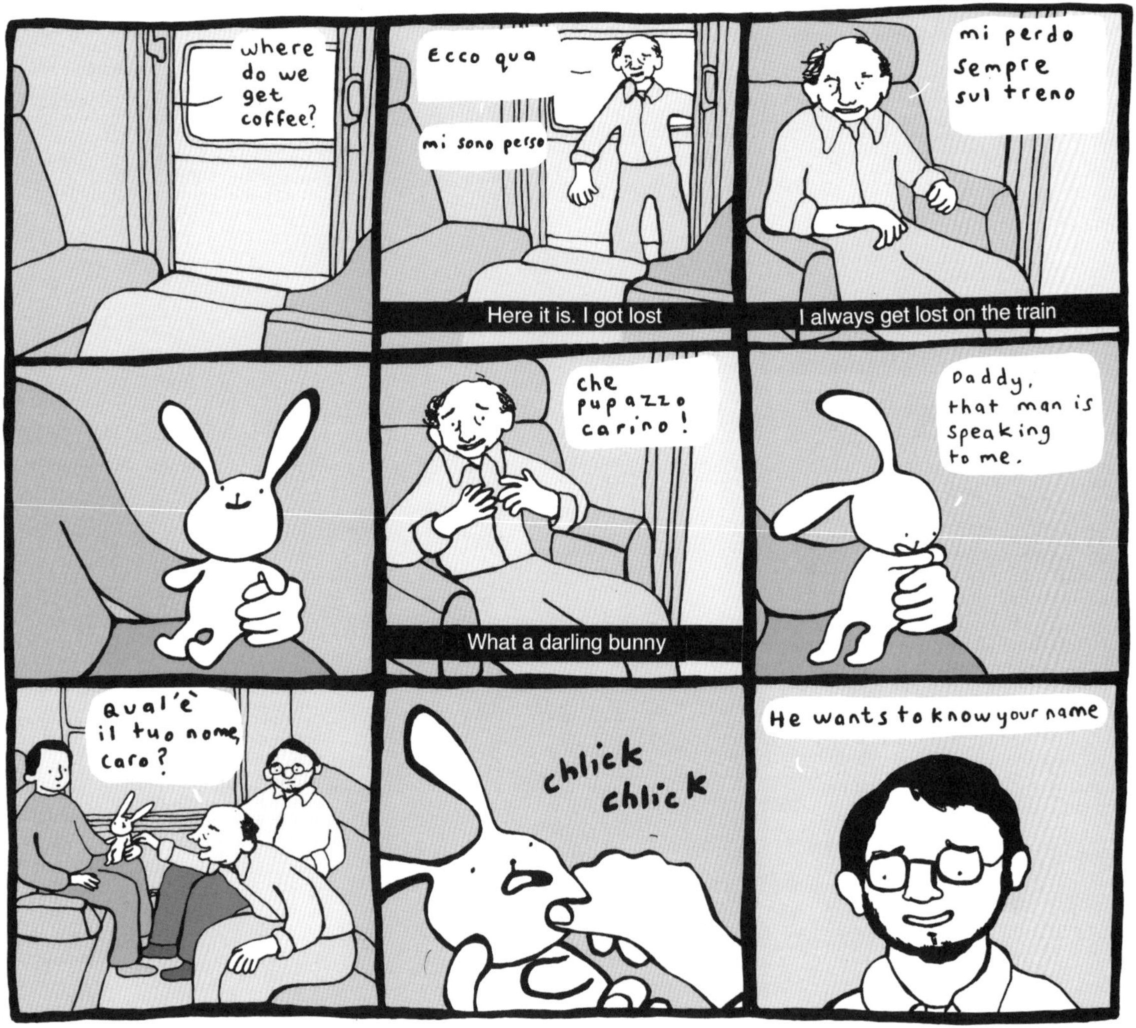
where do we get coffee?
Ecco qua
mi sono perso
Here it is. I got lost
mi perdo sempre sul treno
I always get lost on the train
che pupazzo carino!
What a darling bunny
Daddy, that man is speaking to me.
Qual'è il tuo nome, caro?
chlick chlick
He wants to know your name

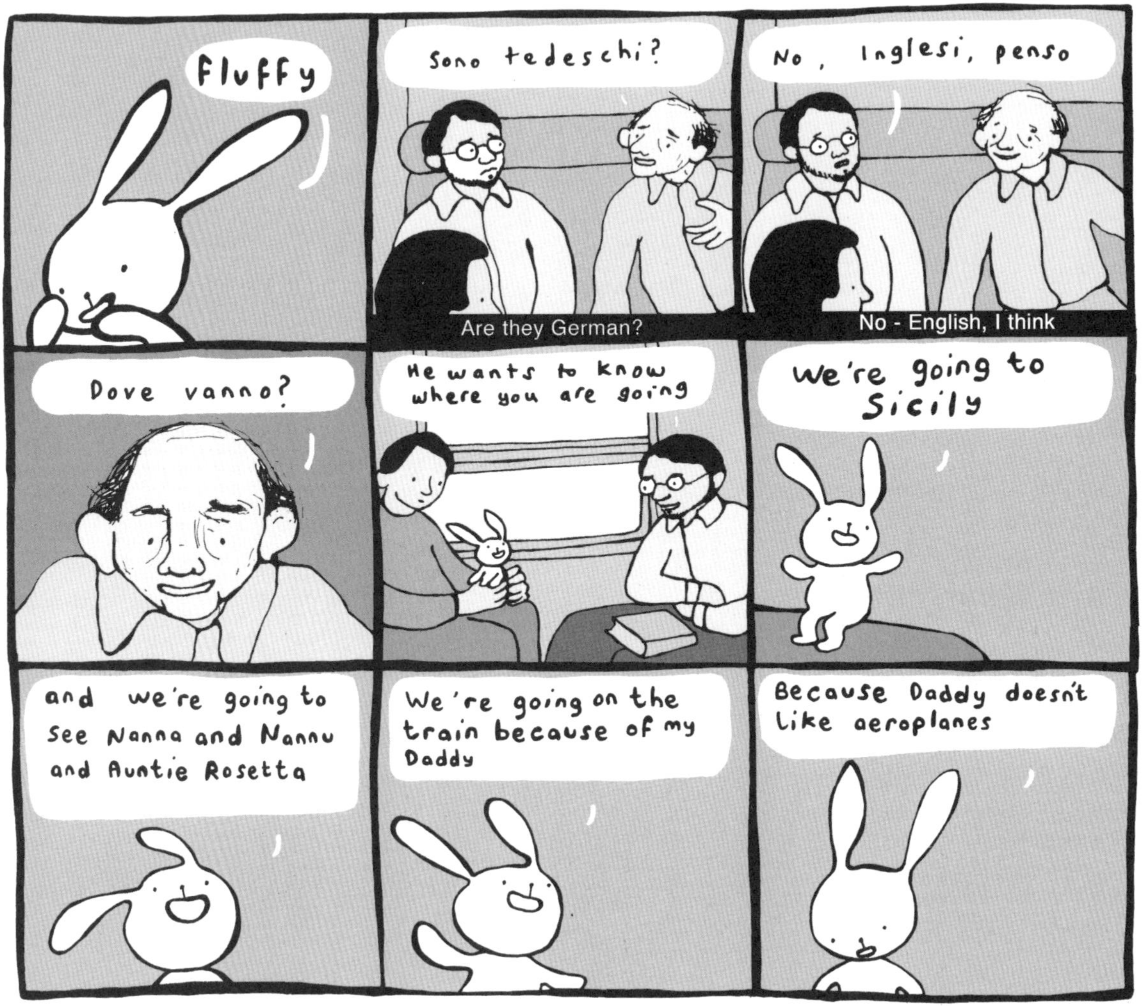
Fluffy
Sono tedeschi?
Are they German?
No, Inglesi, penso
No - English, I think
Dove vanno?
He wants to know where you are going
We're going to Sicily
and we're going to see Nanna and Nannu and Auntie Rosetta
We're going on the train because of my Daddy
Because Daddy doesn't like aeroplanes

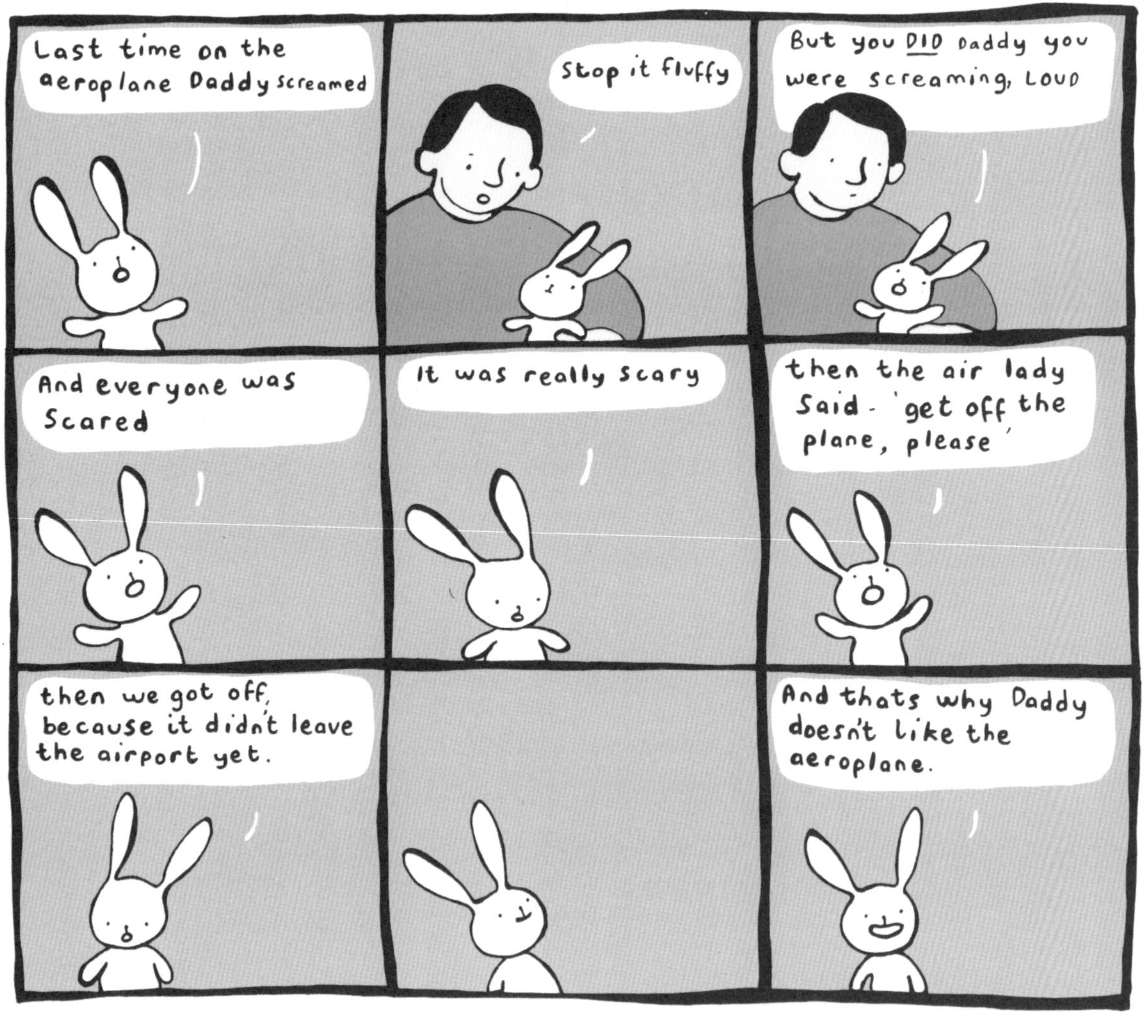
Last time on the aeroplane Daddy screamed
Stop it fluffy
But you DID Daddy you were screaming, LOUD
And everyone was Scared
It was really scary
then the air lady Said - 'get off the plane, please'
then we got off, because it didn't leave the airport yet.
And thats why Daddy doesn't like the aeroplane.

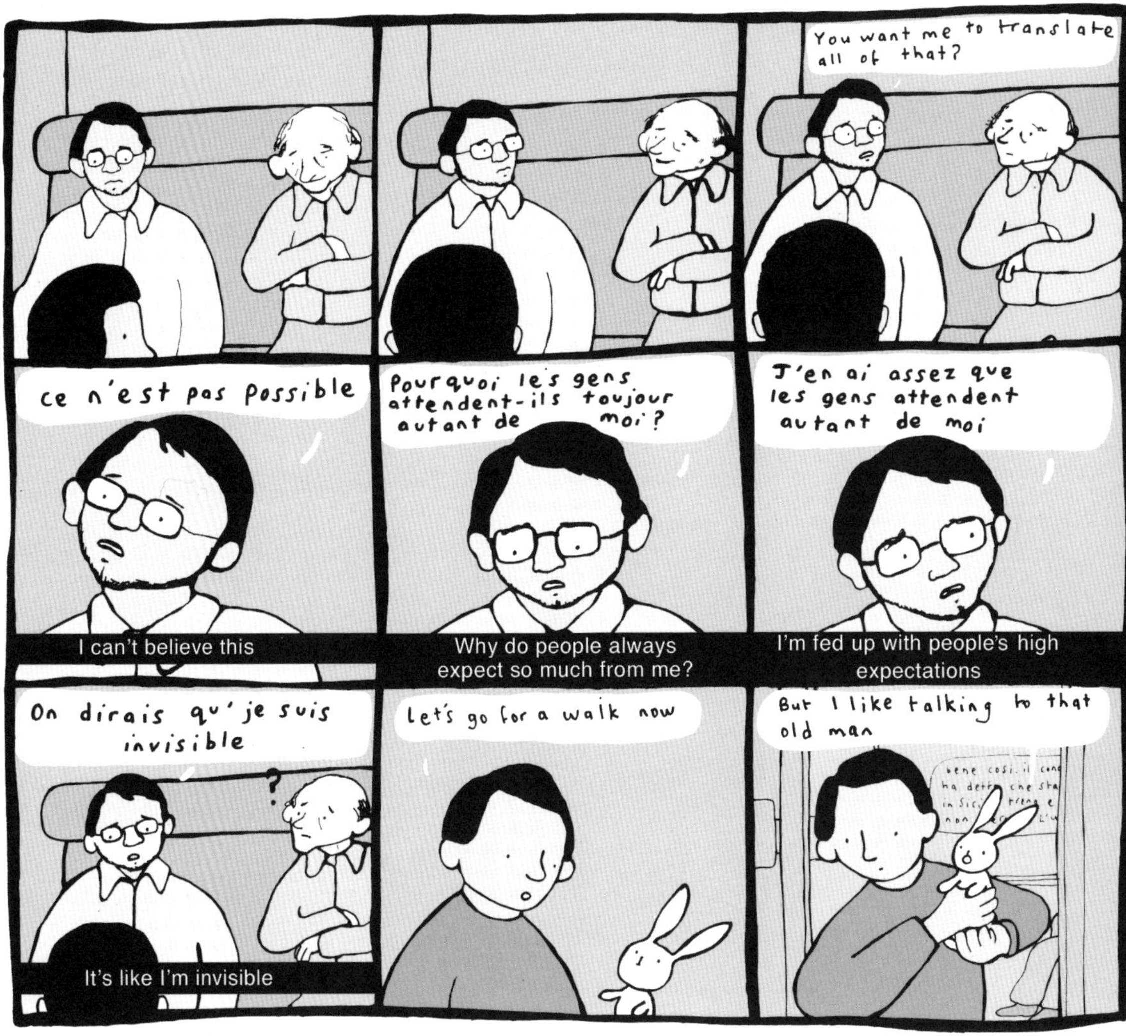

You want me to translate all of that?
ce n'est pas possible
I can't believe this
Pourquoi le's gens attendent-ils toujour autant de moi?
Why do people always expect so much from me?
J'en ai assez que les gens attendent autant de moi
I'm fed up with people's high expectations
On dirais qu' je suis invisible
It's like I'm invisible
Let's go for a walk now
But I like talking to that old man

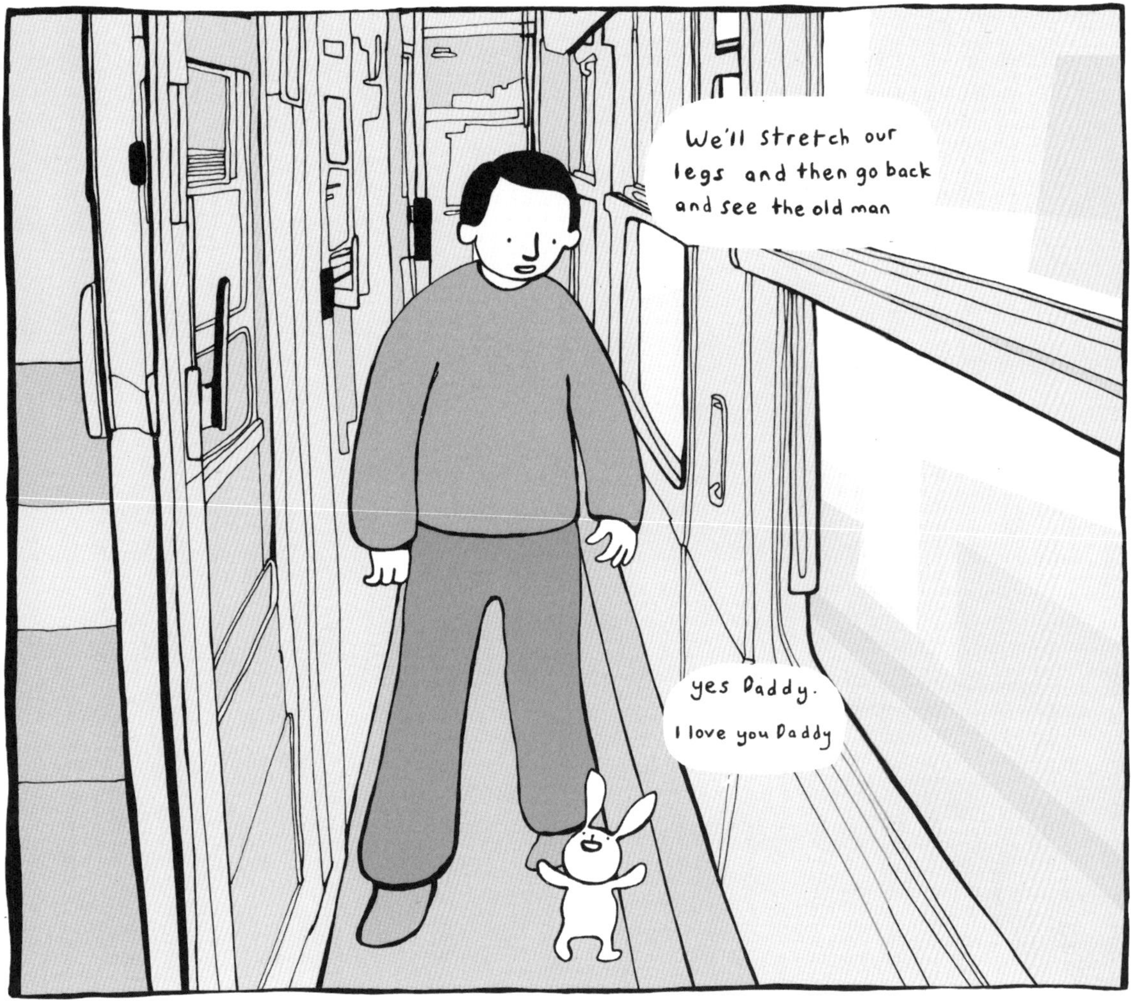
We'll stretch our legs and then go back and see the old man
yes Daddy. I love you Daddy

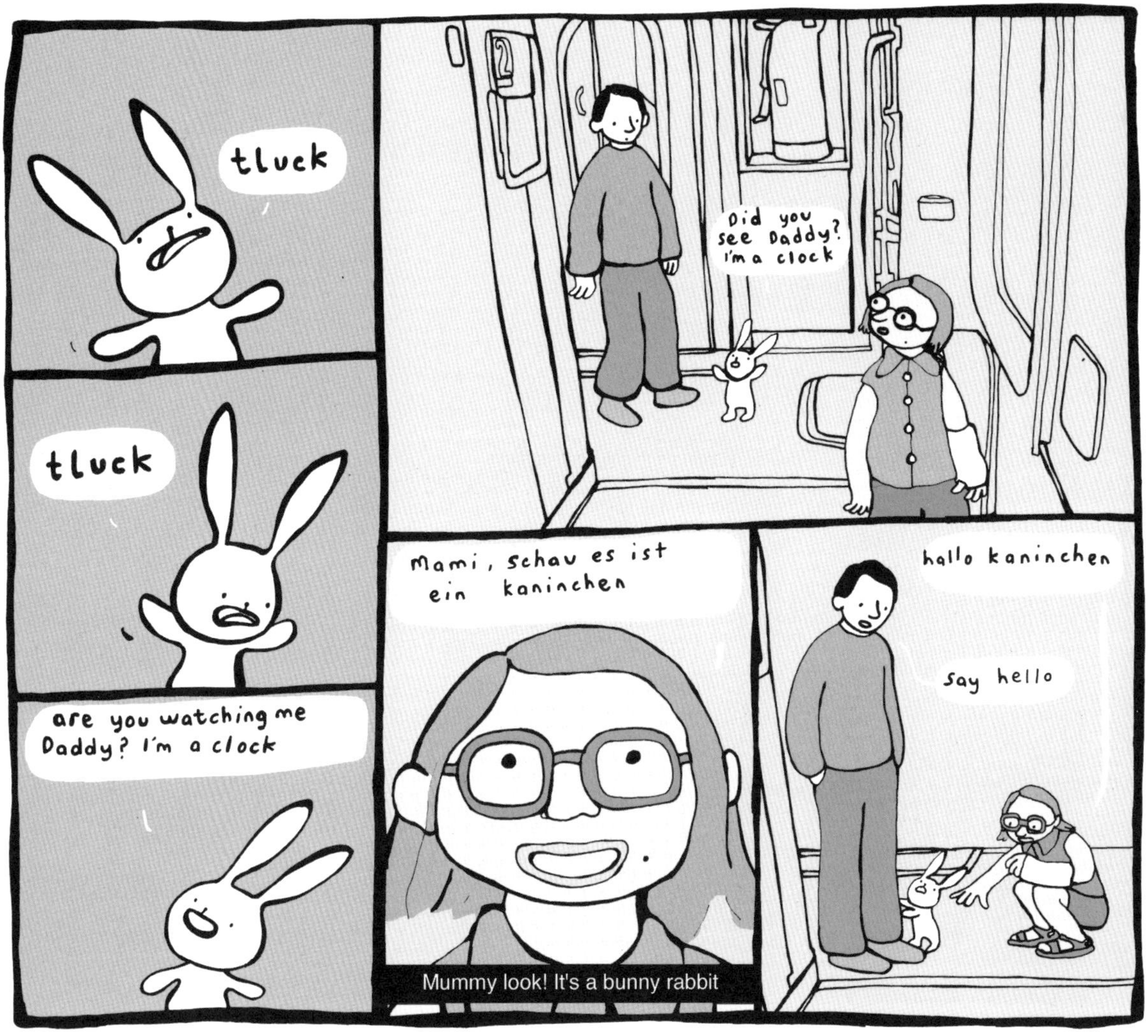
tluck
tluck
are you watching me Daddy? I'm a clock
Did you see Daddy? I'm a clock
Mami, schau es ist ein kaninchen
Mummy look! It's a bunny rabbit
hallo kaninchen
say hello

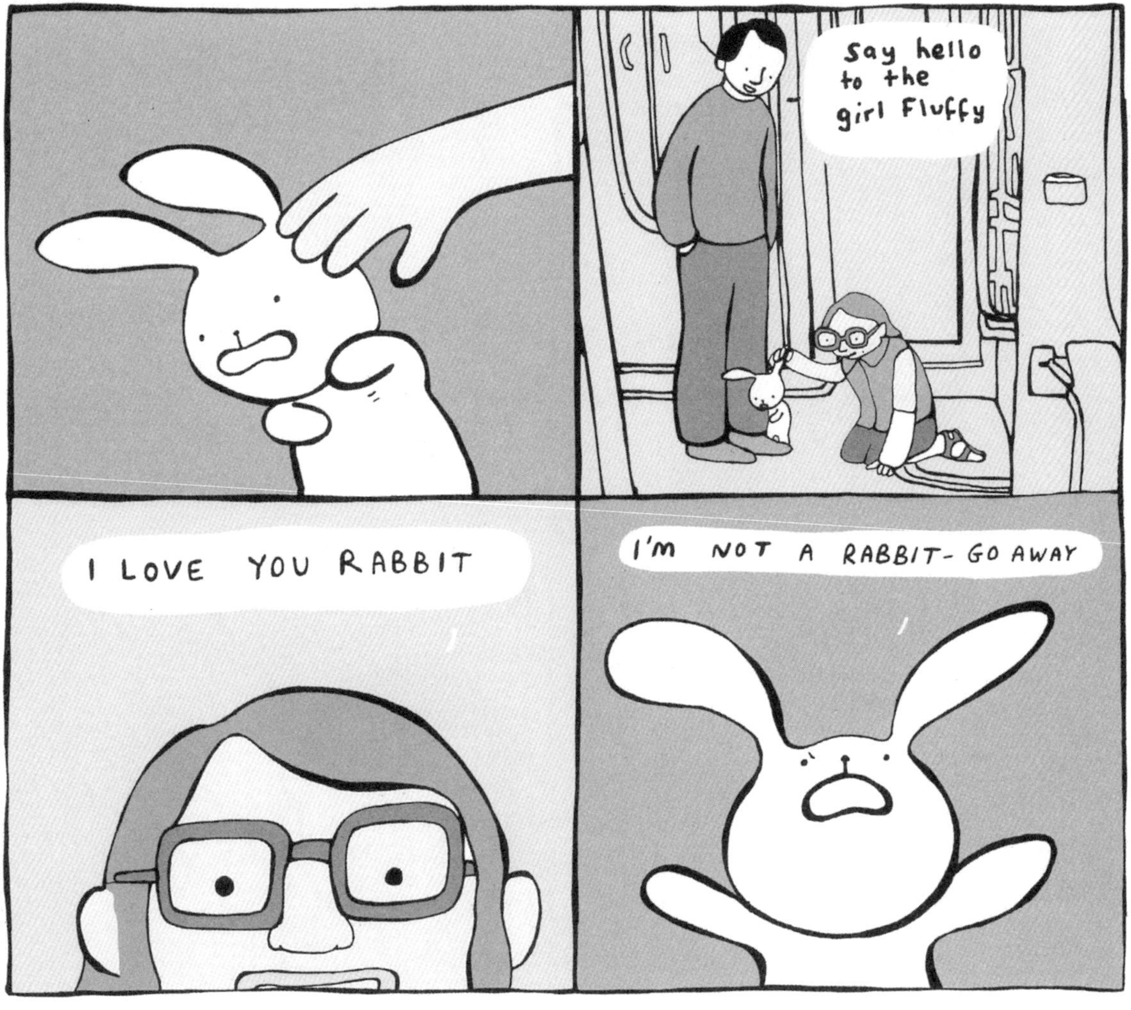
Say hello to the girl Fluffy
I LOVE YOU RABBIT
I'M NOT A RABBIT- GO AWAY

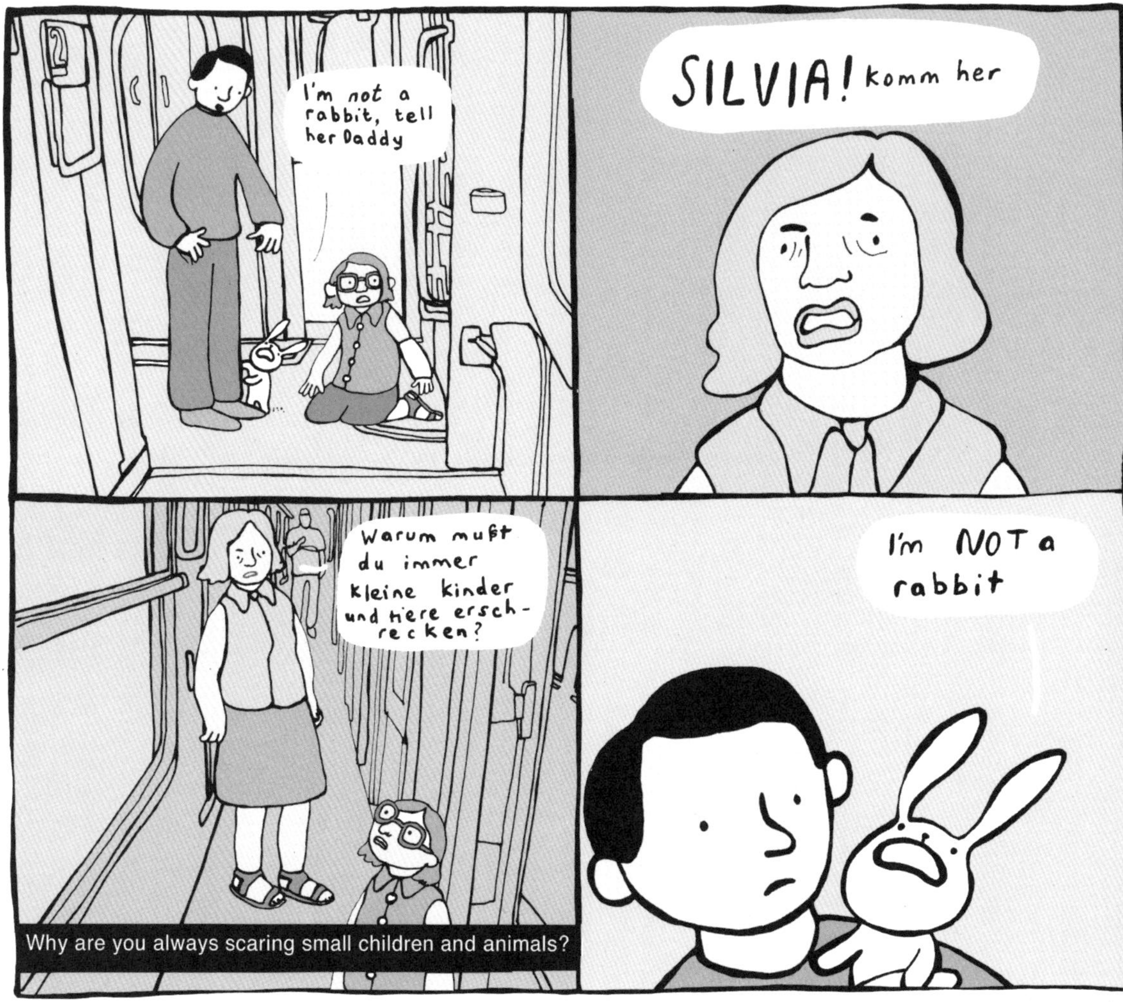
I'm not a rabbit, tell her Daddy
SILVIA! komm her
Warum mußt du immer kleine kinder und tiere ersch-recken?
Why are you always scaring small children and animals?
I'm NOT a rabbit

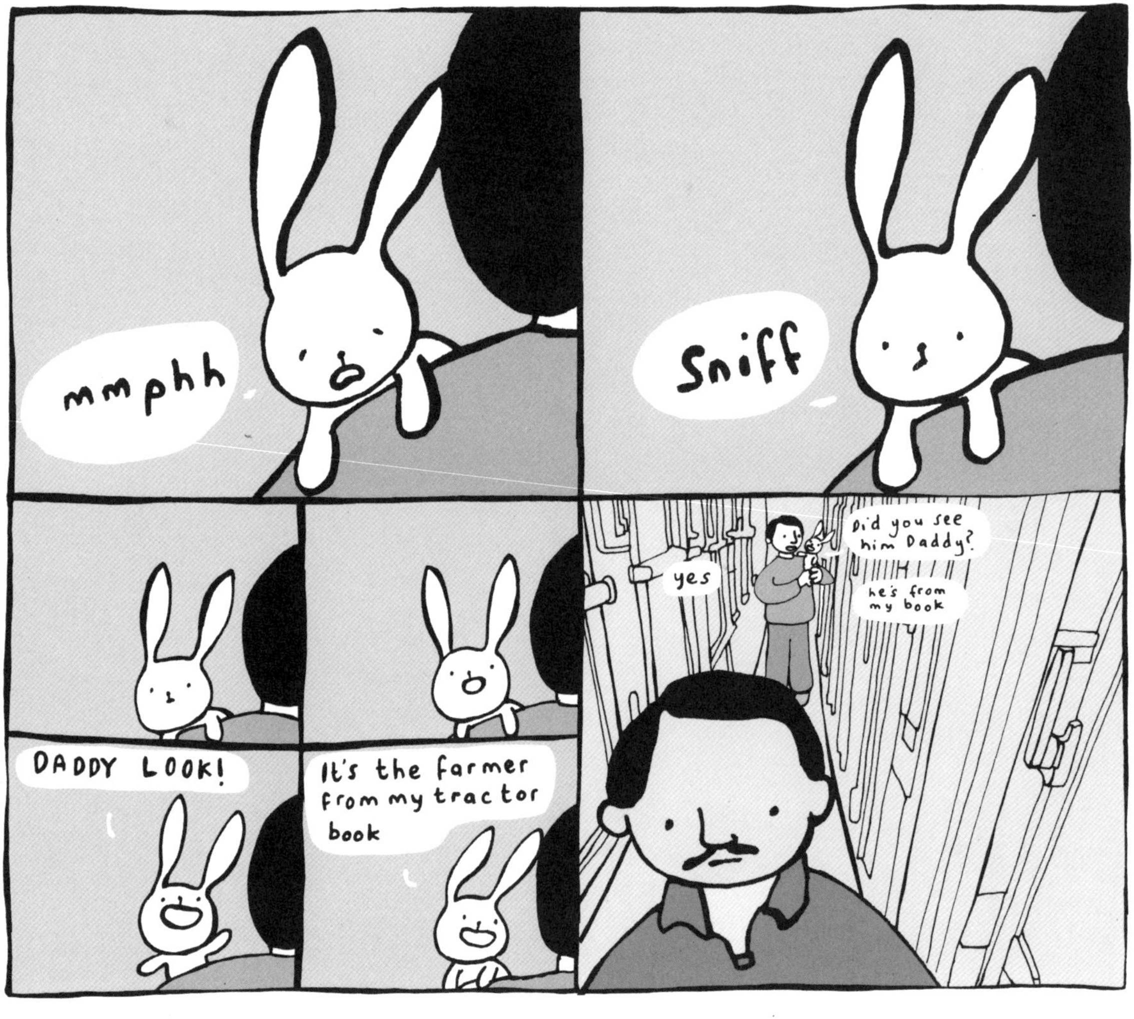
mmphh
Sniff
DADDY LOOK!
It's the farmer from my tractor book
Did you see him Daddy?
yes
he's from my book

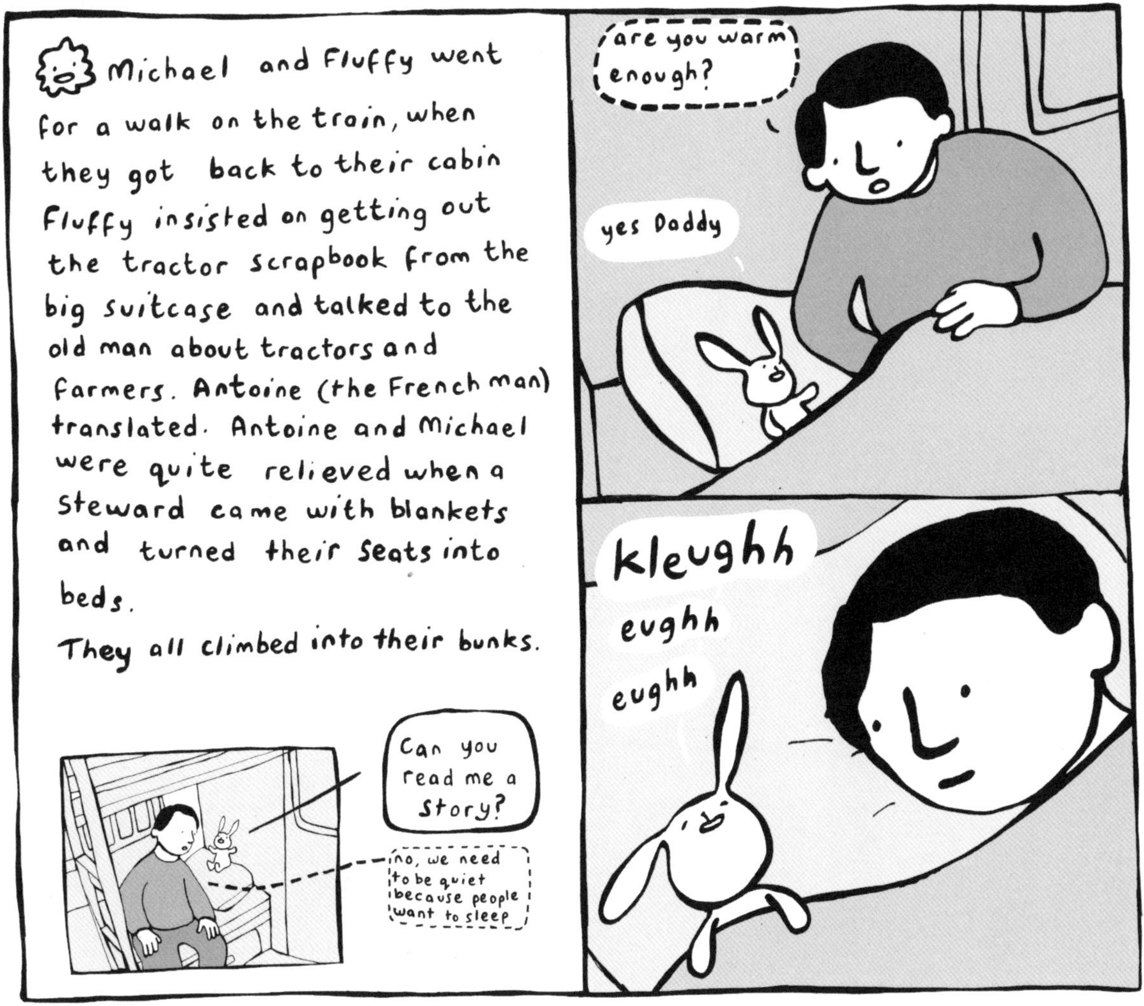
Michael and Fluffy went for a walk on the train, when they got back to their cabin Fluffy insisted on getting out the tractor scrapbook from the big suitcase and talked to the old man about tractors and farmers. Antoine (the French man) translated. Antoine and Michael were quite relieved when a steward came with blankets and turned their seats into beds.
They all climbed into their bunks.
Can you read me a story?
no, we need to be quiet because people want to sleep
are you warm enough?
yes Daddy
kleughh
eughh
eughh

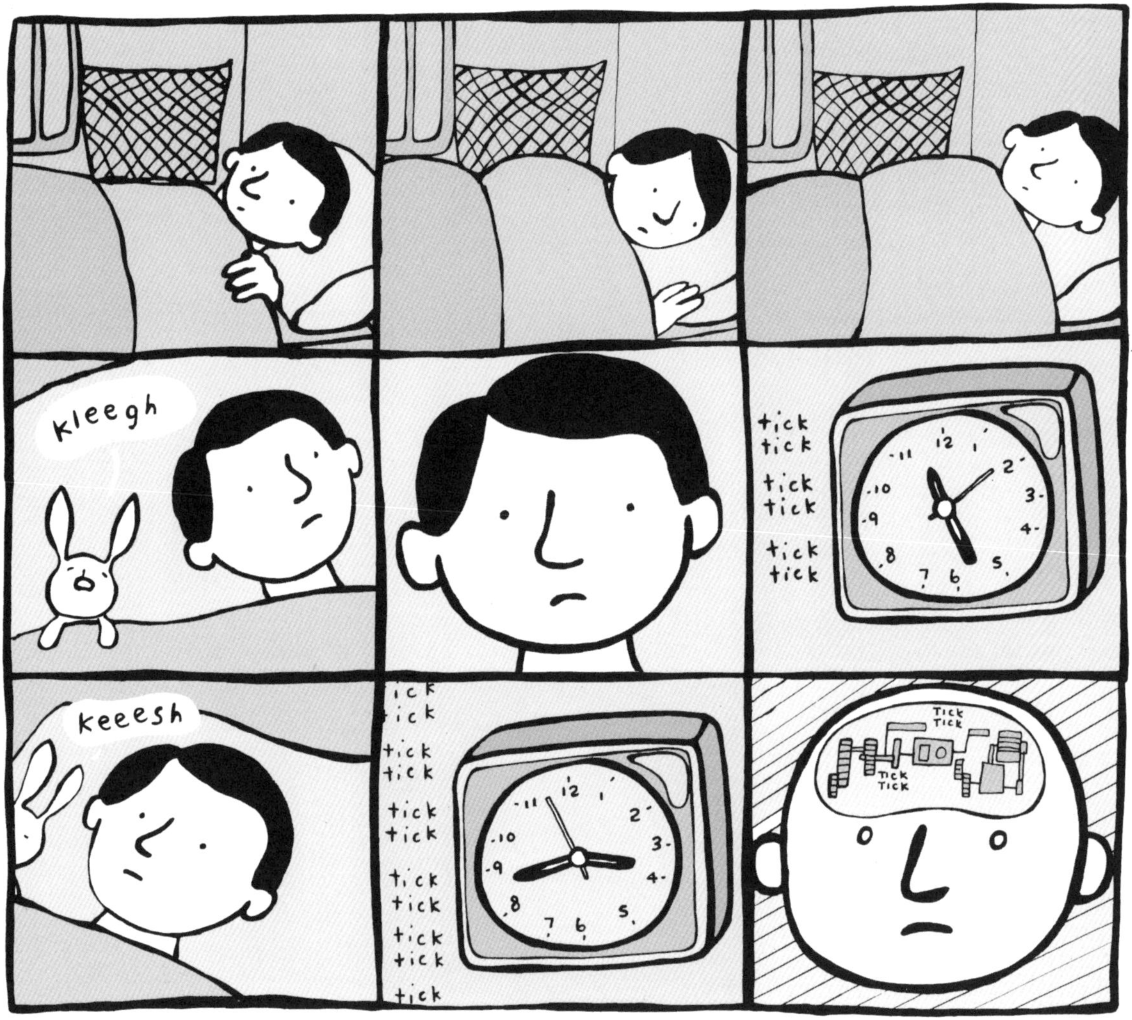
kleegh
tick tick
tick tick
tick tick
keeesh
tick
tick tick
tick tick
tick tick
tick tick
tick
TICK TICK
TICK TICK

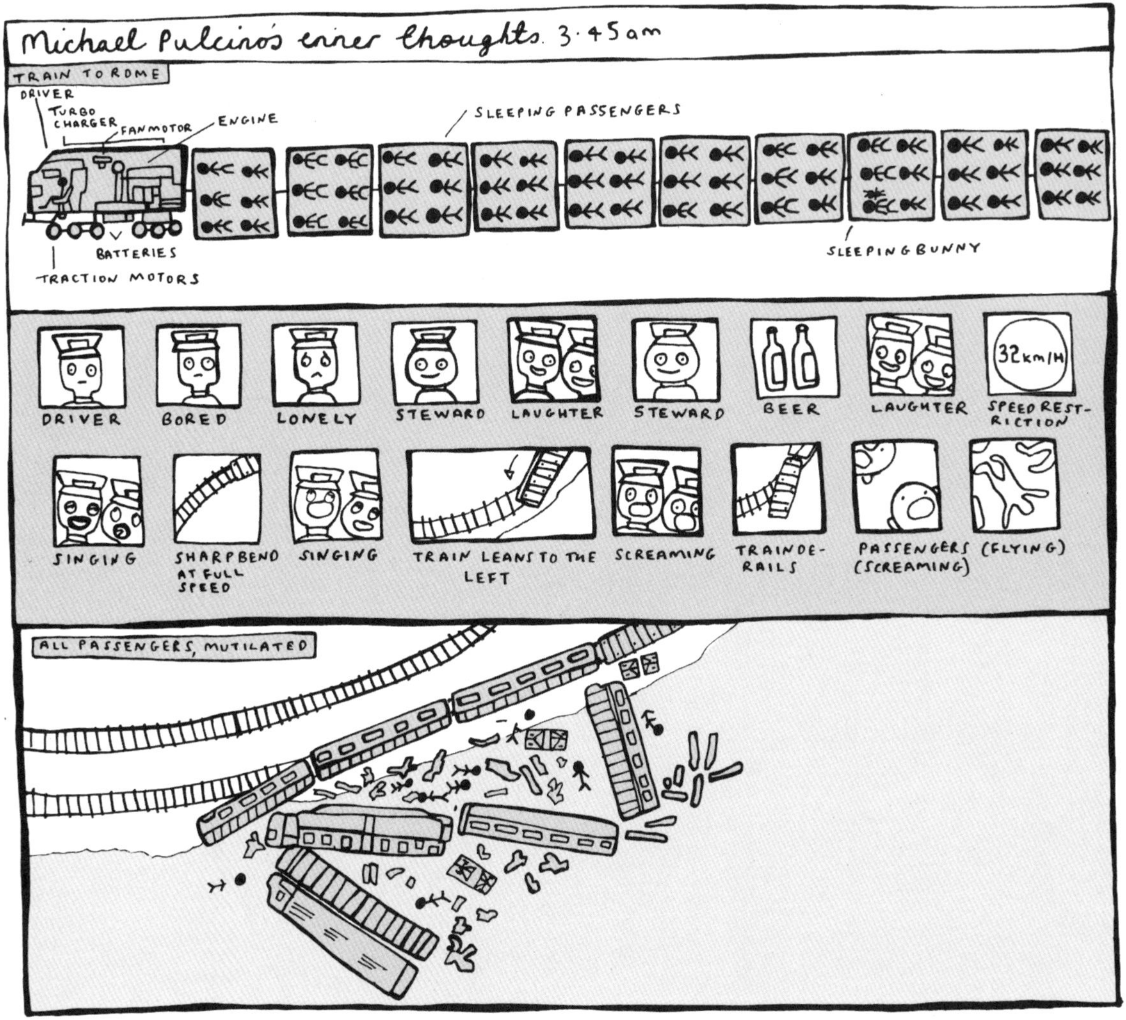
Michael Pulcino's inner thoughts. 3·45am
TRAIN TO ROME
DRIVER
TURBO CHARGER
FANMOTOR
ENGINE
SLEEPING PASSENGERS
BATTERIES
TRACTION MOTORS
SLEEPING BUNNY
DRIVER
BORED
LONELY
STEWARD
LAUGHTER
STEWARD
BEER
LAUGHTER
32km/H
SPEED RESTRICTION
SINGING
SHARPBEND AT FULL SPEED
SINGING
TRAIN LEANS TO THE LEFT
SCREAMING
TRAIN DERAILS
PASSENGERS (SCREAMING)
(FLYING)
ALL PASSENGERS, MUTILATED

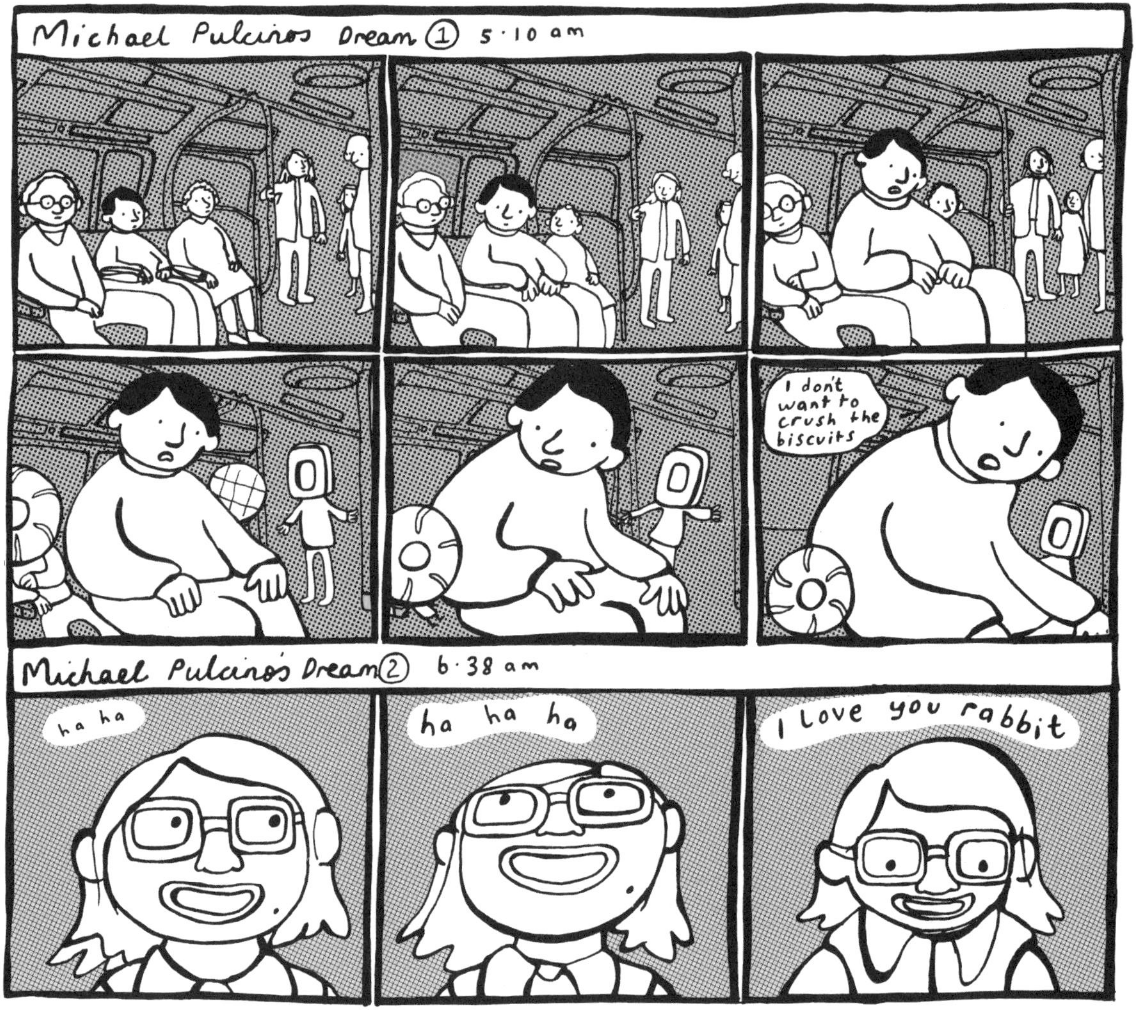
Michael Pulcinos Dream (1) 5·10 am
I don't want to crush the biscuits
Michael Pulcino's Dream (2) 6·38 am
ha ha
ha ha ha
I love you rabbit

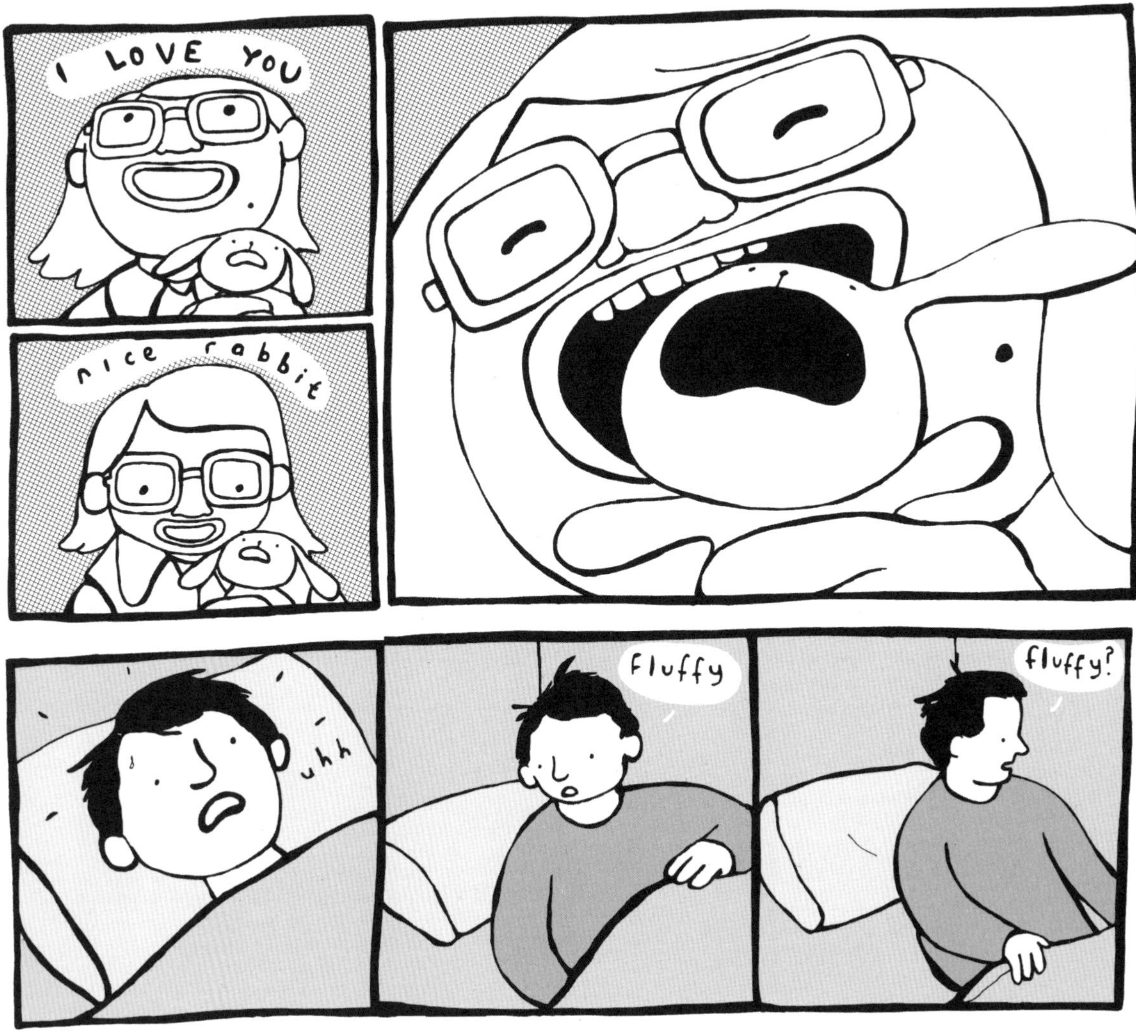
I LOVE YOU
nice rabbit
uhh
fluffy
fluffy?

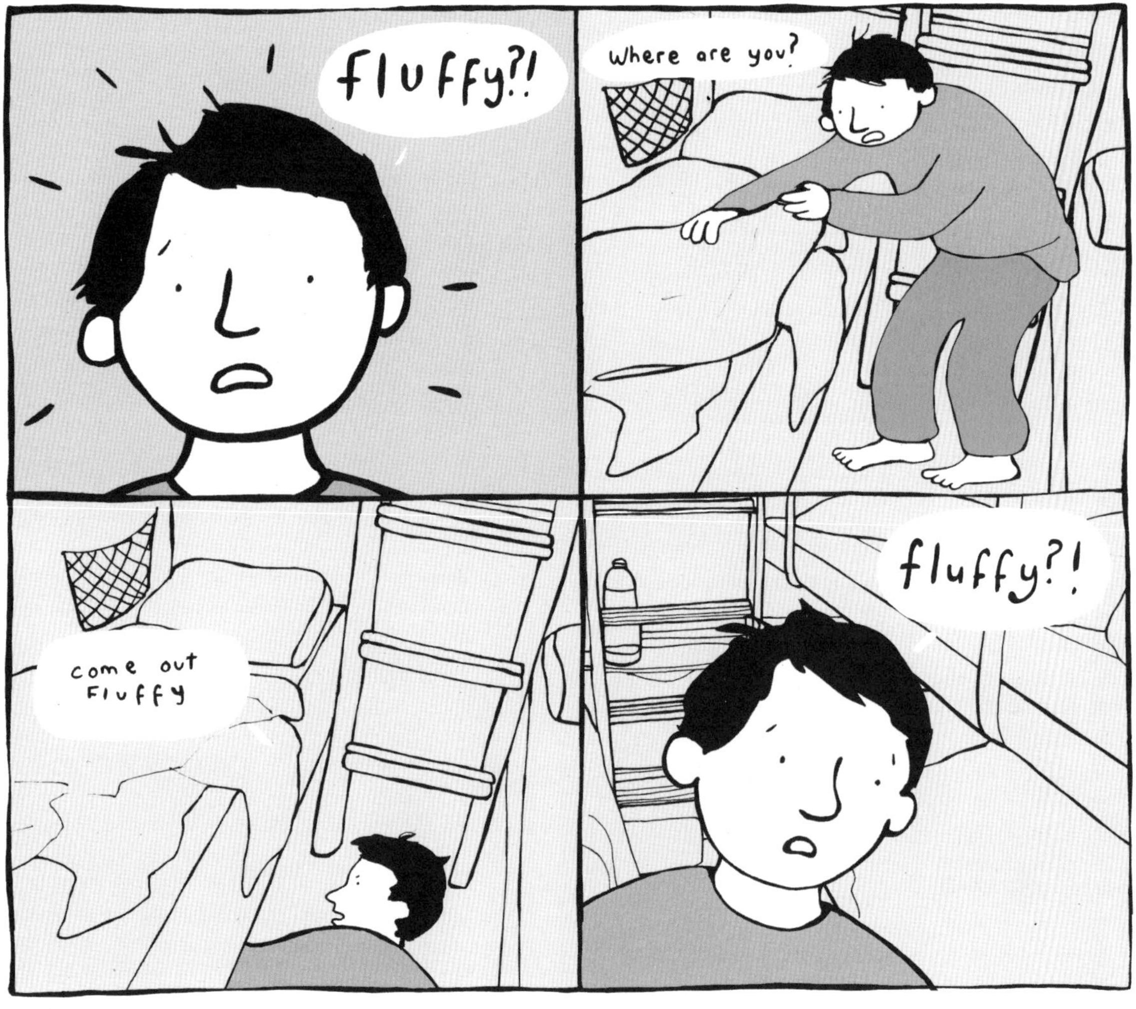
fluffy?!
where are you?
come out fluffy
fluffy?!

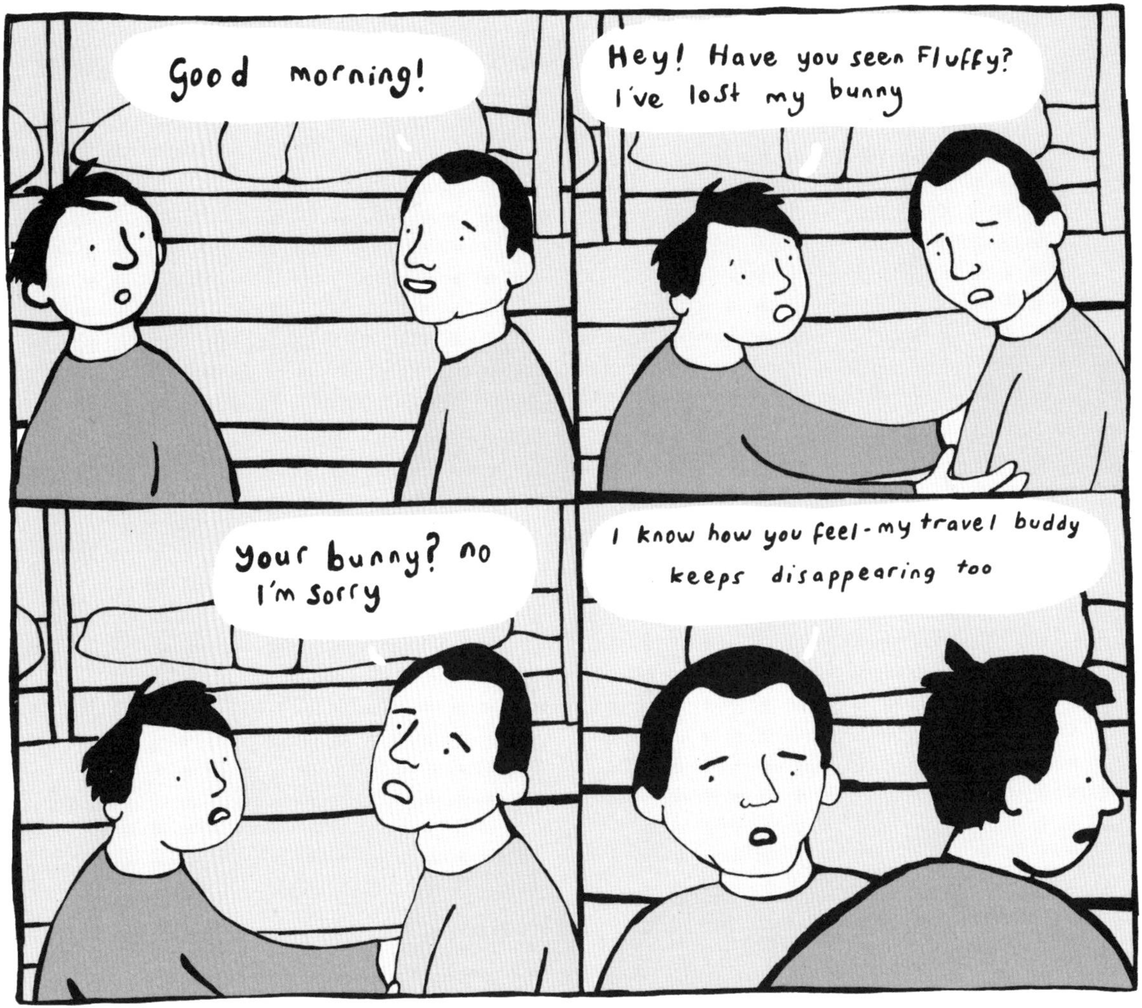
Good morning!
Hey! Have you seen Fluffy? I've lost my bunny
Your bunny? no I'm sorry
I know how you feel-my travel buddy keeps disappearing too

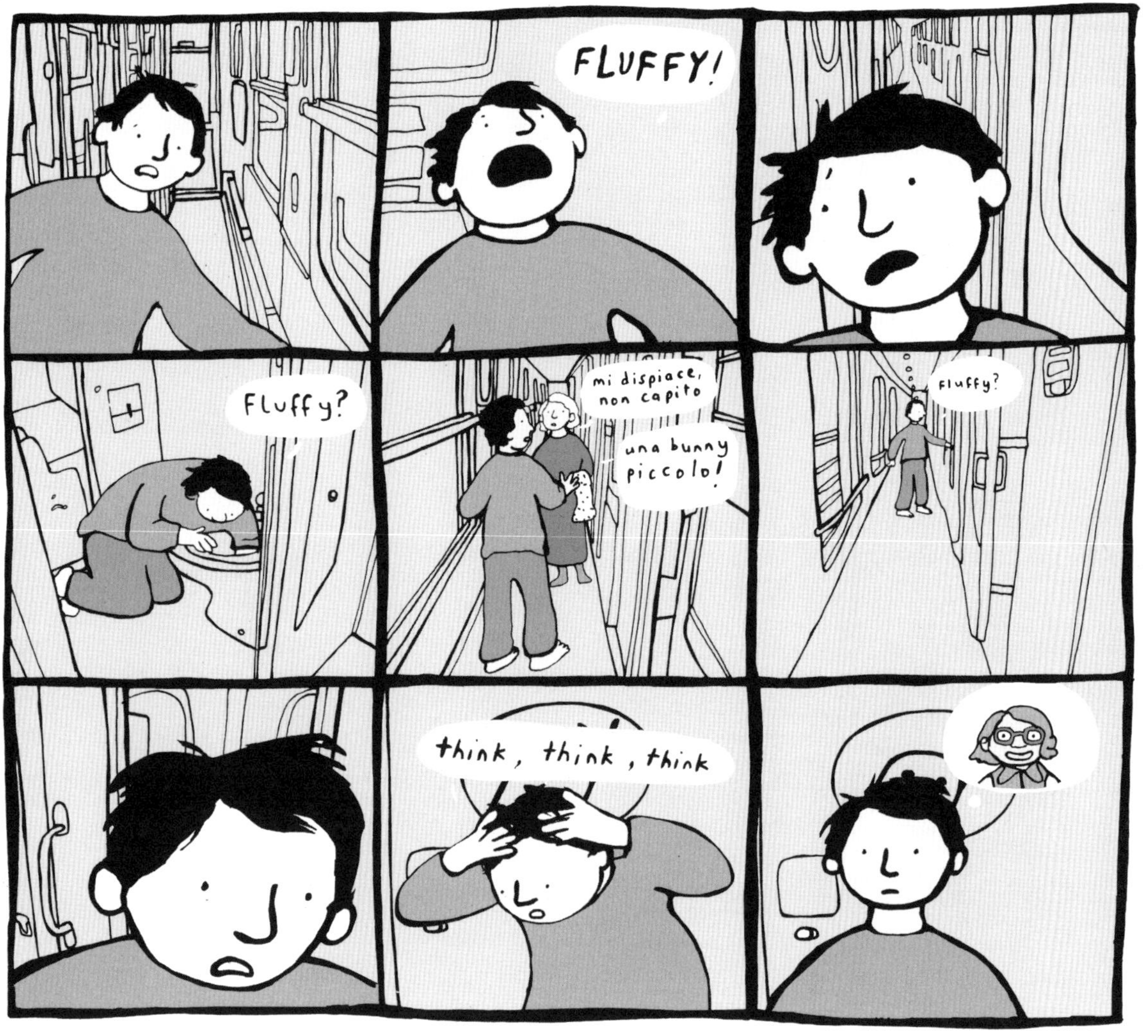
FLUFFY!
Fluffy?
mi dispiace, non capito
una bunny piccolo!
Fluffy?
think, think, think

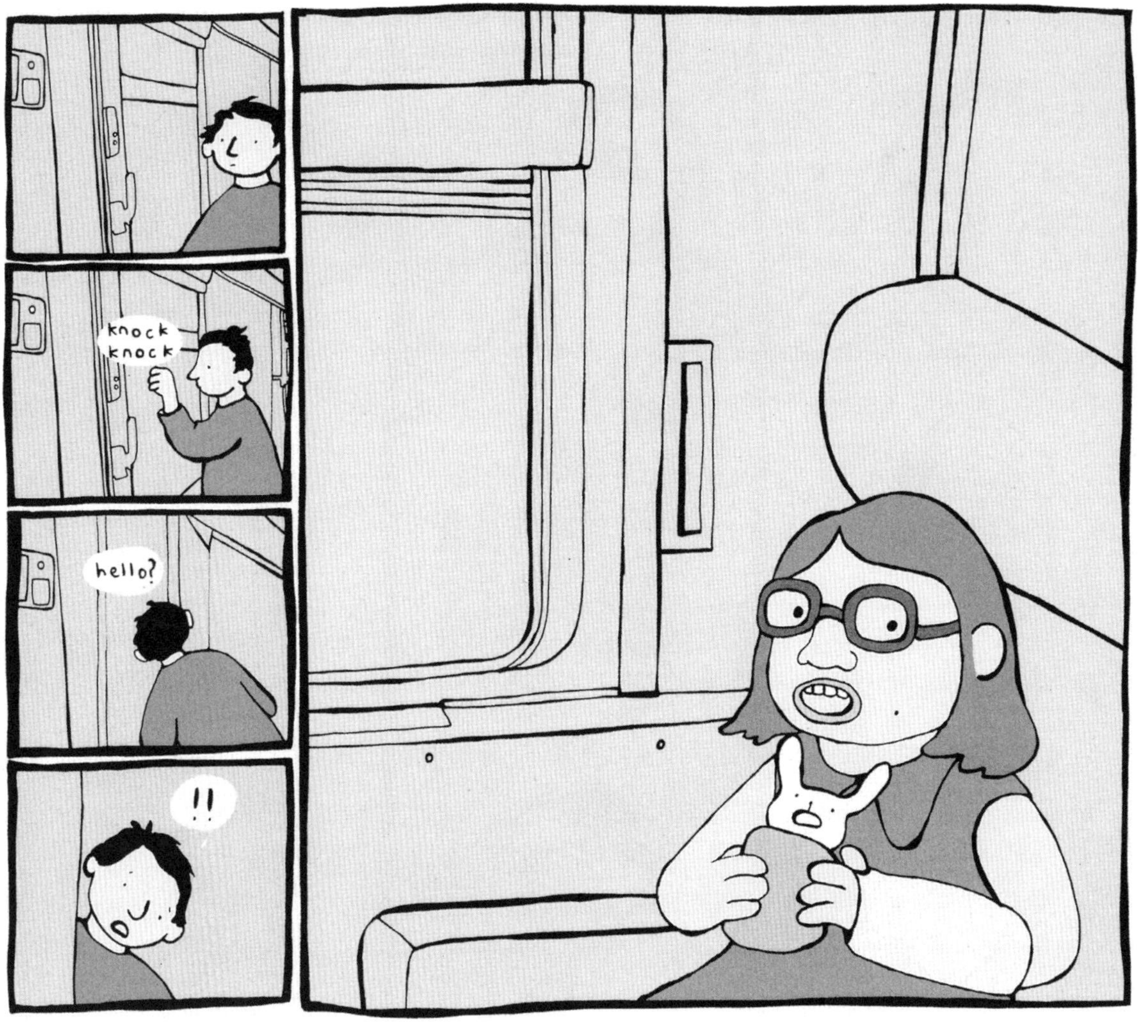
knock
knock
hello?
!!

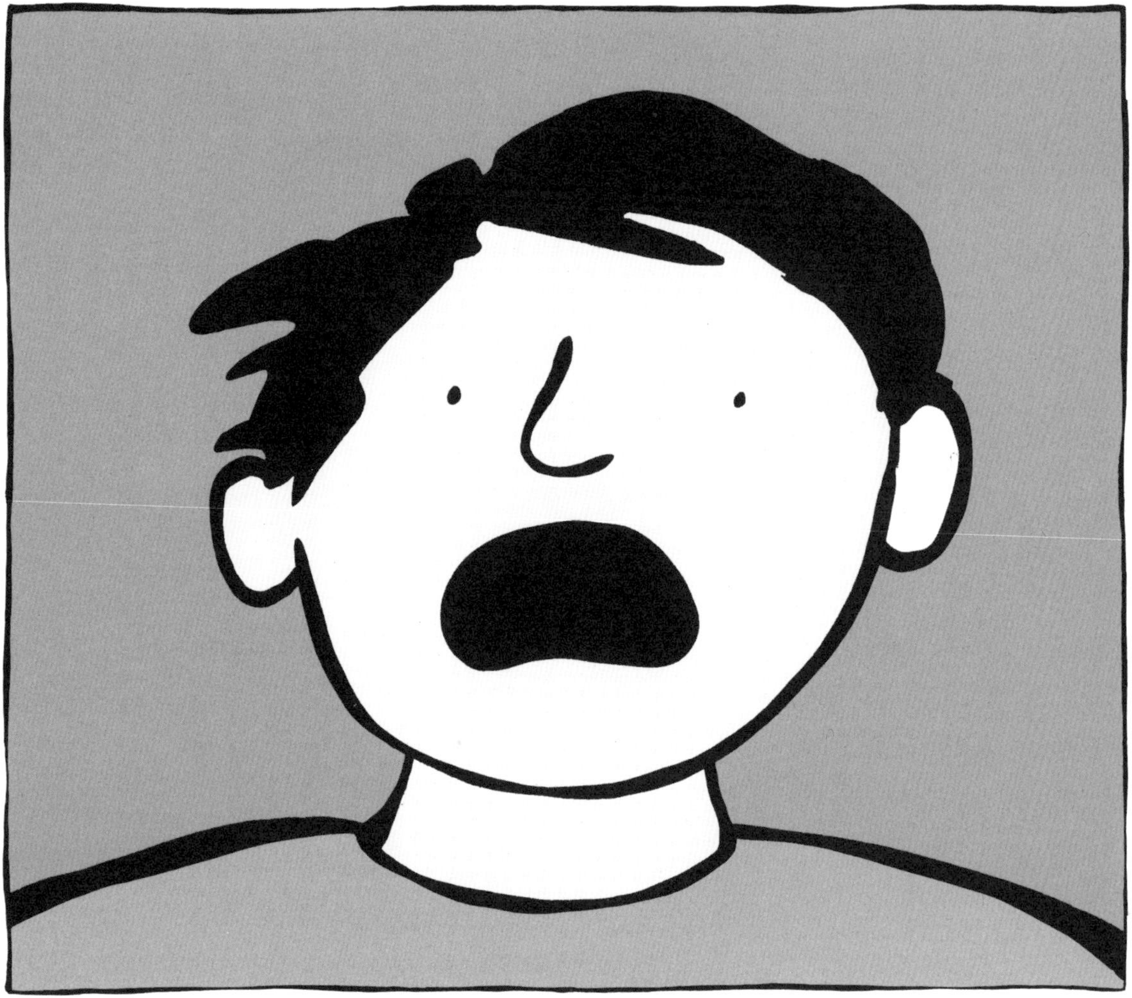

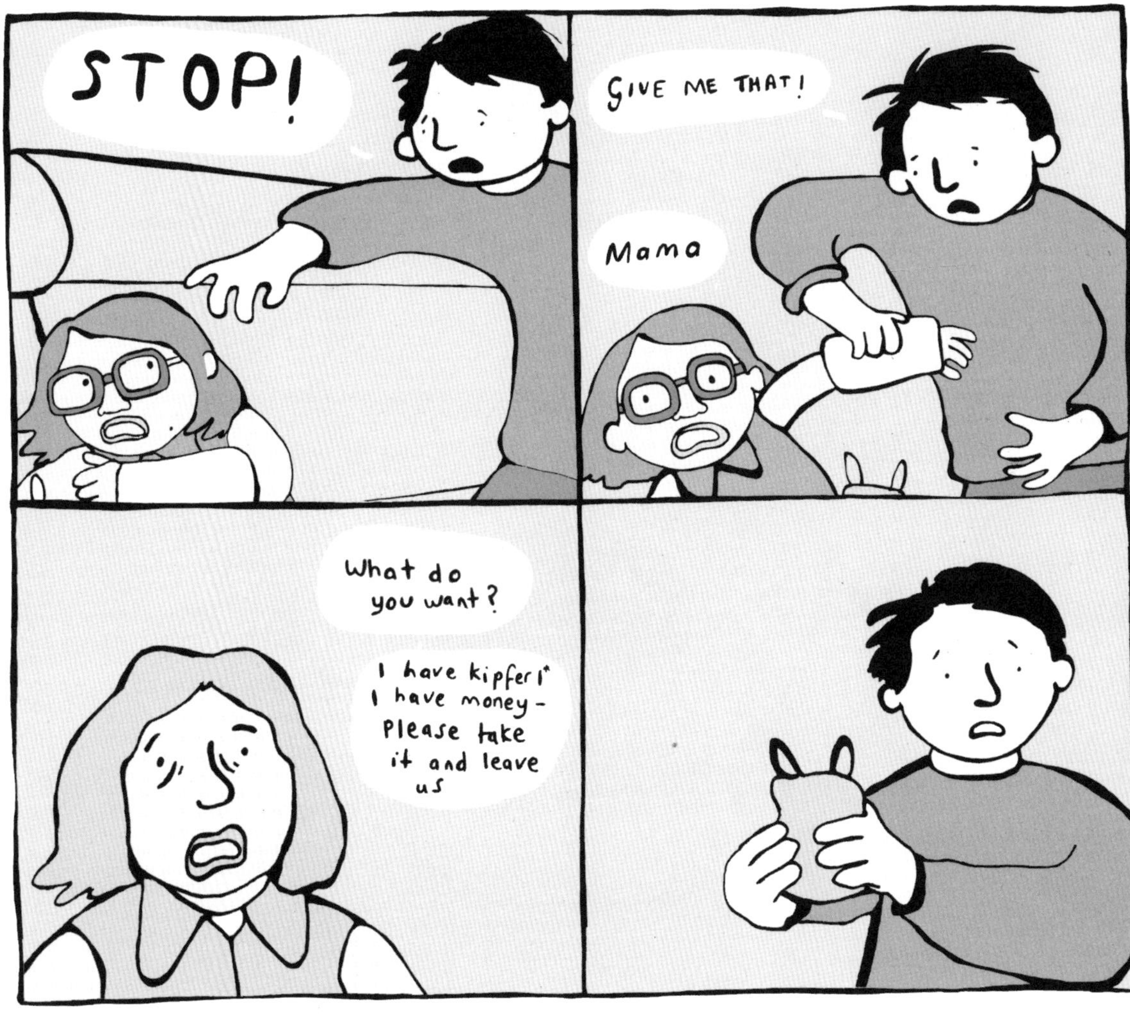
STOP!
GIVE ME THAT!
Mama
What do you want?
I have kipferl* I have money - Please take it and leave us

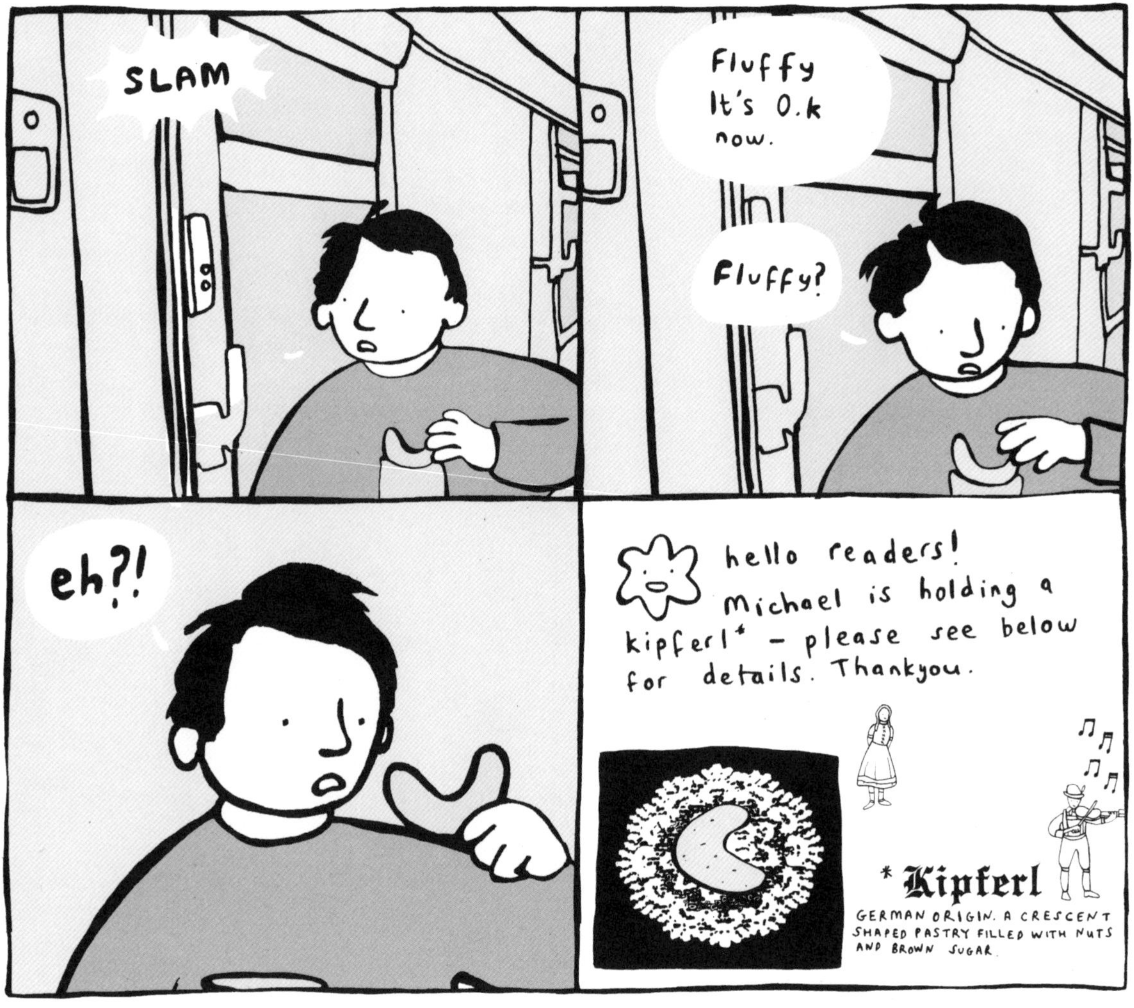
SLAM
Fluffy It's O.k now.
Fluffy?
eh?!
hello readers! Michael is holding a kipferl* - please see below for details. Thankyou.
* Kipferl
GERMAN ORIGIN. A CRESCENT SHAPED PASTRY FILLED WITH NUTS AND BROWN SUGAR.

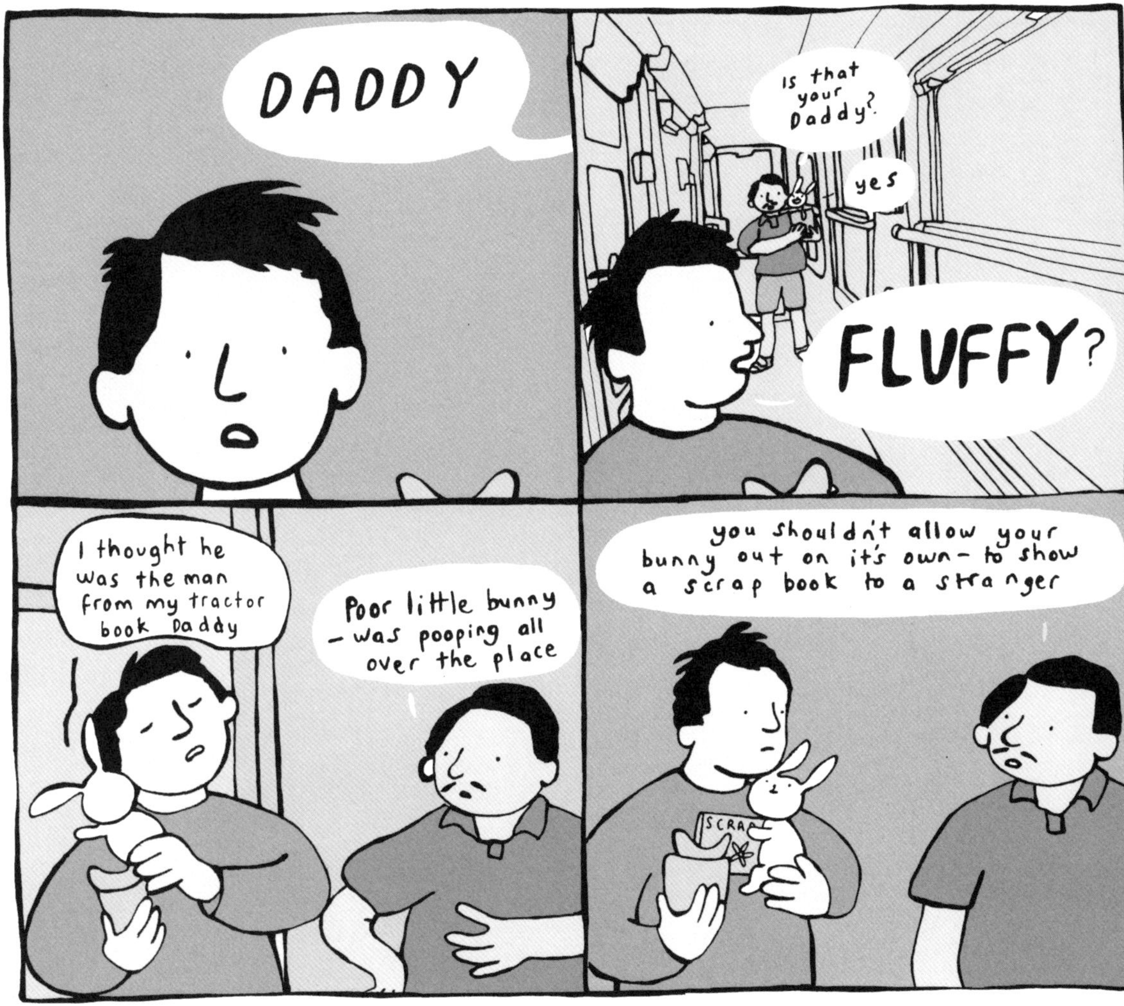
DADDY
Is that your Daddy?
yes
FLUFFY?
I thought he was the man from my tractor book Daddy
Poor little bunny - was pooping all over the place
you shouldn't allow your bunny out on it's own - to show a scrap book to a stranger
SCRAP

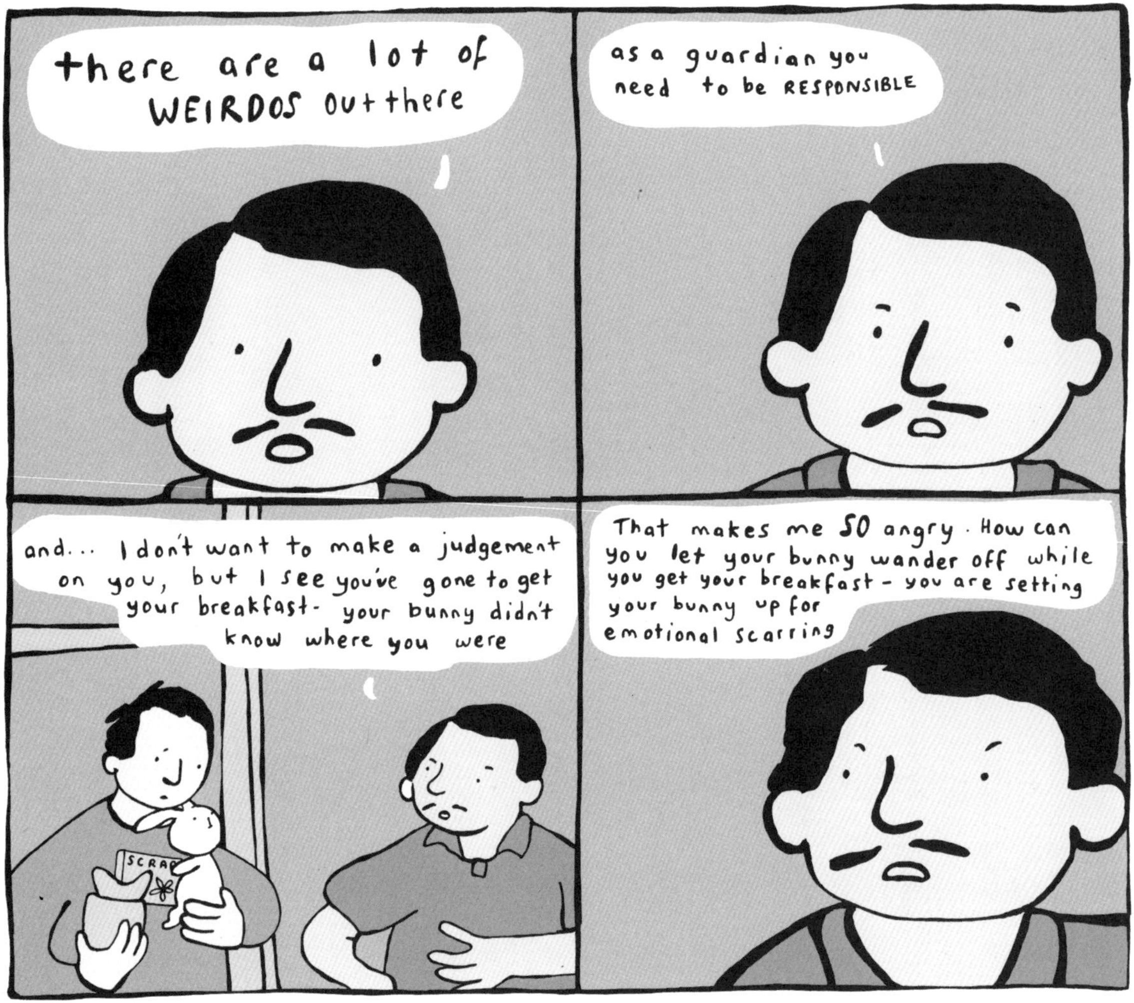
there are a lot of WEIRDOS out there
as a guardian you need to be RESPONSIBLE
and... I don't want to make a judgement on you, but I see you've gone to get your breakfast- your bunny didn't know where you were
SCRAP
That makes me SO angry. How can you let your bunny wander off while you get your breakfast - you are setting your bunny up for emotional scarring

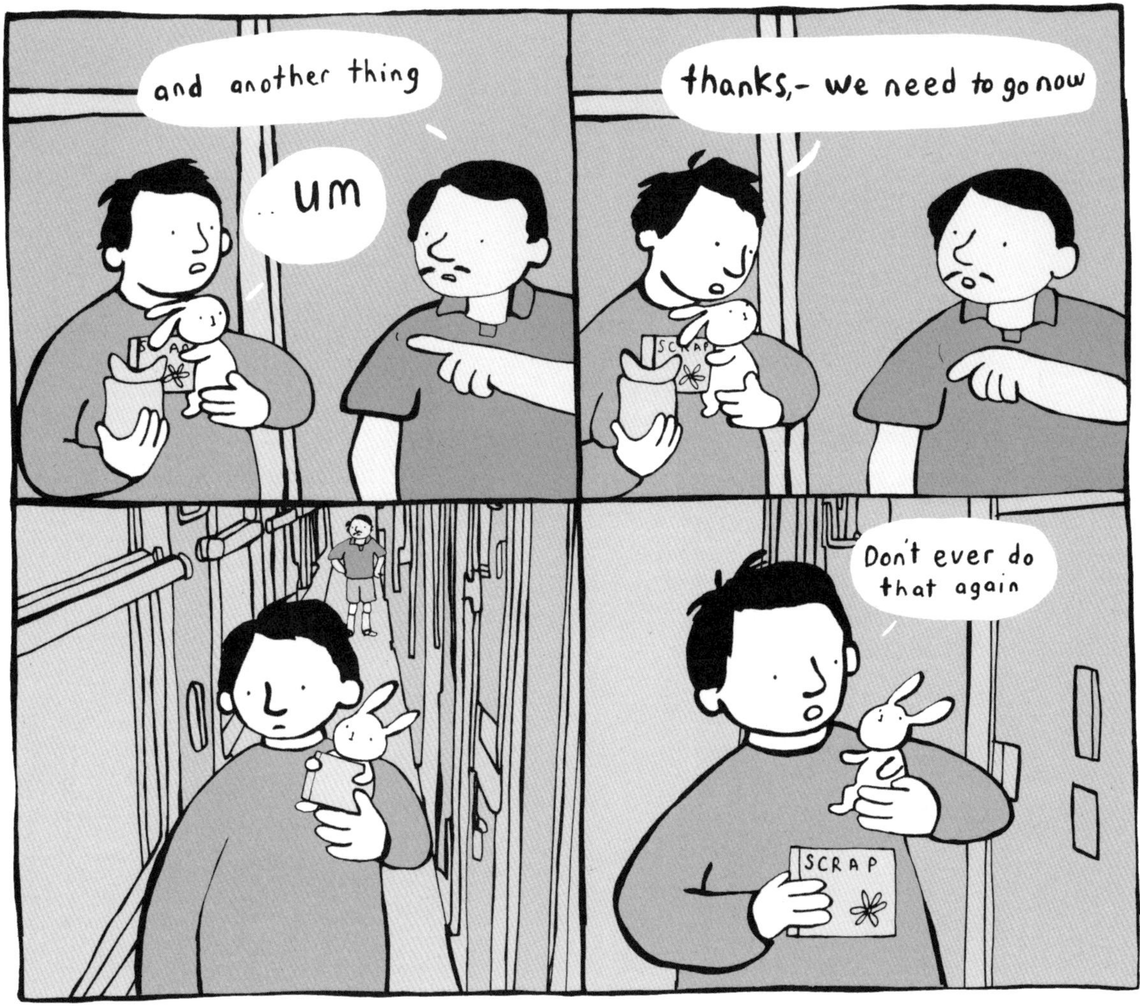

and another thing
um
thanks,- we need to go now
Don't ever do that again
SCRAP

And that's just about all there is to this chapter.

The rest of the journey went very smoothly. Michael and Fluffy had a very nice time and it was almost like a normal holiday with fun things happening.

My cousin Sebastion is training to be a reportage photographer and he took some photos of the rest of the journey.

Here are some of his snaps- (the blurry ones are michael's).

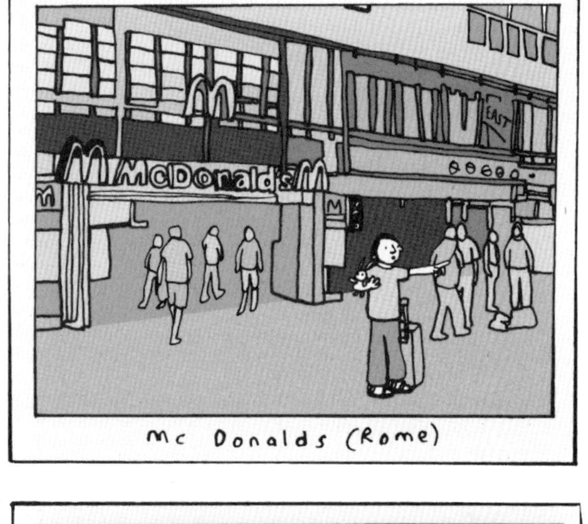
McDonald's
EAST
Mc Donalds (Rome)

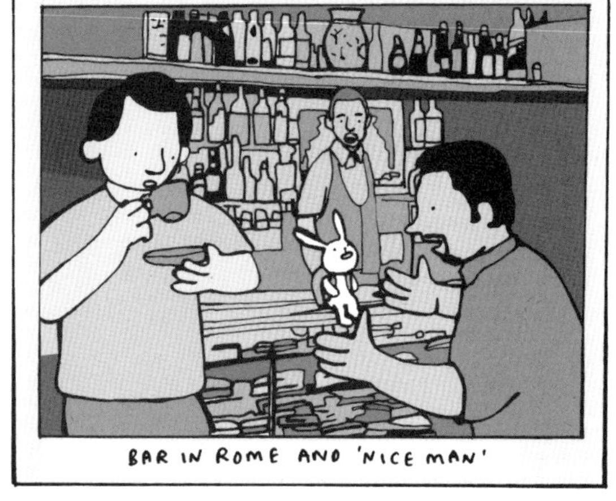
BAR IN ROME AND 'NICE MAN'

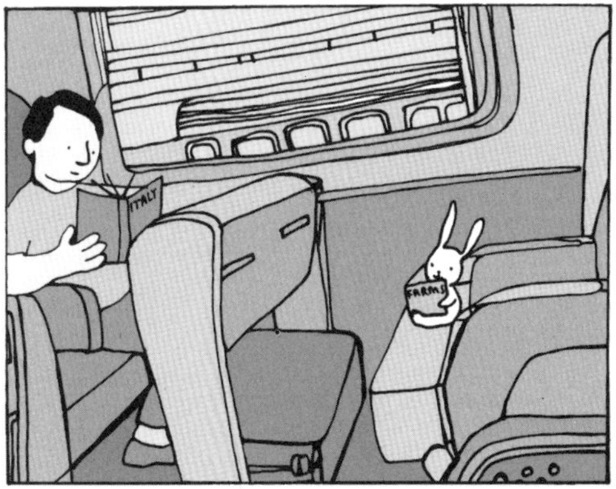
ITALY
FARMS

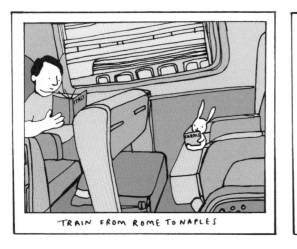

TRAIN FROM ROME TO NAPLES

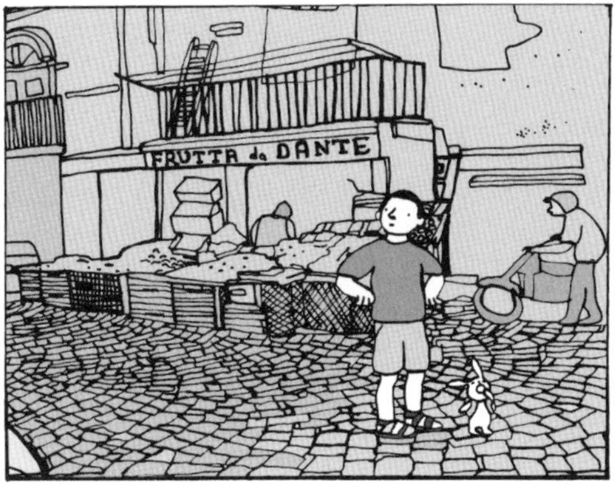
FRUTTA da DANTE

PLACE OF INTEREST: QUIET STREET

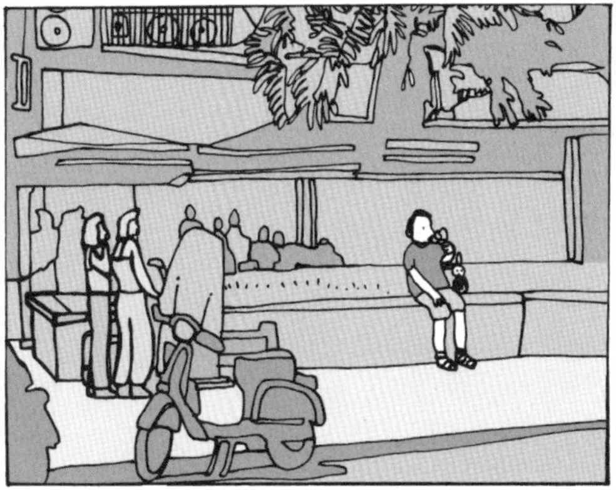

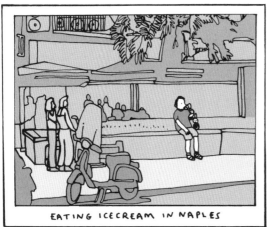

EATING ICECREAM IN NAPLES

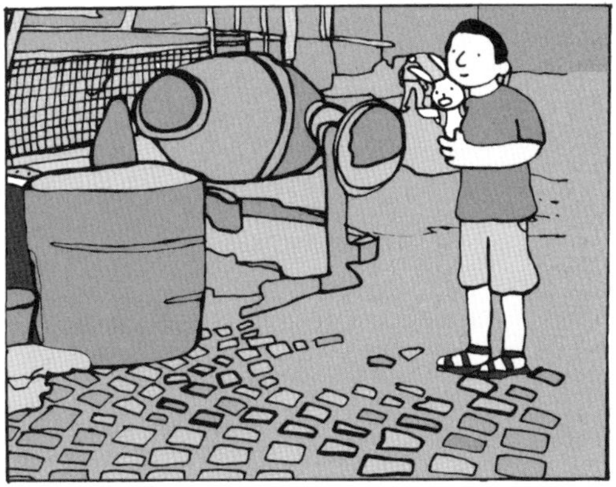

PLACE OF INTEREST: CONSTRUCTION SITE

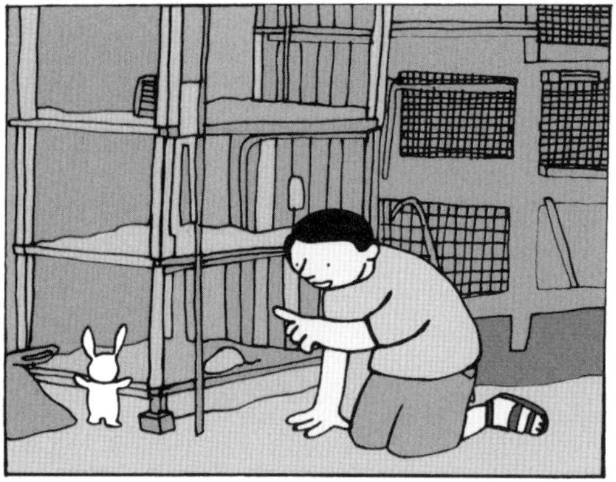

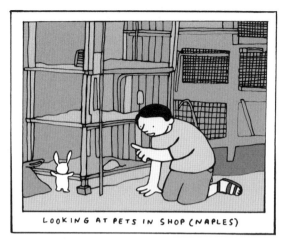

LOOKING AT PETS IN SHOP (NAPLES)

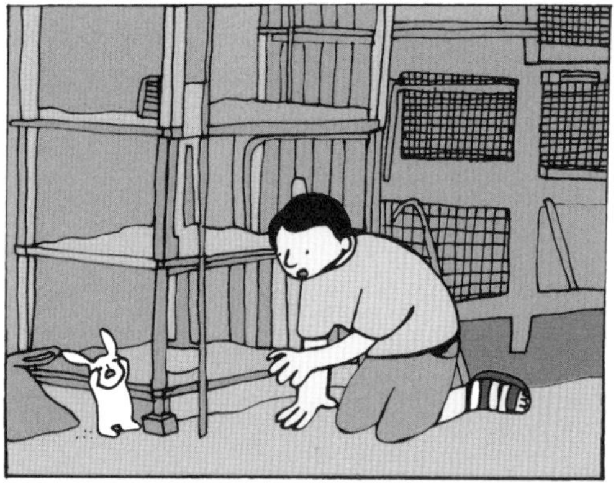

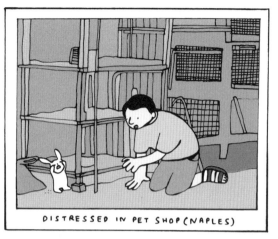

DISTRESSED IN PET SHOP (NAPLES)

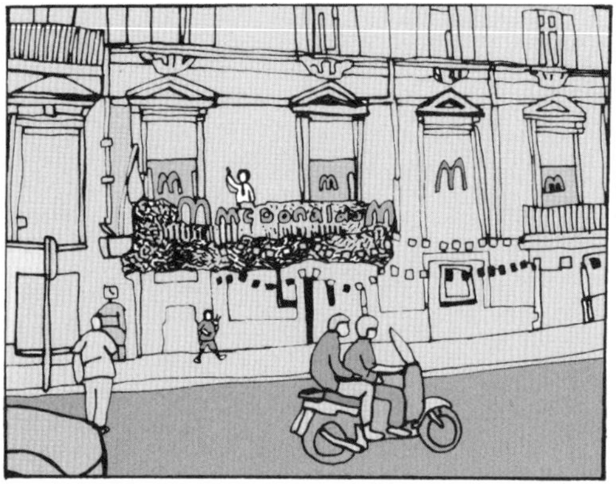

VISIT TO MC DONALDS (NAPLES)

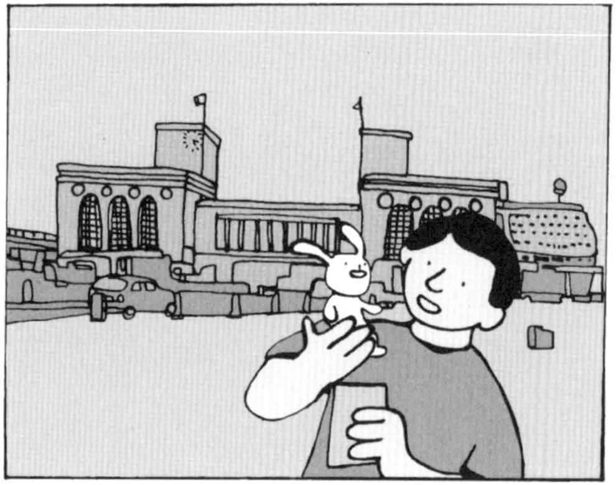

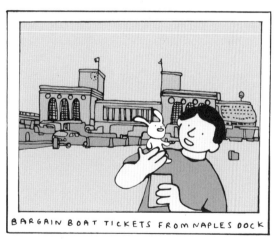

BARGAIN BOAT TICKETS FROM NAPLES DOCK

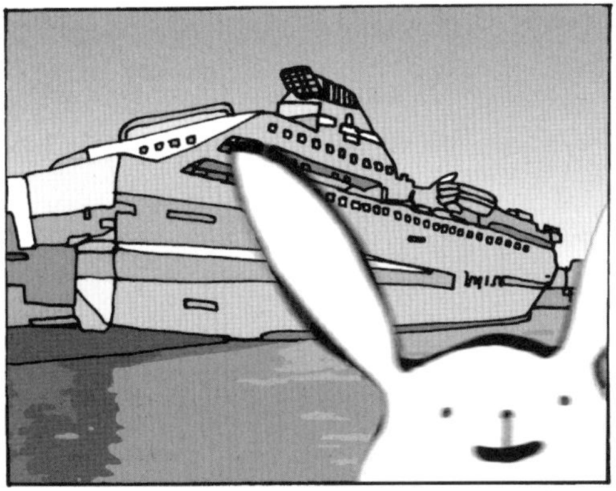

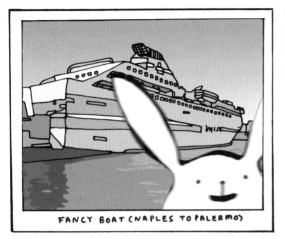

FANCY BOAT (NAPLES TO PALERMO)

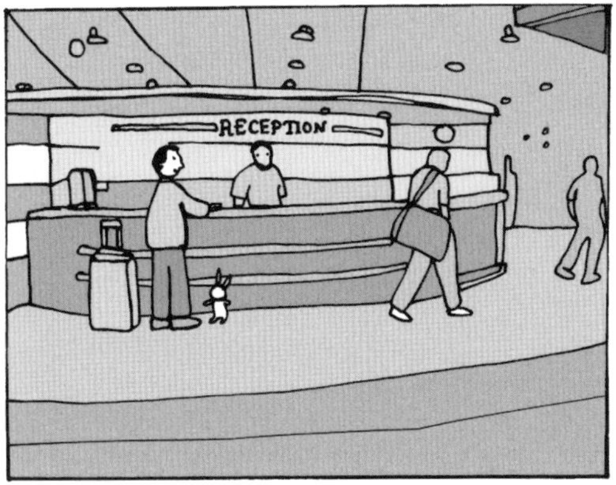
RECEPTION

RECEPTION ON FANCY BOAT

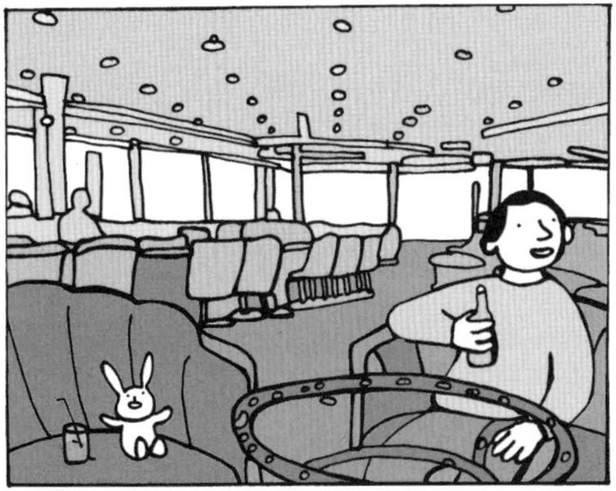

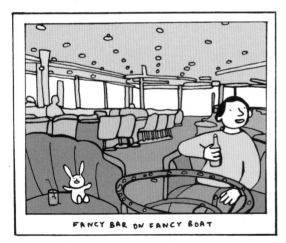

FANCY BAR ON FANCY BOAT

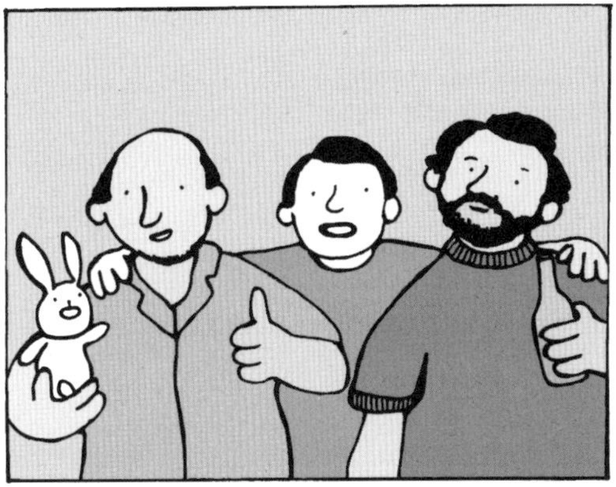

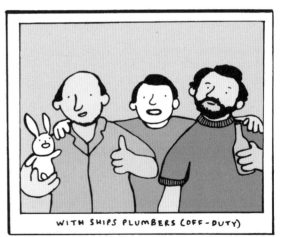

WITH SHIPS PLUMBERS (OFF-DUTY)

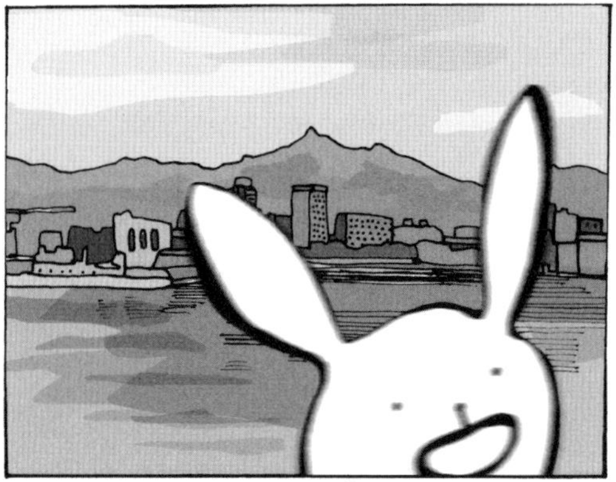

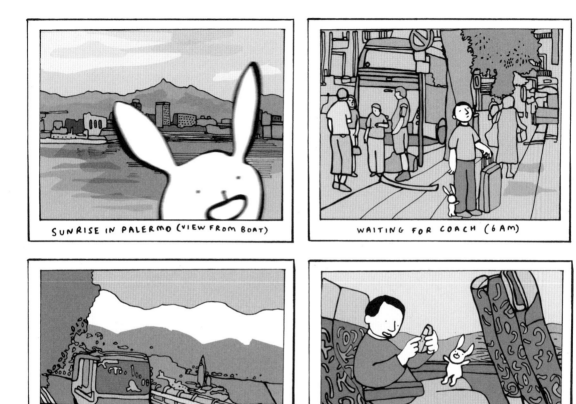

SUNRISE IN PALERMO (VIEW FROM BOAT)

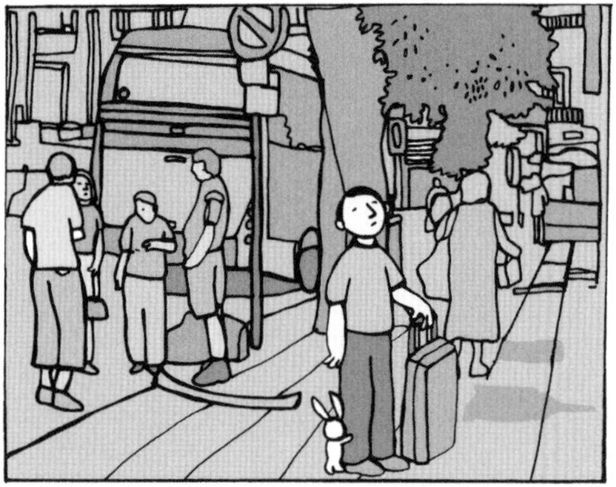

WAITING FOR COACH (6 AM)

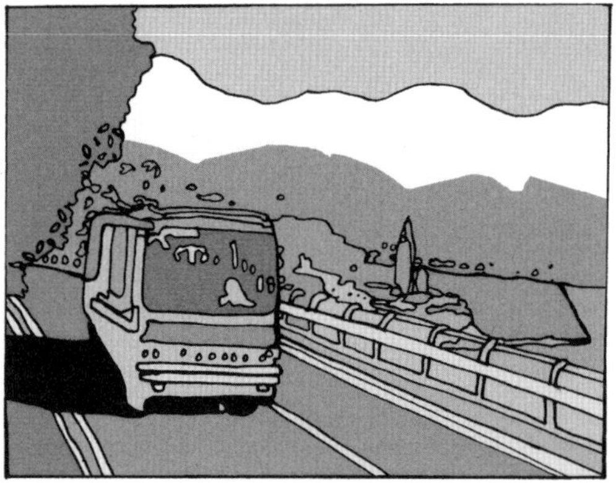

PALERMO TO CATANIA

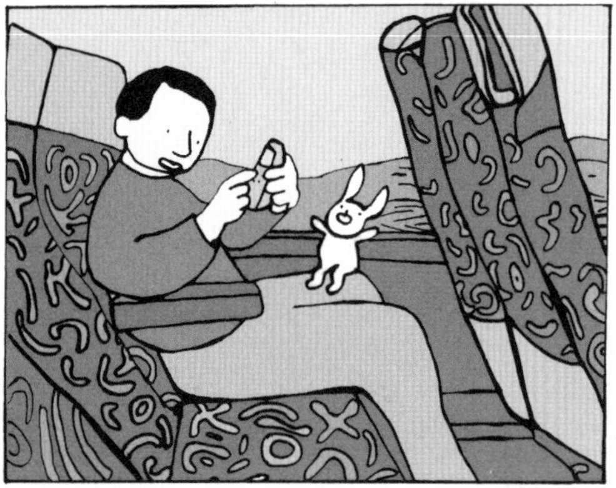

TRYING OUT ROAMING FEATURE ON PHONE

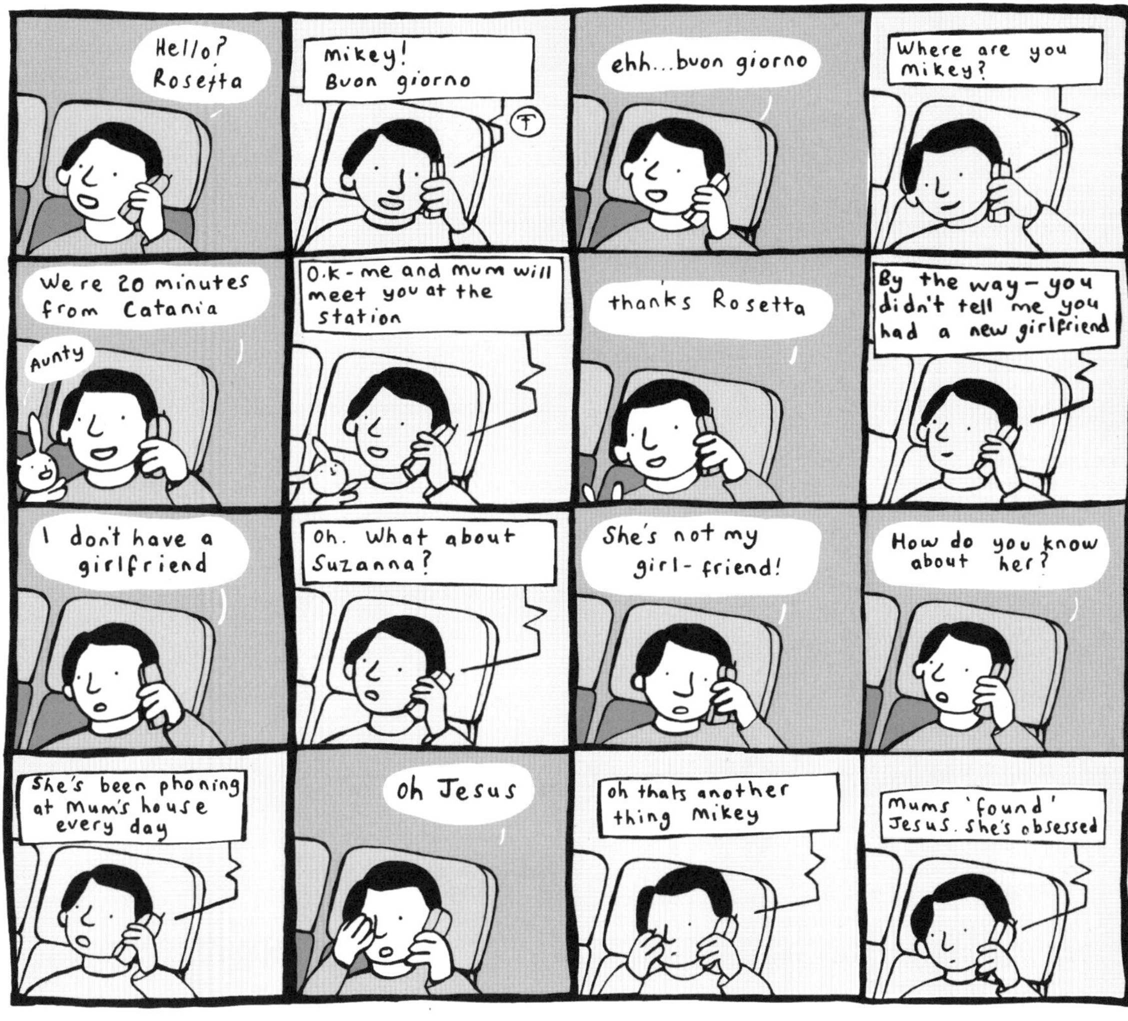

Hello? Rosetta
mikey! Buon giorno
ehh...buon giorno
Where are you mikey?
We're 20 minutes from Catania
Aunty
O.k - me and mum will meet you at the station
thanks Rosetta
By the way - you didn't tell me you had a new girlfriend
I don't have a girlfriend
Oh. What about Suzanna?
She's not my girl-friend!
How do you know about her?
She's been phoning at Mum's house every day
oh Jesus
oh thats another thing Mikey
Mums 'found' Jesus. She's obsessed

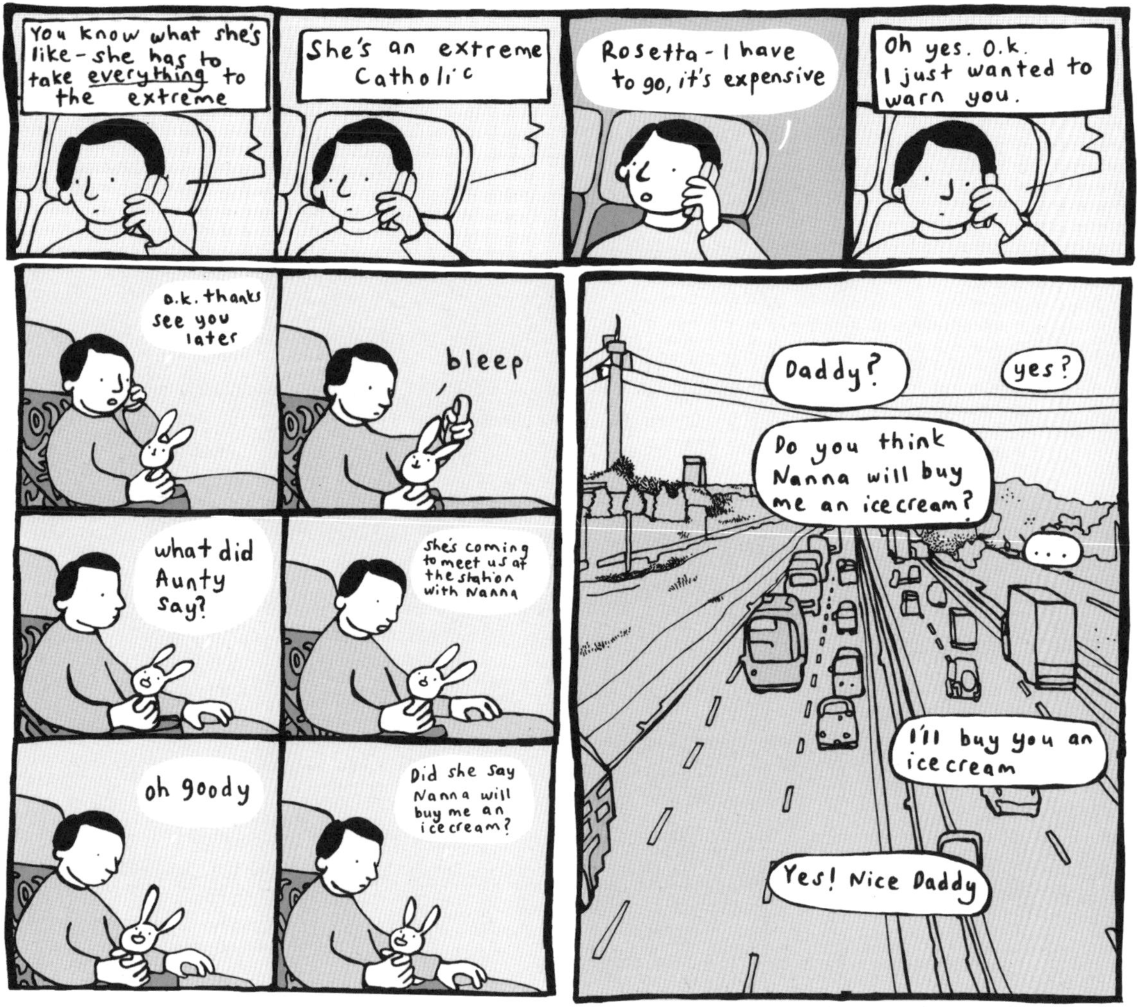
You know what she's like - she has to take everything to the extreme
She's an extreme Catholic
Rosetta - I have to go, it's expensive
Oh yes. O.k. I just wanted to warn you.
o.k. thanks see you later
bleep
what did Aunty say?
She's coming to meet us at the station with Nanna
oh goody
Did she say Nanna will buy me an icecream?
Daddy?
yes?
Do you think Nanna will buy me an icecream?
...
I'll buy you an icecream
Yes! Nice Daddy

and that's it -
it really is the
end of fluffy part 2
it's goodbye from me
but fluffy will be
back in part 3.

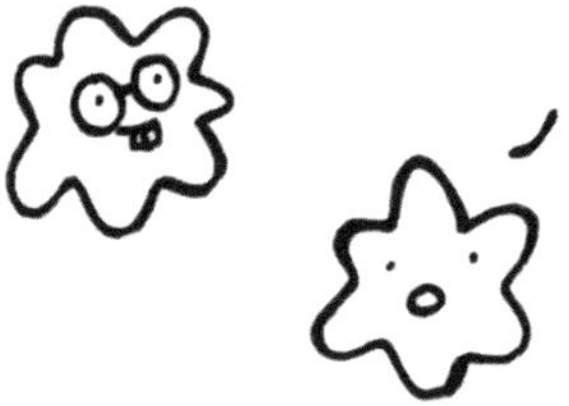

Thanks for reading -
I'm off to hang out
with my friends.
Byee.

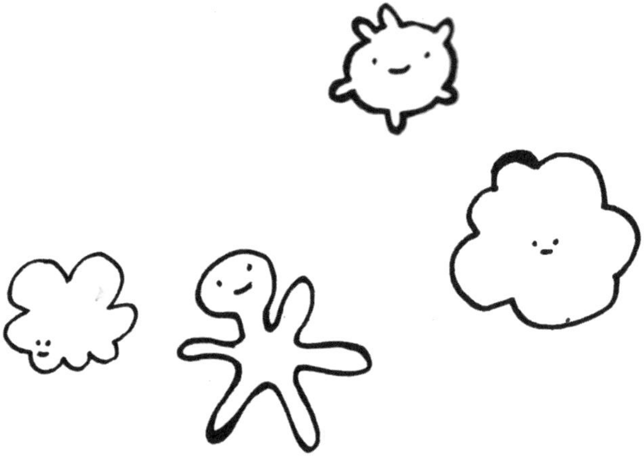

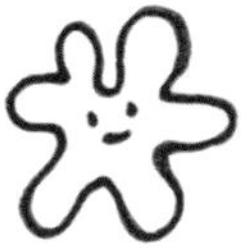

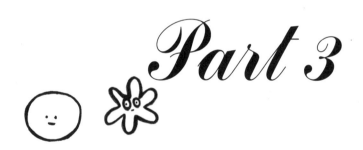

Part 3

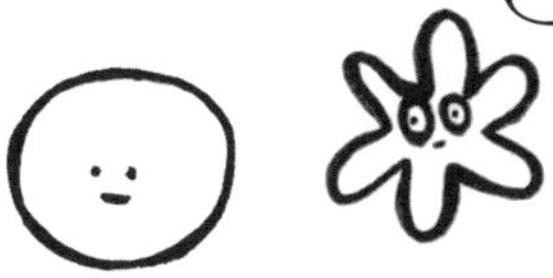

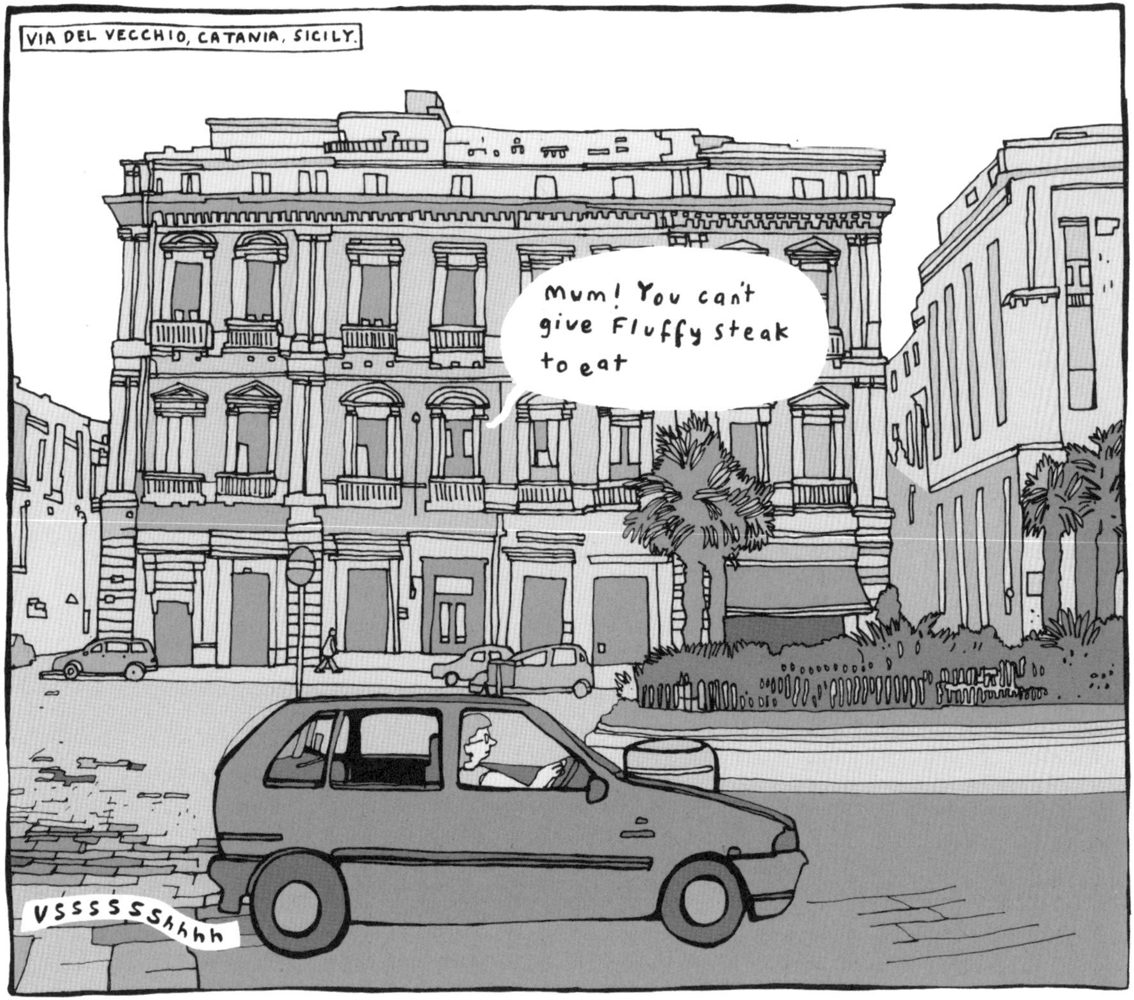
VIA DEL VECCHIO, CATANIA, SICILY.
Mum! You can't give Fluffy steak to eat
VSSSSSSShhhh

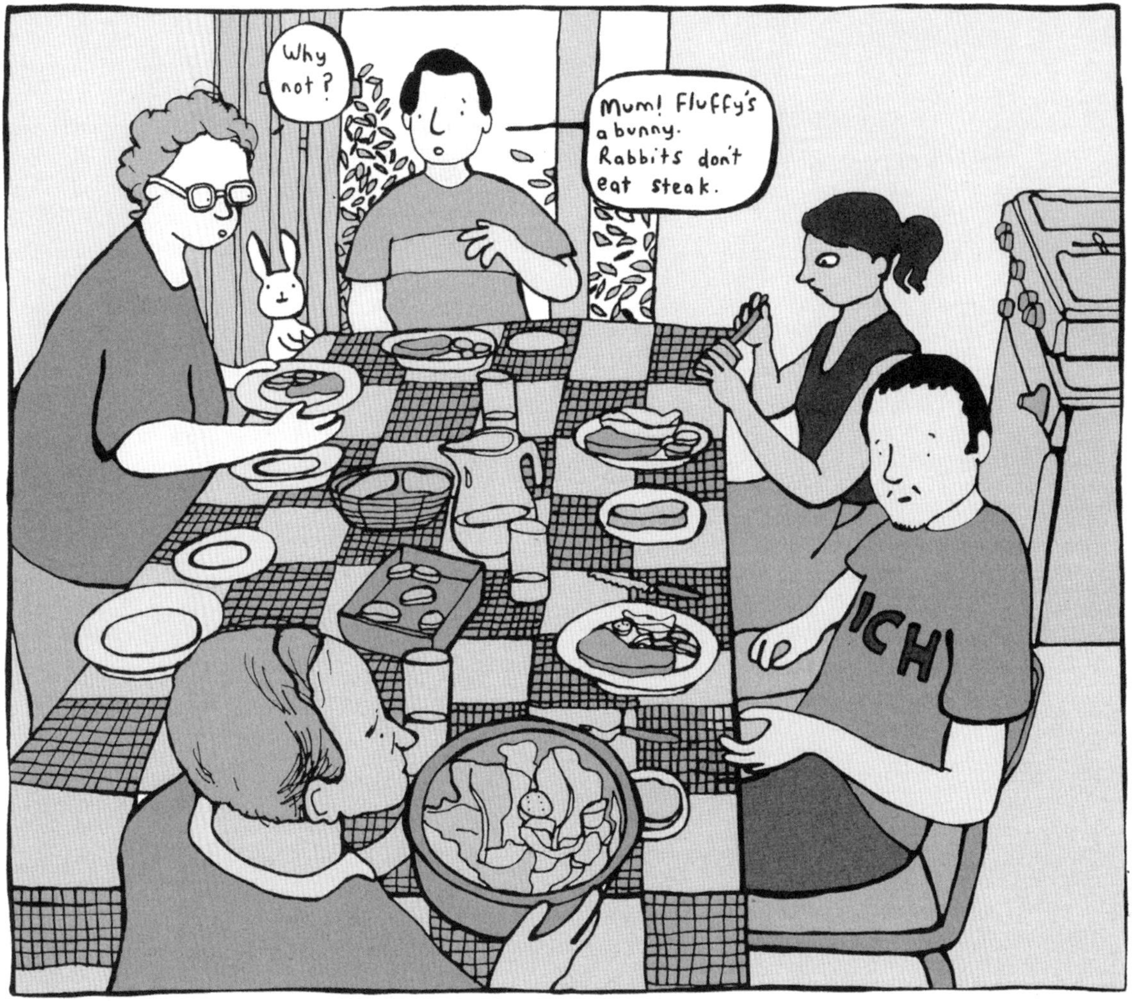
Why not?
Mum! Fluffy's a bunny. Rabbits don't eat steak.
ICH

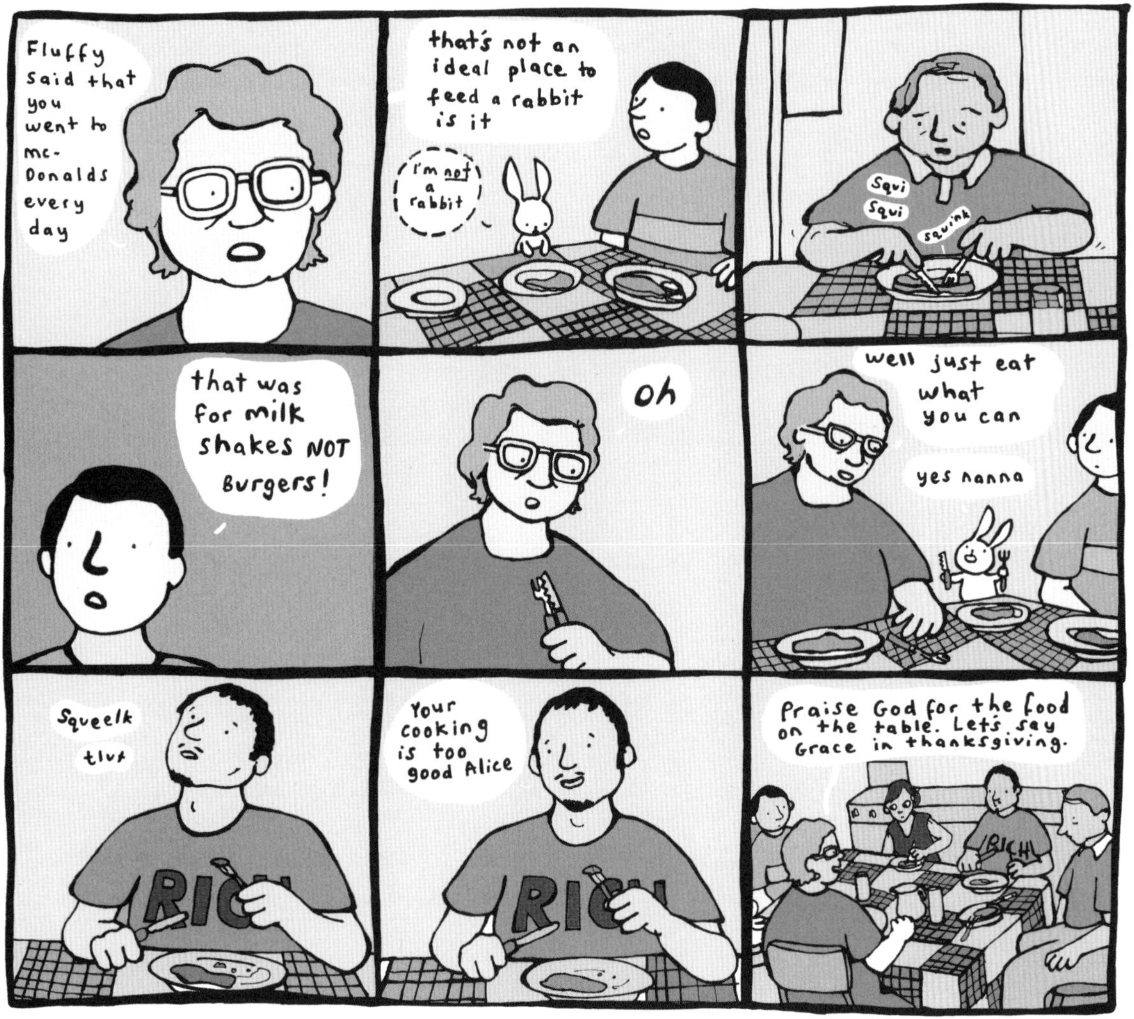
Fluffy said that you went to mc-Donalds every day
that's not an ideal place to feed a rabbit is it
I'm not a rabbit
Squi
Squi
squink
that was for milk shakes NOT Burgers!
Oh
well just eat what you can
yes nanna
Squeelk
tluk
Your cooking is too good Alice
Praise God for the food on the table. Let's say Grace in thanksgiving.
RICH
RICH
RICH

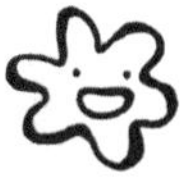

Hi! it's me again. I'm the dust particle from the last chapter. I wasn't supposed to be in this chapter. They hired a flake of dandruff to be guest narrator but he had mood swings and was a bit too disruptive for the crew. So, to my surprise and delight I received a call to work again in this chapter. I'm SO happy to be back!

And so, with the story- Michael and Fluffy have made it to Sicily and they are with Michael's family:-

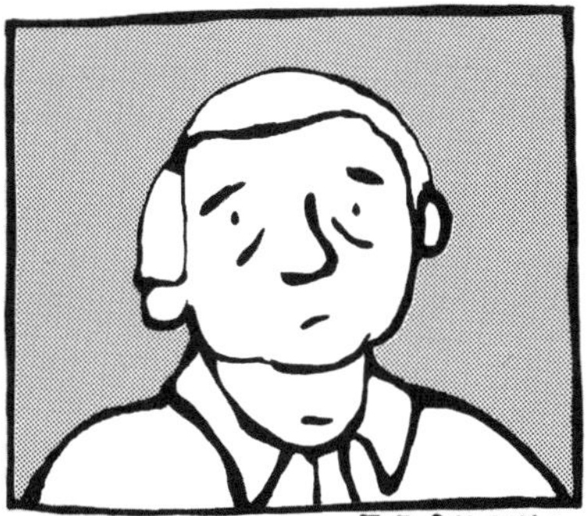

JOE PULCINO

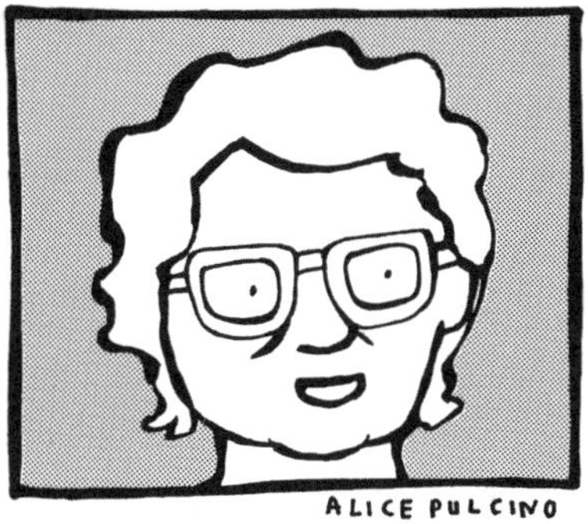

ALICE PULCINO

This is Michael's Dad, Guiseppe (Joe) Pulcino. He is from Sicily but went to England when he was 18 to find work. He met Alice at a bus-stop in Brixton, they got married and had three children. Joe worked with the same company for 31 years as an engineer and then took early retirement. Now they live 6 months in Surrey and 6 months in Sicily in this flat that belongs to Joe's Uncle. Joe really likes bell ringing and spends a lot of time in church towers. Alice never did understand his fascination with bells but she didn't have much to do when they were spending time in Sicily and so she started going with him. And that's when she had a life transforming conversion to the Catholic church. Suddenly life had meaning and she found a new undiscovered talent for painting.

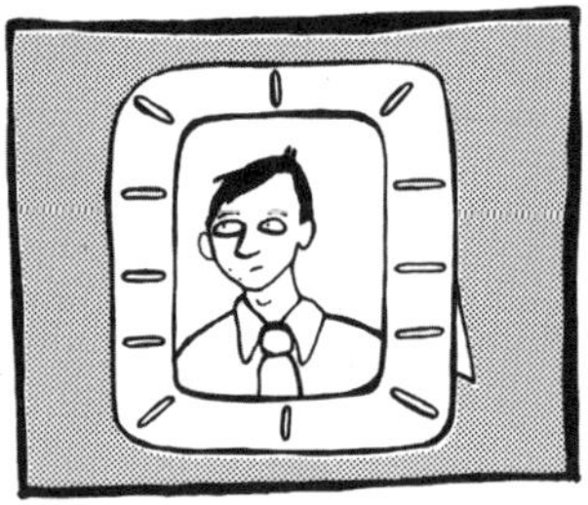

David Pulcino

This is David Pulcino, he is the eldest son. He hasn't been in touch with the family for 16 years. He was stealing cars at the age of 15, his parents were shocked and confused by his behaviour. They later regretted it, but they threw him out of the house when he was 17. They heard afterwards that he had left for America.

He isn't in this story but sometimes it's interesting to know these things and pretend to be a psychiatrist or something. No. More likely it's very intrusive, like going through a drawer in someone's house when they've left the room.

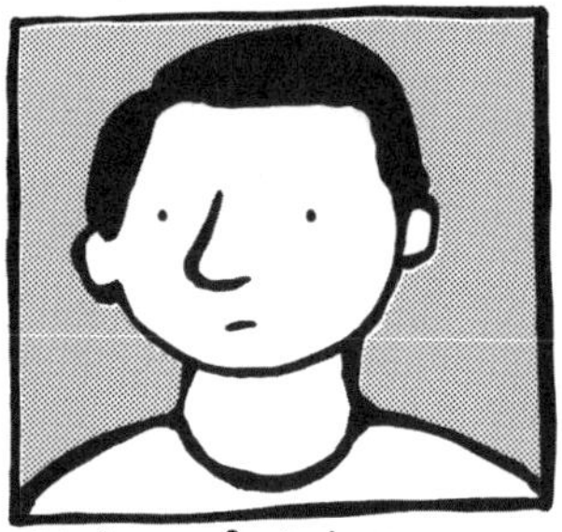

Michael Pulcino

This is Michael Pulcino. He lives in South London and works from home as an architect. He mostly gets projects designing conservatories for small businesses and rich people. He finds his work very boring but can't work out what else he might be good at, so he sticks to the conservatories. He doesn't have a girlfriend but is the victim of an unhealthy relationship with Fluffy's nursery school teacher. He passively tries to stop the relationship, he doesn't call her, he tries to avoid seeing or speaking to her but she's just 'there' and won't go away.

His resignation of not being able to find a real girlfriend and the fear of being alone keeps him uncomfortably entangled with Suzanna Owers.

This is Fluffy. Fluffy is a small white bunny and has a deep fascination with tractors. This came about after Michael took Fluffy to visit a friend from college who lived in Yorkshire. His friend lived next to a farm and the friend took Fluffy to meet the farmer who showed them around his farm. Fluffy also developed a fascination for pylons but soon forgot about them when they returned to London. Fluffy also likes light switches (switching them off and on), swings in the playground and people who have broken legs in plaster and need to use crutches.

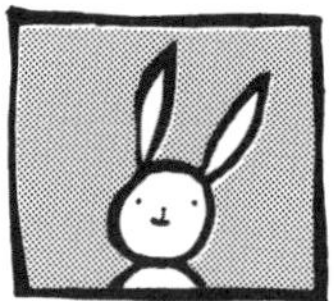

Fluffy

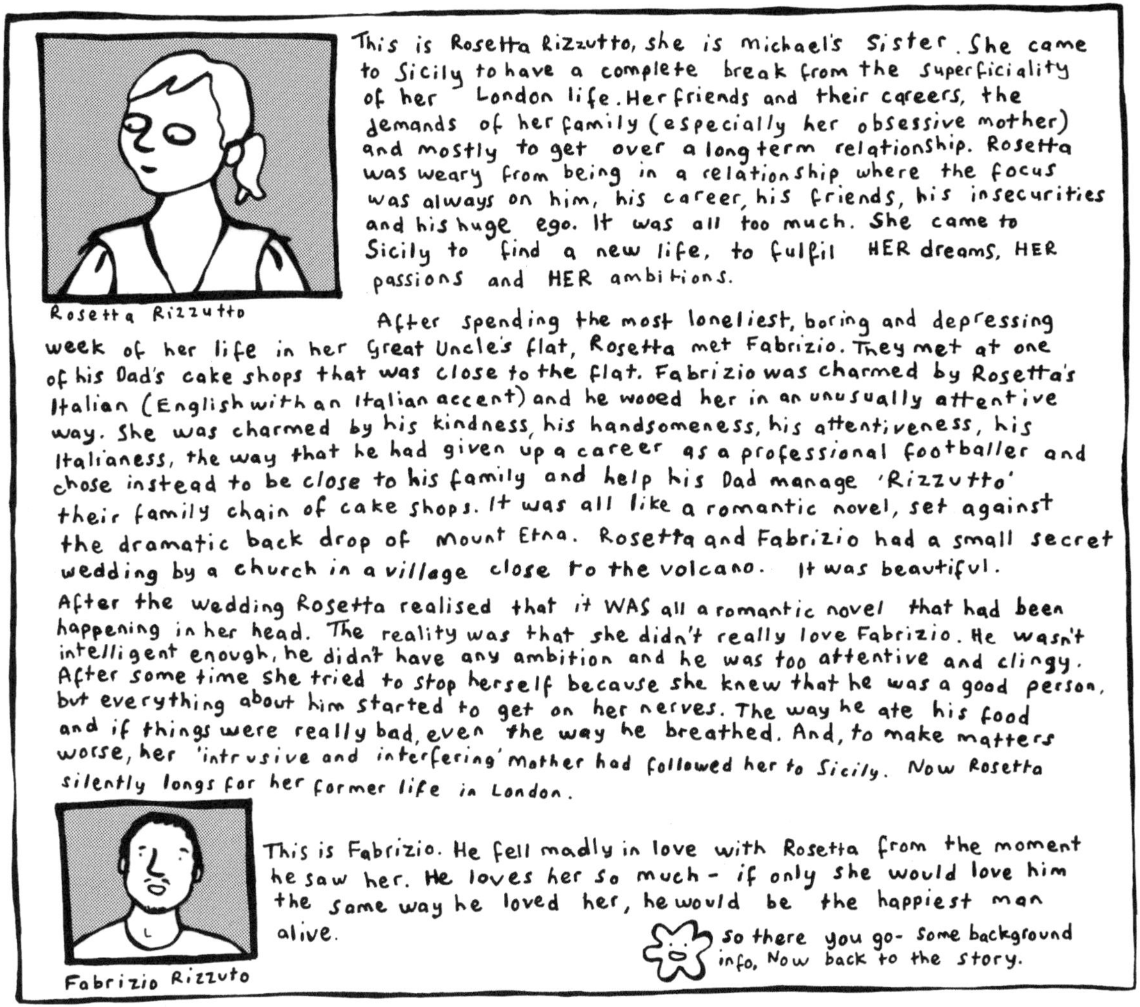
This is Rosetta Rizzutto, she is michael's sister. She came to Sicily to have a complete break from the superficiality of her London life. Her friends and their careers, the demands of her family (especially her obsessive mother) and mostly to get over a long term relationship. Rosetta was weary from being in a relationship where the focus was always on him, his career, his friends, his insecurities and his huge ego. It was all too much. She came to Sicily to find a new life, to fulfil HER dreams, HER passions and HER ambitions.
Rosetta Rizzutto
After spending the most loneliest, boring and depressing week of her life in her Great Uncle's flat, Rosetta met Fabrizio. They met at one of his Dad's cake shops that was close to the flat. Fabrizio was charmed by Rosetta's Italian (English with an Italian accent) and he wooed her in an unusually attentive way. She was charmed by his kindness, his handsomeness, his attentiveness, his Italianess, the way that he had given up a career as a professional footballer and chose instead to be close to his family and help his Dad manage 'Rizzutto' their family chain of cake shops. It was all like a romantic novel, set against the dramatic back drop of Mount Etna. Rosetta and Fabrizio had a small secret wedding by a church in a village close to the volcano. It was beautiful.
After the wedding Rosetta realised that it WAS all a romantic novel that had been happening in her head. The reality was that she didn't really love Fabrizio. He wasn't intelligent enough, he didn't have any ambition and he was too attentive and clingy. After some time she tried to stop herself because she knew that he was a good person, but everything about him started to get on her nerves. The way he ate his food and if things were really bad, even the way he breathed. And, to make matters worse, her 'intrusive and interfering' mother had followed her to Sicily. Now Rosetta silently longs for her former life in London.
This is Fabrizio. He fell madly in love with Rosetta from the moment he saw her. He loves her so much - if only she would love him the same way he loved her, he would be the happiest man alive.
Fabrizio Rizzuto
So there you go- some background info. Now back to the story.

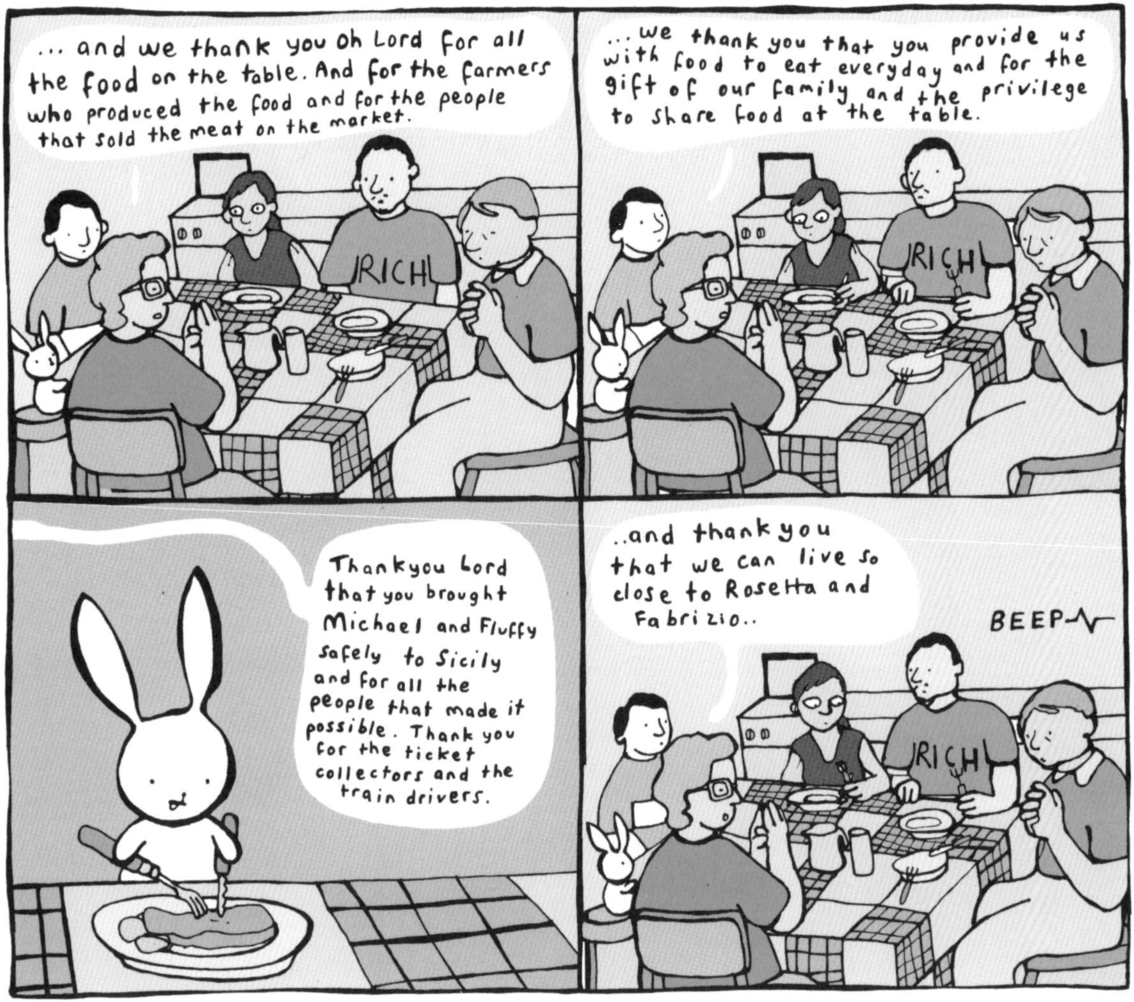
... and we thank you Oh Lord for all the food on the table. And for the farmers who produced the food and for the people that sold the meat on the market.
... we thank you that you provide us with food to eat everyday and for the gift of our family and the privilege to share food at the table.
Thankyou Lord that you brought Michael and Fluffy safely to Sicily and for all the people that made it possible. Thank you for the ticket collectors and the train drivers.
..and thank you that we can live so close to Rosetta and Fabrizio..
BEEP
RICH

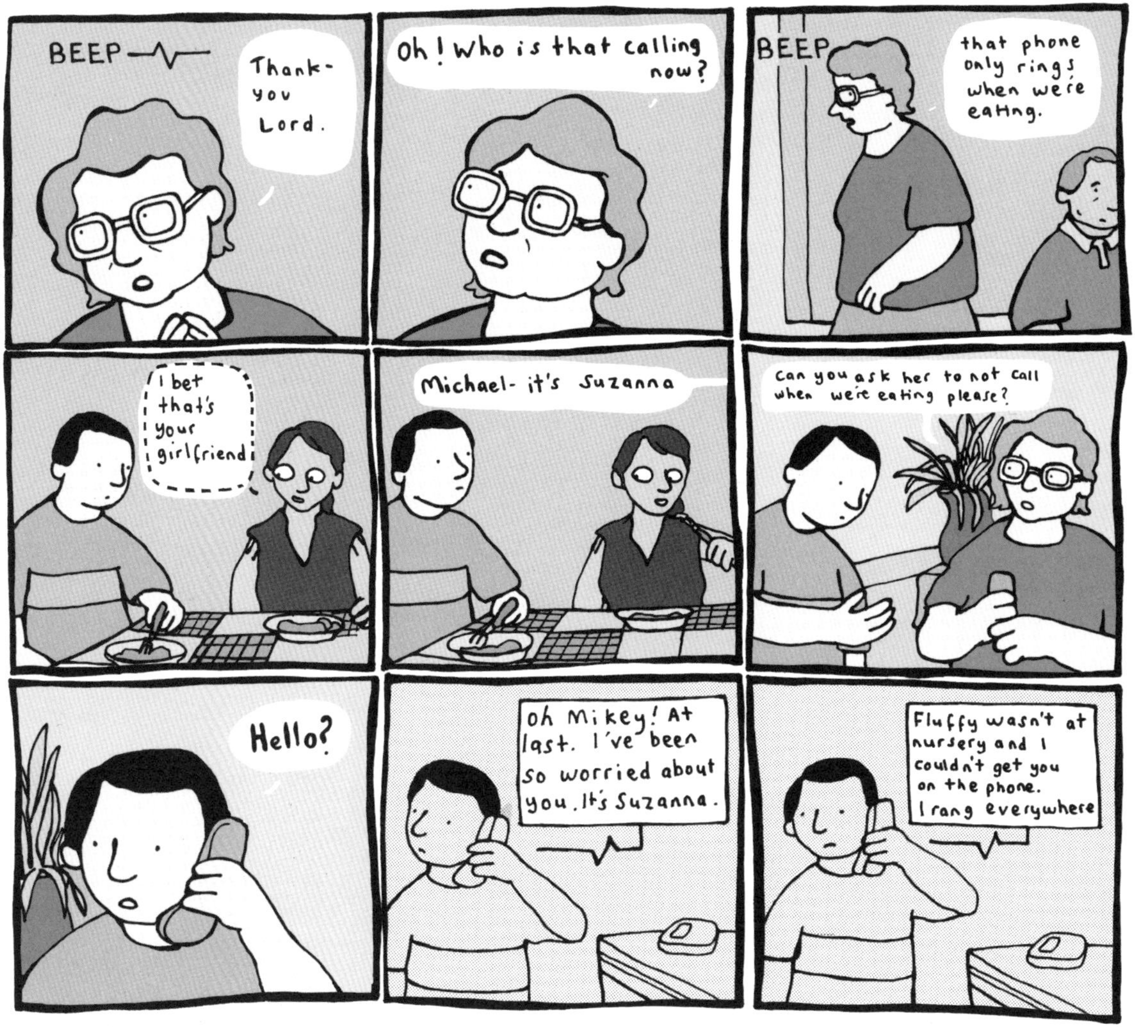
BEEP
Thank-you Lord.
Oh! Who is that calling now?
BEEP
that phone only rings when we're eating.
I bet that's your girlfriend
Michael- it's Suzanna
Can you ask her to not call when we're eating please?
Hello?
Oh Mikey! At last. I've been so worried about you. It's Suzanna.
Fluffy wasn't at nursery and I couldn't get you on the phone. I rang everywhere

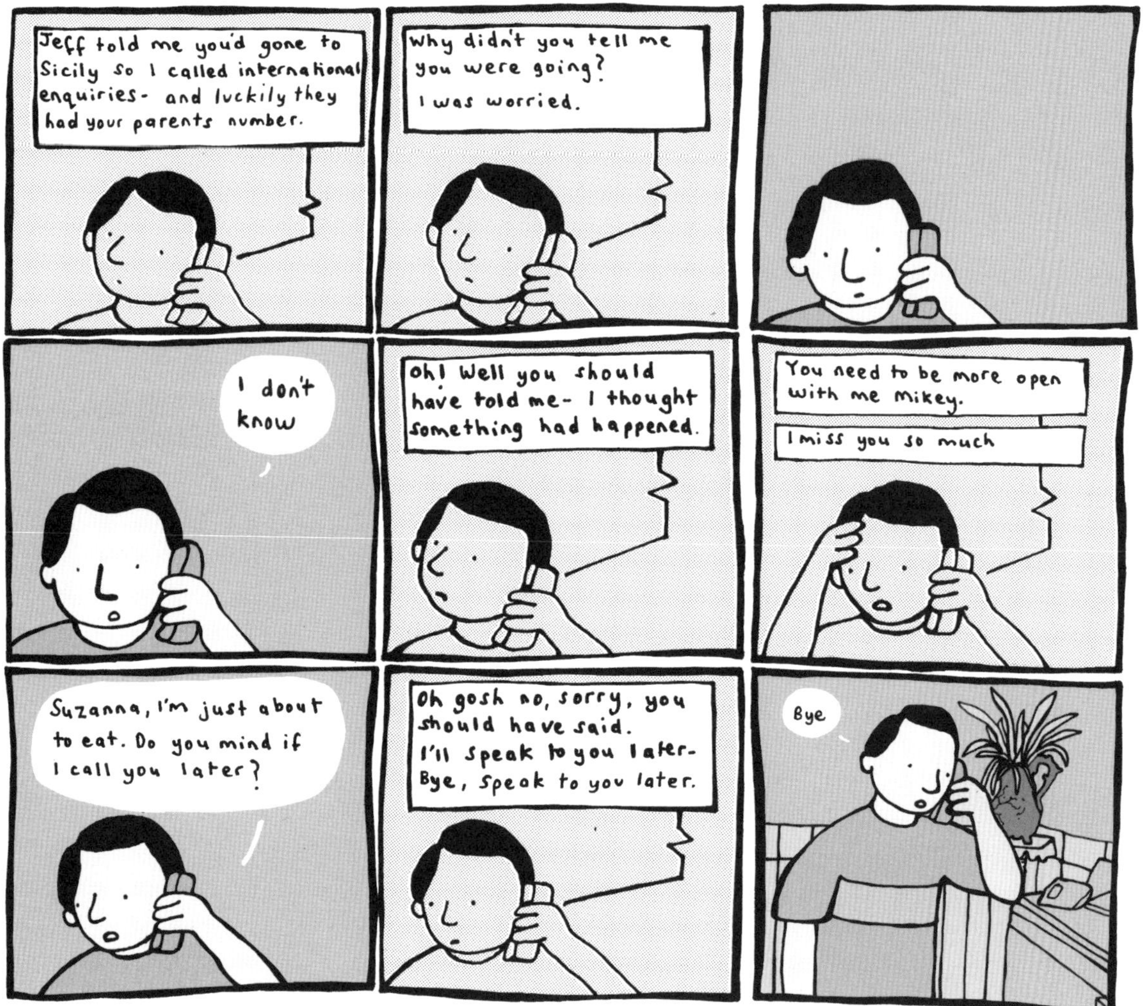
Jeff told me you'd gone to Sicily so I called international enquiries- and luckily they had your parents number.
Why didn't you tell me you were going?
I was worried.
I don't know
Oh! Well you should have told me- I thought something had happened.
You need to be more open with me Mikey.
I miss you so much
Suzanna, I'm just about to eat. Do you mind if I call you later?
Oh gosh no, sorry, you should have said. I'll speak to you later- Bye, speak to you later.
Bye

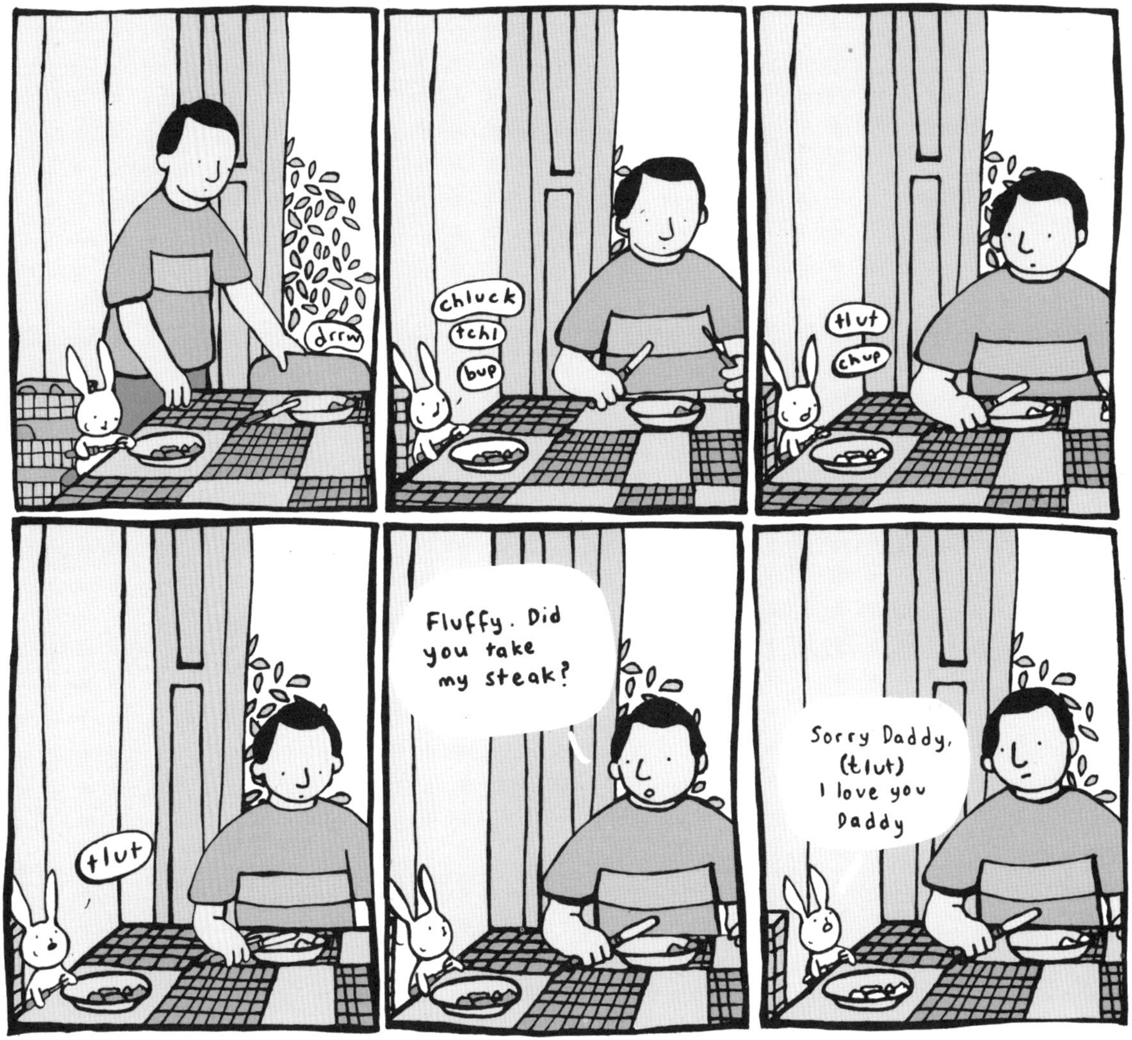
drrw
chluck
tchl
bup
tlut
chup
tlut
Fluffy. Did you take my steak?
Sorry Daddy, (tlut) I love you Daddy

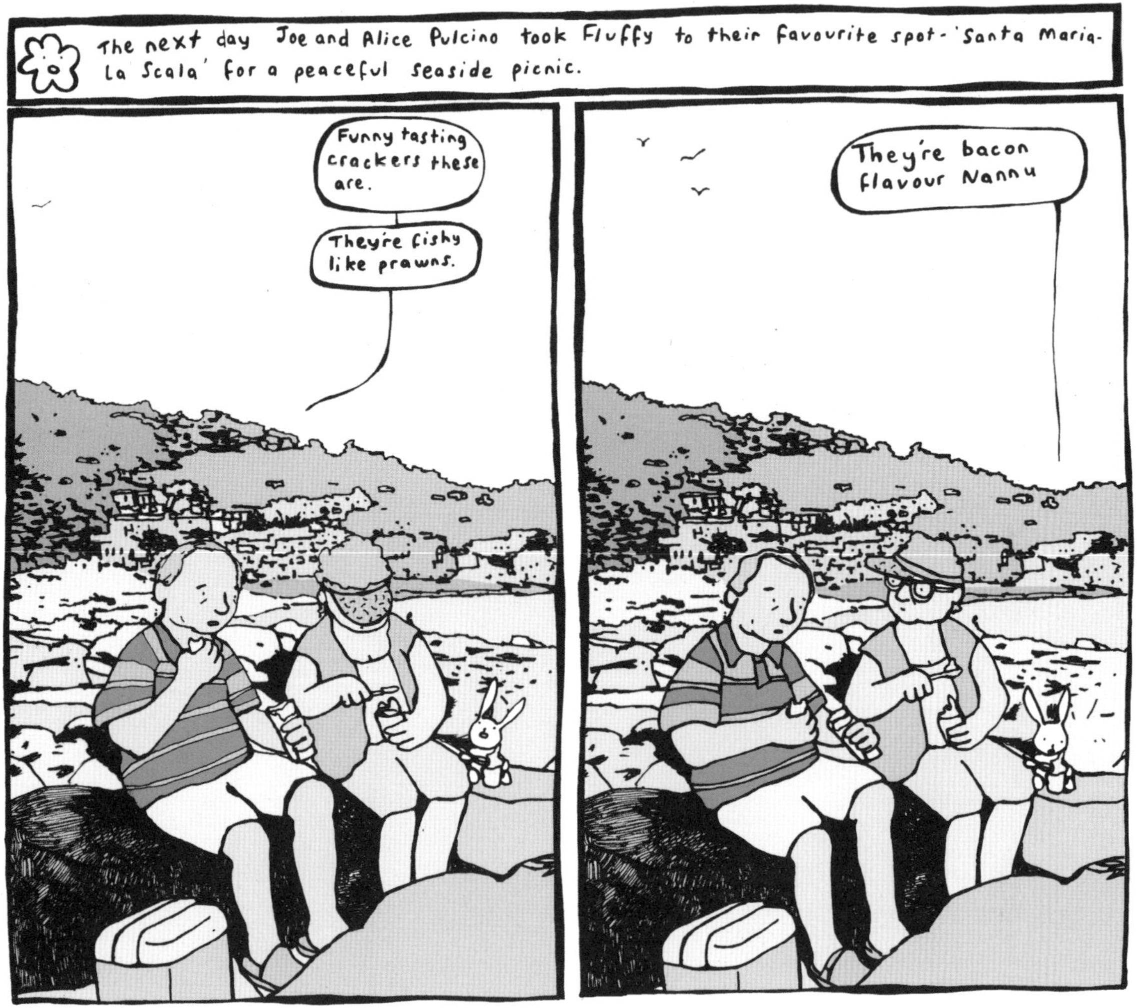
The next day Joe and Alice Pulcino took Fluffy to their favourite spot - 'Santa Maria-la Scala' for a peaceful seaside picnic.
Funny tasting crackers these are.
They're fishy like prawns.
They're bacon flavour Nannu

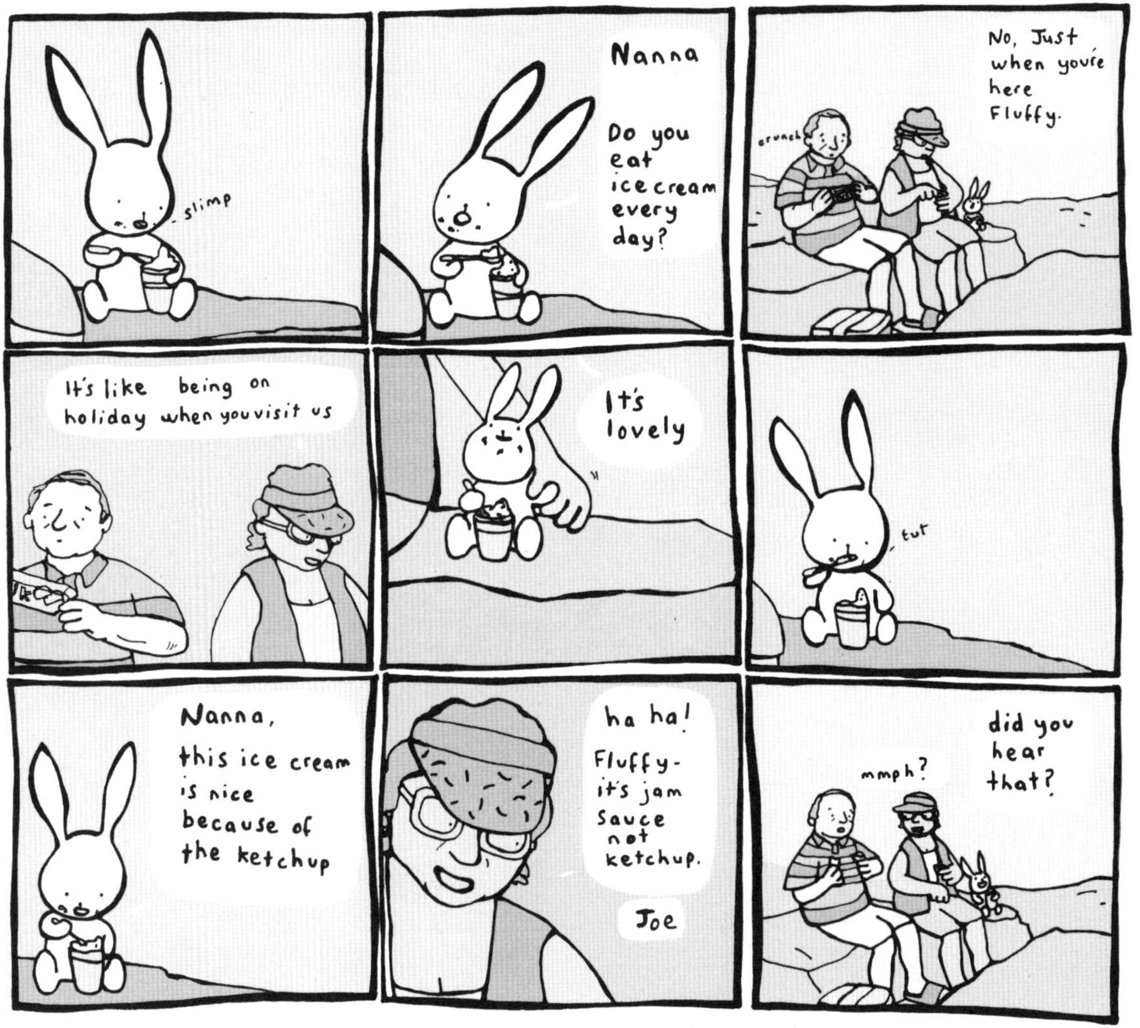
slimp
Nanna
Do you eat ice cream every day?
crunch
No, Just when you're here Fluffy.
It's like being on holiday when you visit us
It's lovely
tut
Nanna,
this ice cream is nice because of the ketchup
ha ha!
Fluffy- it's jam sauce not ketchup.
Joe
mmph?
did you hear that?

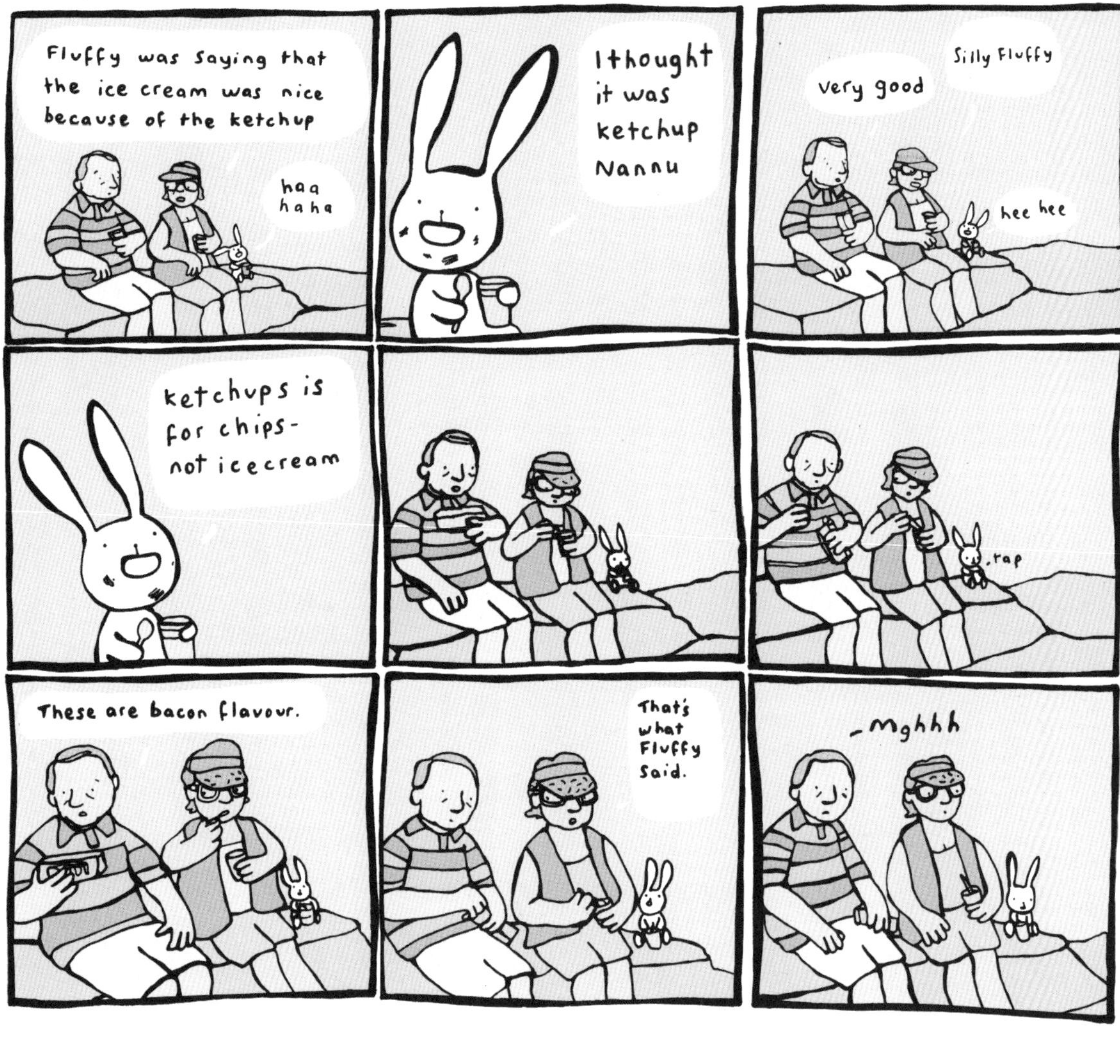
Fluffy was saying that the ice cream was nice because of the ketchup
haa haha
I thought it was ketchup Nannu
Silly Fluffy
very good
hee hee
ketchups is for chips- not icecream
rap
These are bacon flavour.
That's what Fluffy said.
-Mghhh

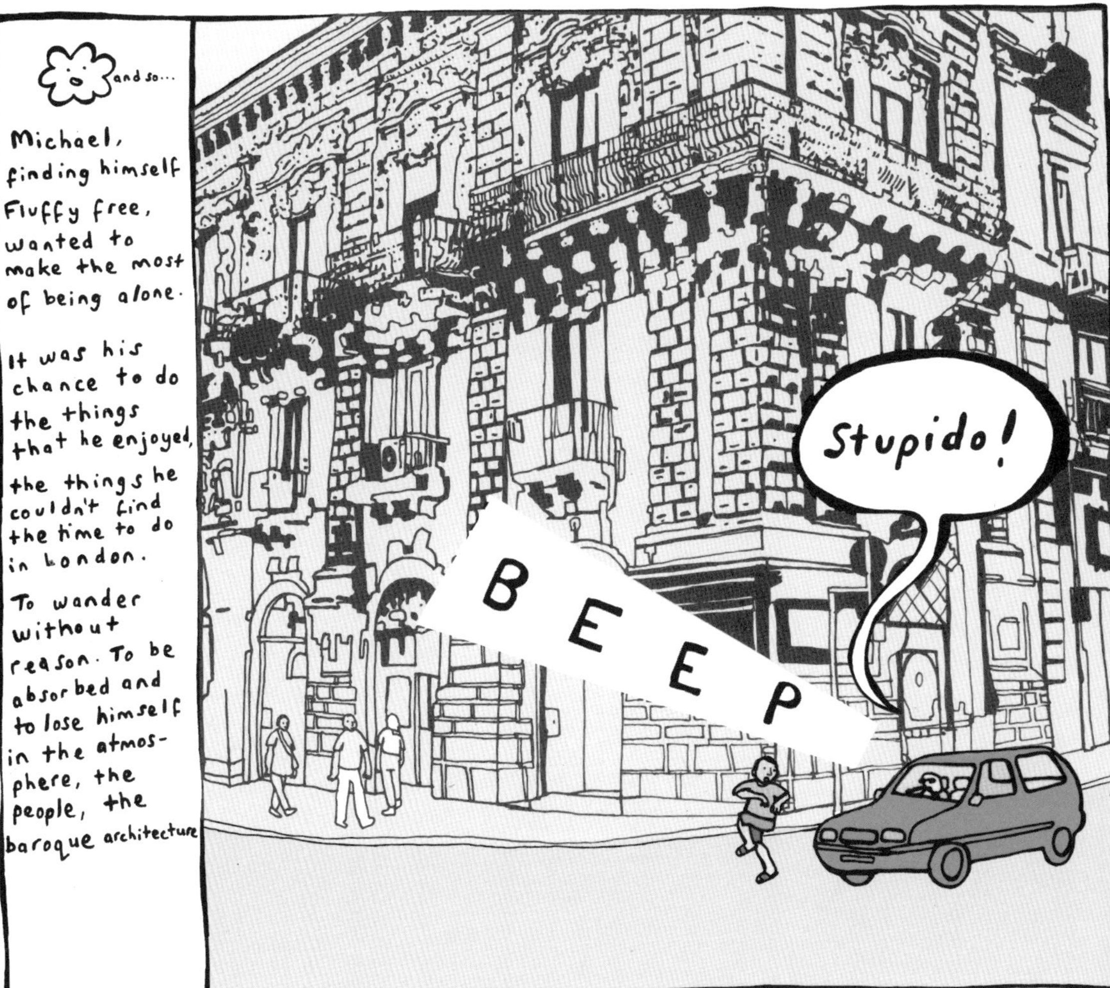
and so...
Michael, finding himself Fluffy free, wanted to make the most of being alone.
It was his chance to do the things that he enjoyed, the things he couldn't find the time to do in London.
To wander without reason. To be absorbed and to lose himself in the atmosphere, the people, the baroque architecture
BEEP
Stupido!

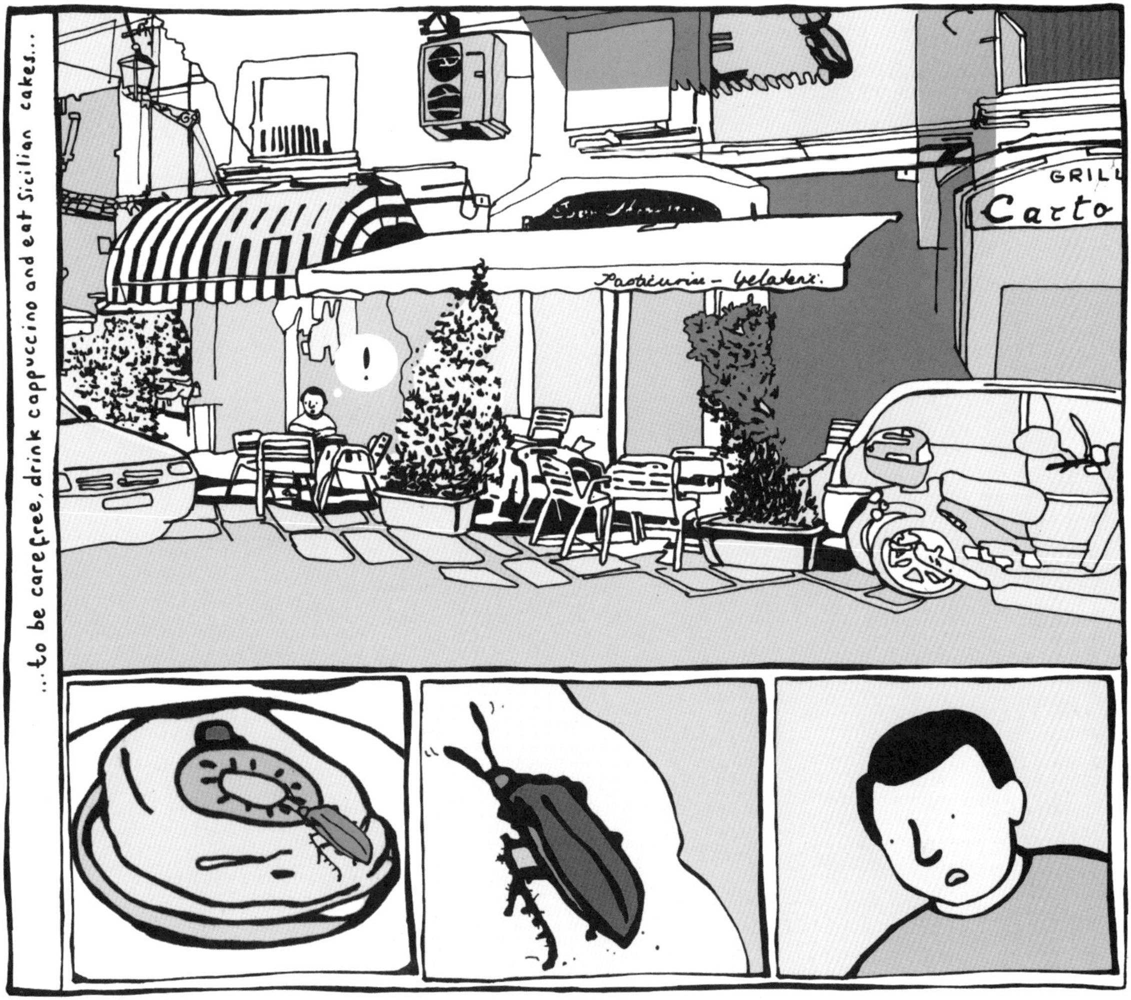
...to be carefree, drink cappuccino and eat Sicilian cakes...
!
GRILL
Carto

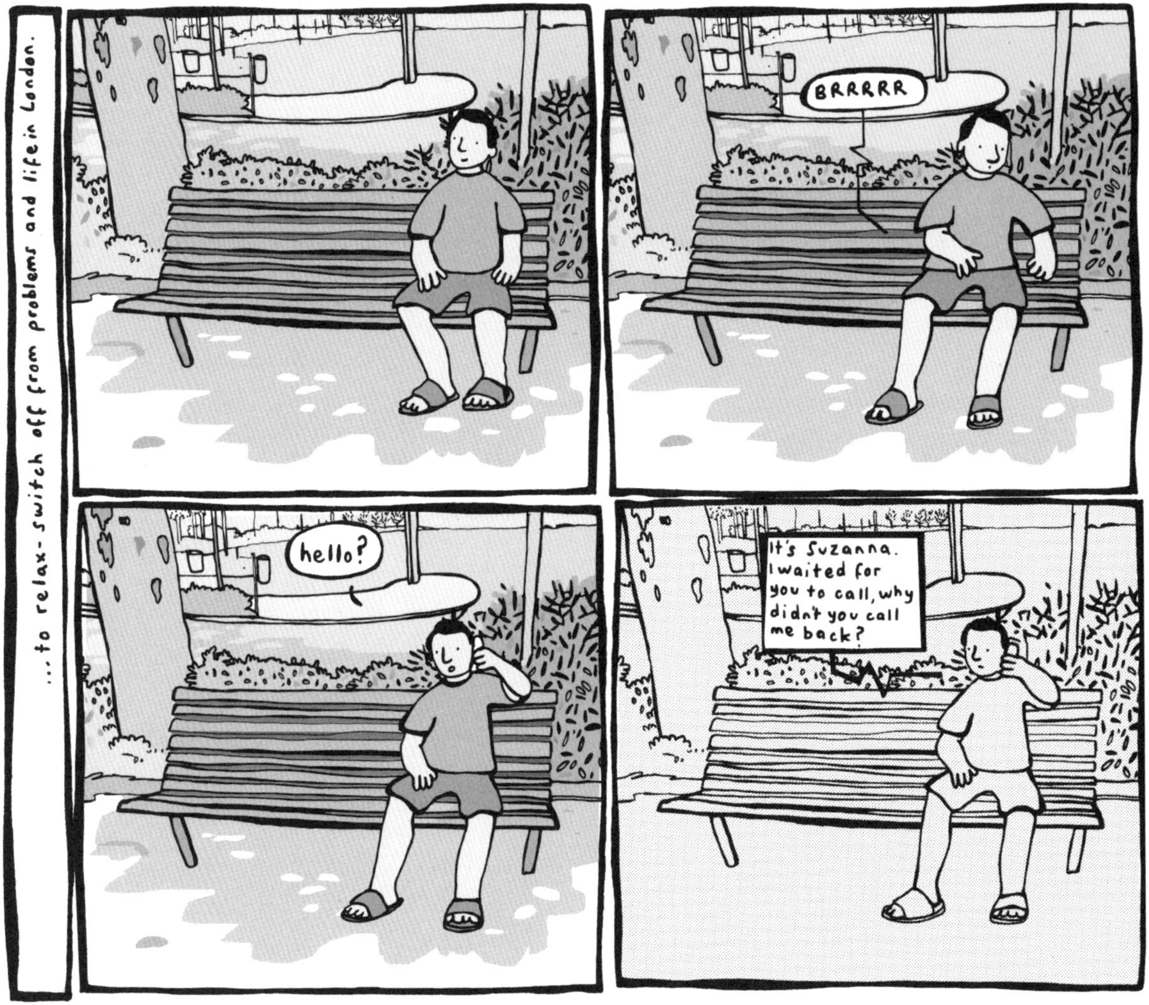
...to relax- switch off from problems and life in London.
BRRRRR
hello?
It's Suzanna. I waited for you to call, why didn't you call me back?

Panel 1: Ahem! - My name is Flake O'Dandy. I was the guest narrator for this chapter.

Panel 2: That lying dust particle implied that I was sacked. It's not true - I quit.

Panel 3: I have no interest in working with such bland and unchallenging scripts, nor with hopeless amateurs.

Panel 4: Oh hi flake of dandruff. They let you back in! Are you going to help me narrate? -

Panel 5: You've got to be joking. I want nothing more to do with this amateur production.

Panel 6: Oh deary me. Well... on with the story.

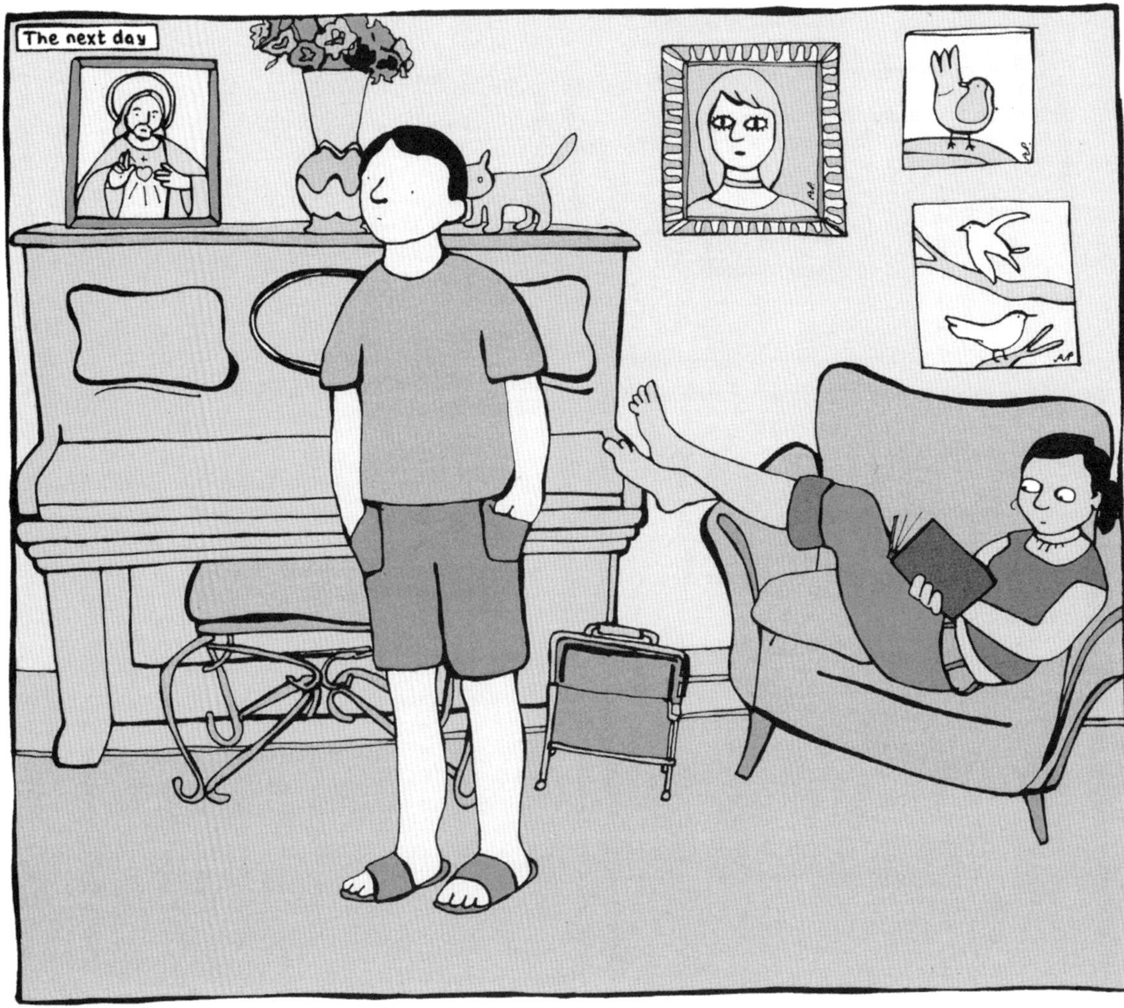
The next day

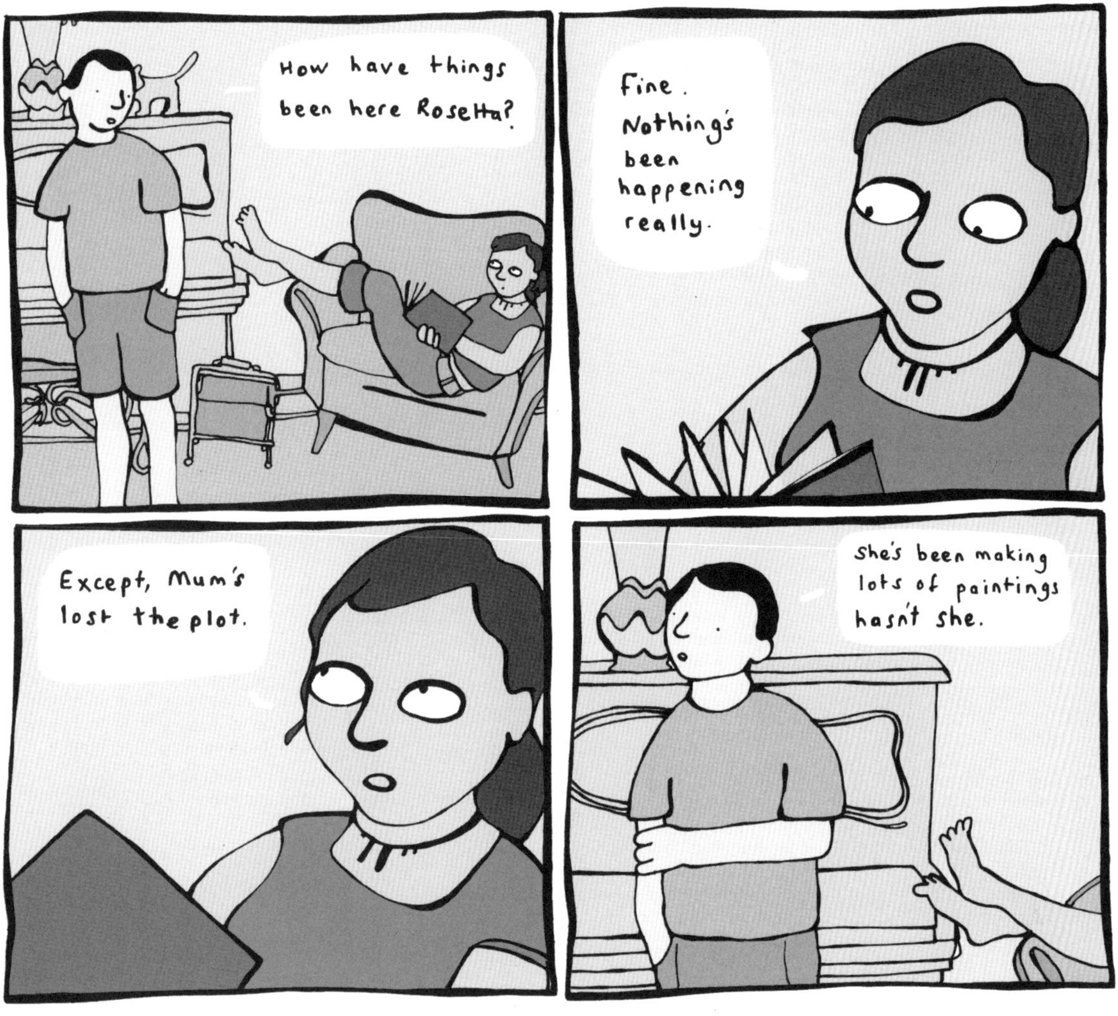
How have things been here Rosetta?
Fine. Nothing's been happening really.
Except, Mum's lost the plot.
She's been making lots of paintings hasn't she.

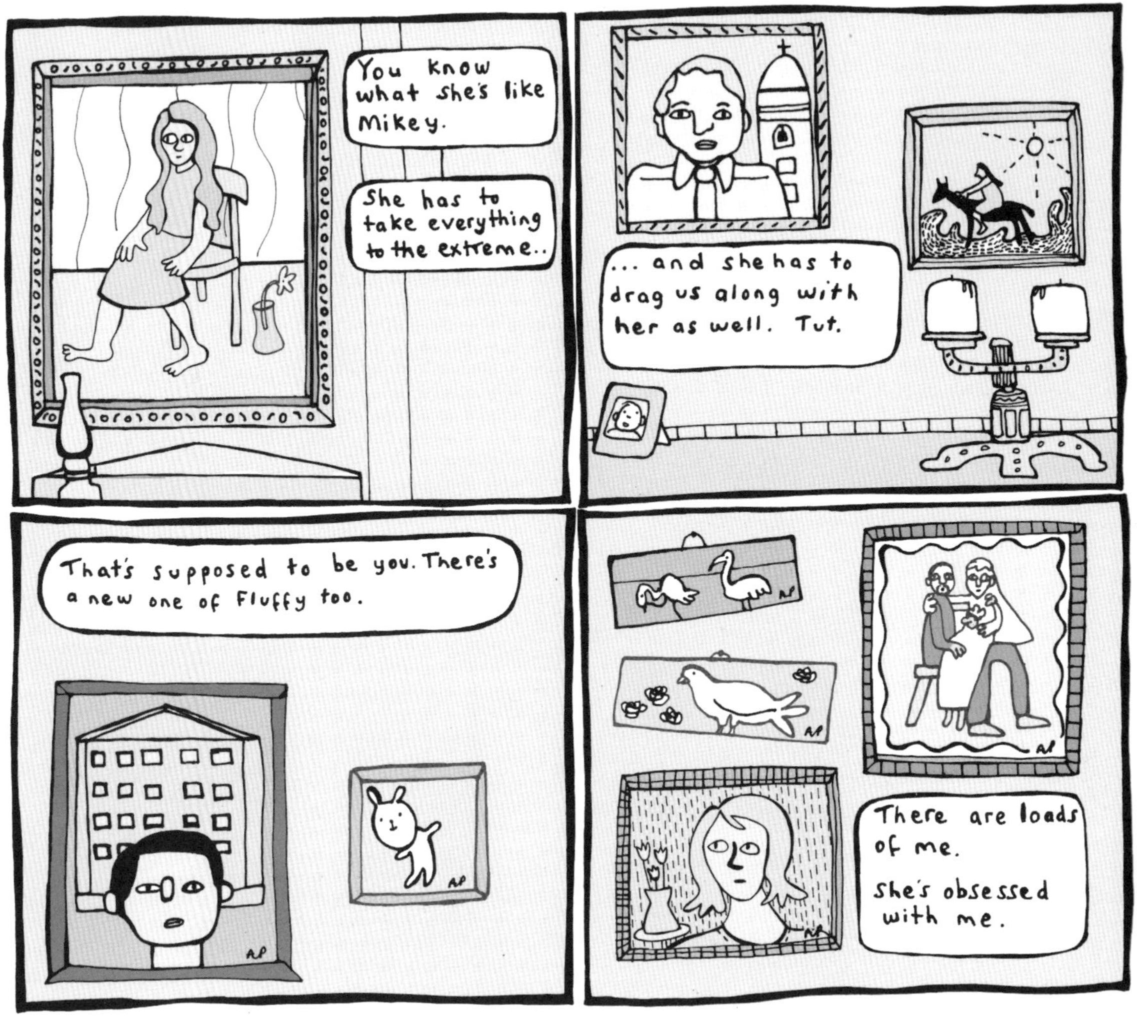
You know what she's like Mikey.
She has to take everything to the extreme..
... and she has to drag us along with her as well. Tut.
That's supposed to be you. There's a new one of Fluffy too.
There are loads of me.
She's obsessed with me.

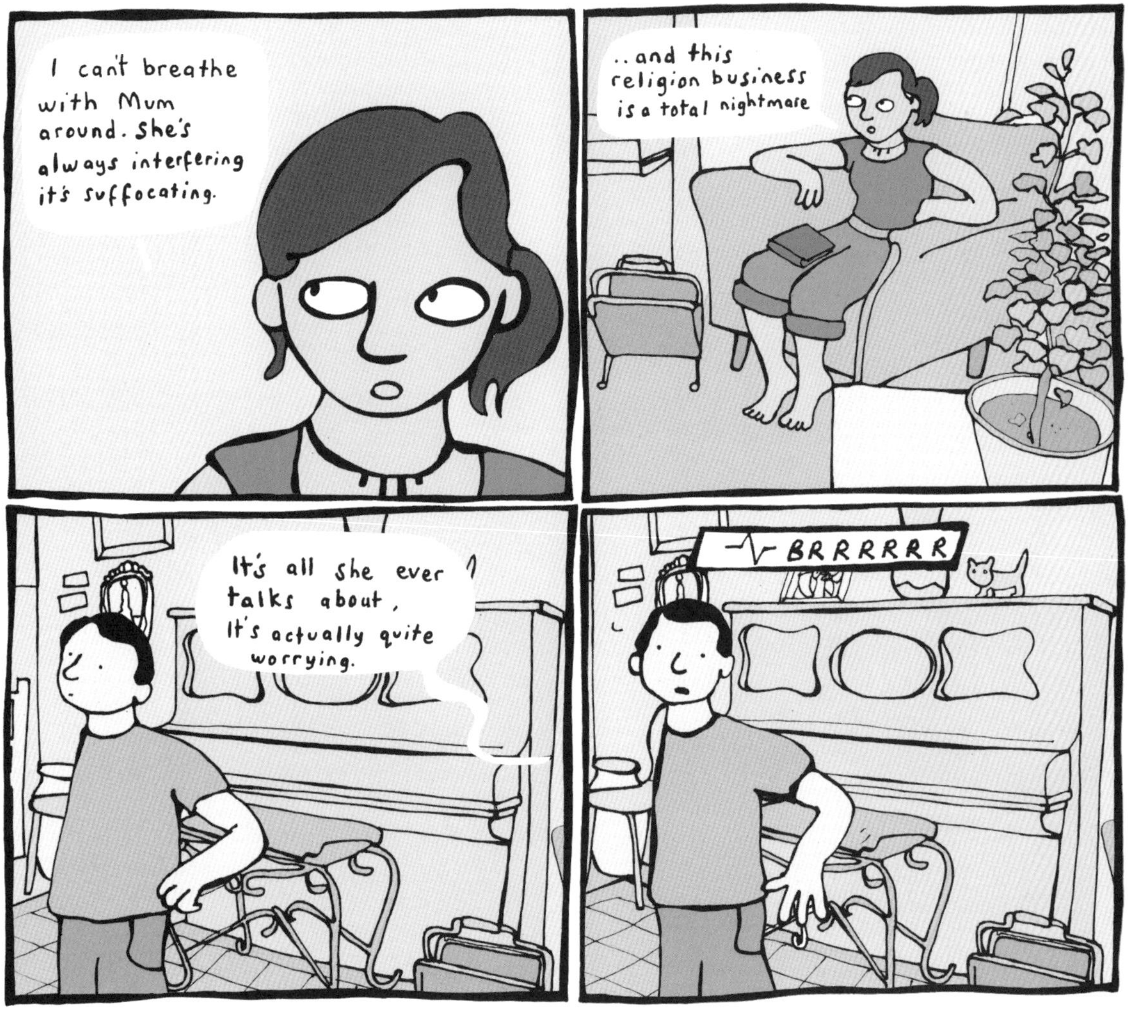
I can't breathe with Mum around. She's always interfering it's suffocating.
..and this religion business is a total nightmare
It's all she ever talks about, It's actually quite worrying.
BRRRRRR

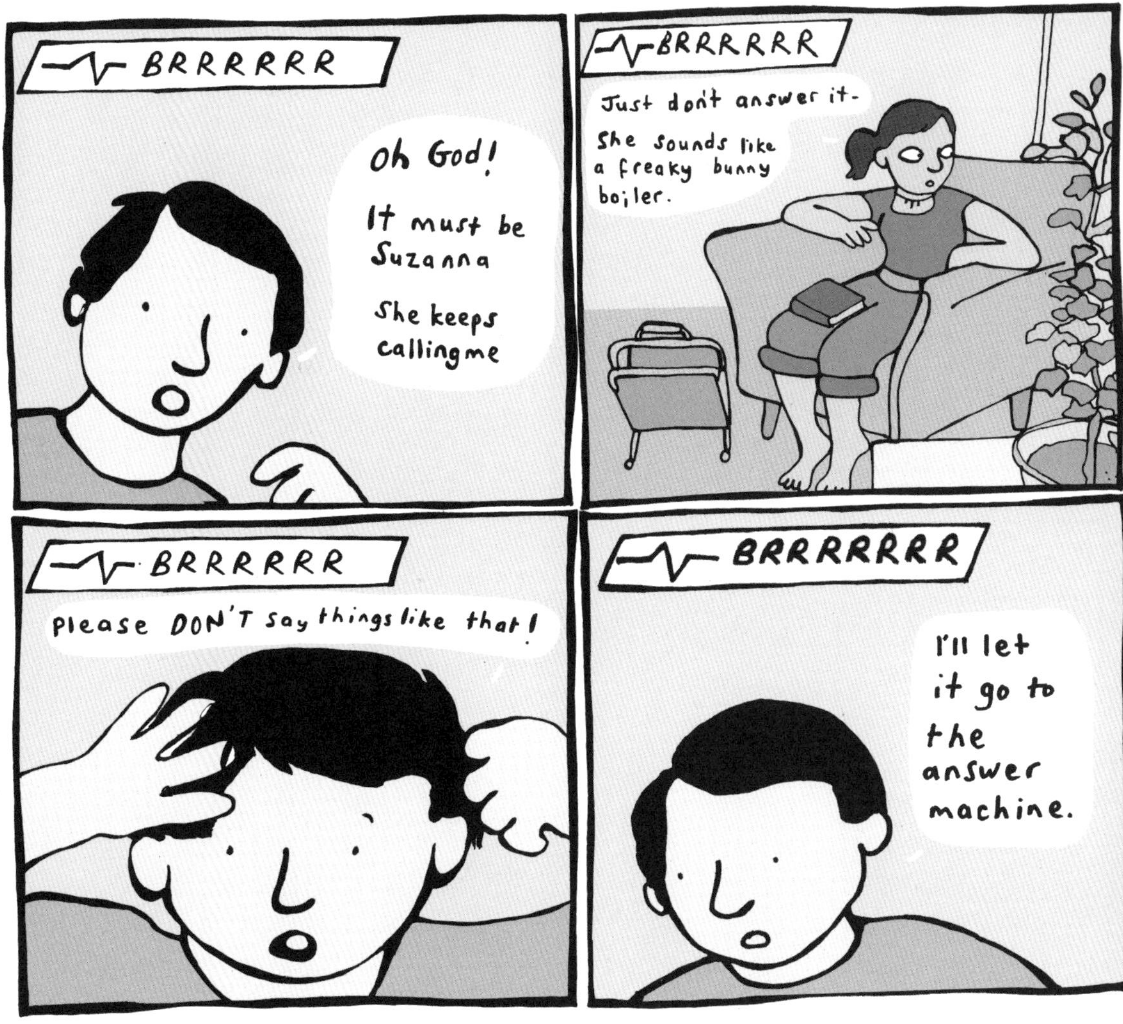
BRRRRRR
Oh God!
It must be Suzanna
She keeps callingme
BRRRRRR
Just don't answer it-
She sounds like a freaky bunny boiler.
BRRRRRR
Please DON'T say things like that!
BRRRRRRR
I'll let it go to the answer machine.

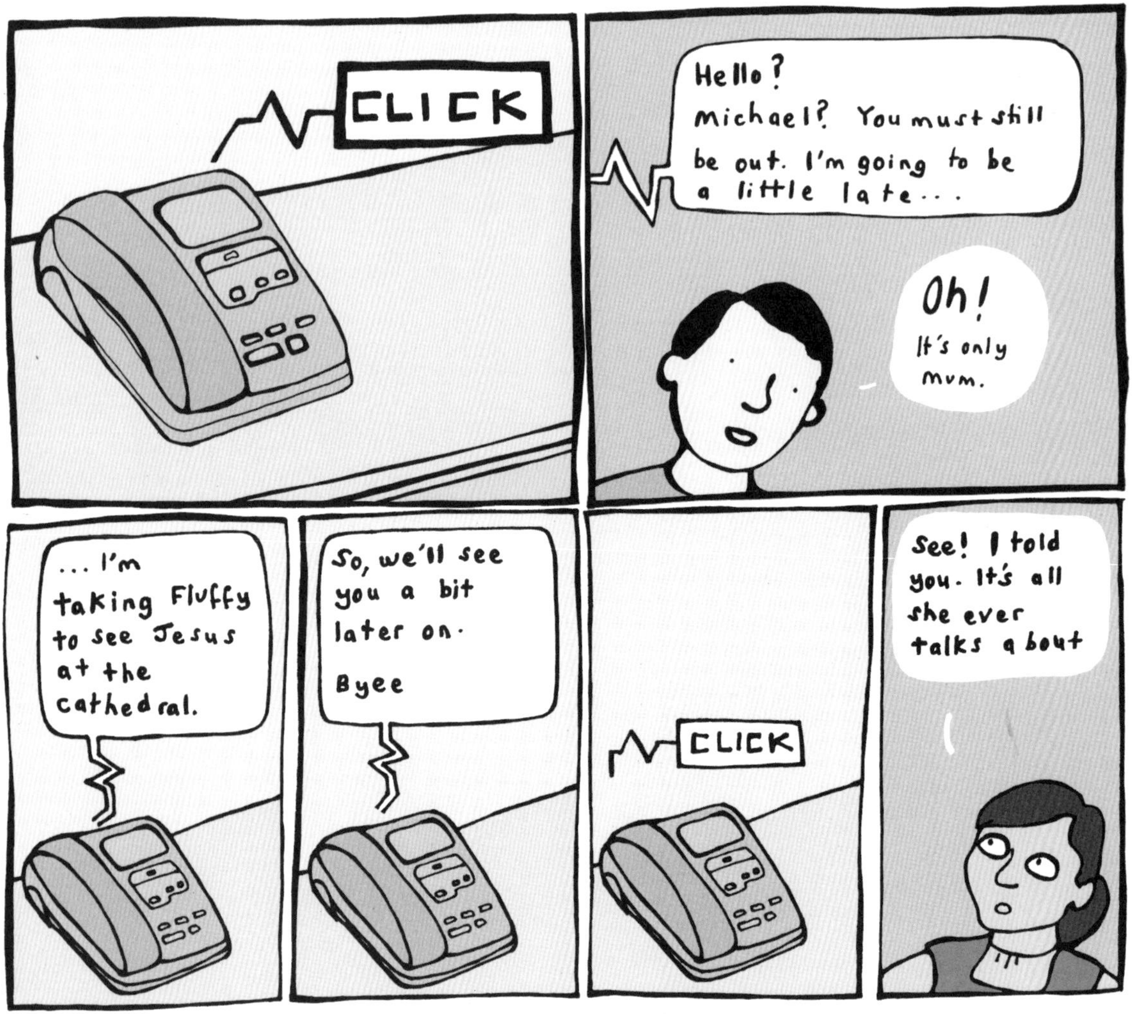

CLICK
Hello? michael? You must still be out. I'm going to be a little late...
Oh! It's only mum.
... I'm taking Fluffy to see Jesus at the cathedral.
So, we'll see you a bit later on. Byee
CLICK
See! I told you. It's all she ever talks about

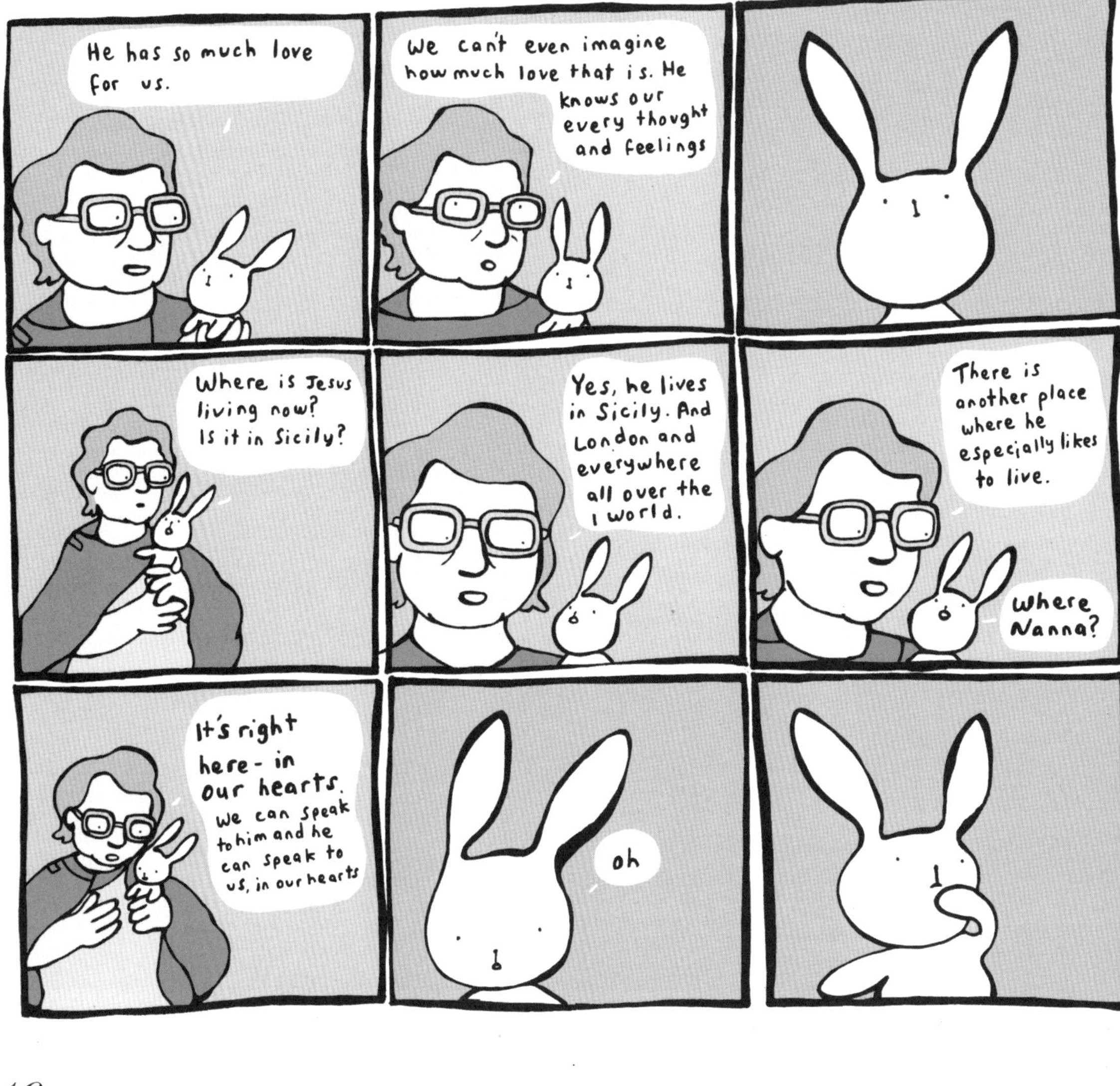
He has so much love for us.
We can't even imagine how much love that is. He knows our every thought and feelings
Where is Jesus living now? Is it in Sicily?
Yes, he lives in Sicily. And London and everywhere all over the world.
There is another place where he especially likes to live.
Where Nanna?
It's right here - in our hearts. We can speak to him and he can speak to us, in our hearts
oh

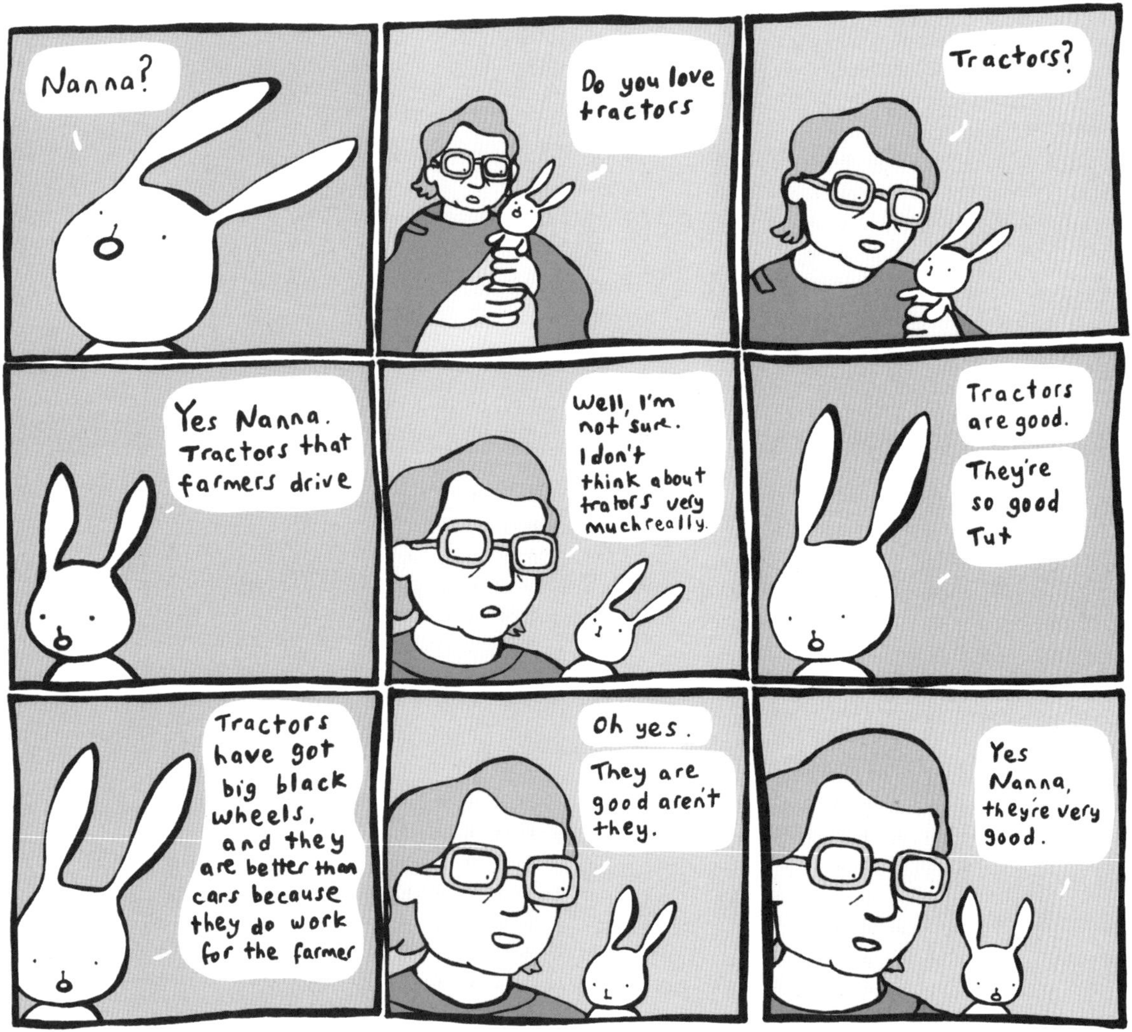
Nanna?
Do you love tractors
Tractors?
Yes Nanna. Tractors that farmers drive
Well, I'm not sure. I don't think about trators very much really.
Tractors are good.
They're so good Tut
Tractors have got big black wheels, and they are better than cars because they do work for the farmer
Oh yes.
They are good aren't they.
Yes Nanna, they're very good.

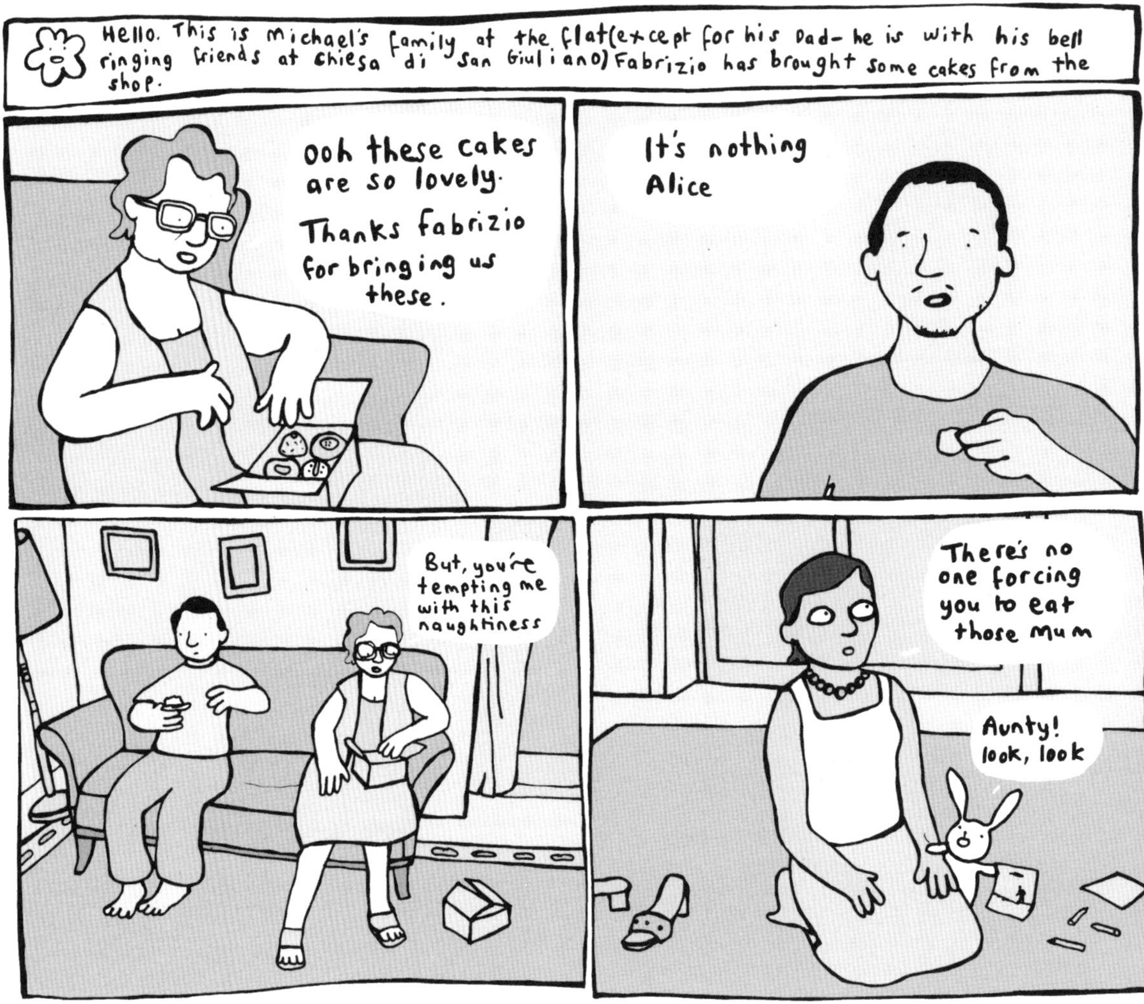
Hello. This is Michael's family at the flat (except for his Dad - he is with his bell ringing friends at Chiesa di San Giuliano) Fabrizio has brought some cakes from the shop.
Ooh these cakes are so lovely. Thanks Fabrizio for bringing us these.
It's nothing Alice
But, you're tempting me with this naughtiness
There's no one forcing you to eat those Mum
Aunty! look, look

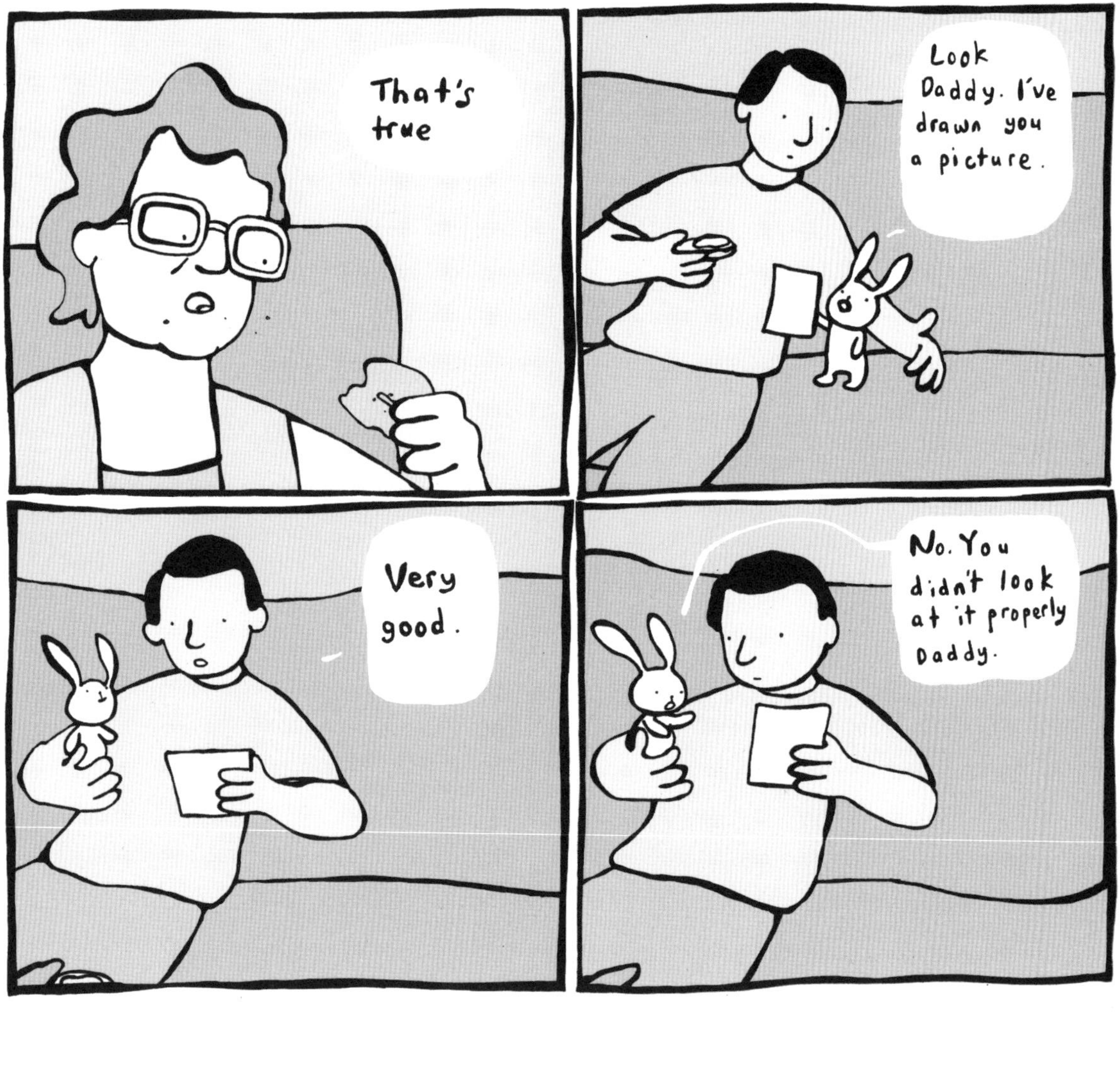
That's true
Look Daddy. I've drawn you a picture.
Very good.
No. You didn't look at it properly Daddy.

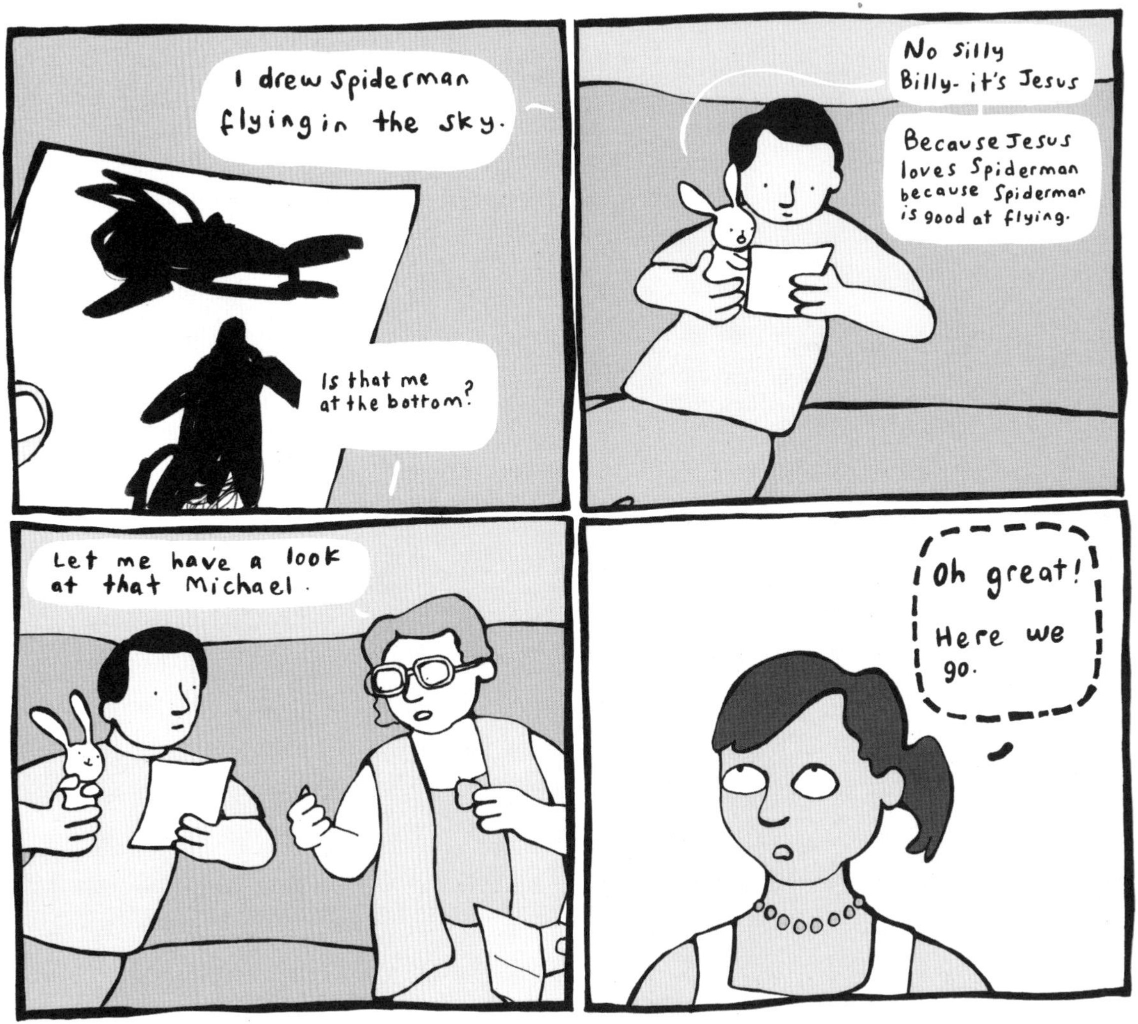
I drew Spiderman flying in the sky.
Is that me at the bottom?
No silly Billy- it's Jesus
Because Jesus loves Spiderman because Spiderman is good at flying.
Let me have a look at that Michael.
Oh great! Here we go.

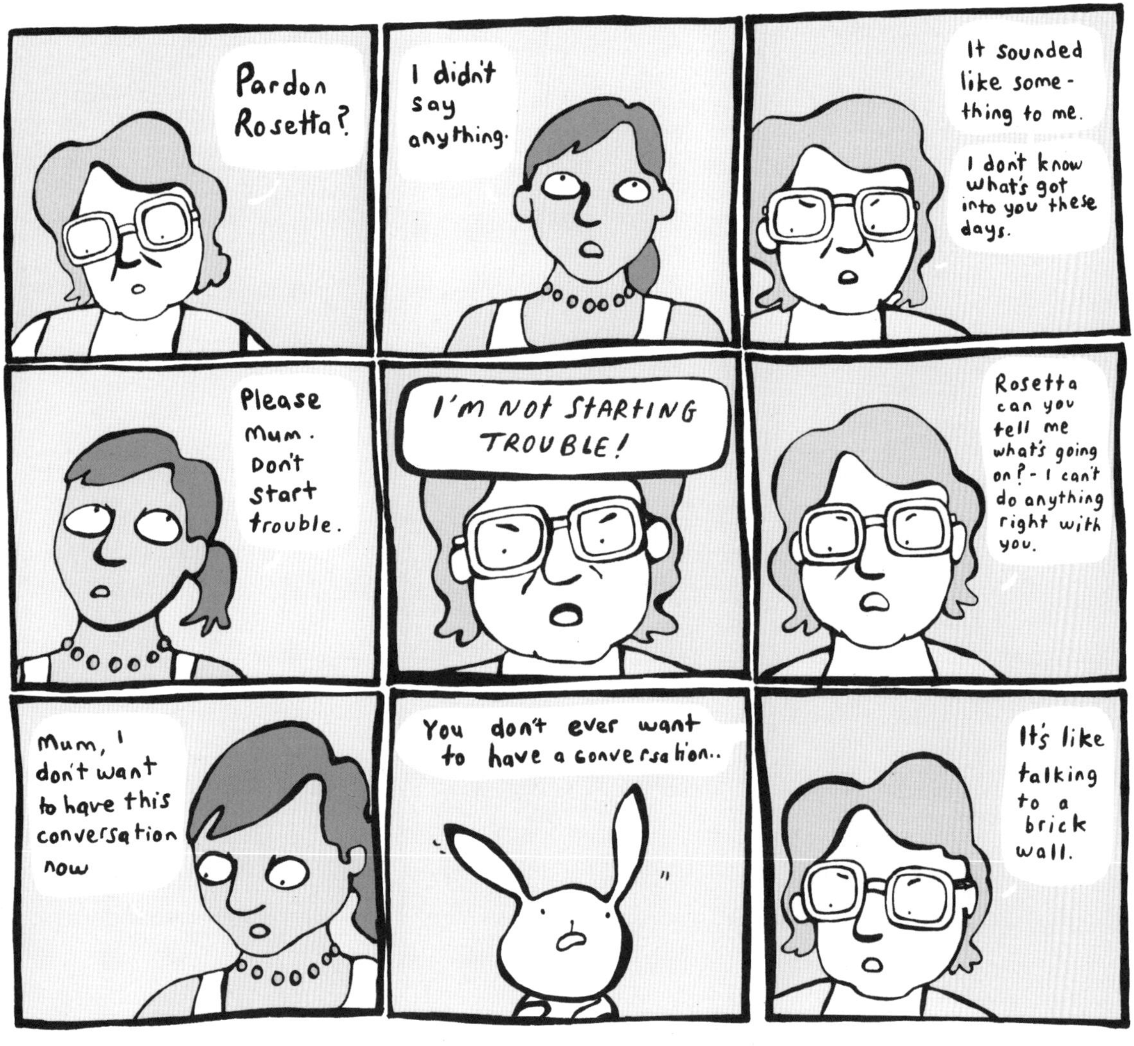
Pardon Rosetta?
I didn't say anything.
It sounded like some-thing to me.
I don't know what's got into you these days.
Please Mum. Don't start trouble.
I'M NOT STARTING TROUBLE!
Rosetta can you tell me what's going on? - I can't do anything right with you.
Mum, I don't want to have this conversation now
You don't ever want to have a conversation..
It's like talking to a brick wall.

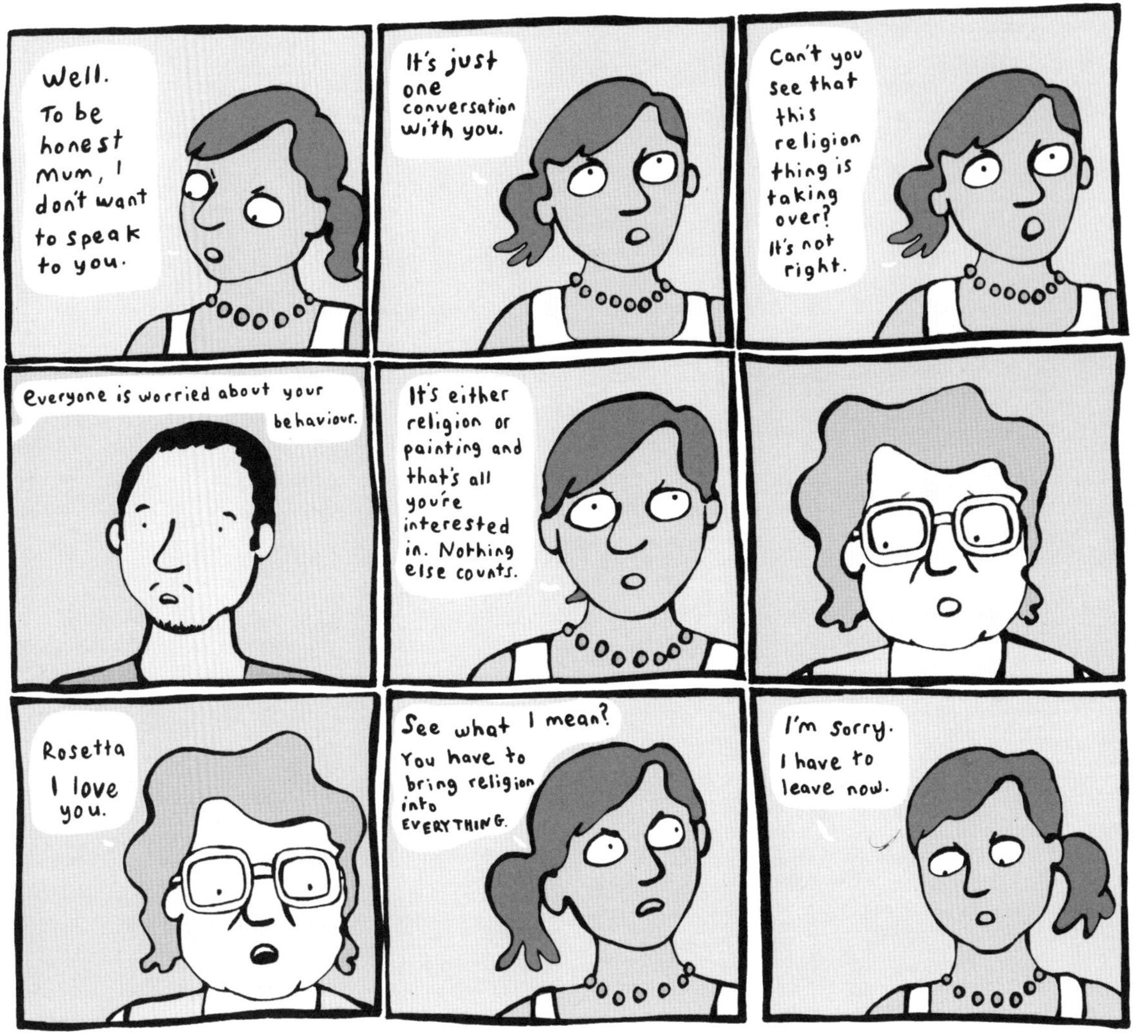
Well. To be honest Mum, I don't want to speak to you.
It's just one conversation with you.
Can't you see that this religion thing is taking over? It's not right.
Everyone is worried about your behaviour.
It's either religion or painting and that's all you're interested in. Nothing else counts.
Rosetta I love you.
See what I mean? You have to bring religion into EVERYTHING.
I'm sorry. I have to leave now.

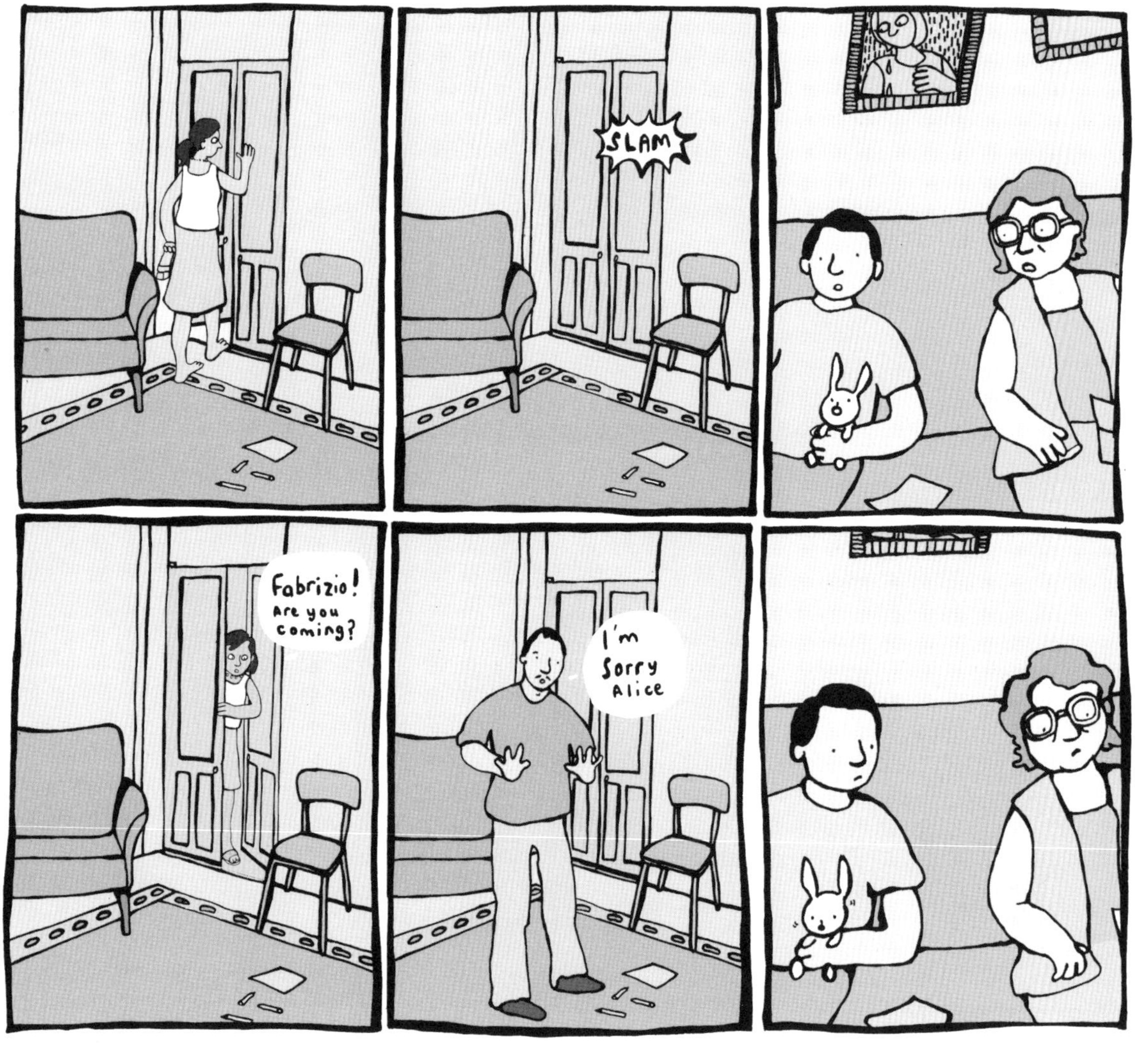
SLAM
Fabrizio! Are you coming?
I'm Sorry Alice

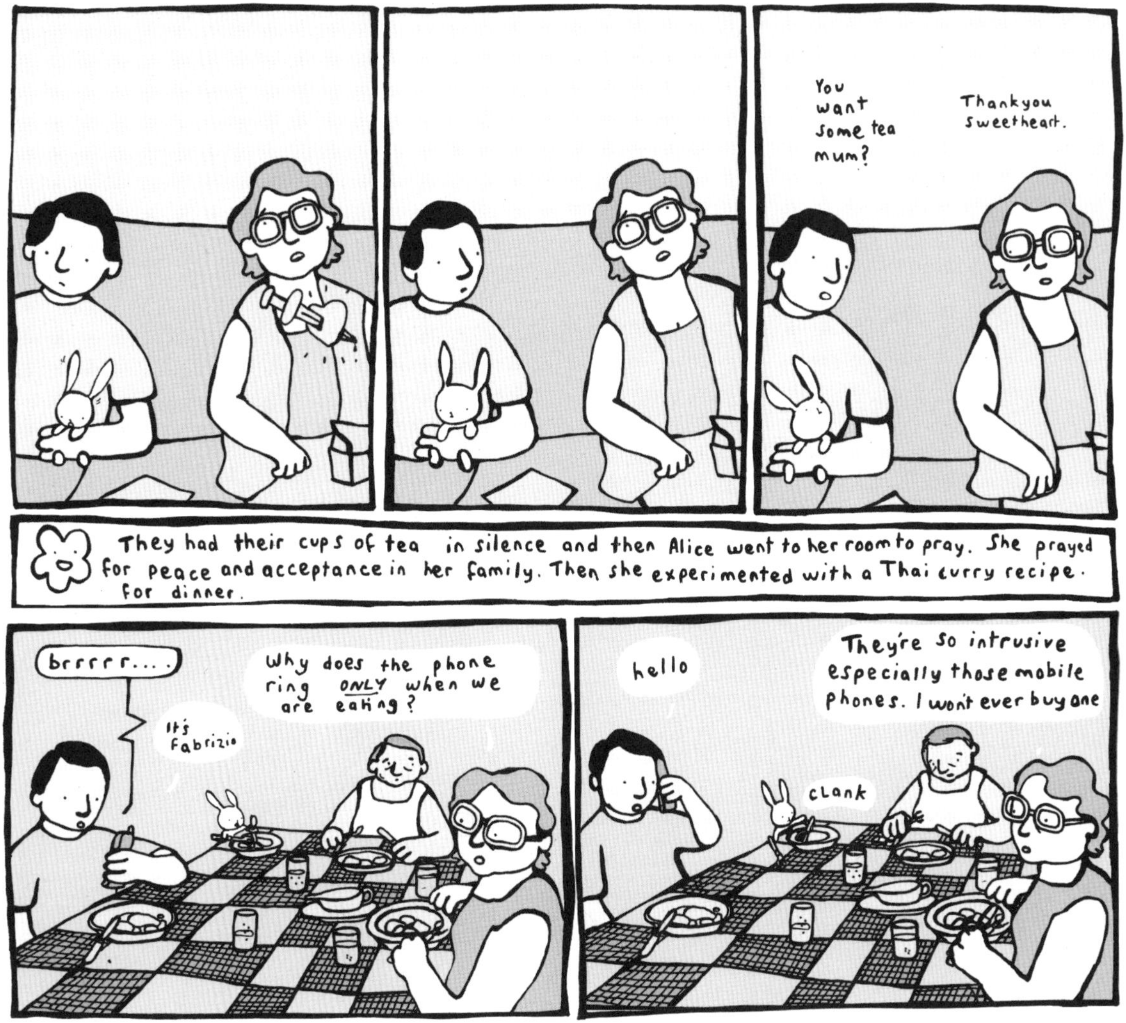
You want some tea mum?
Thankyou sweetheart.
They had their cups of tea in silence and then Alice went to her room to pray. She prayed for peace and acceptance in her family. Then she experimented with a Thai curry recipe. for dinner.
brrrrr....
It's Fabrizio
Why does the phone ring ONLY when we are eating?
hello
clank
They're so intrusive especially those mobile phones. I won't ever buy one

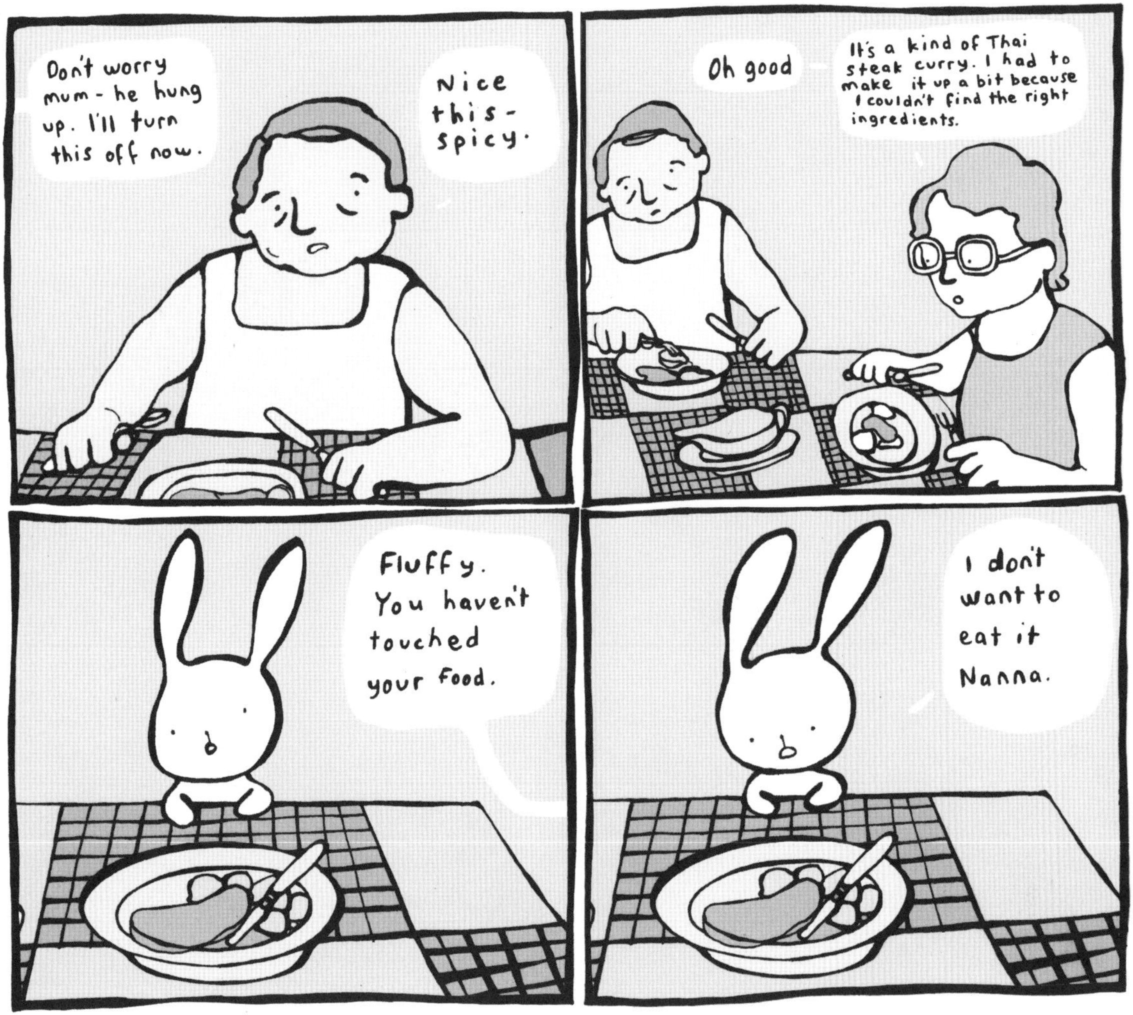

Don't worry mum - he hung up. I'll turn this off now.
Nice this - spicy.
Oh good
It's a kind of Thai steak curry. I had to make it up a bit because I couldn't find the right ingredients.
Fluffy. You haven't touched your food.
I don't want to eat it Nanna.

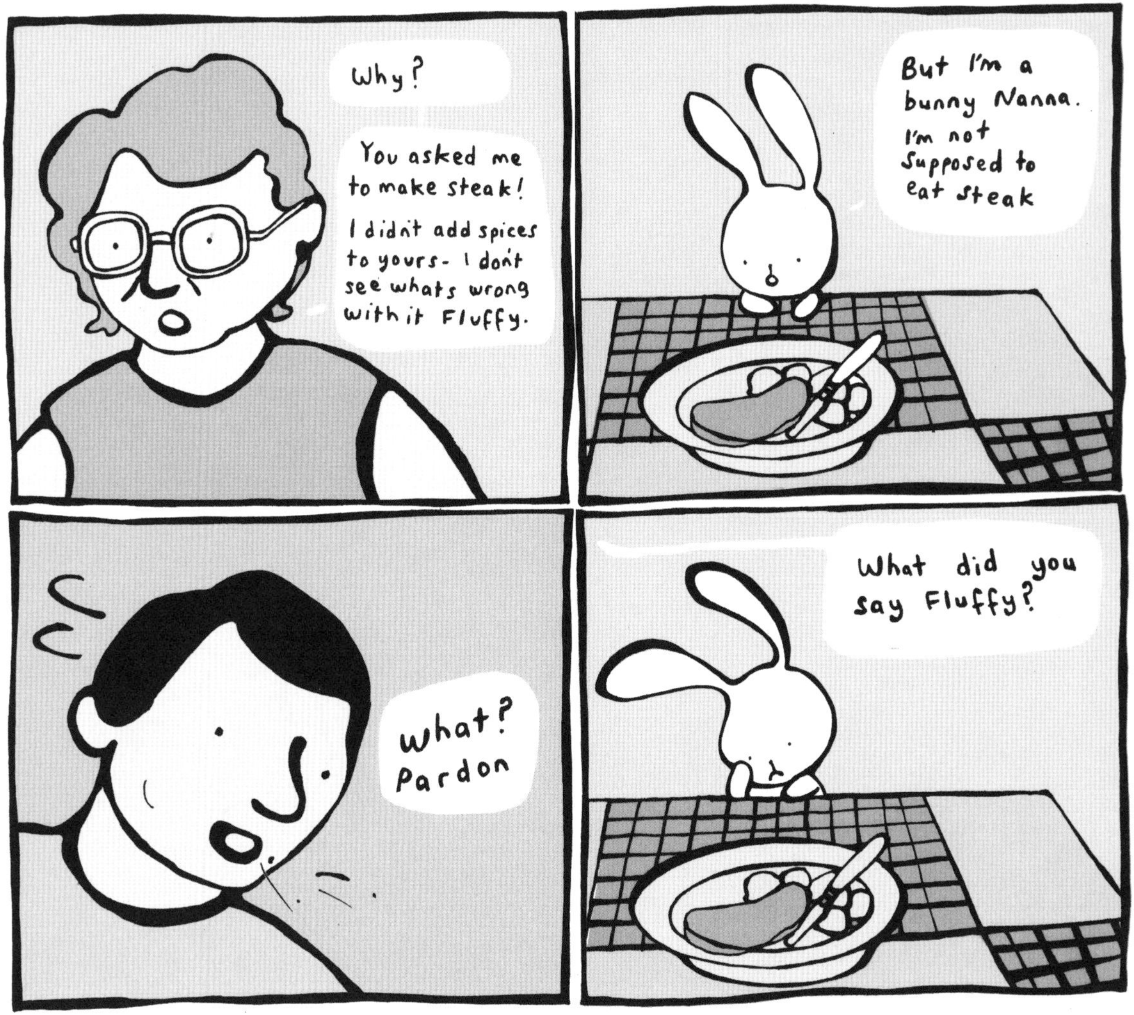
Why?
You asked me to make steak!
I didn't add spices to yours- I don't see whats wrong with it Fluffy.
But I'm a bunny Nanna. I'm not supposed to eat steak
what? Pardon
What did you say Fluffy?

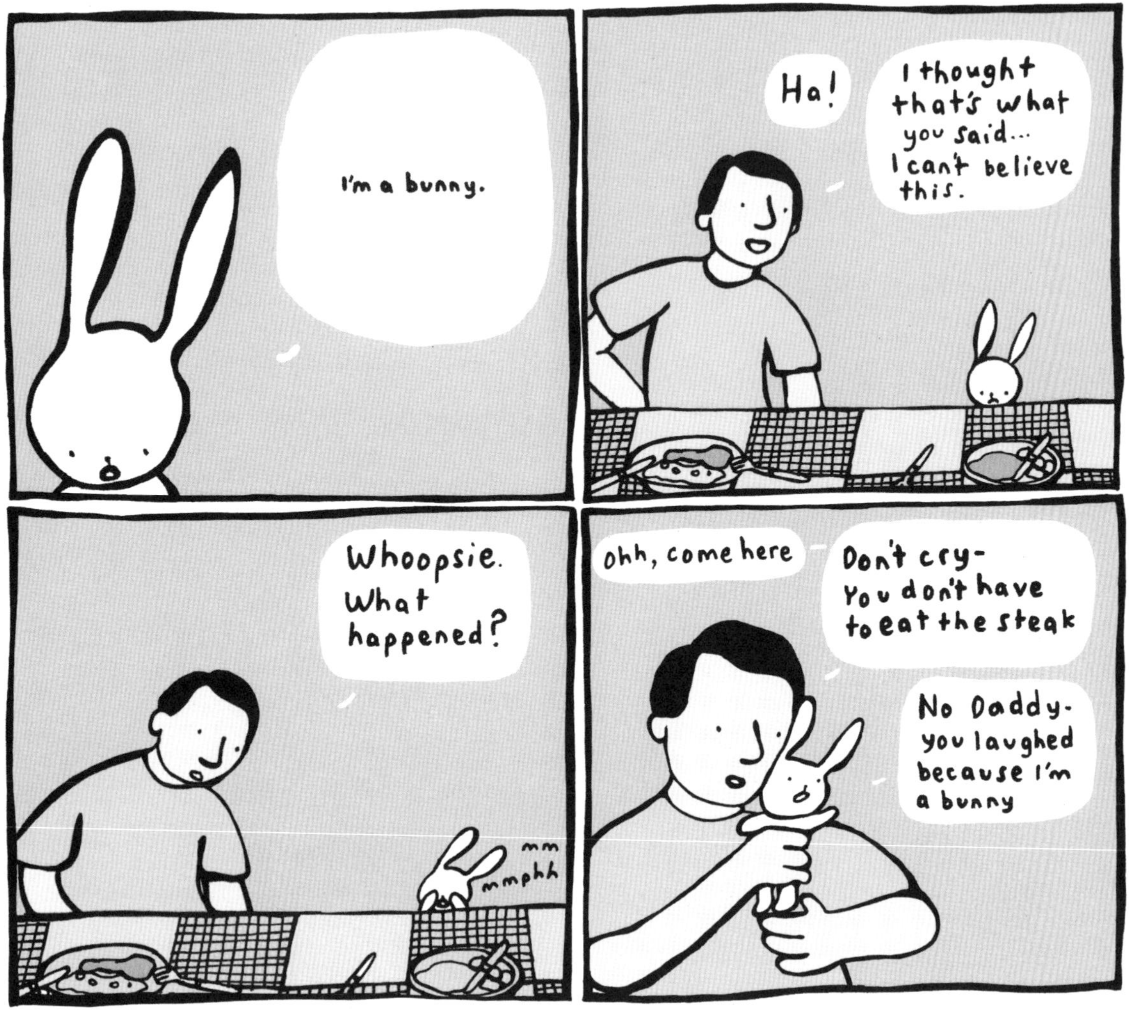
I'm a bunny.
Ha!
I thought that's what you said... I can't believe this.
Whoopsie. What happened?
mm mmphh
Ohh, come here
Don't cry- You don't have to eat the steak
No Daddy- you laughed because I'm a bunny

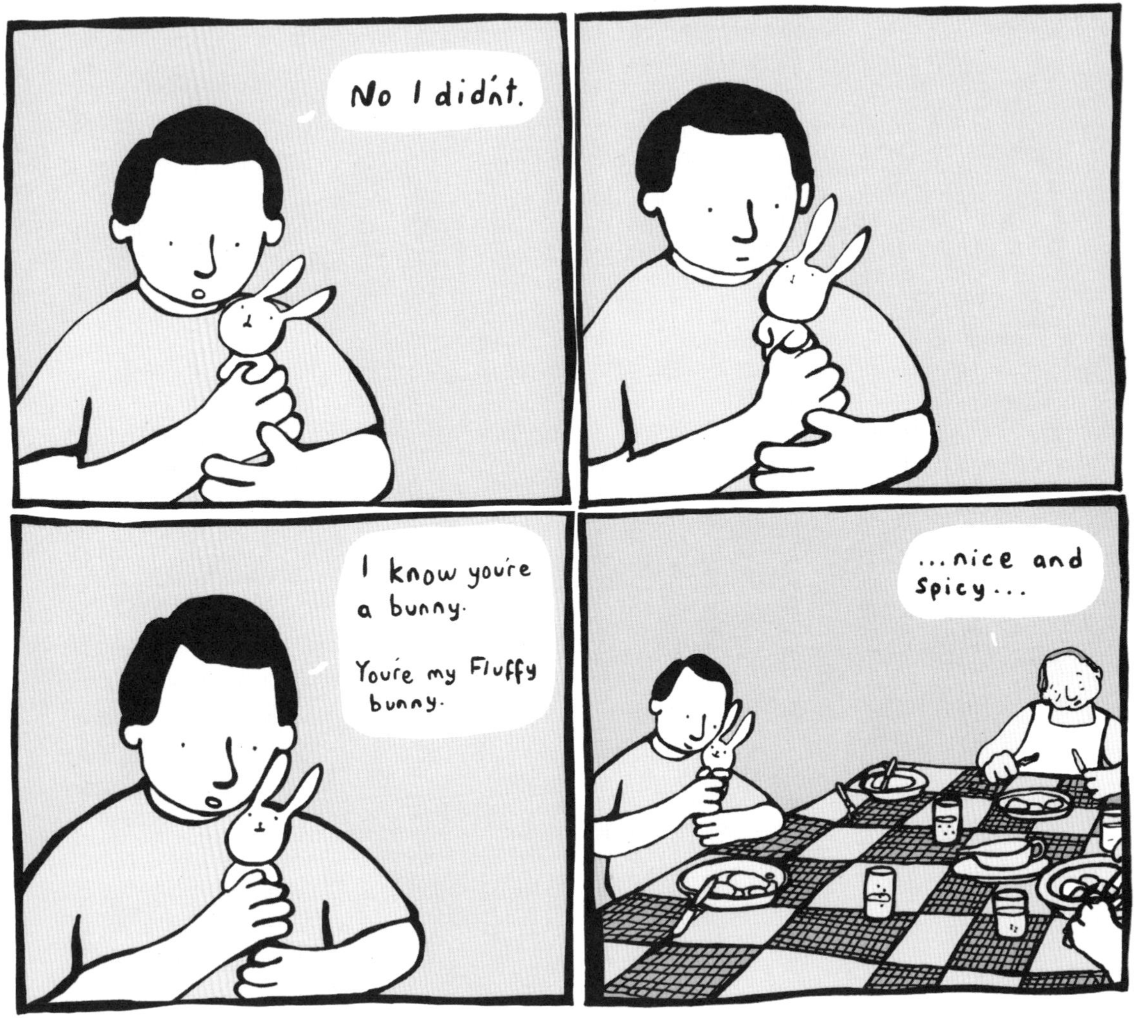
No I didn't.
I know you're a bunny.
You're my Fluffy bunny.
...nice and spicy...

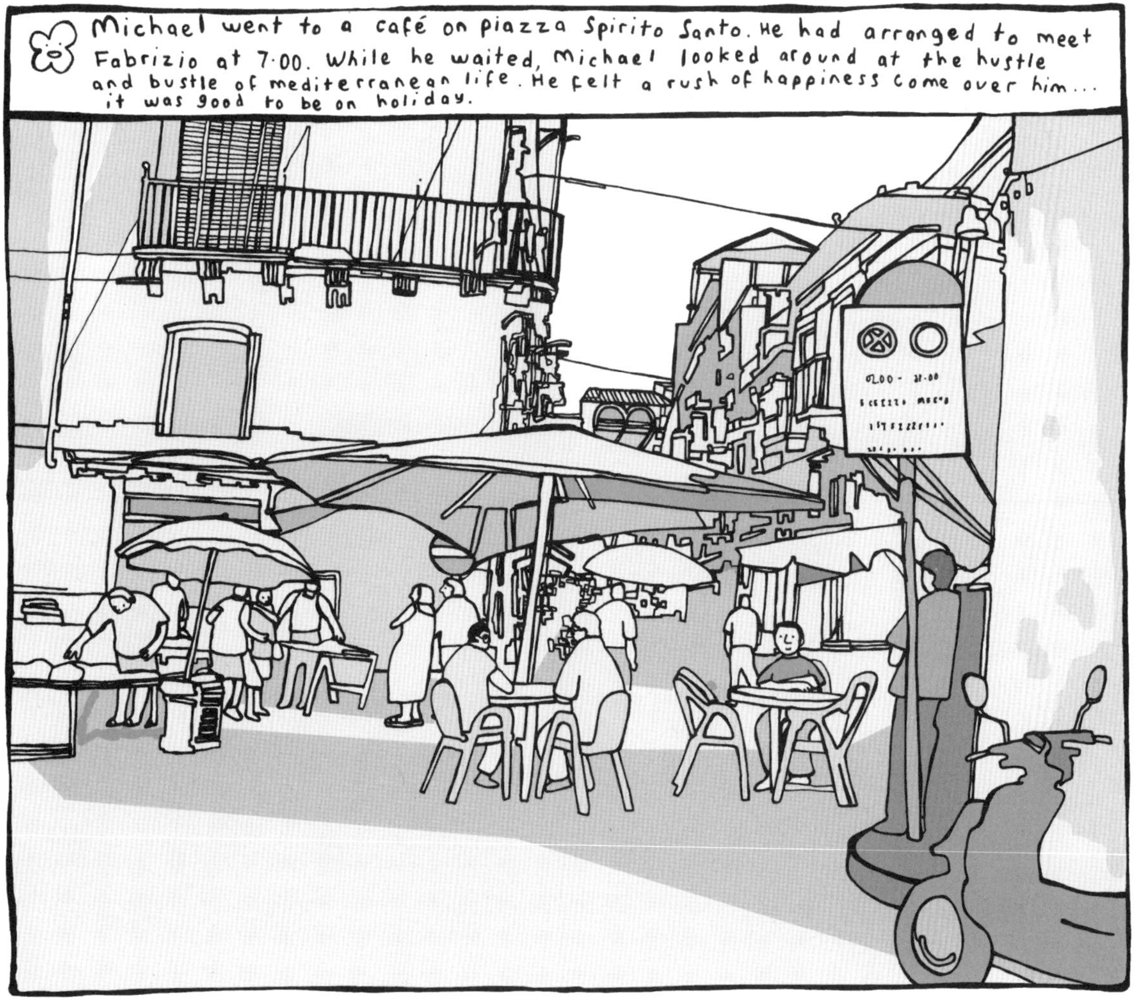
Michael went to a café on piazza Spirito Santo. He had arranged to meet Fabrizio at 7.00. While he waited, Michael looked around at the hustle and bustle of mediterranean life. He felt a rush of happiness come over him... it was good to be on holiday.

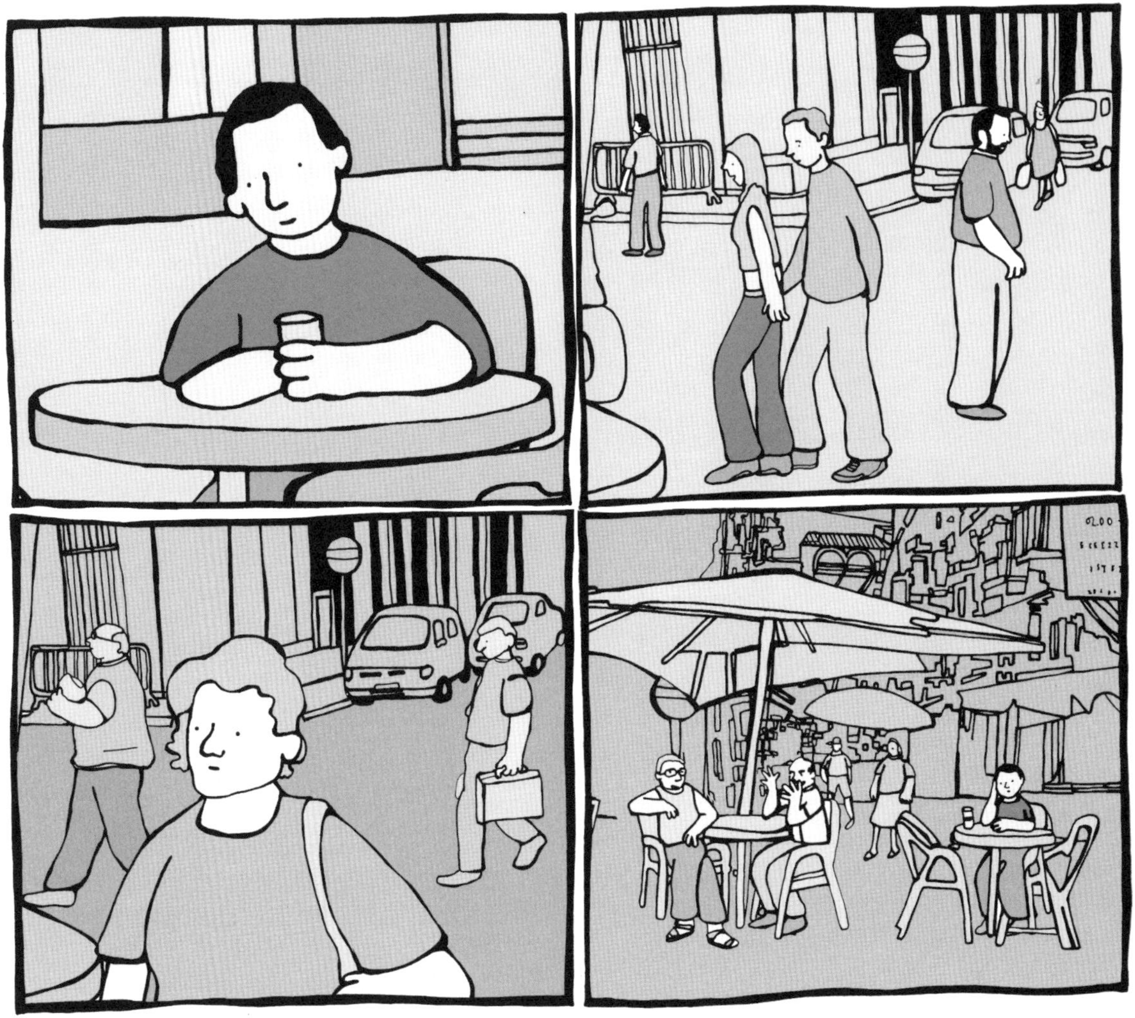

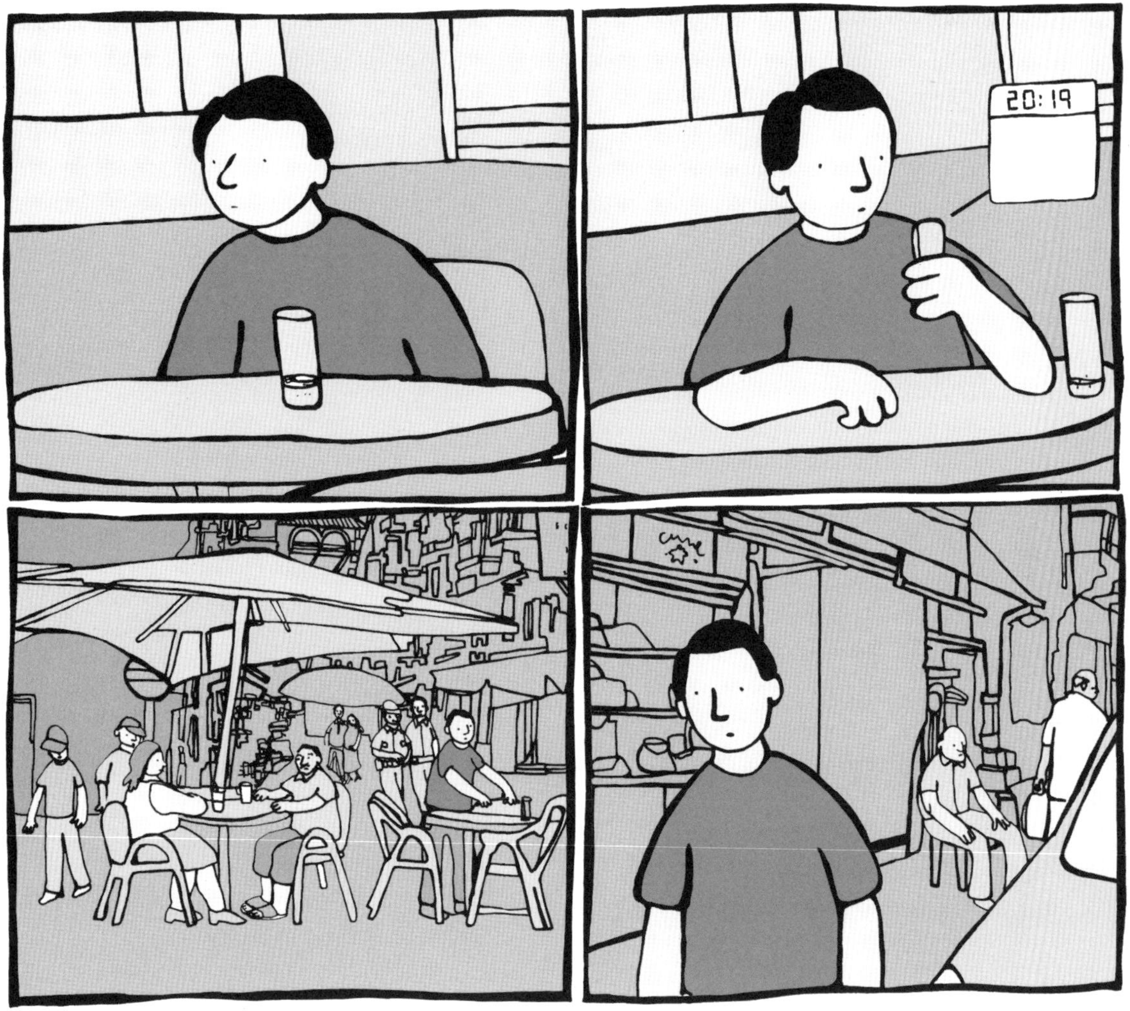
20:19

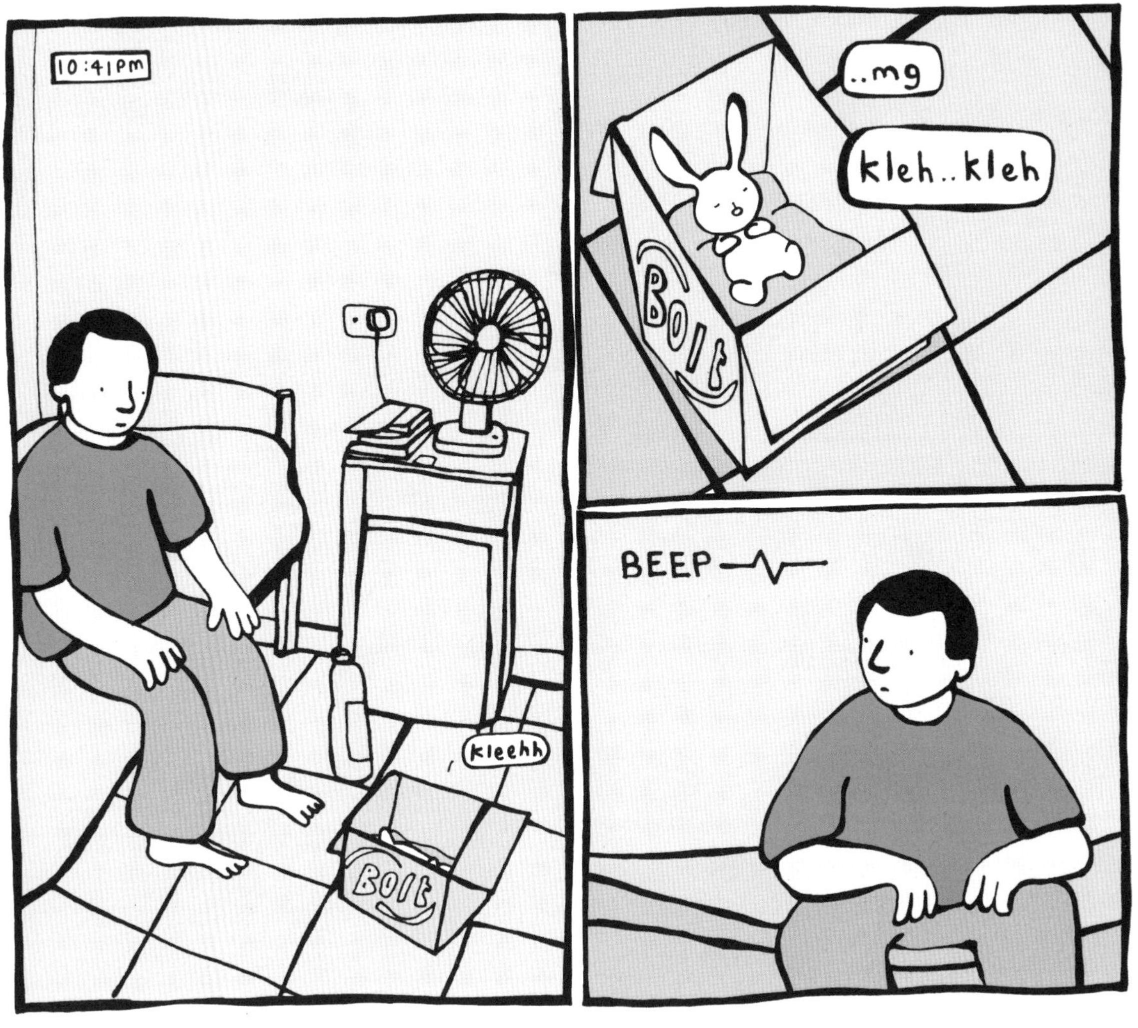
10:41PM
kleehh
..mg
kleh..kleh
BEEP

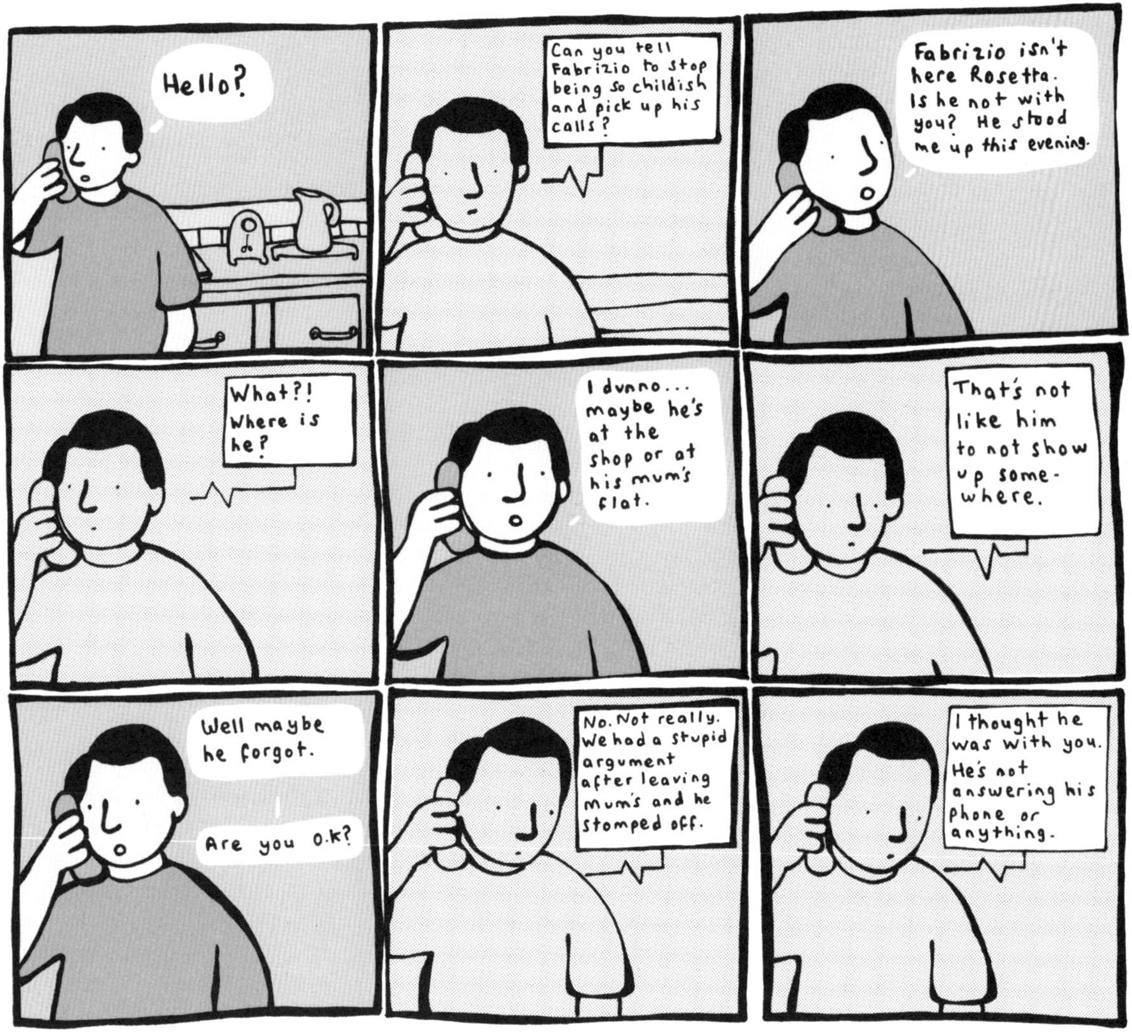
Hello?
Can you tell Fabrizio to stop being so childish and pick up his calls?
Fabrizio isn't here Rosetta. Is he not with you? He stood me up this evening.
What?! Where is he?
I dunno... maybe he's at the shop or at his mum's flat.
That's not like him to not show up some-where.
Well maybe he forgot.
Are you O.K?
No. Not really. We had a stupid argument after leaving mum's and he stomped off.
I thought he was with you. He's not answering his phone or anything.

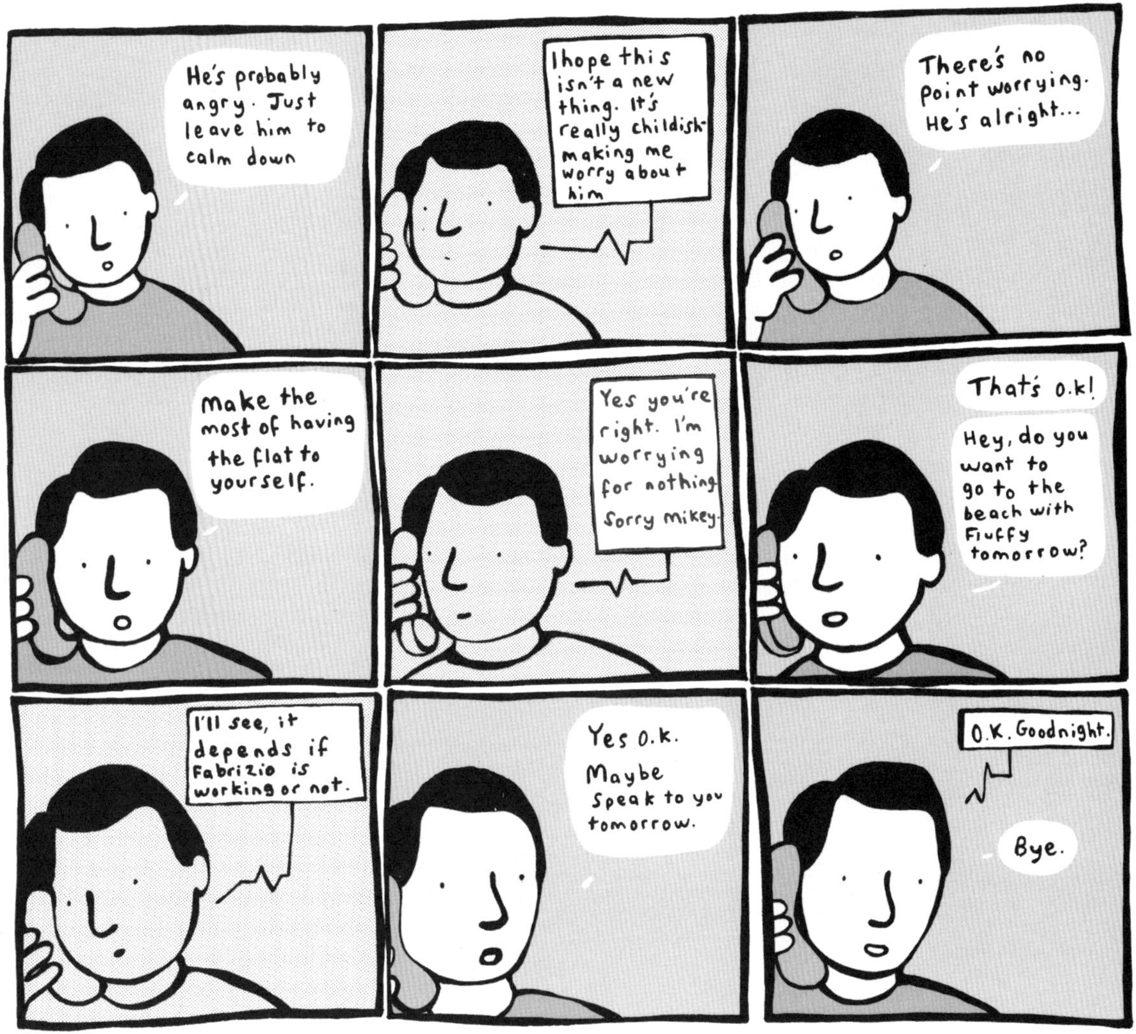
He's probably angry. Just leave him to calm down
I hope this isn't a new thing. It's really childish- making me worry about him
There's no point worrying. He's alright...
Make the most of having the flat to yourself.
Yes you're right. I'm worrying for nothing
Sorry mikey.
That's o.k!
Hey, do you want to go to the beach with Fluffy tomorrow?
I'll see, it depends if Fabrizio is working or not.
Yes o.k.
Maybe speak to you tomorrow.
O.K. Goodnight.
Bye.

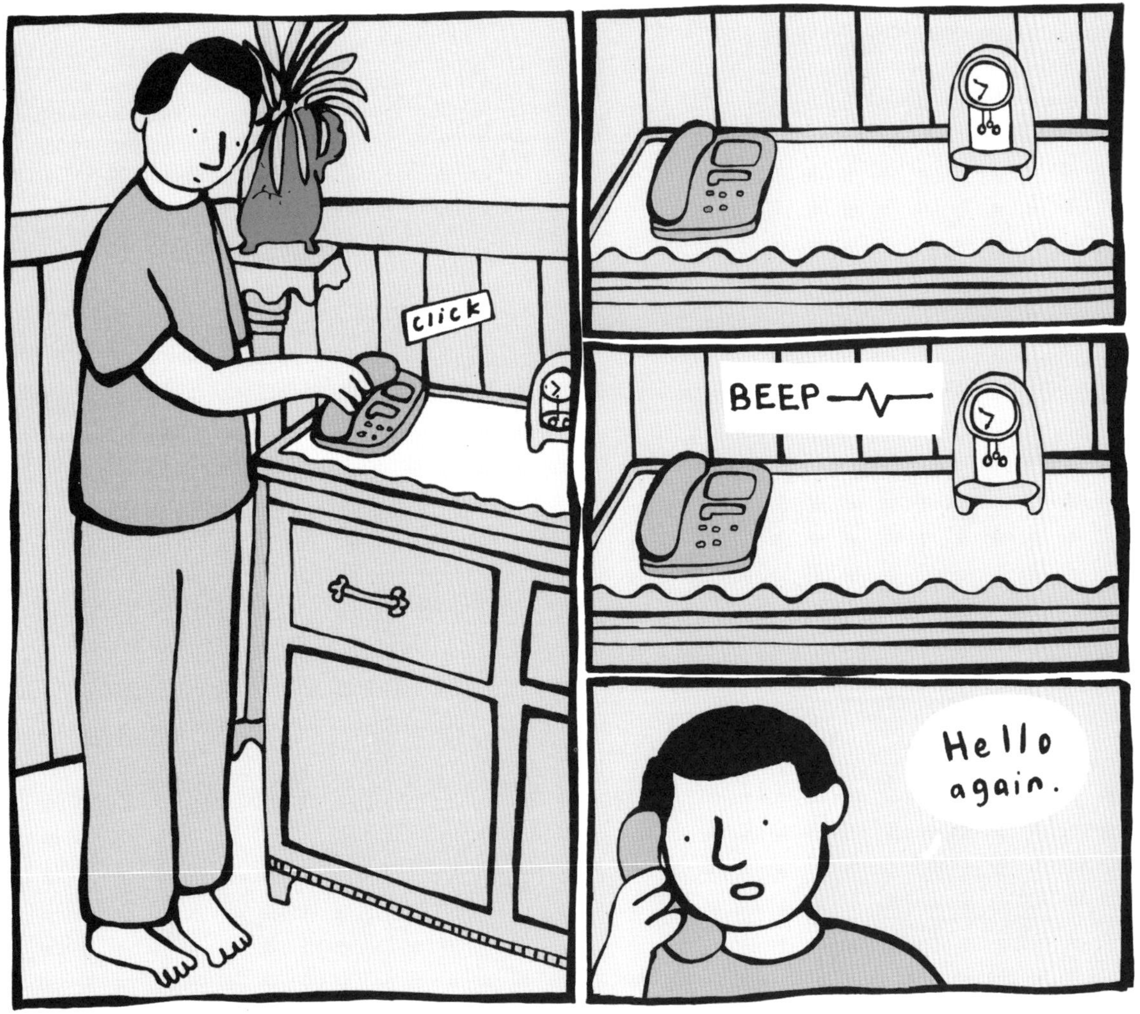
click
BEEP
Hello again.

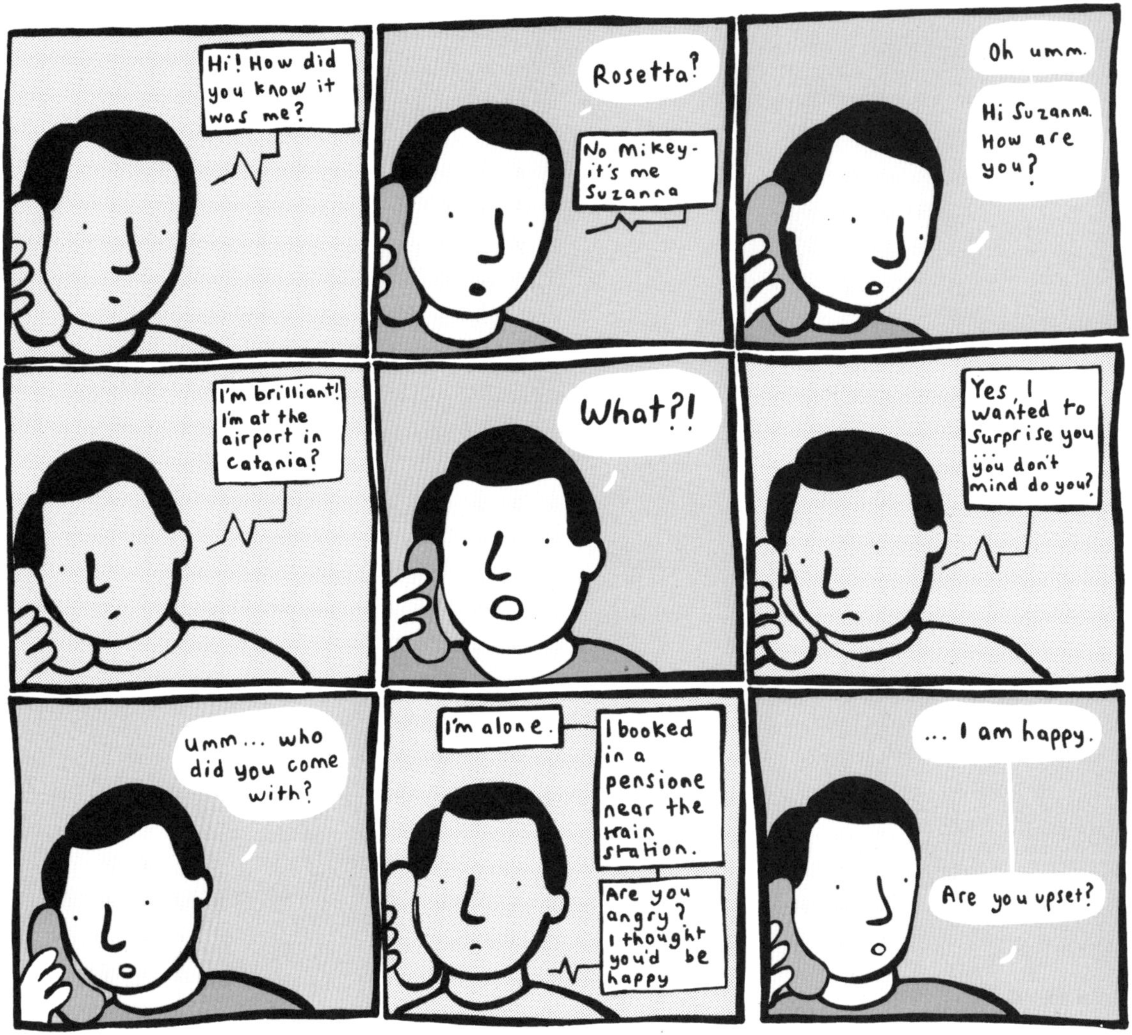
Hi! How did you know it was me?
Rosetta?
No Mikey - it's me Suzanna
Oh umm.
Hi Suzanna. How are you?
I'm brilliant! I'm at the airport in Catania?
What?!
Yes, I wanted to surprise you ... you don't mind do you?
umm... who did you come with?
I'm alone.
I booked in a pensione near the train station.
Are you angry? I thought you'd be happy
... I am happy.
Are you upset?

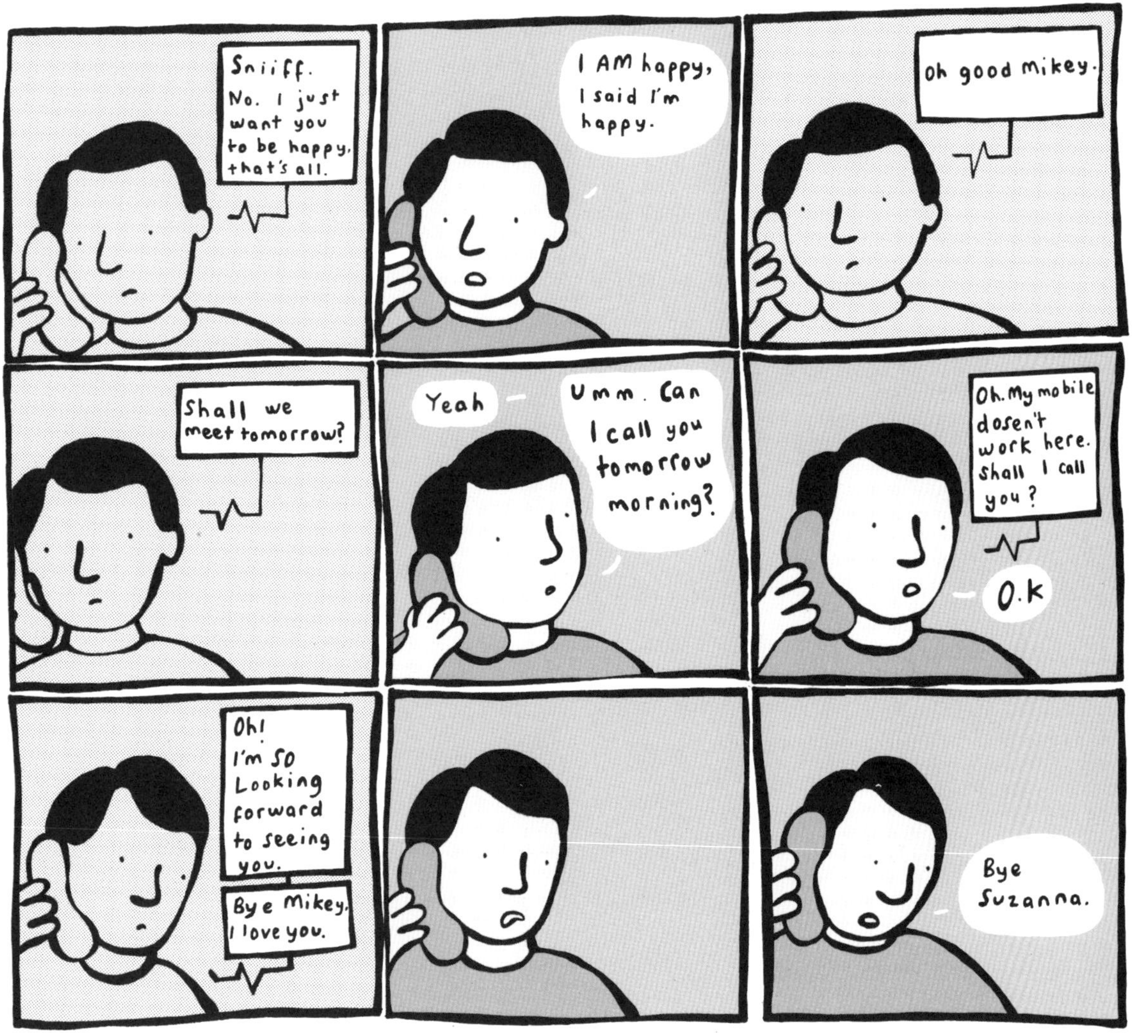
Sniiff.
No. I just want you to be happy, that's all.
I AM happy, I said I'm happy.
Oh good mikey.
Shall we meet tomorrow?
Yeah
Umm. Can I call you tomorrow morning?
Oh. My mobile dosen't work here. Shall I call you?
O.K
Oh! I'm SO Looking forward to seeing you.
Bye Mikey, I love you.
Bye Suzanna.

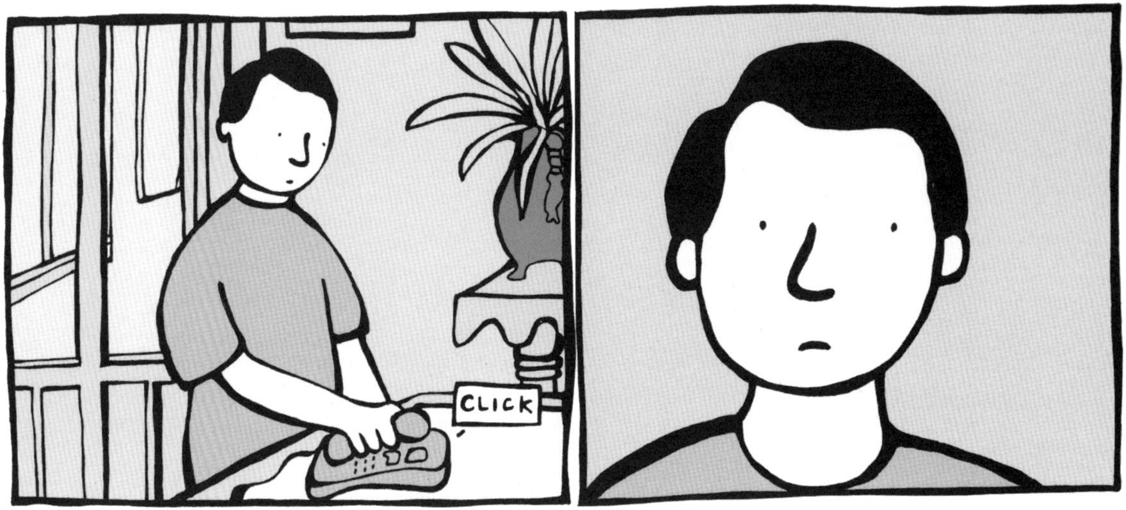
CLICK

Part 4

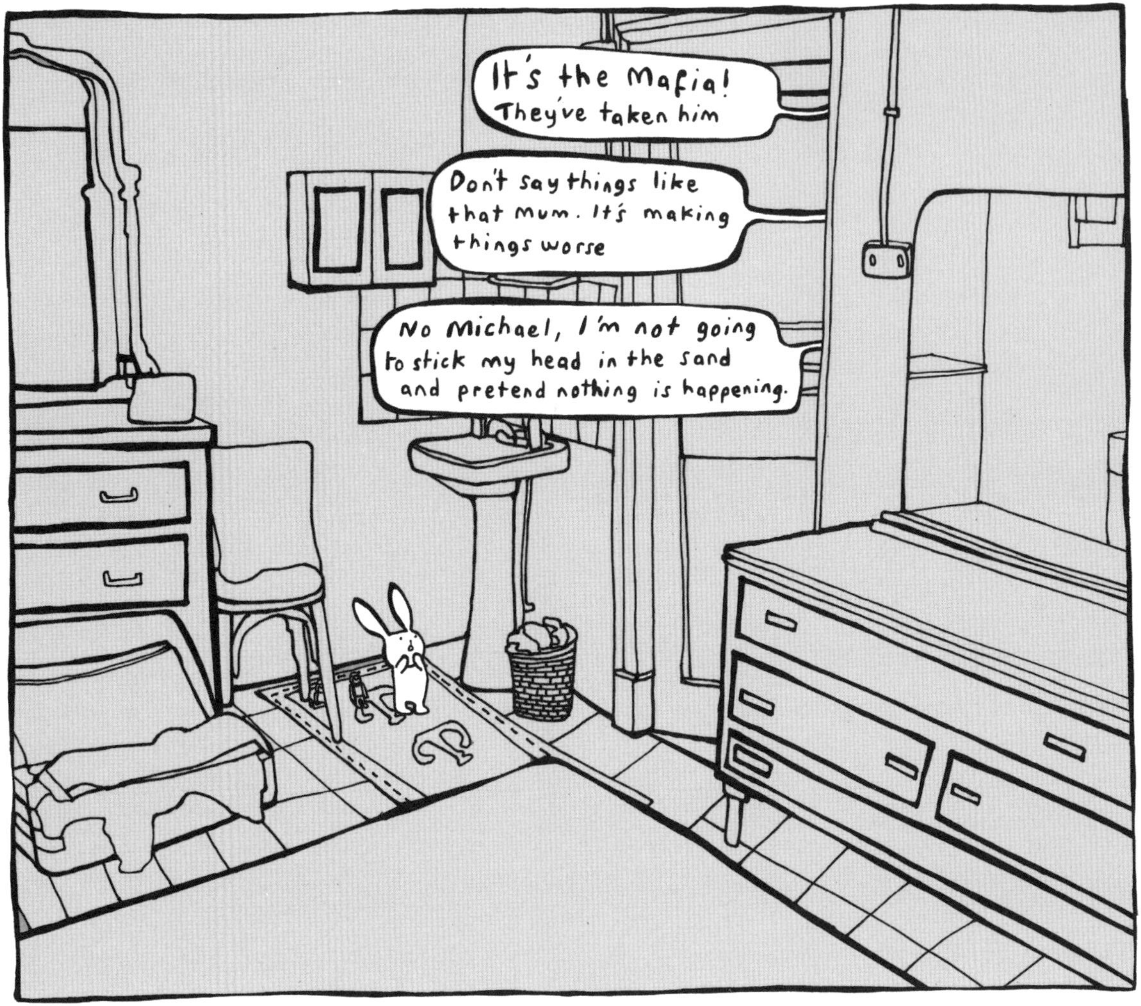
It's the Mafia! They've taken him
Don't say things like that mum. It's making things worse
No Michael, I'm not going to stick my head in the sand and pretend nothing is happening.

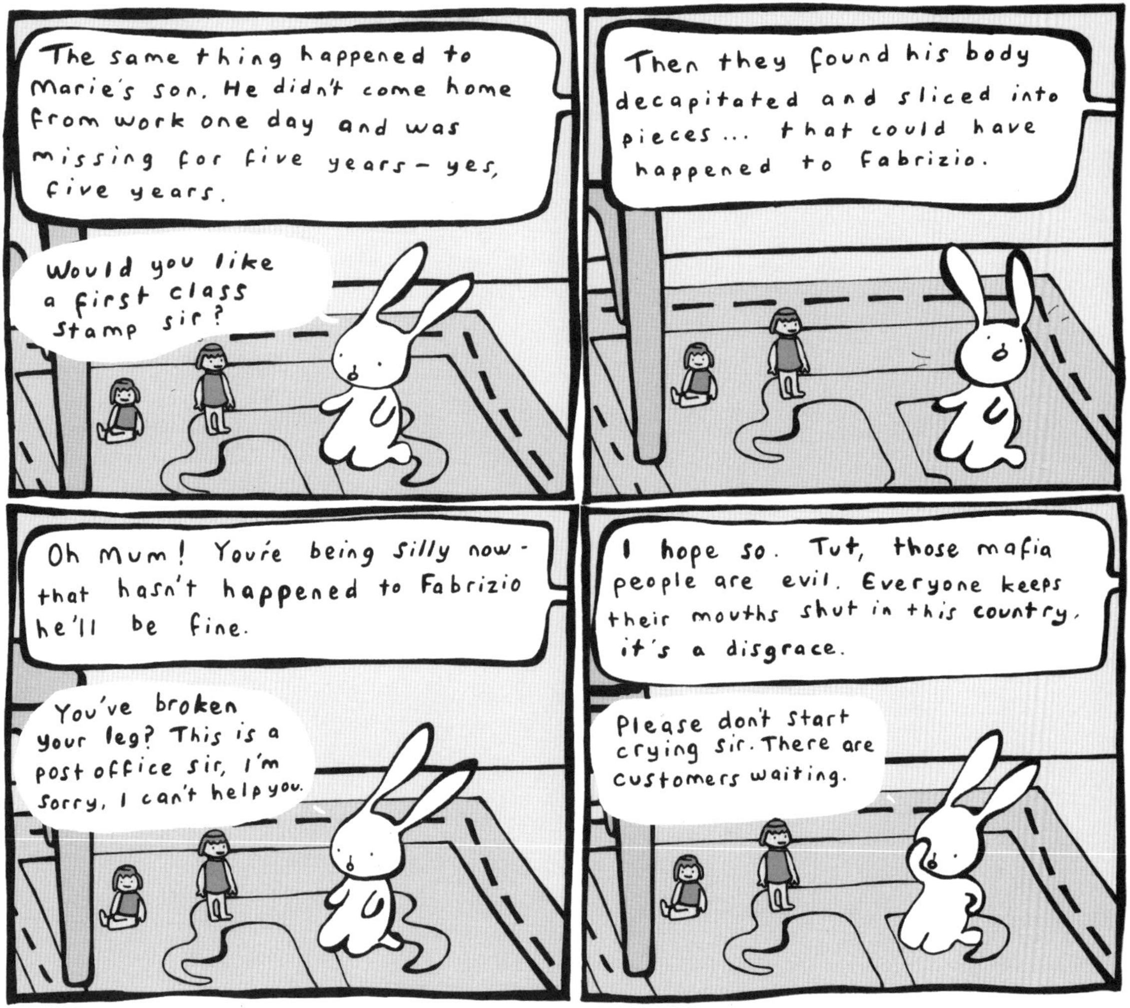
The same thing happened to Marie's son. He didn't come home from work one day and was missing for five years – yes, five years.
Would you like a first class stamp sir?
Then they found his body decapitated and sliced into pieces... that could have happened to Fabrizio.
Oh Mum! You're being silly now - that hasn't happened to Fabrizio he'll be fine.
You've broken your leg? This is a post office sir, I'm sorry, I can't help you.
I hope so. Tut, those mafia people are evil. Everyone keeps their mouths shut in this country, it's a disgrace.
Please don't start crying sir. There are customers waiting.

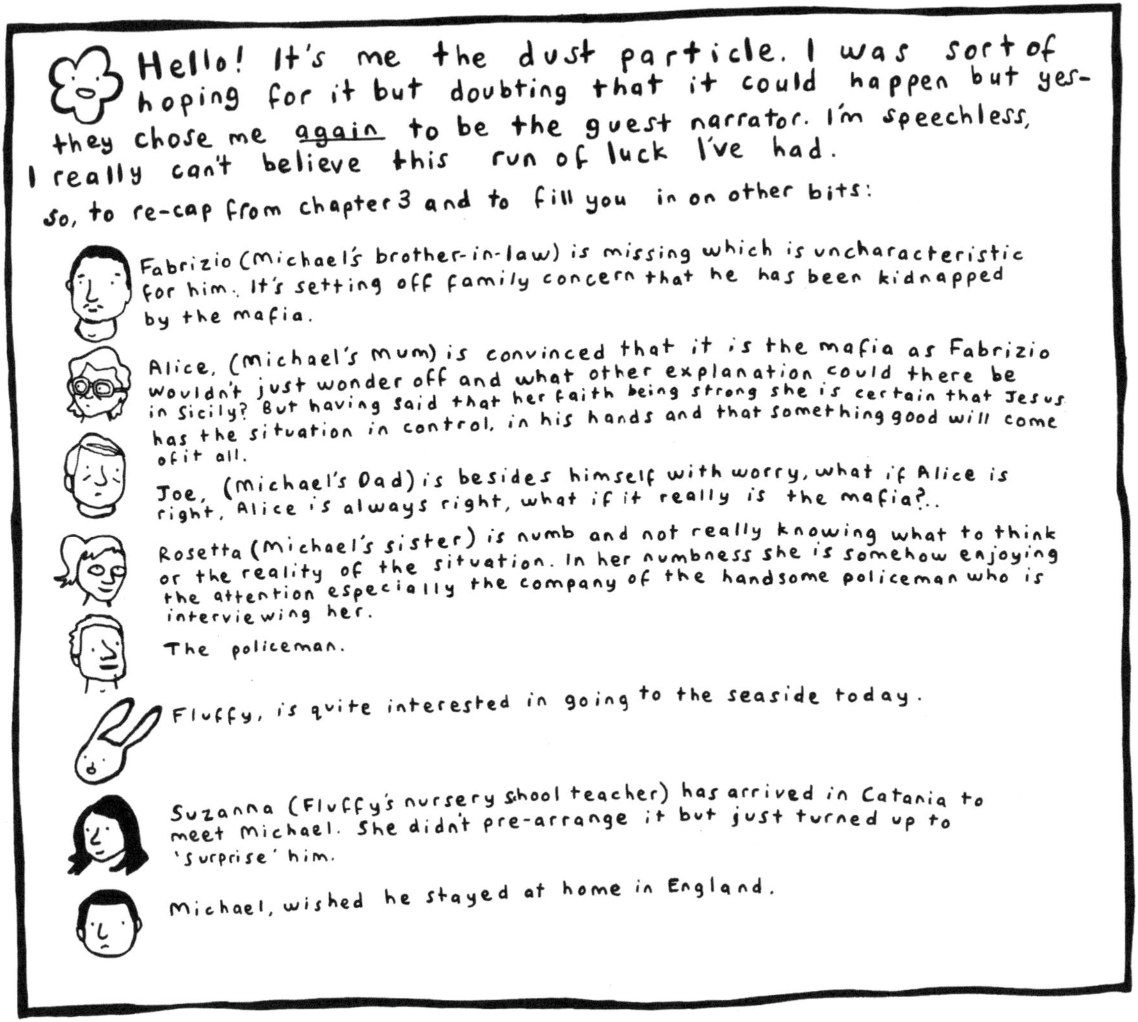
Hello! It's me the dust particle. I was sort of hoping for it but doubting that it could happen but yes- they chose me again to be the guest narrator. I'm speechless, I really can't believe this run of luck I've had.
So, to re-cap from chapter 3 and to fill you in on other bits:
Fabrizio (Michael's brother-in-law) is missing which is uncharacteristic for him. It's setting off family concern that he has been kidnapped by the mafia.
Alice, (Michael's Mum) is convinced that it is the mafia as Fabrizio wouldn't just wonder off and what other explanation could there be in Sicily? But having said that her faith being strong she is certain that Jesus has the situation in control, in his hands and that something good will come of it all.
Joe, (Michael's Dad) is besides himself with worry, what if Alice is right, Alice is always right, what if it really is the mafia?..
Rosetta (Michael's sister) is numb and not really knowing what to think or the reality of the situation. In her numbness she is somehow enjoying the attention especially the company of the handsome policeman who is interviewing her.
The policeman.
Fluffy, is quite interested in going to the seaside today.
Suzanna (Fluffy's nursery school teacher) has arrived in Catania to meet Michael. She didn't pre-arrange it but just turned up to 'surprise' him.
Michael, wished he stayed at home in England.

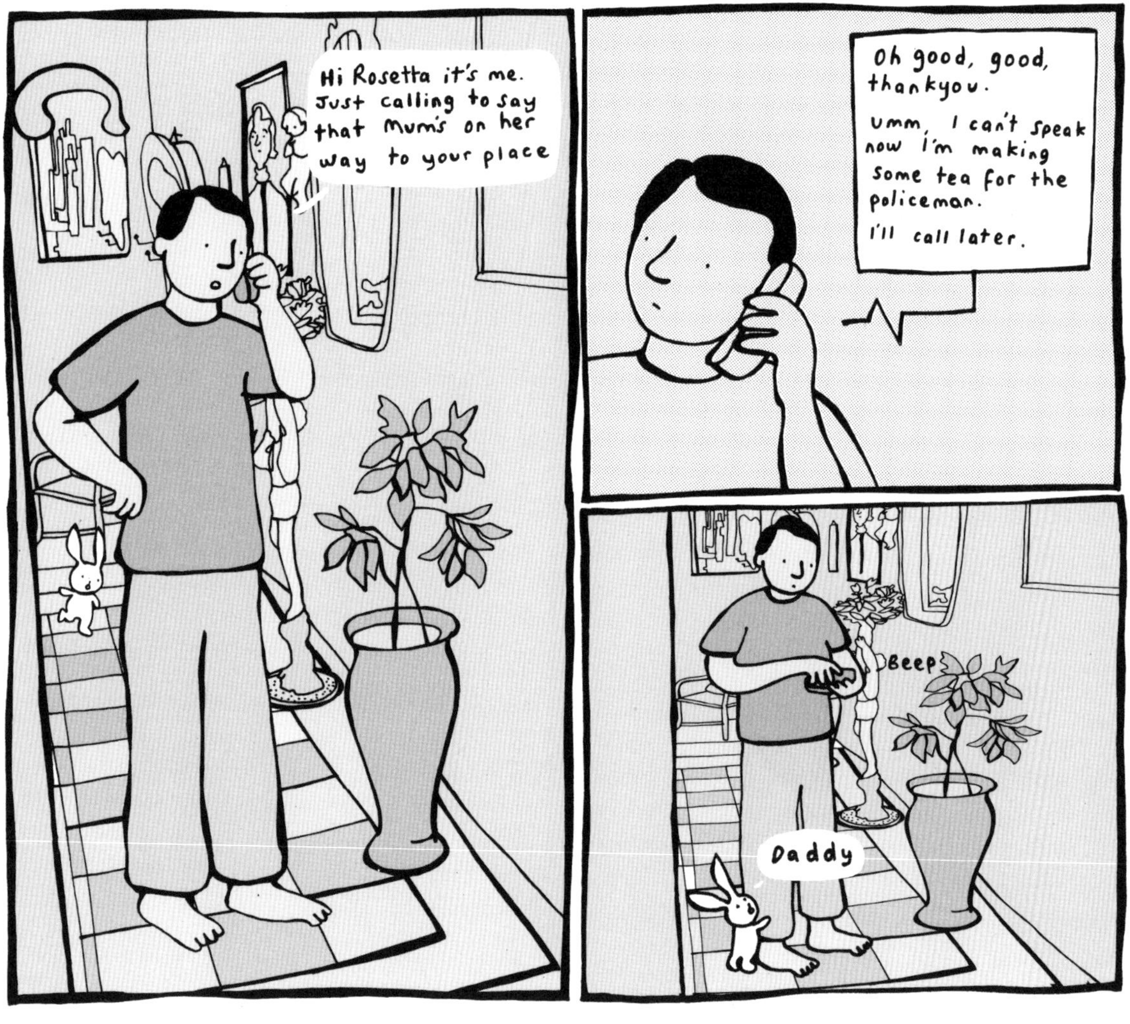
Hi Rosetta it's me. Just calling to say that Mum's on her way to your place
Oh good, good, thankyou.
umm, I can't speak now I'm making some tea for the policeman.
I'll call later.
Beep
Daddy

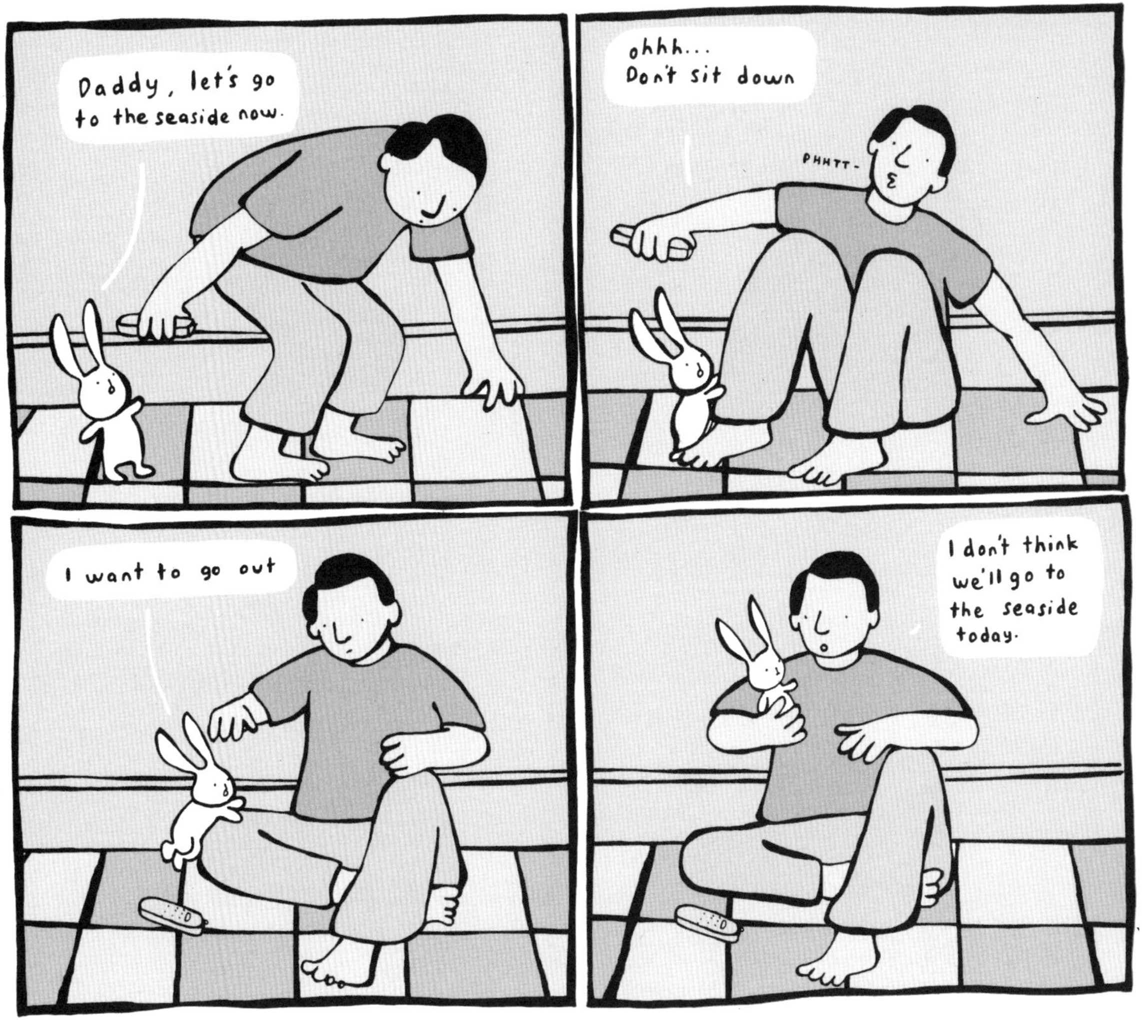
Daddy, let's go to the seaside now.
ohhh...
Don't sit down
PHHTT-
I want to go out
I don't think we'll go to the seaside today.

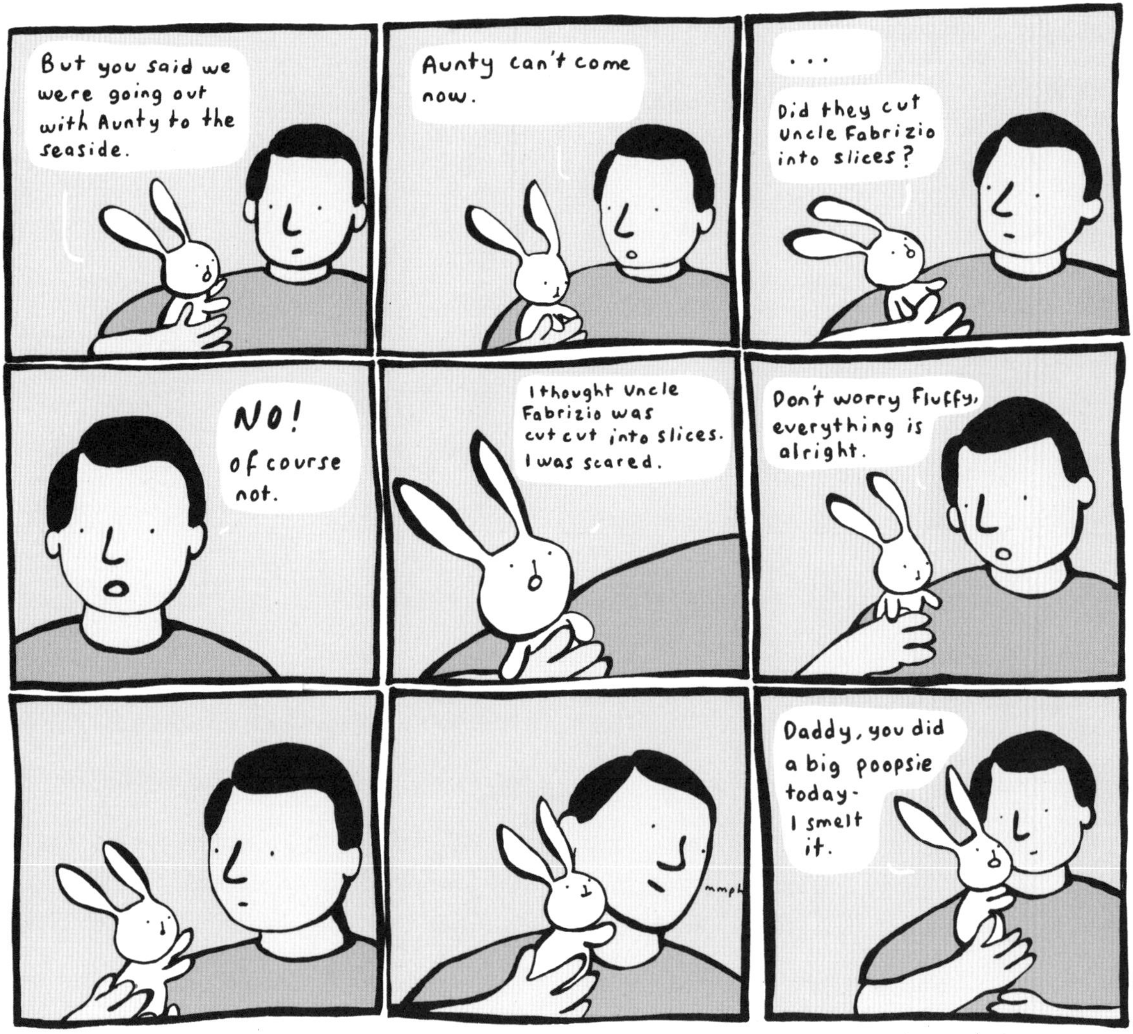
But you said we were going out with Aunty to the seaside.
Aunty can't come now.
. . .
Did they cut Uncle Fabrizio into slices?
NO!
of course not.
I thought Uncle Fabrizio was cut cut into slices.
I was scared.
Don't worry Fluffy, everything is alright.
mmph
Daddy, you did a big poopsie today-
I smelt it.

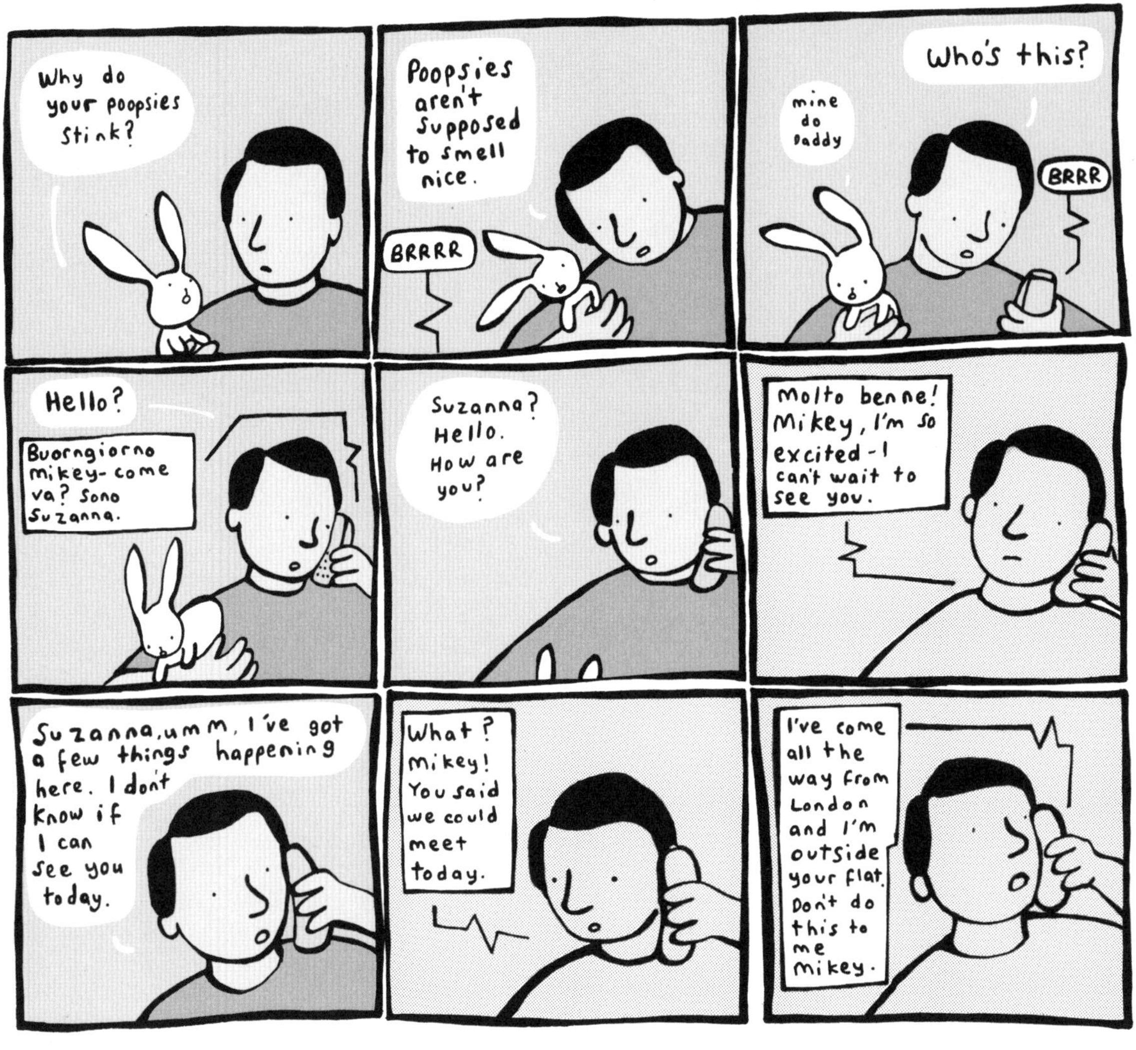
Why do your poopsies stink?
Poopsies aren't supposed to smell nice.
BRRRR
Who's this?
mine do Daddy
BRRR
Hello?
Buorngiorno mikey- come va? Sono Suzanna.
Suzanna? Hello. How are you?
Molto benne! Mikey, I'm so excited - I can't wait to see you.
Suzanna, umm, I've got a few things happening here. I don't know if I can see you today.
What? Mikey! You said we could meet today.
I've come all the way from London and I'm outside your flat. Don't do this to me mikey.

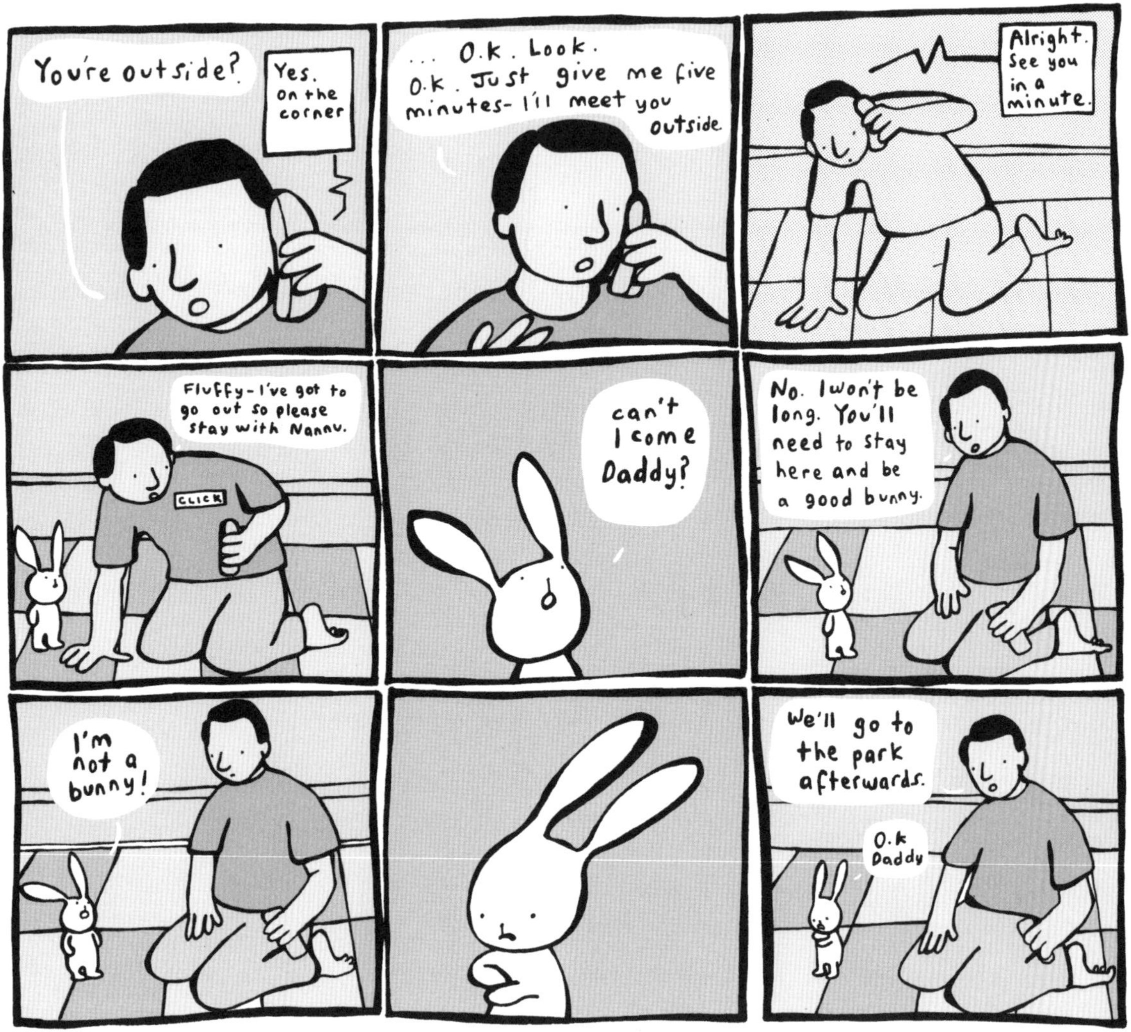
You're outside?
Yes. on the corner
... O.k. Look. O.k. Just give me five minutes- I'll meet you outside.
Alright. See you in a minute.
Fluffy- I've got to go out so please stay with Nannu.
CLICK
can't I come Daddy?
No. I won't be long. You'll need to stay here and be a good bunny.
I'm not a bunny!
We'll go to the park afterwards.
O.k Daddy

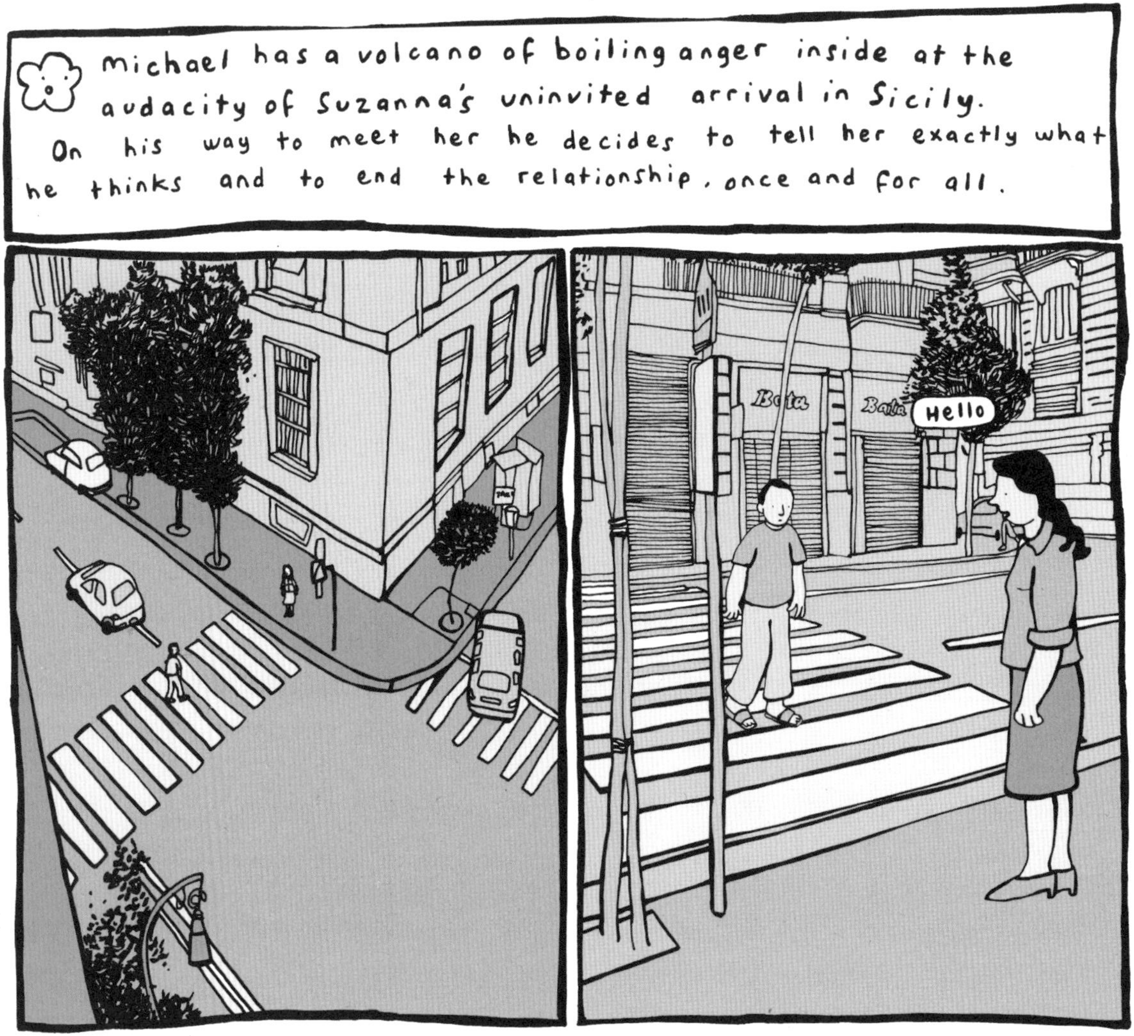
michael has a volcano of boiling anger inside at the audacity of Suzanna's uninvited arrival in Sicily. On his way to meet her he decides to tell her exactly what he thinks and to end the relationship, once and for all.
Bata
Bata
Hello

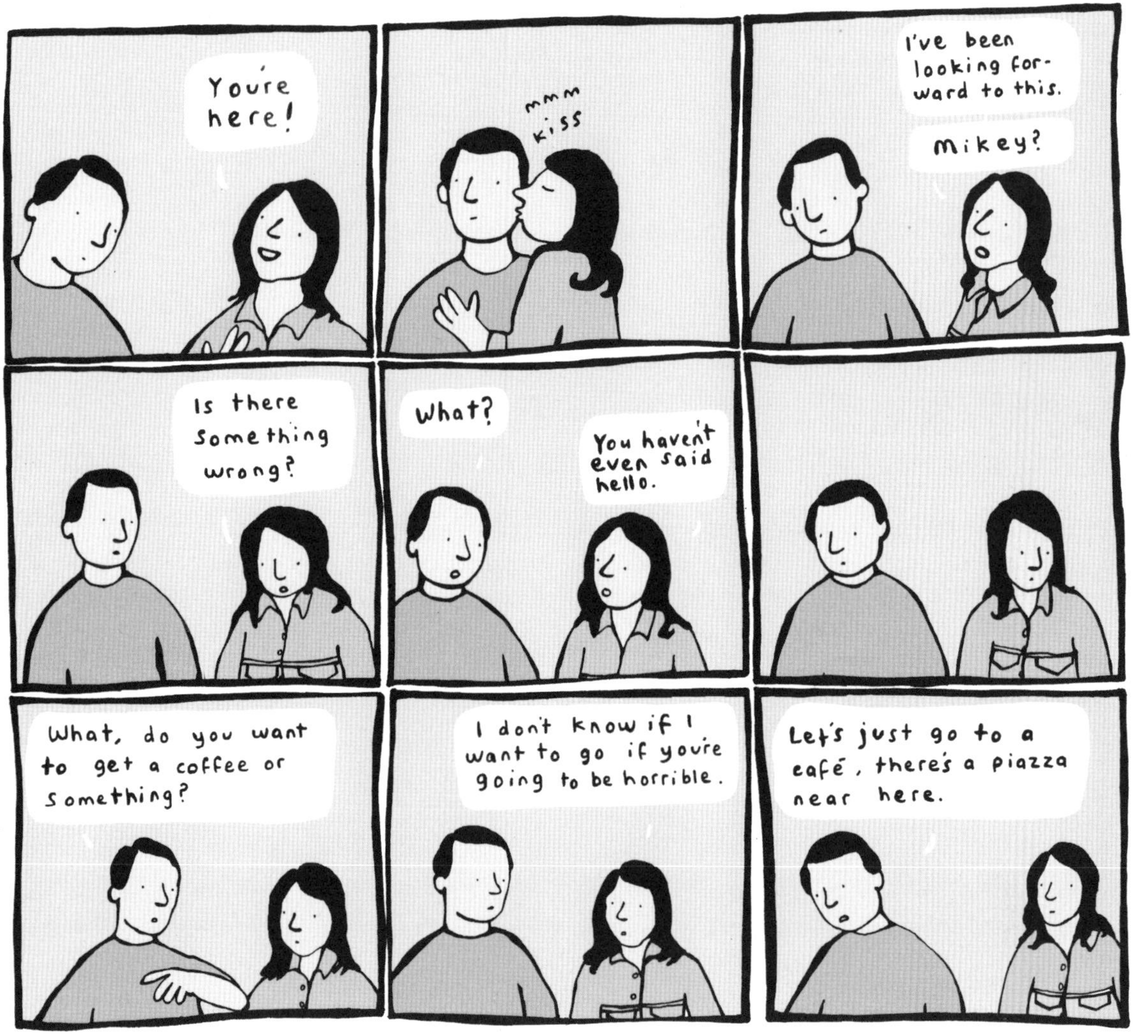
You're here!
mmm kiss
I've been looking forward to this.
Mikey?
Is there something wrong?
What?
You haven't even said hello.
What, do you want to get a coffee or something?
I don't know if I want to go if you're going to be horrible.
Let's just go to a café, there's a piazza near here.

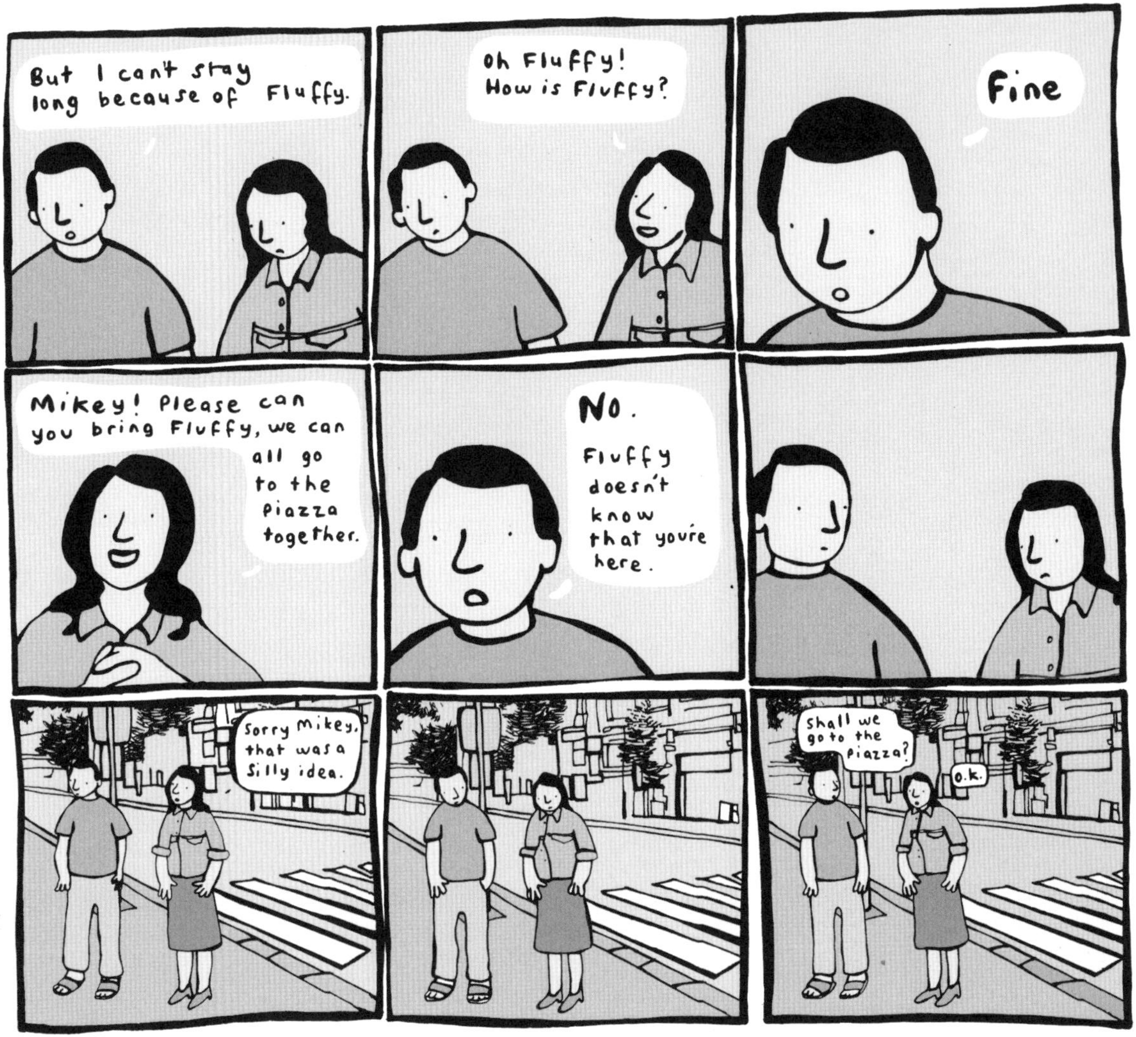
But I can't stay long because of Fluffy.
Oh Fluffy! How is Fluffy?
Fine
Mikey! Please can you bring Fluffy, we can all go to the piazza together.
No.
Fluffy doesn't know that you're here.
Sorry Mikey, that was a silly idea.
Shall we go to the piazza?
O.K.

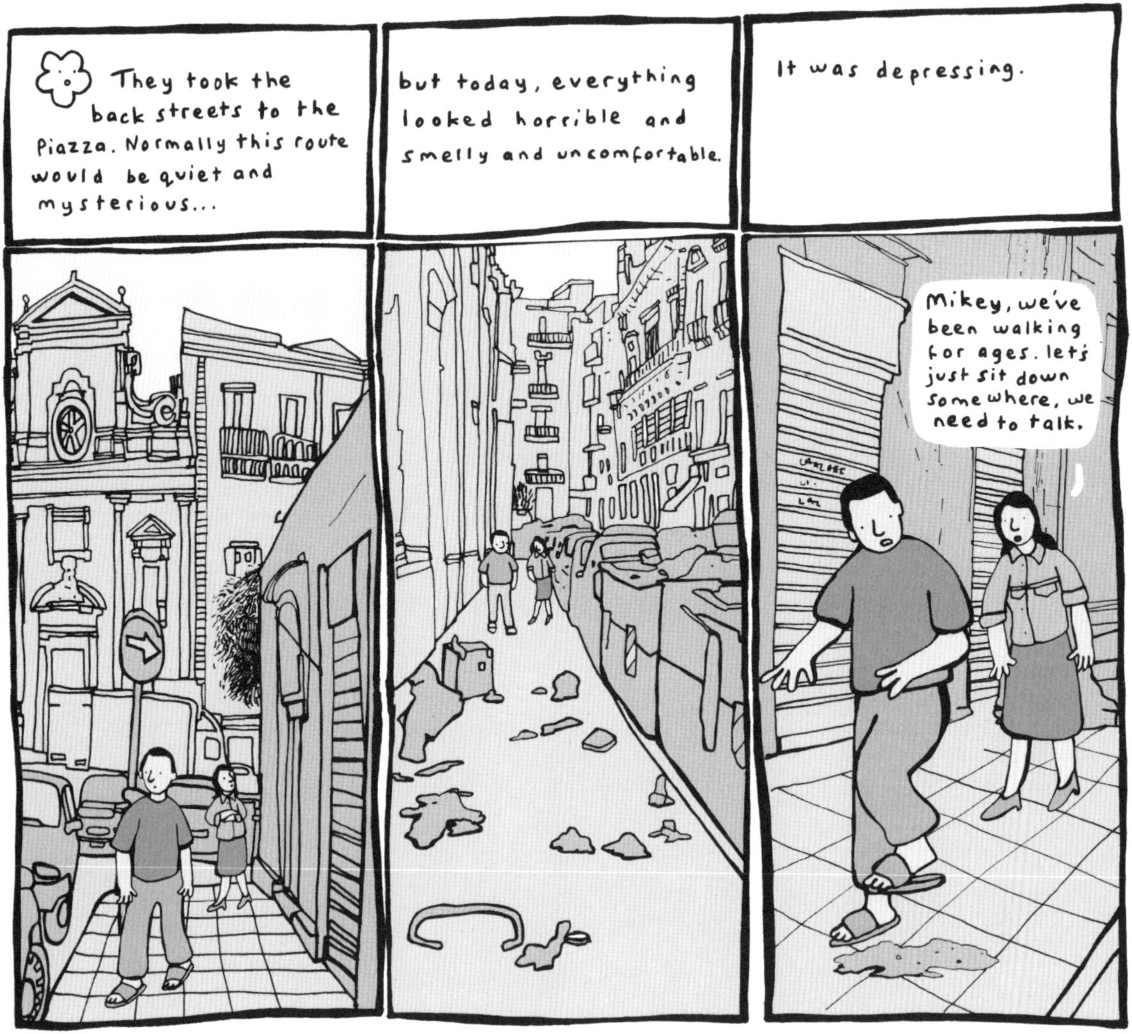
They took the back streets to the Piazza. Normally this route would be quiet and mysterious...
but today, everything looked horrible and smelly and uncomfortable.
It was depressing.
Mikey, we've been walking for ages. let's just sit down somewhere, we need to talk.

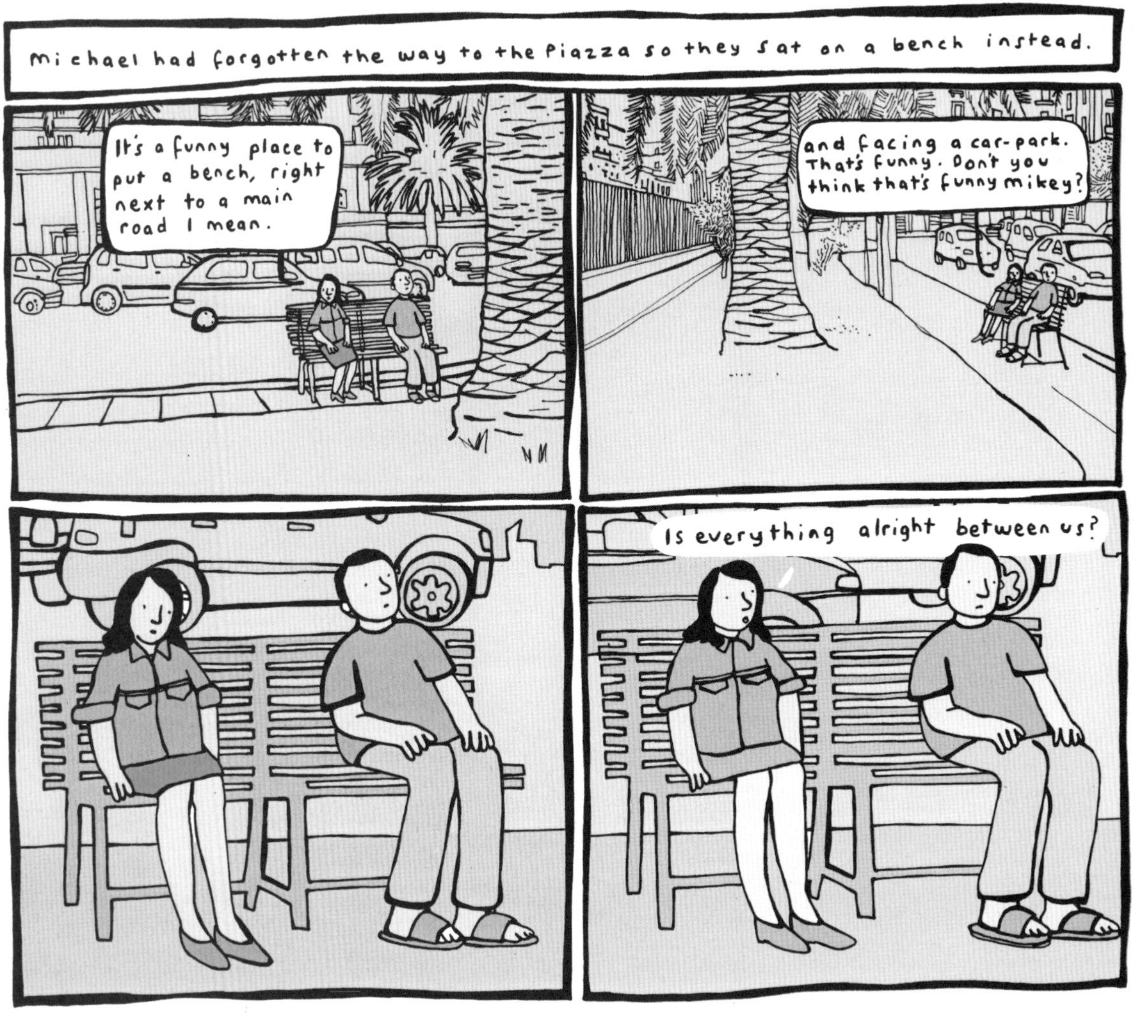
michael had forgotten the way to the piazza so they sat on a bench instead.
It's a funny place to put a bench, right next to a main road I mean.
and facing a car-park. That's funny. Don't you think that's funny mikey?
Is everything alright between us?

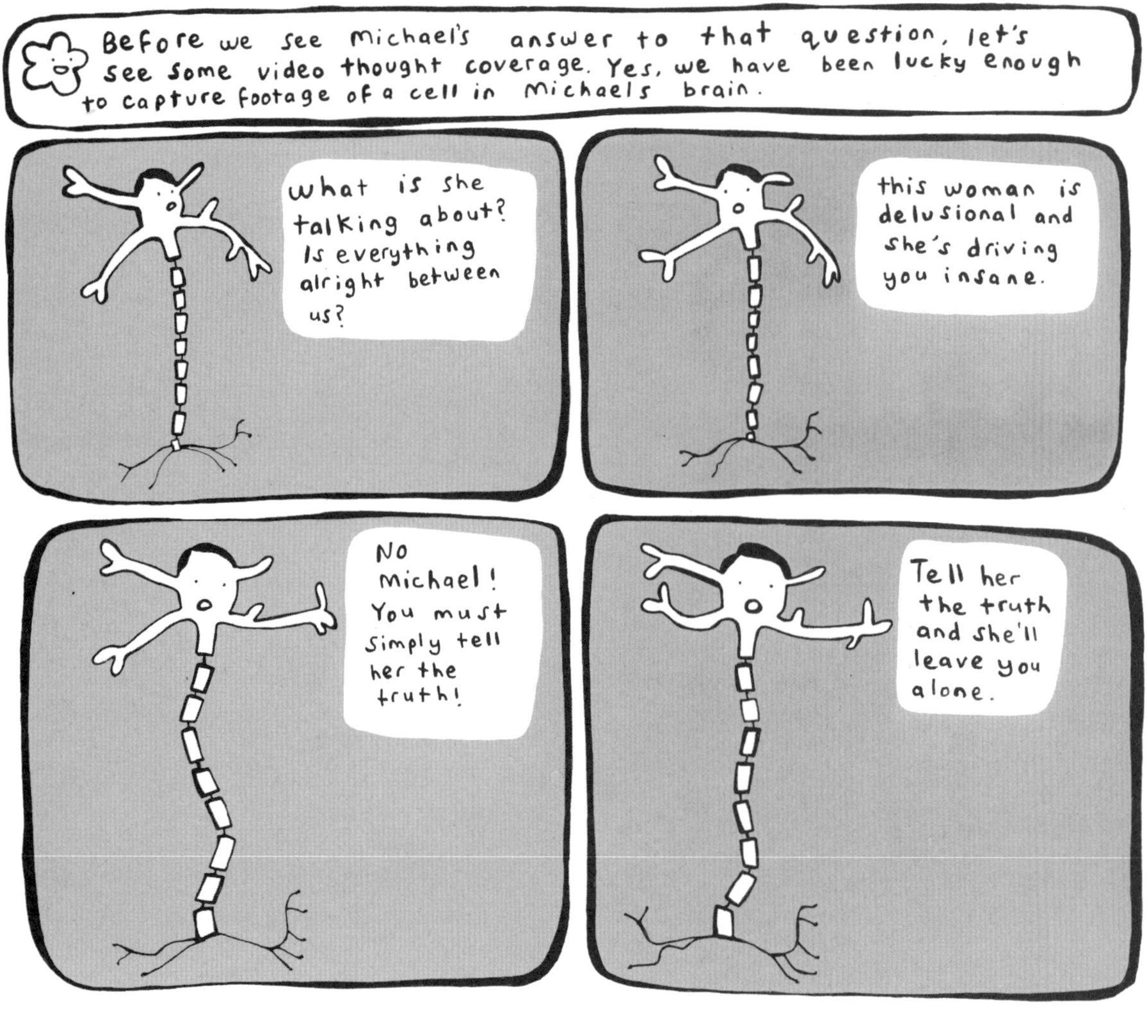
Before we see michael's answer to that question, let's see some video thought coverage. Yes, we have been lucky enough to capture footage of a cell in Michaels brain.
what is she talking about? Is everything alright between us?
this woman is delusional and she's driving you insane.
No Michael! You must simply tell her the truth!
Tell her the truth and she'll leave you alone.

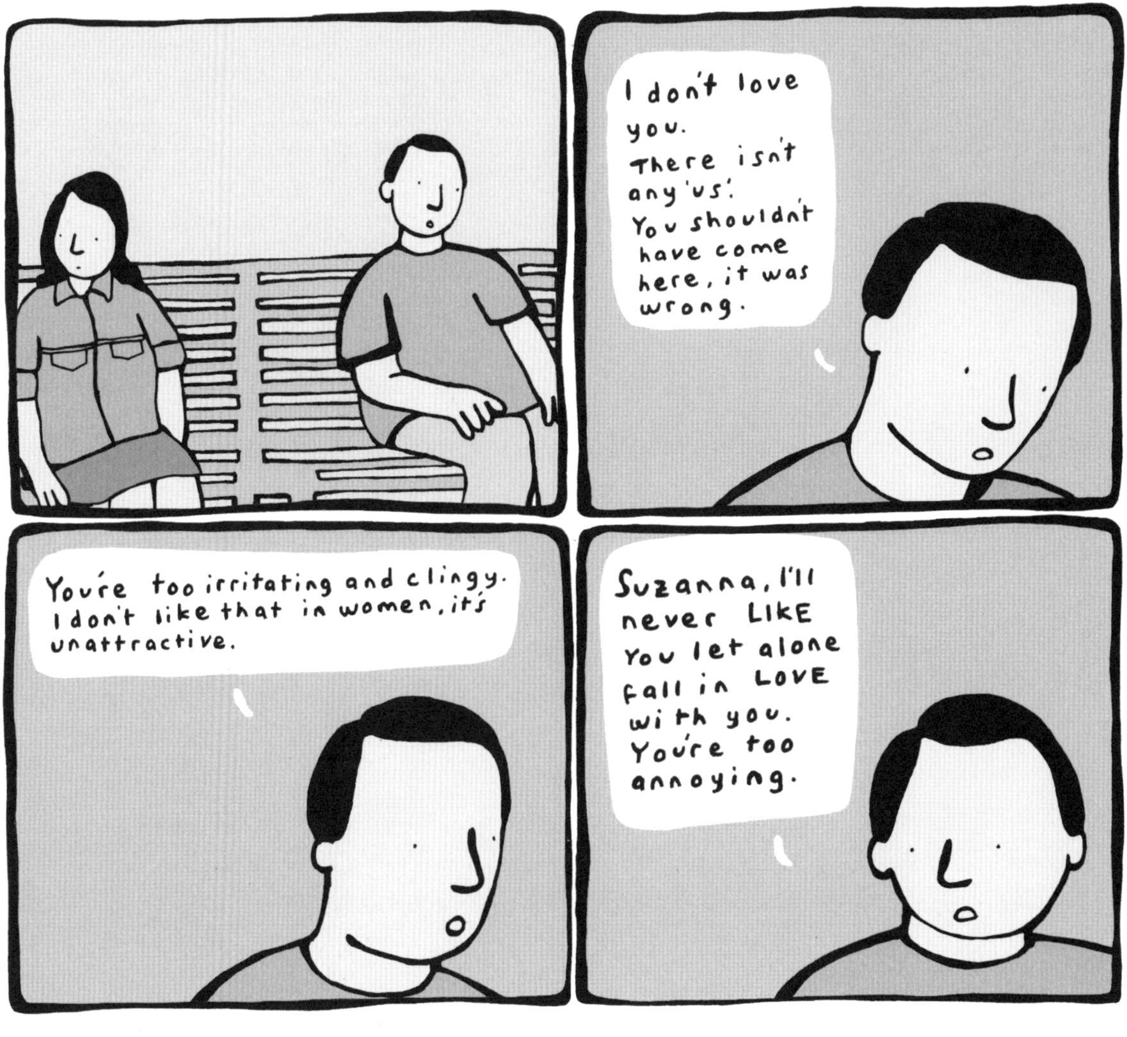
I don't love you. There isn't any 'us'. You shouldn't have come here, it was wrong.
You're too irritating and clingy. I don't like that in women, it's unattractive.
Suzanna, I'll never LIKE you let alone fall in LOVE with you. You're too annoying.

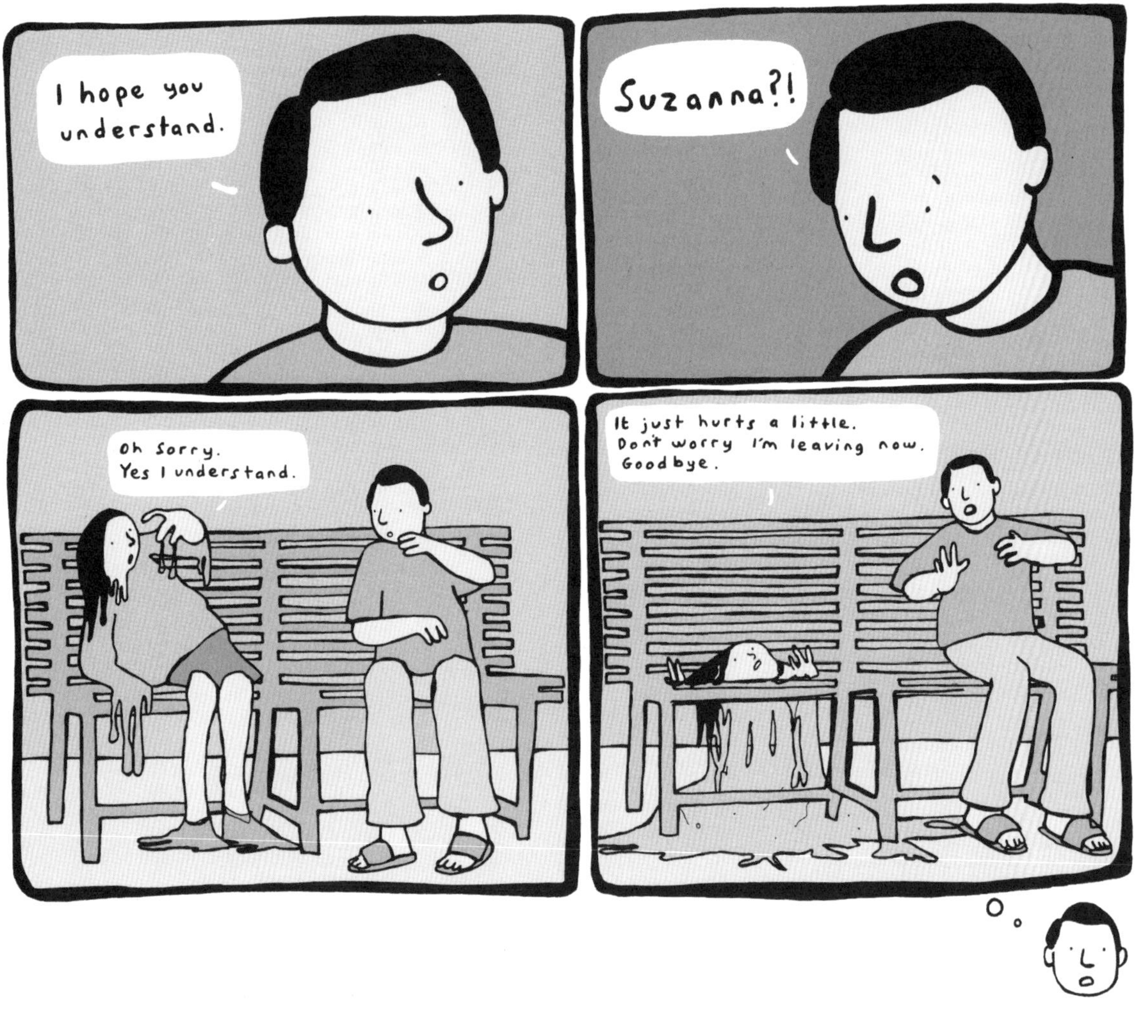
I hope you understand.
Suzanna?!
Oh Sorry.
Yes I understand.
It just hurts a little.
Don't worry I'm leaving now.
Goodbye.

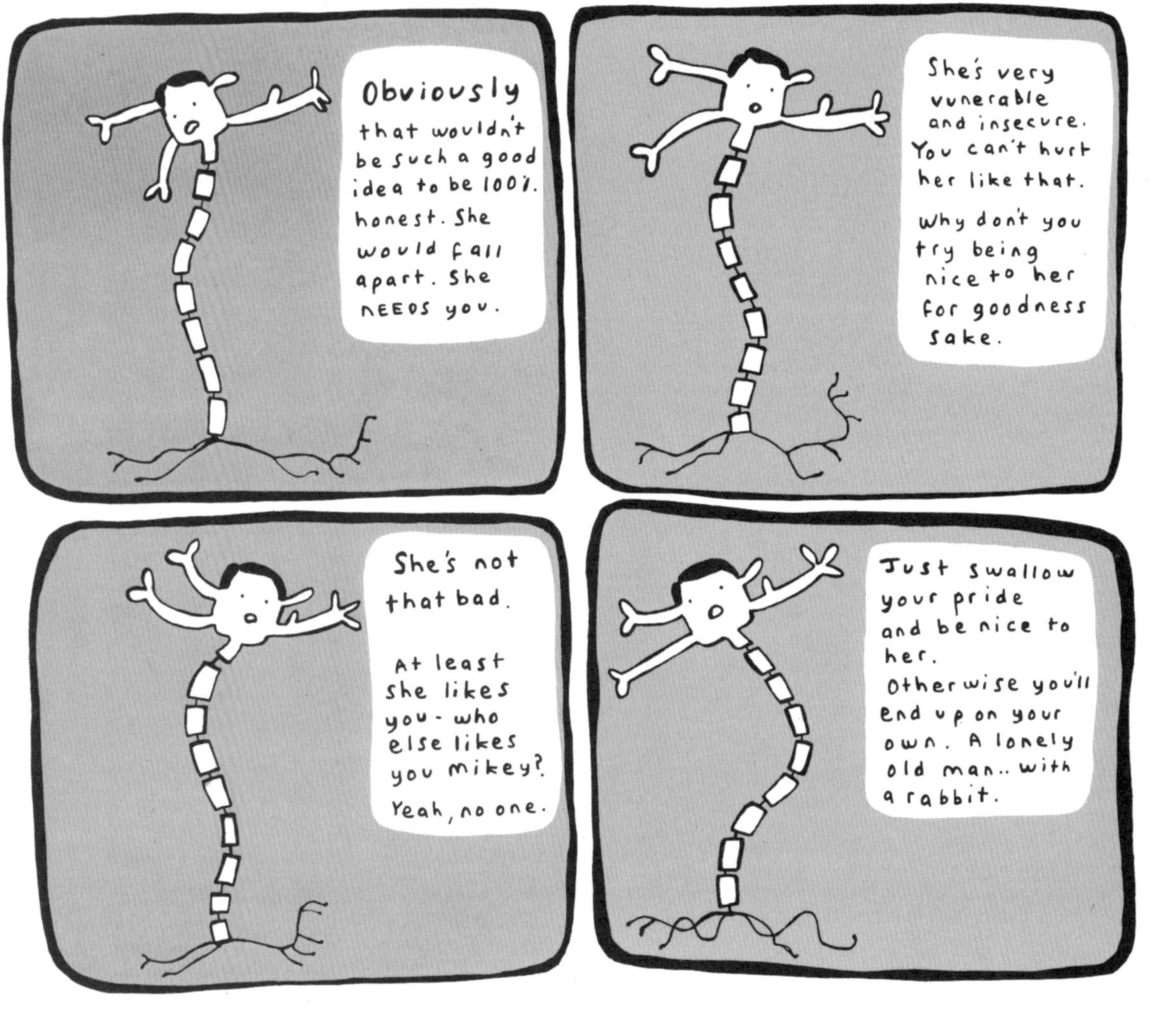
Obviously that wouldn't be such a good idea to be 100%. honest. She would fall apart. She NEEDS you.
She's very vunerable and insecure. You can't hurt her like that.
Why don't you try being nice to her for goodness sake.
She's not that bad.
At least she likes you - who else likes you mikey?
Yeah, no one.
Just swallow your pride and be nice to her.
Otherwise you'll end up on your own. A lonely old man.. with a rabbit.

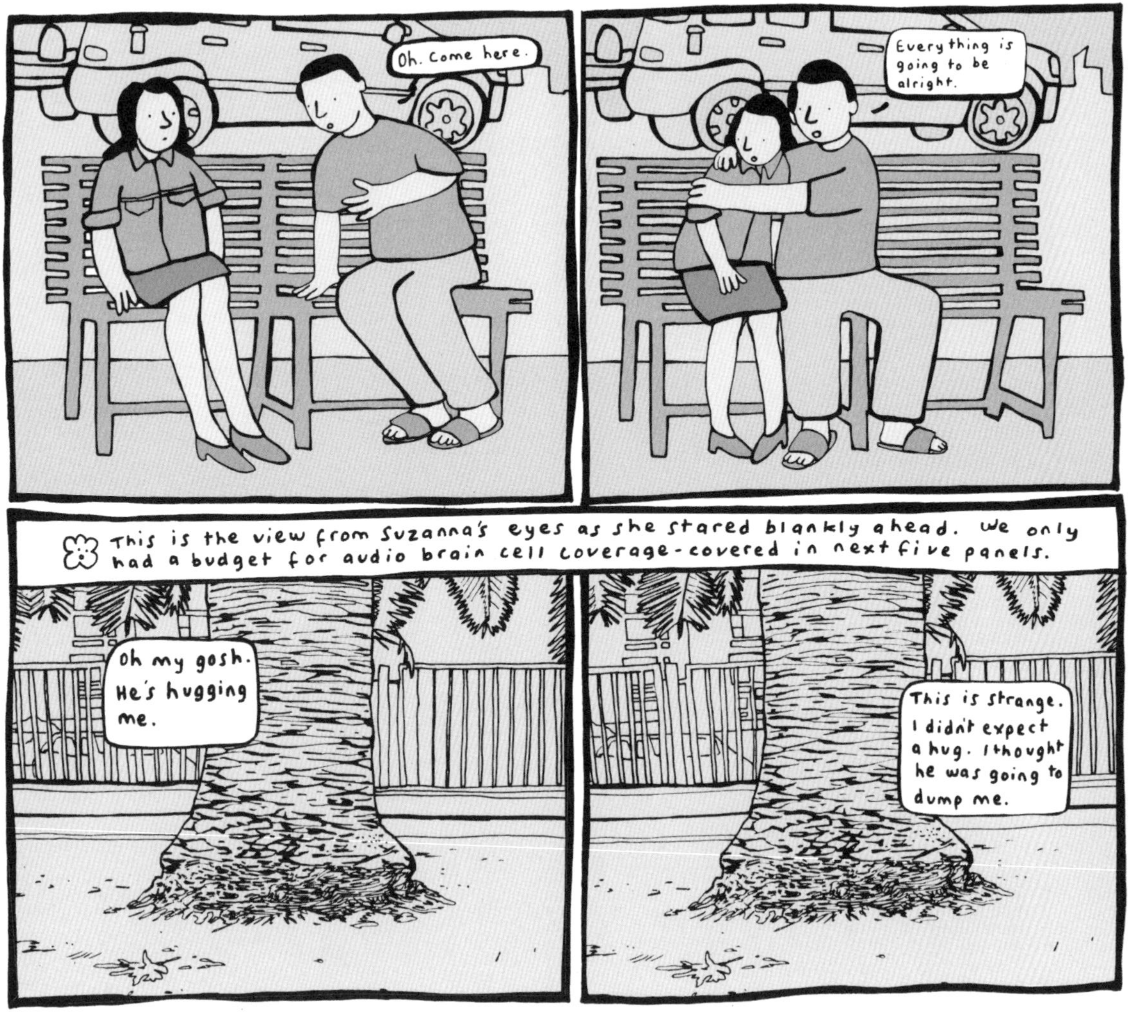
Oh. Come here.
Everything is going to be alright.
This is the view from Suzanna's eyes as she stared blankly ahead. We only had a budget for audio brain cell coverage - covered in next five panels.
Oh my gosh. He's hugging me.
This is strange. I didn't expect a hug. I thought he was going to dump me.

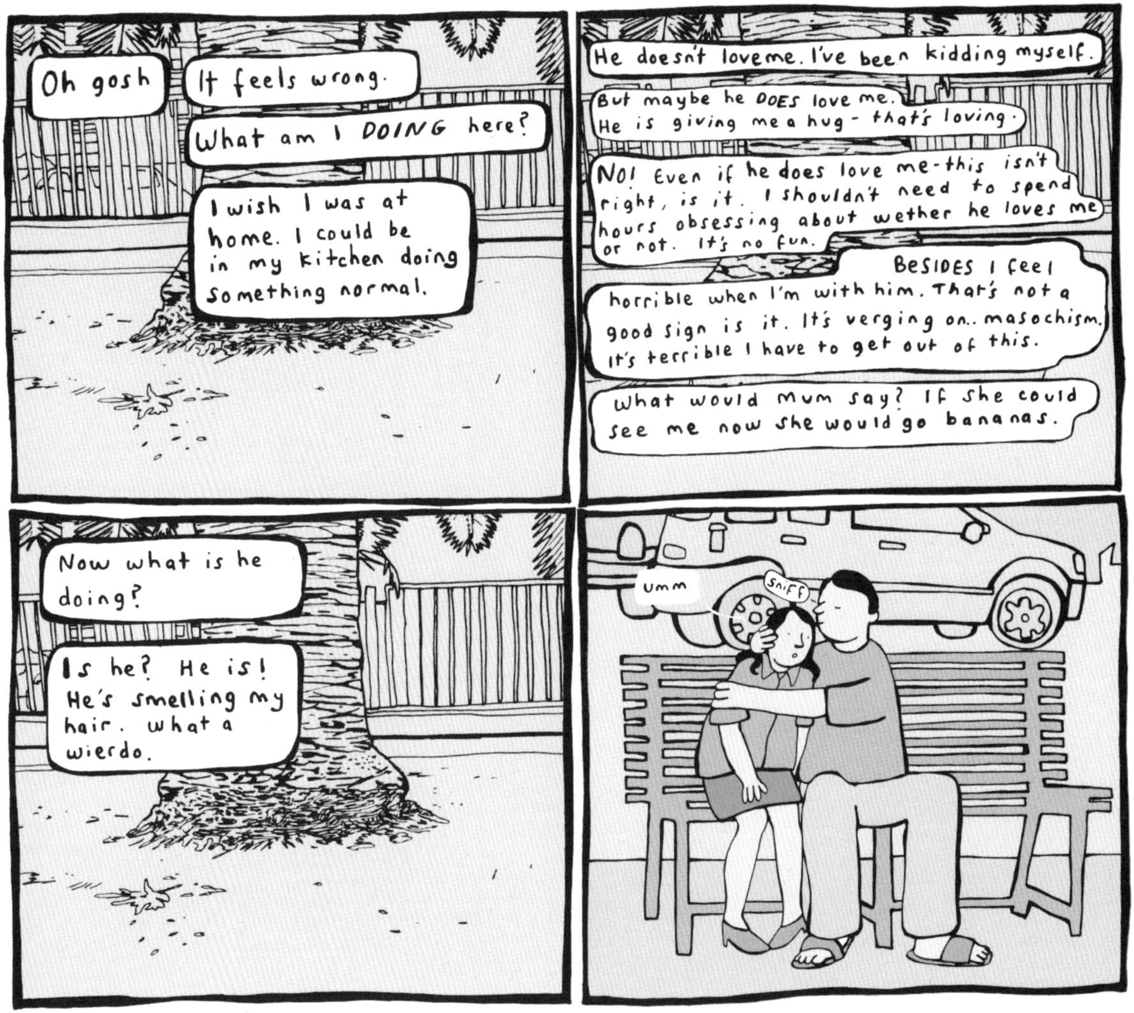
Oh gosh
It feels wrong.
What am I DOING here?
I wish I was at home. I could be in my kitchen doing something normal.
He doesn't love me. I've been kidding myself.
But maybe he DOES love me. He is giving me a hug - that's loving.
NO! Even if he does love me - this isn't right, is it. I shouldn't need to spend hours obsessing about wether he loves me or not. It's no fun.
BESIDES I feel horrible when I'm with him. That's not a good sign is it. It's verging on.. masochism. It's terrible I have to get out of this.
What would Mum say? If she could see me now she would go bananas.
Now what is he doing?
Is he? He is! He's smelling my hair. What a wierdo.
umm
sniff

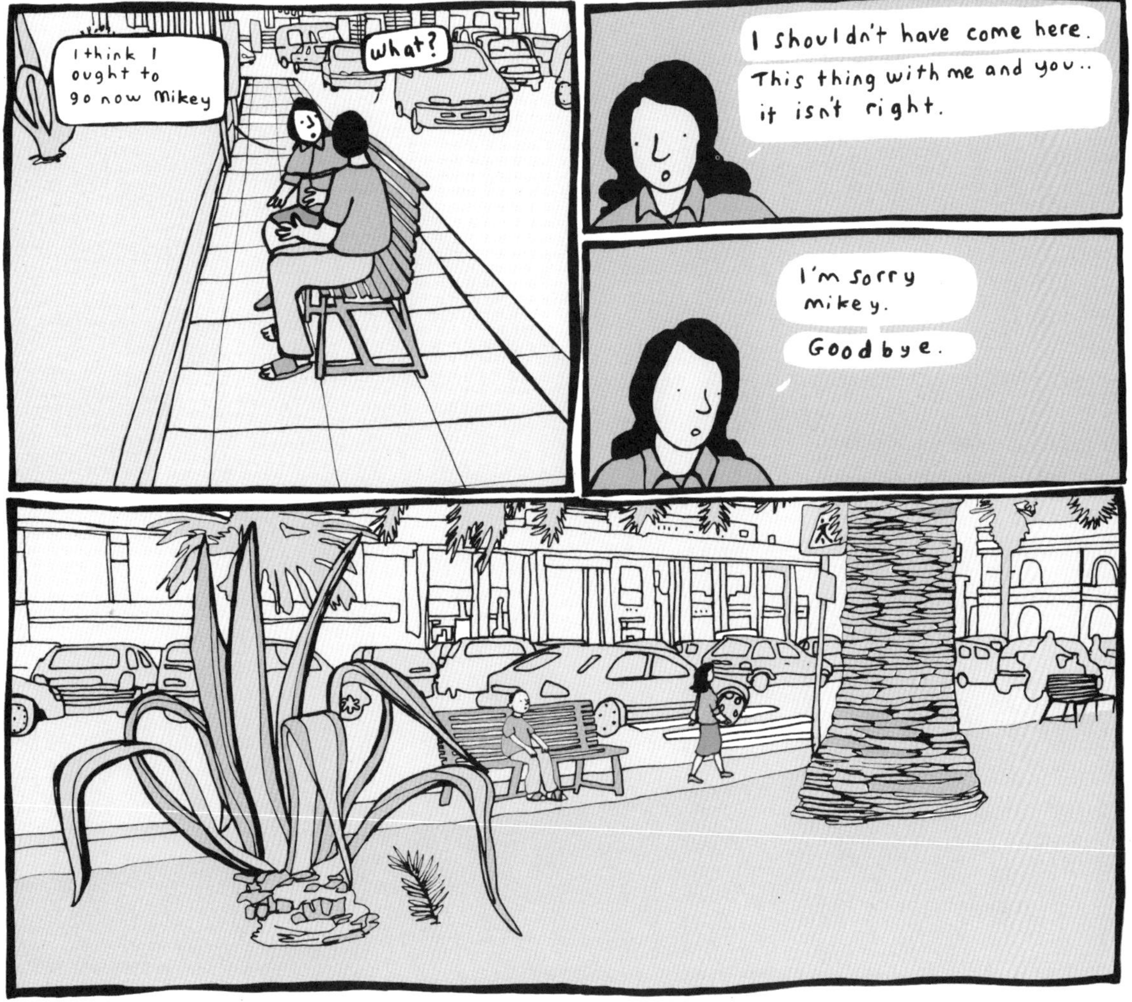
I think I ought to go now Mikey
what?
I shouldn't have come here.
This thing with me and you.. it isn't right.
I'm sorry mikey.
Goodbye.

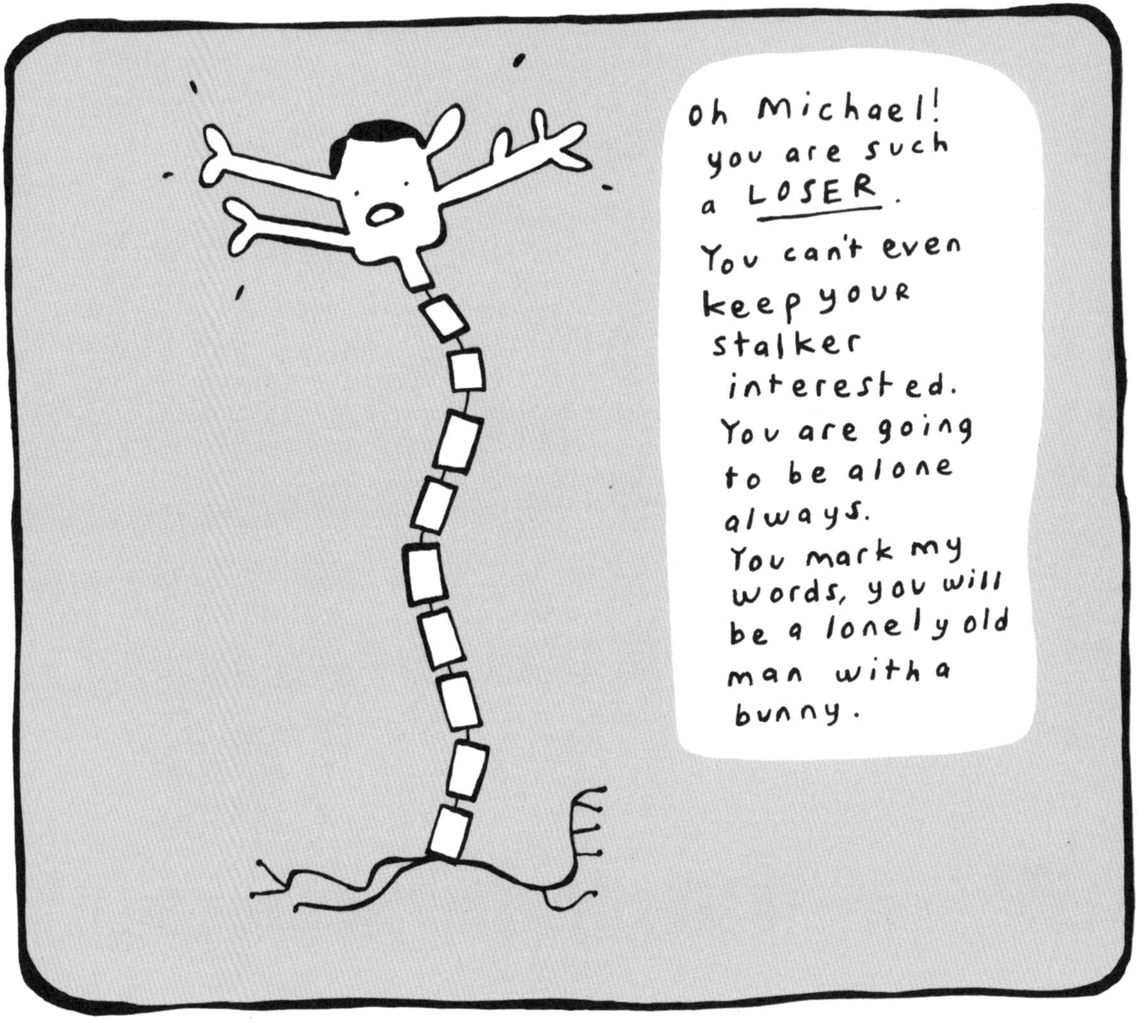
oh Michael! you are such a LOSER. You can't even keep your stalker interested. You are going to be alone always. You mark my words, you will be a lonely old man with a bunny.

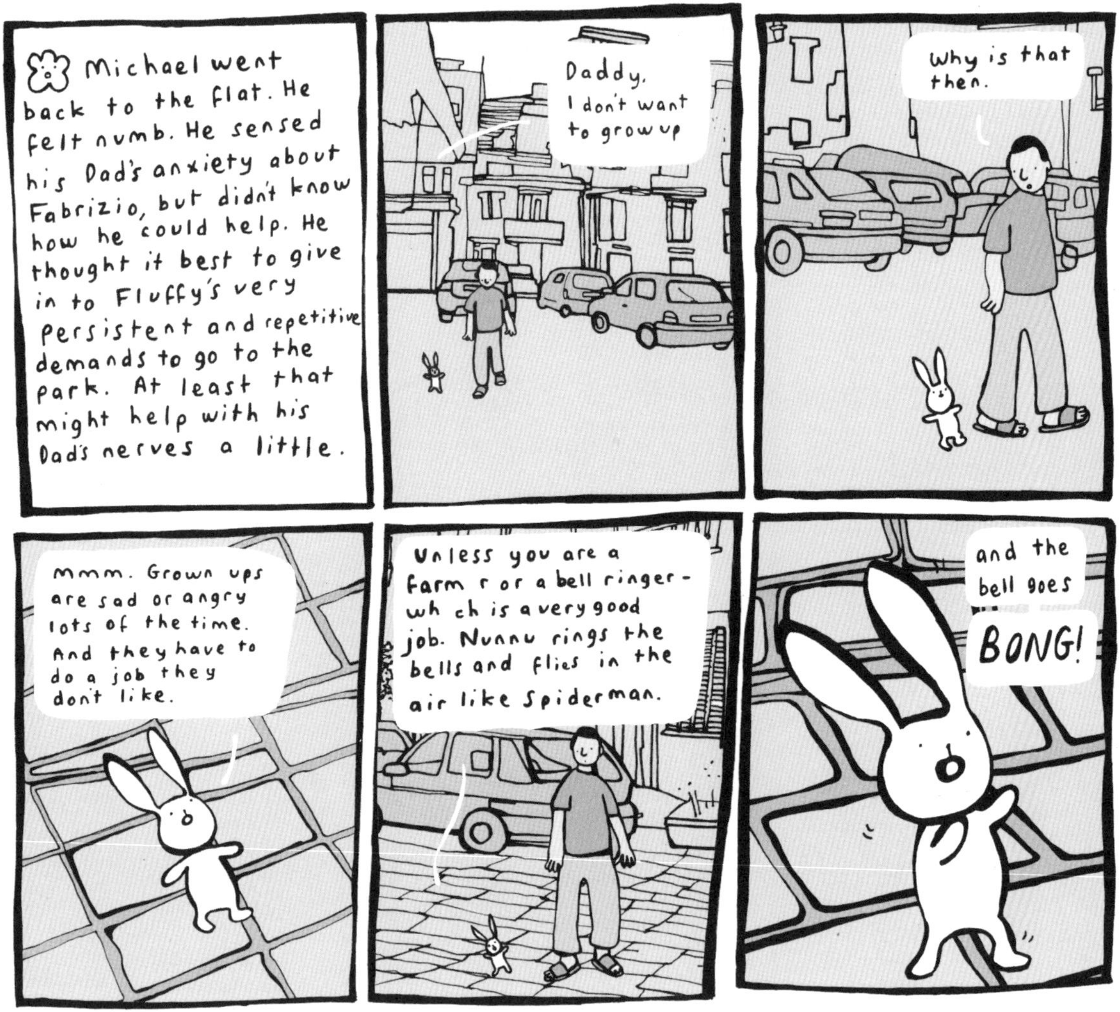
Michael went back to the flat. He felt numb. He sensed his Dad's anxiety about Fabrizio, but didn't know how he could help. He thought it best to give in to Fluffy's very persistent and repetitive demands to go to the park. At least that might help with his Dad's nerves a little.
Daddy, I don't want to grow up
Why is that then.
mmm. Grown ups are sad or angry lots of the time. And they have to do a job they don't like.
Unless you are a farm r or a bell ringer - wh ch is a very good job. Nunnu rings the bells and flies in the air like Spiderman.
and the bell goes
BONG!

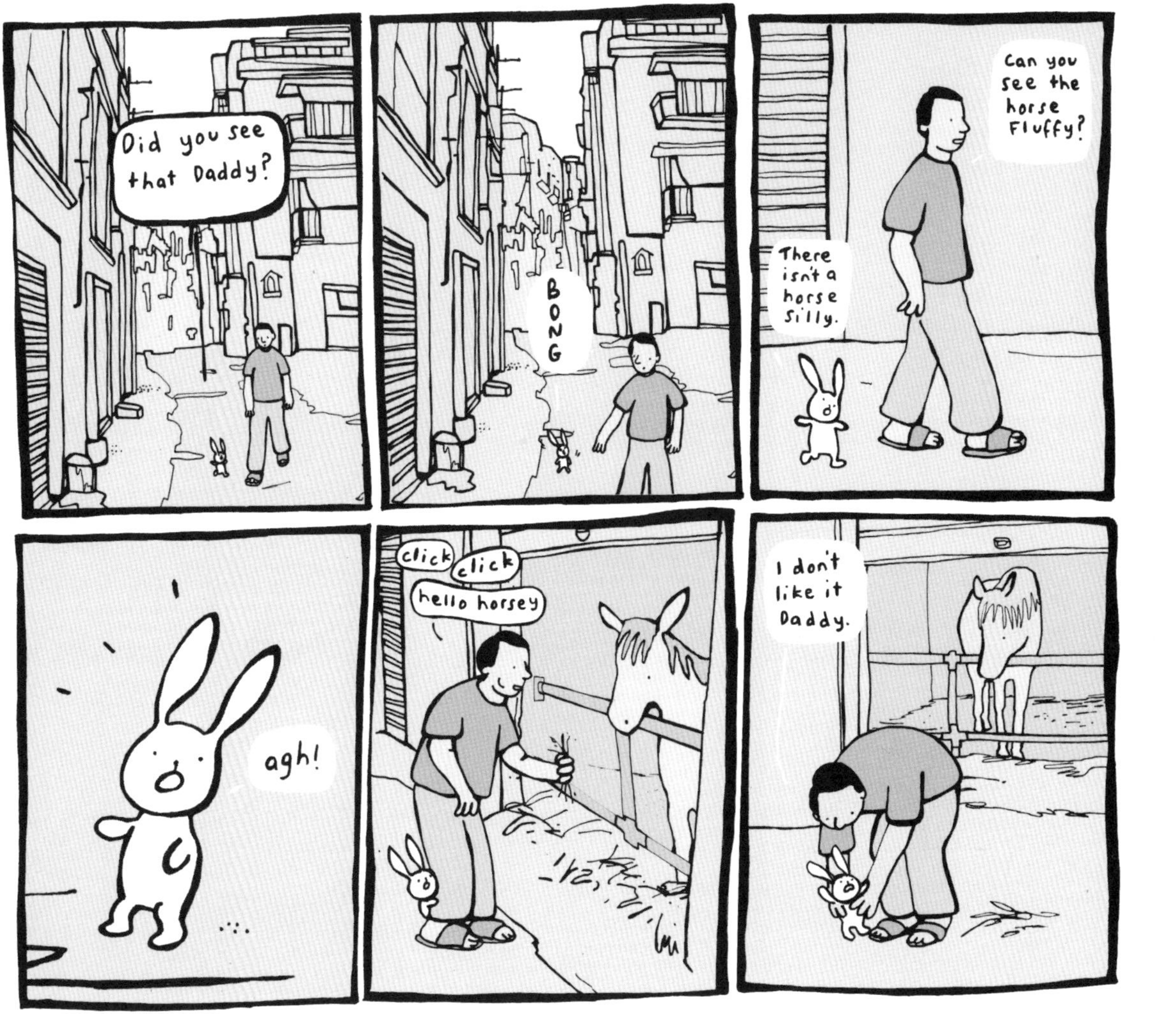
Did you see that Daddy?
BONG
Can you see the horse Fluffy?
There isn't a horse silly.
agh!
click
click
hello horsey
I don't like it Daddy.

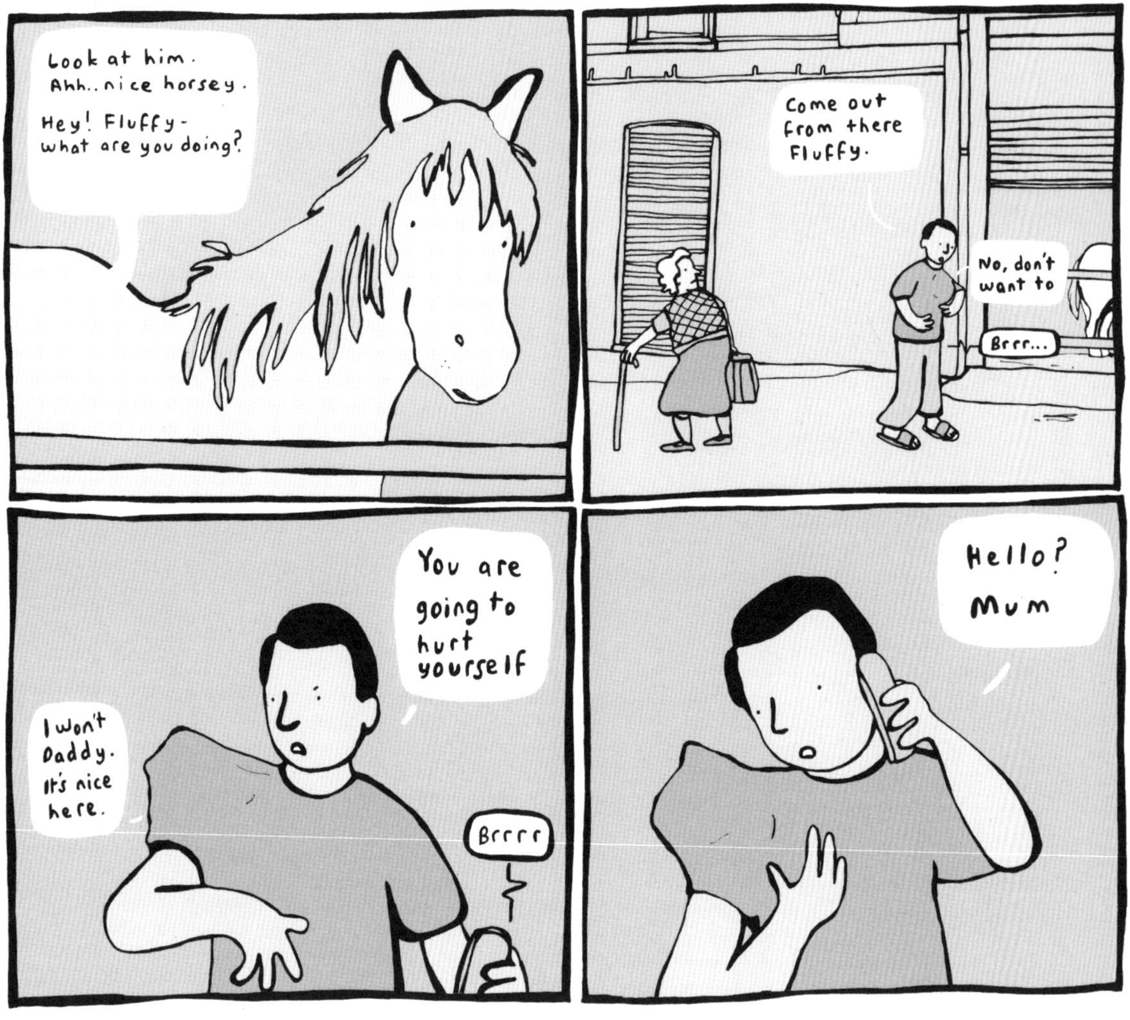
Look at him. Ahh.. nice horsey. Hey! Fluffy- what are you doing?
Come out from there Fluffy.
No, don't want to
Brrr...
You are going to hurt yourself
I won't Daddy. It's nice here.
Brrrr
Hello? Mum

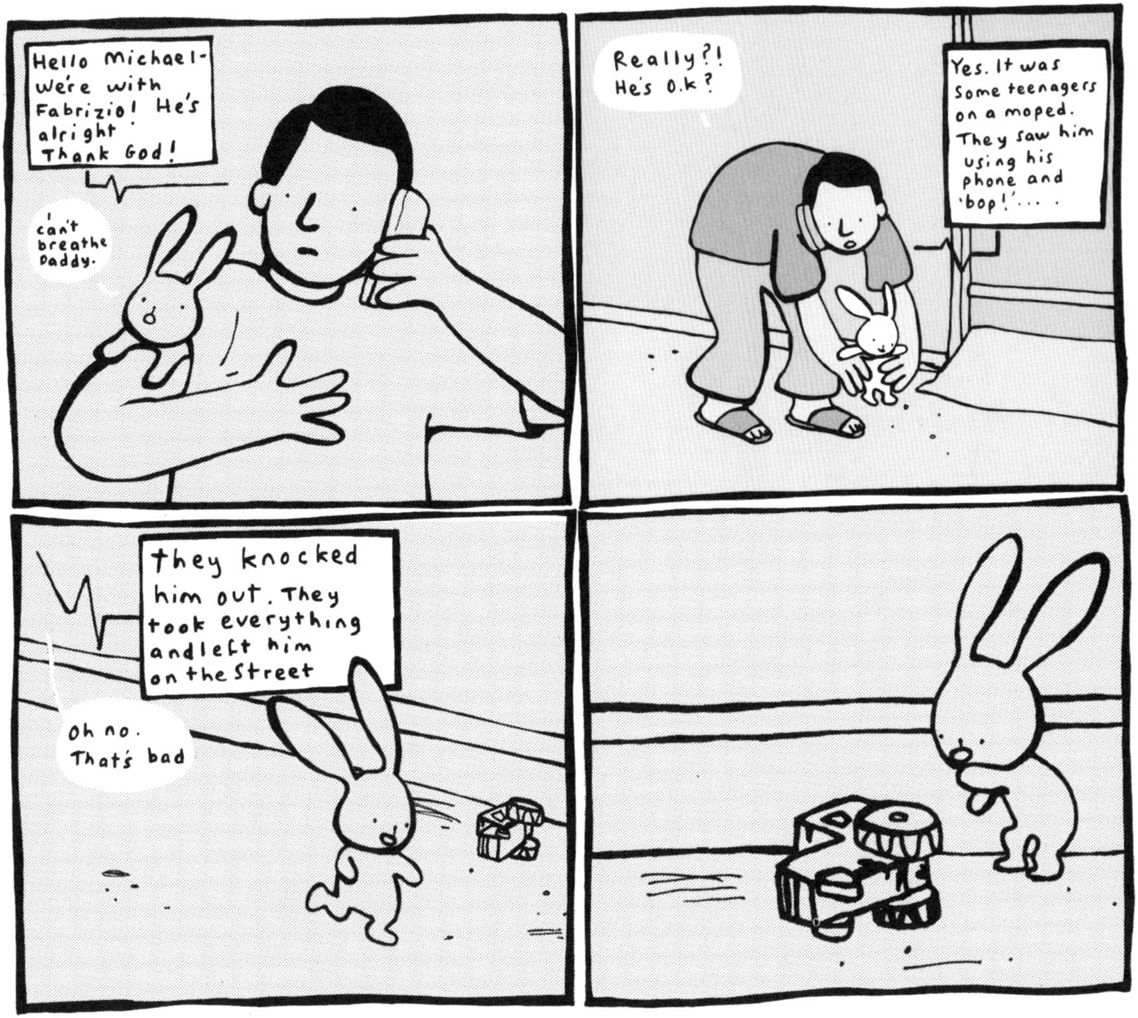
Hello Michael- We're with Fabrizio! He's alright Thank God!
I can't breathe Daddy.
Really?! He's O.k?
Yes. It was some teenagers on a moped. They saw him using his phone and 'bop!'...
they knocked him out. They took everything and left him on the Street
Oh no. That's bad

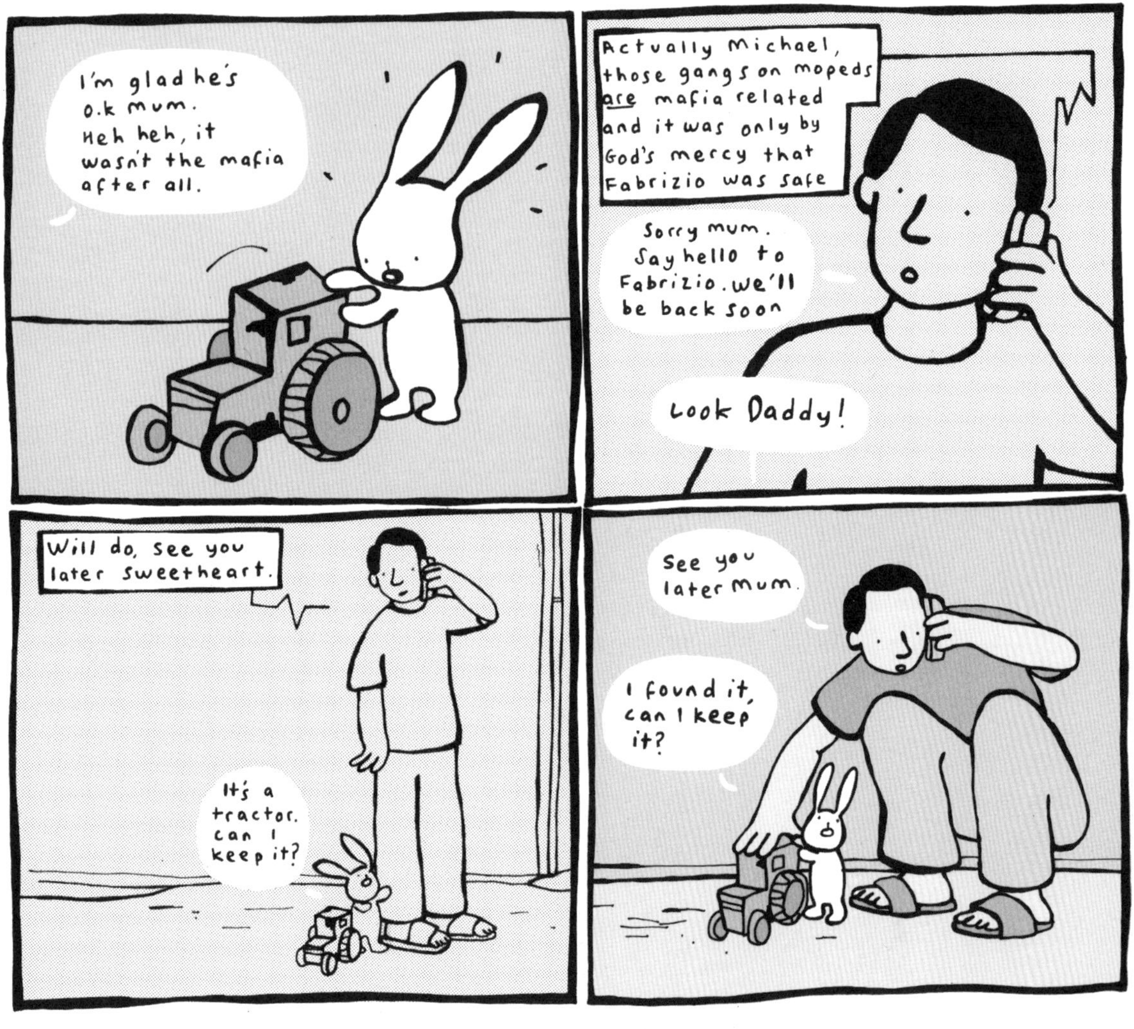
I'm glad he's o.k mum. Heh heh, it wasn't the mafia after all.
Actually Michael, those gangs on mopeds are mafia related and it was only by God's mercy that Fabrizio was safe
Sorry mum. Say hello to Fabrizio. We'll be back soon
Look Daddy!
Will do, see you later sweetheart.
It's a tractor. can I keep it?
See you later Mum.
I found it, can I keep it?

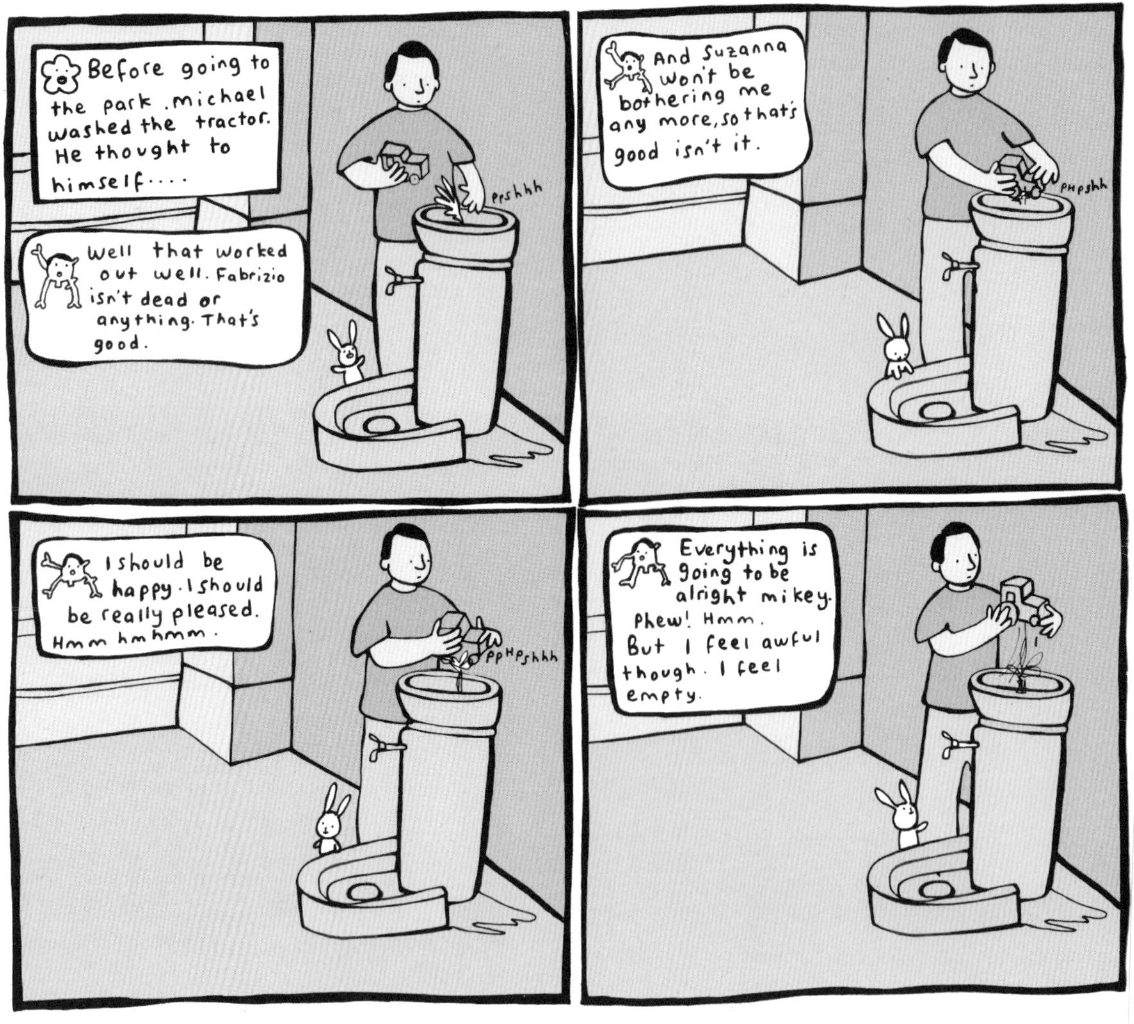

Before going to the park. michael washed the tractor. He thought to himself....
Well that worked out well. Fabrizio isn't dead or anything. That's good.
Prshhh
And Suzanna won't be bothering me any more, so that's good isn't it.
PHpshh
I should be happy. I should be really pleased. Hmm hmhmm.
ppHPshhh
Everything is going to be alright mikey. Phew! Hmm. But I feel awful though. I feel empty.

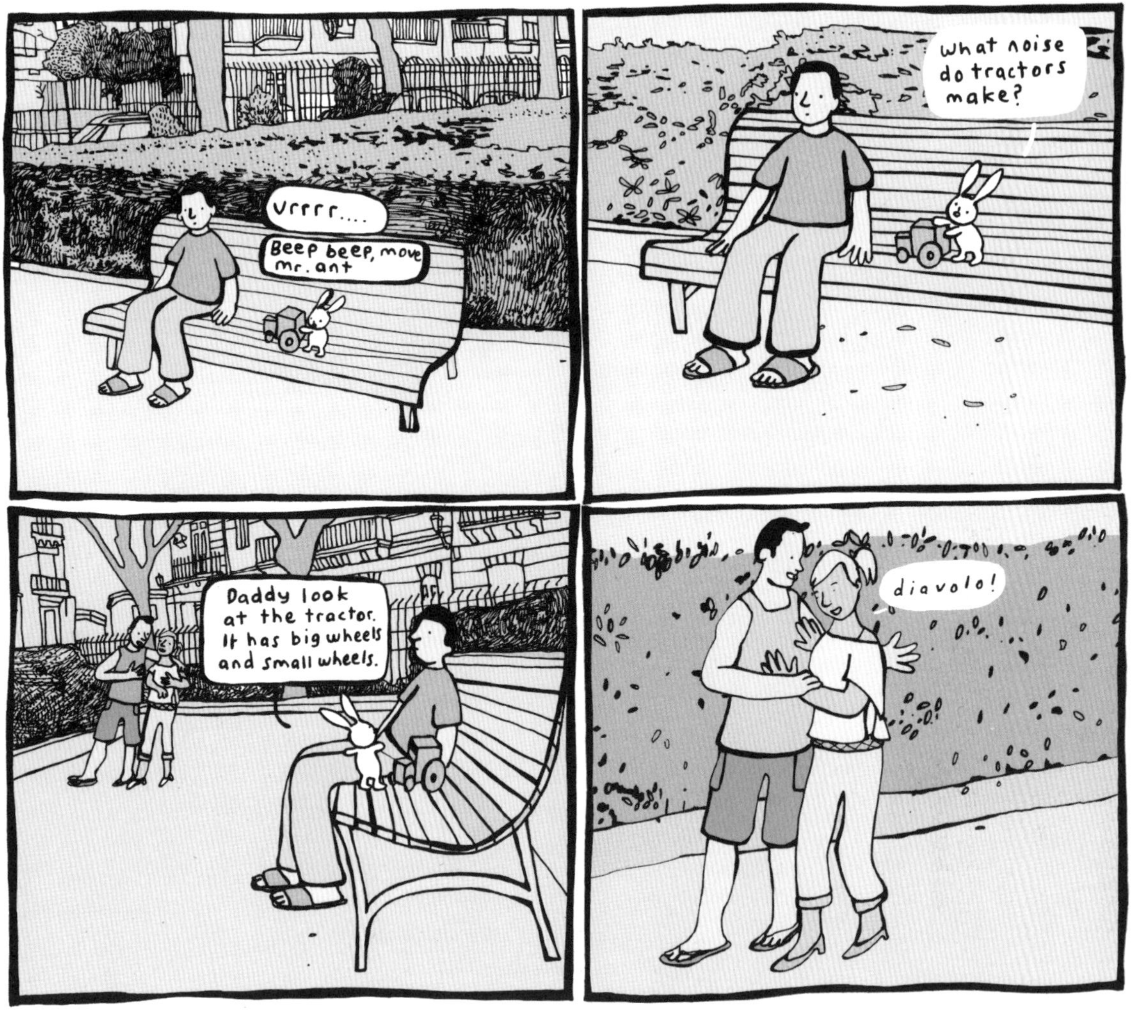
vrrrr....
Beep beep, move mr. ant
what noise do tractors make?
Daddy look at the tractor. It has big wheels and small wheels.
diavolo!

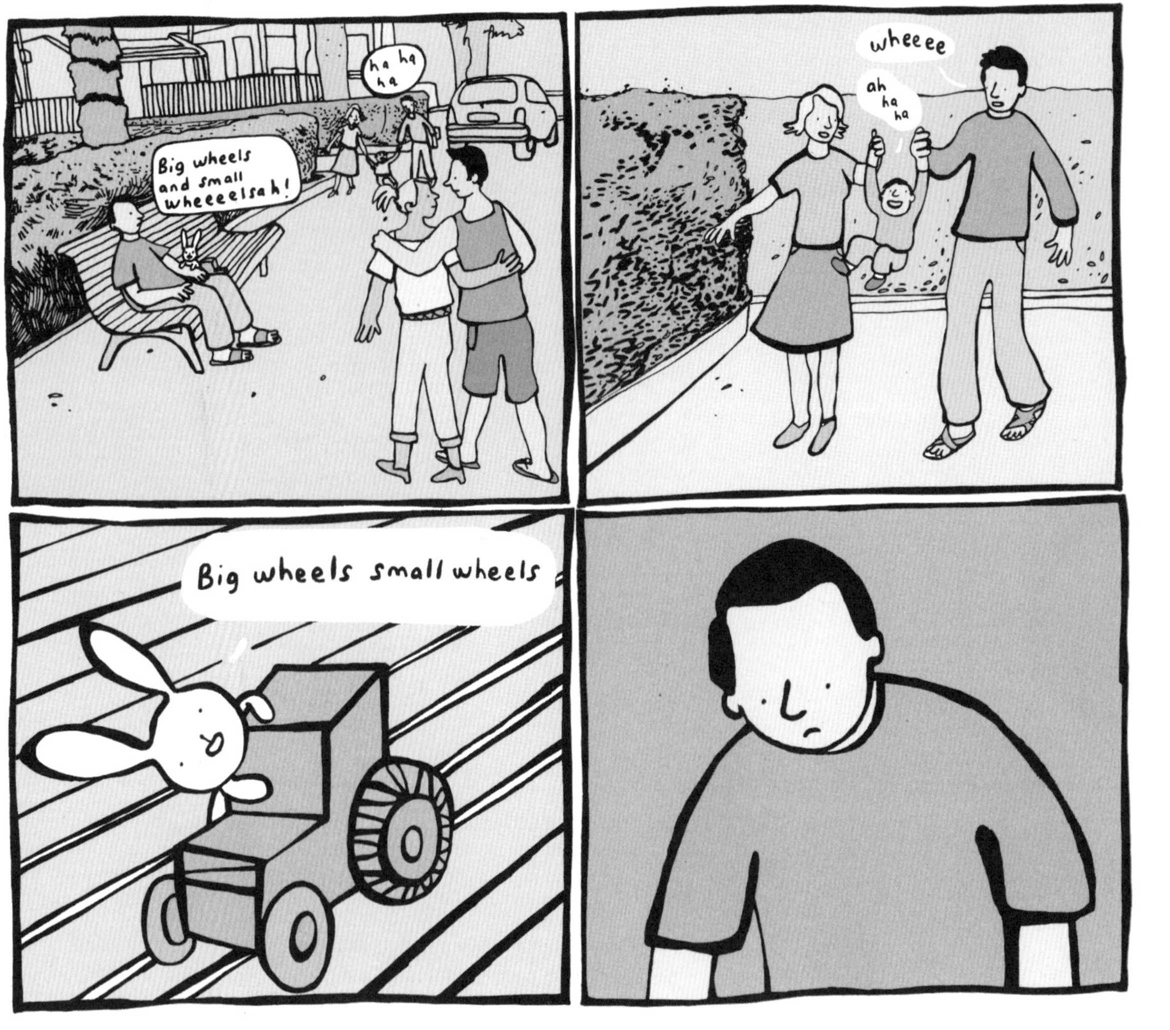

ha ha ha
Big wheels and small wheeeelsah!
wheeee
ah ha ha
Big wheels small wheels

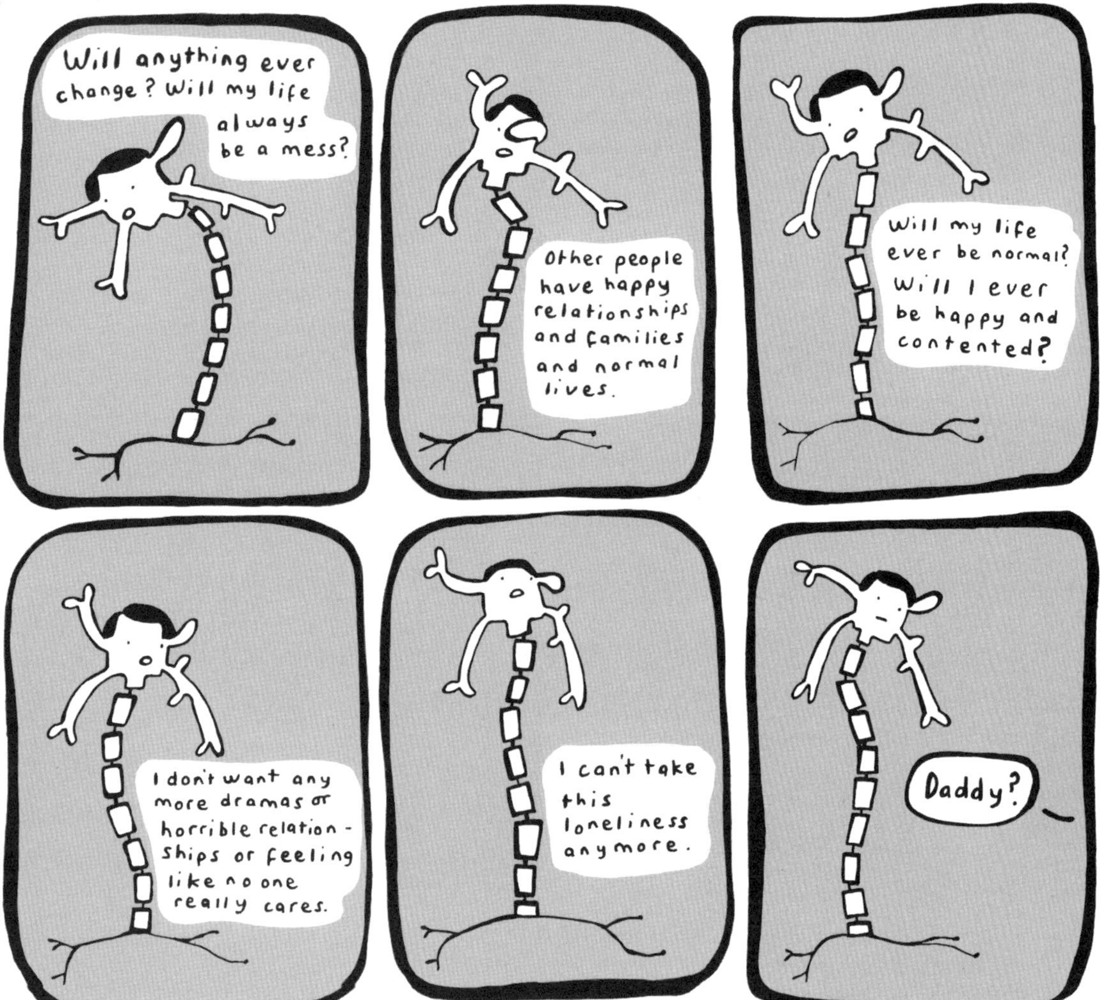
Will anything ever change? Will my life always be a mess?
Other people have happy relationships and families and normal lives.
Will my life ever be normal? Will I ever be happy and contented?
I don't want any more dramas or horrible relation-ships or feeling like no one really cares.
I can't take this loneliness anymore.
Daddy?

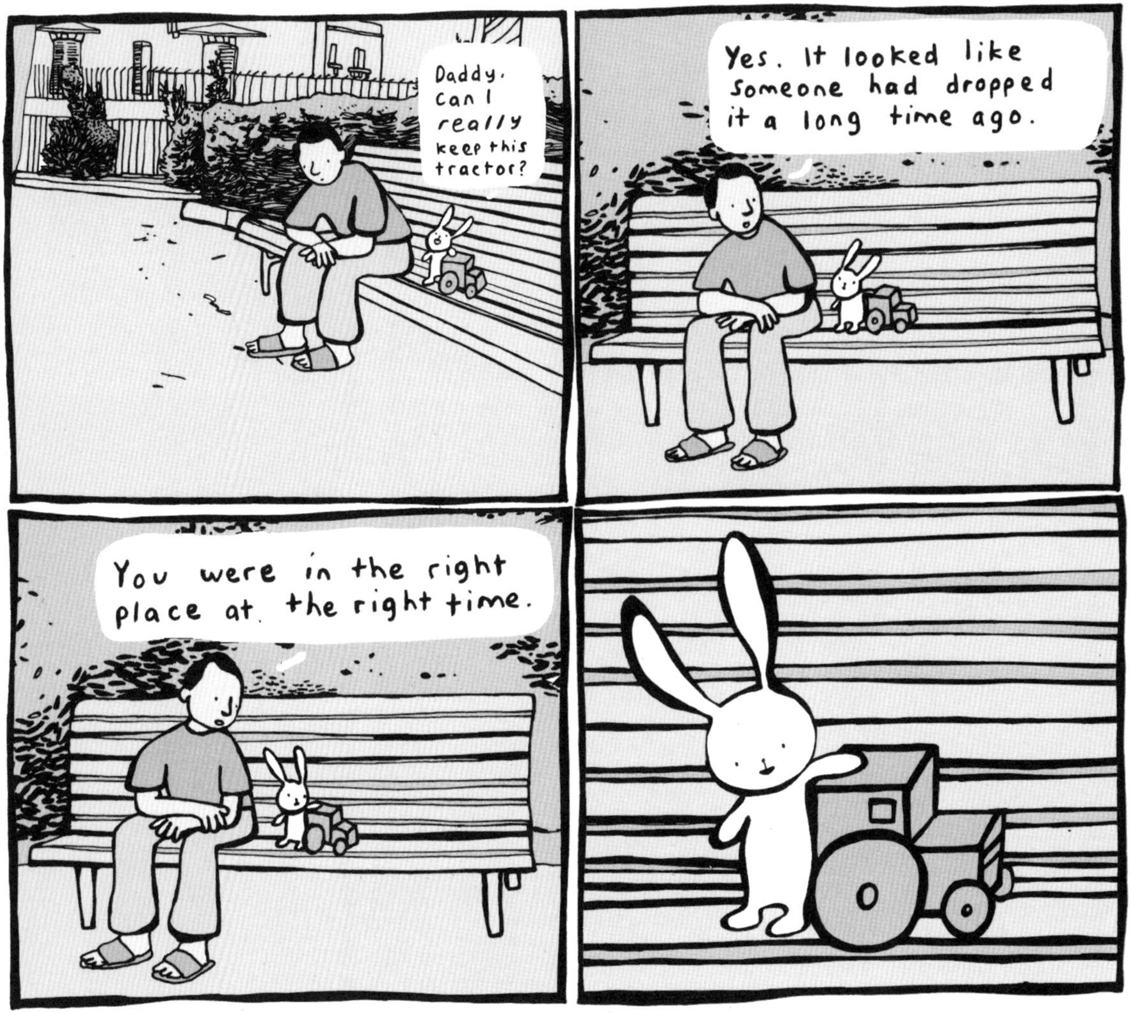
Daddy, can I really keep this tractor?
Yes. It looked like someone had dropped it a long time ago.
You were in the right place at the right time.

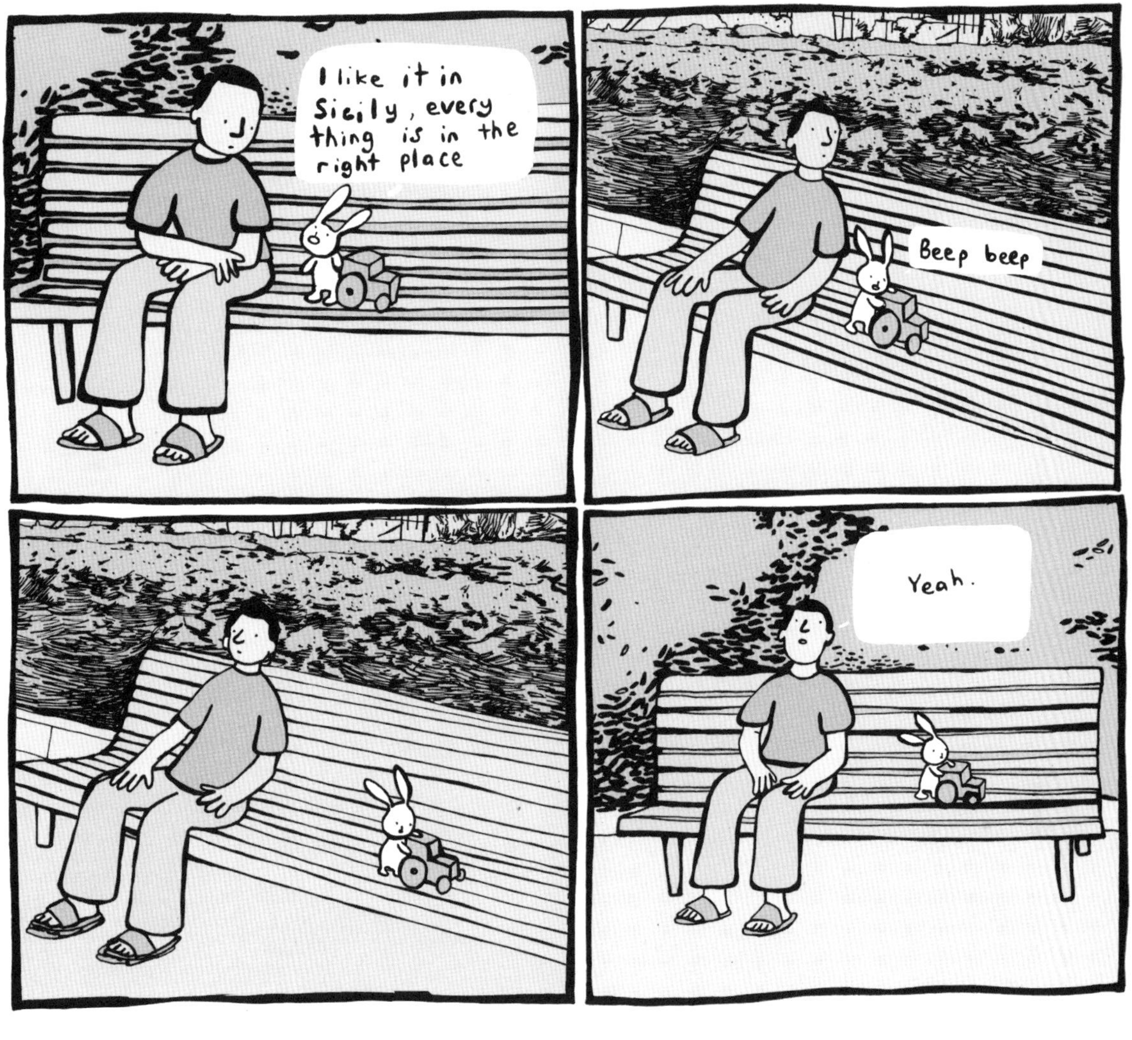
I like it in Sicily, every thing is in the right place
Beep beep
Yeah.

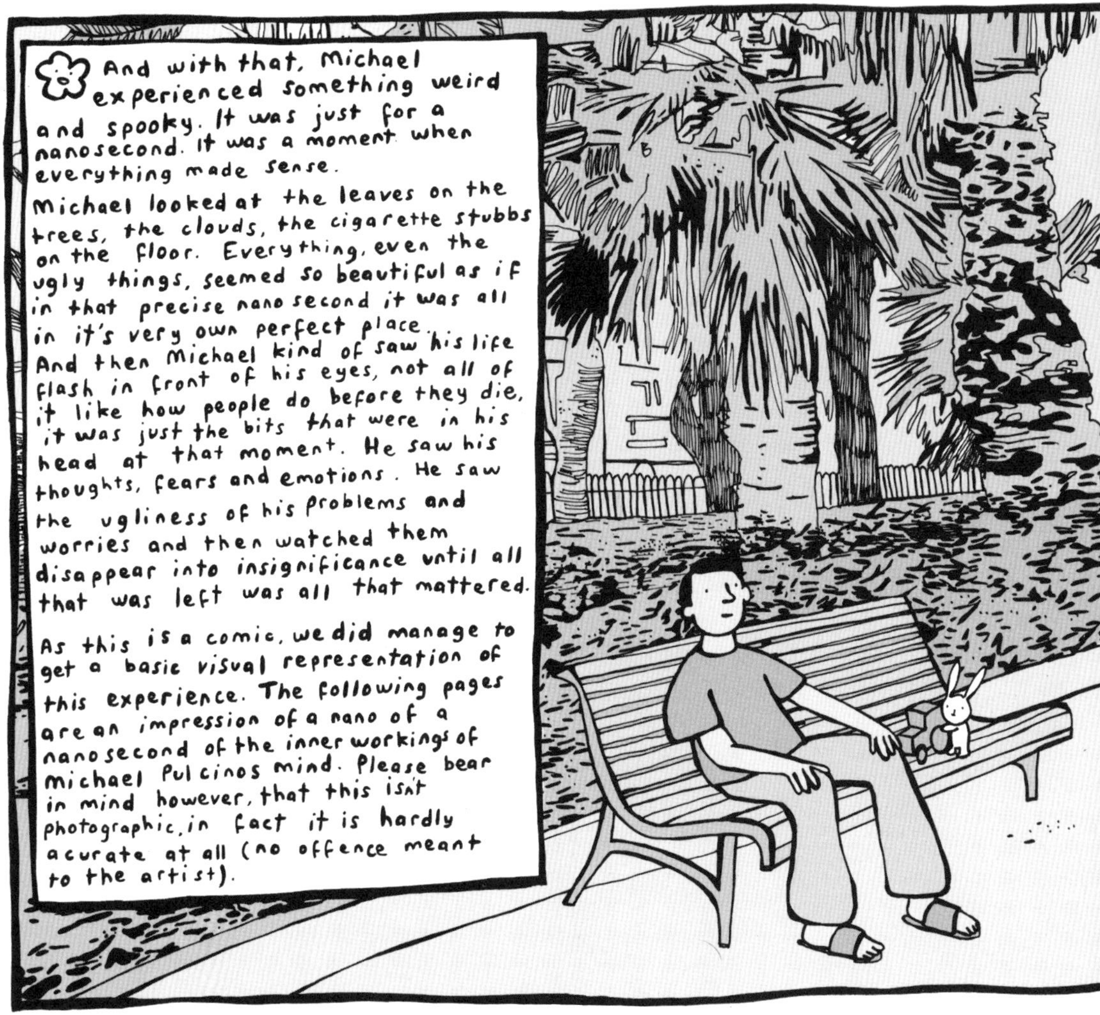
And with that, Michael experienced something weird and spooky. It was just for a nanosecond. It was a moment when everything made sense.
Michael looked at the leaves on the trees, the clouds, the cigarette stubbs on the floor. Everything, even the ugly things, seemed so beautiful as if in that precise nano second it was all in it's very own perfect place.
And then Michael kind of saw his life flash in front of his eyes, not all of it like how people do before they die, it was just the bits that were in his head at that moment. He saw his thoughts, fears and emotions. He saw the ugliness of his problems and worries and then watched them disappear into insignificance until all that was left was all that mattered.
As this is a comic, we did manage to get a basic visual representation of this experience. The following pages are an impression of a nano of a nanosecond of the inner workings of Michael Pulcinos mind. Please bear in mind however, that this isn't photographic, in fact it is hardly acurate at all (no offence meant to the artist).

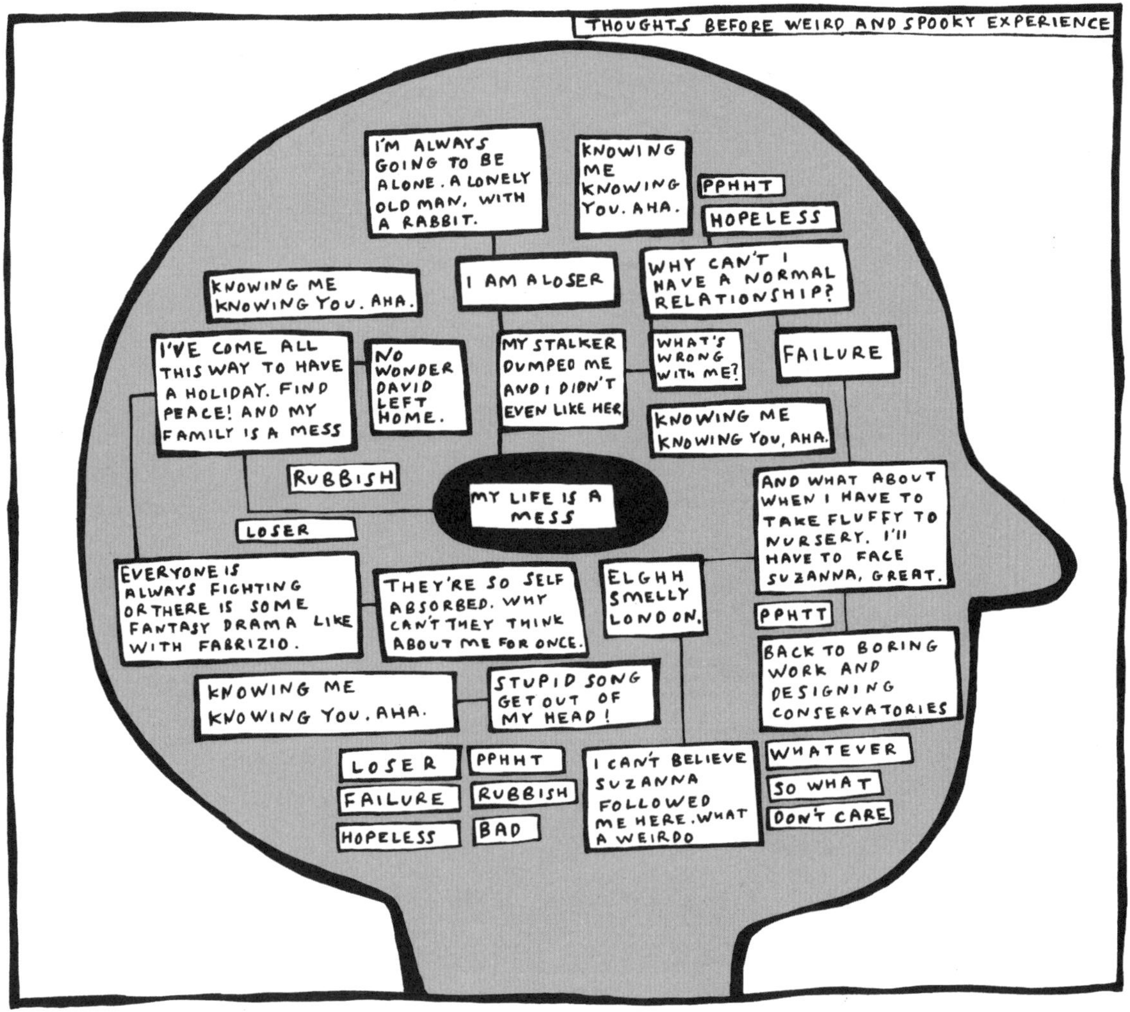
THOUGHTS BEFORE WEIRD AND SPOOKY EXPERIENCE
I'M ALWAYS GOING TO BE ALONE. A LONELY OLD MAN, WITH A RABBIT.
KNOWING ME KNOWING YOU. AHA.
PPHHT
HOPELESS
I AM A LOSER
WHY CAN'T I HAVE A NORMAL RELATIONSHIP?
KNOWING ME KNOWING YOU. AHA.
I'VE COME ALL THIS WAY TO HAVE A HOLIDAY. FIND PEACE! AND MY FAMILY IS A MESS
NO WONDER DAVID LEFT HOME.
MY STALKER DUMPED ME AND I DIDN'T EVEN LIKE HER
WHAT'S WRONG WITH ME?
FAILURE
KNOWING ME KNOWING YOU, AHA.
RUBBISH
MY LIFE IS A MESS
AND WHAT ABOUT WHEN I HAVE TO TAKE FLUFFY TO NURSERY. I'll HAVE TO FACE SUZANNA, GREAT.
LOSER
EVERYONE IS ALWAYS FIGHTING OR THERE IS SOME FANTASY DRAMA LIKE WITH FABRIZIO.
THEY'RE SO SELF ABSORBED. WHY CAN'T THEY THINK ABOUT ME FOR ONCE.
ELGHH SMELLY LONDON.
PPHTT
BACK TO BORING WORK AND DESIGNING CONSERVATORIES
KNOWING ME KNOWING YOU. AHA.
STUPID SONG GET OUT OF MY HEAD!
LOSER
PPHHT
FAILURE
RUBBISH
HOPELESS
BAD
I CAN'T BELIEVE SUZANNA FOLLOWED ME HERE. WHAT A WEIRDO
WHATEVER
SO WHAT
DON'T CARE

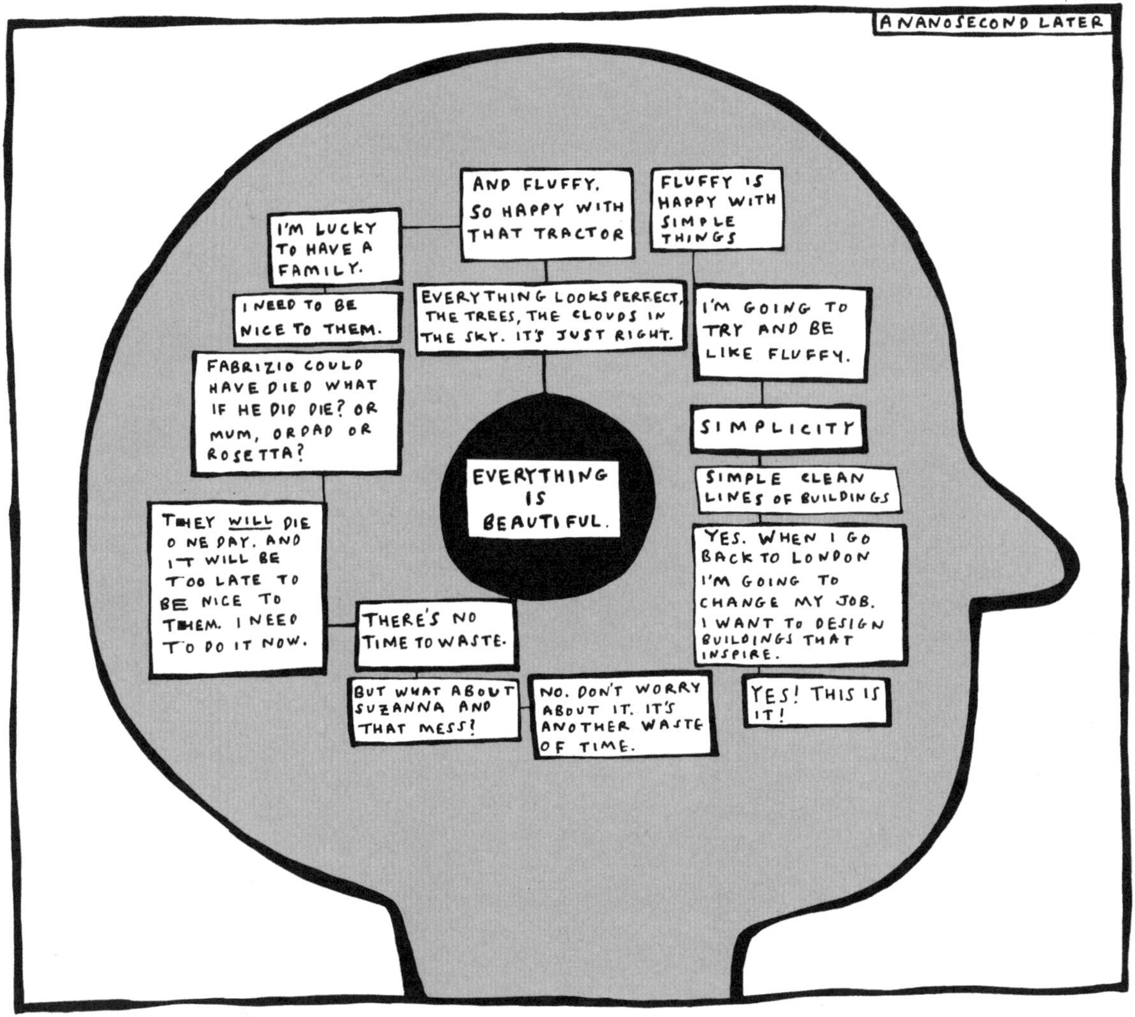
A NANOSECOND LATER
EVERYTHING IS BEAUTIFUL.
EVERYTHING LOOKS PERFECT, THE TREES, THE CLOUDS IN THE SKY. IT'S JUST RIGHT.
AND FLUFFY. SO HAPPY WITH THAT TRACTOR
I'M LUCKY TO HAVE A FAMILY.
I NEED TO BE NICE TO THEM.
FABRIZIO COULD HAVE DIED WHAT IF HE DID DIE? OR MUM, OR DAD OR ROSETTA?
THEY WILL DIE ONE DAY. AND IT WILL BE TOO LATE TO BE NICE TO THEM. I NEED TO DO IT NOW.
THERE'S NO TIME TO WASTE.
BUT WHAT ABOUT SUZANNA AND THAT MESS?
NO. DON'T WORRY ABOUT IT. IT'S ANOTHER WASTE OF TIME.
FLUFFY IS HAPPY WITH SIMPLE THINGS
I'M GOING TO TRY AND BE LIKE FLUFFY.
SIMPLICITY
SIMPLE CLEAN LINES OF BUILDINGS
YES. WHEN I GO BACK TO LONDON I'M GOING TO CHANGE MY JOB. I WANT TO DESIGN BUILDINGS THAT INSPIRE.
YES! THIS IS IT!

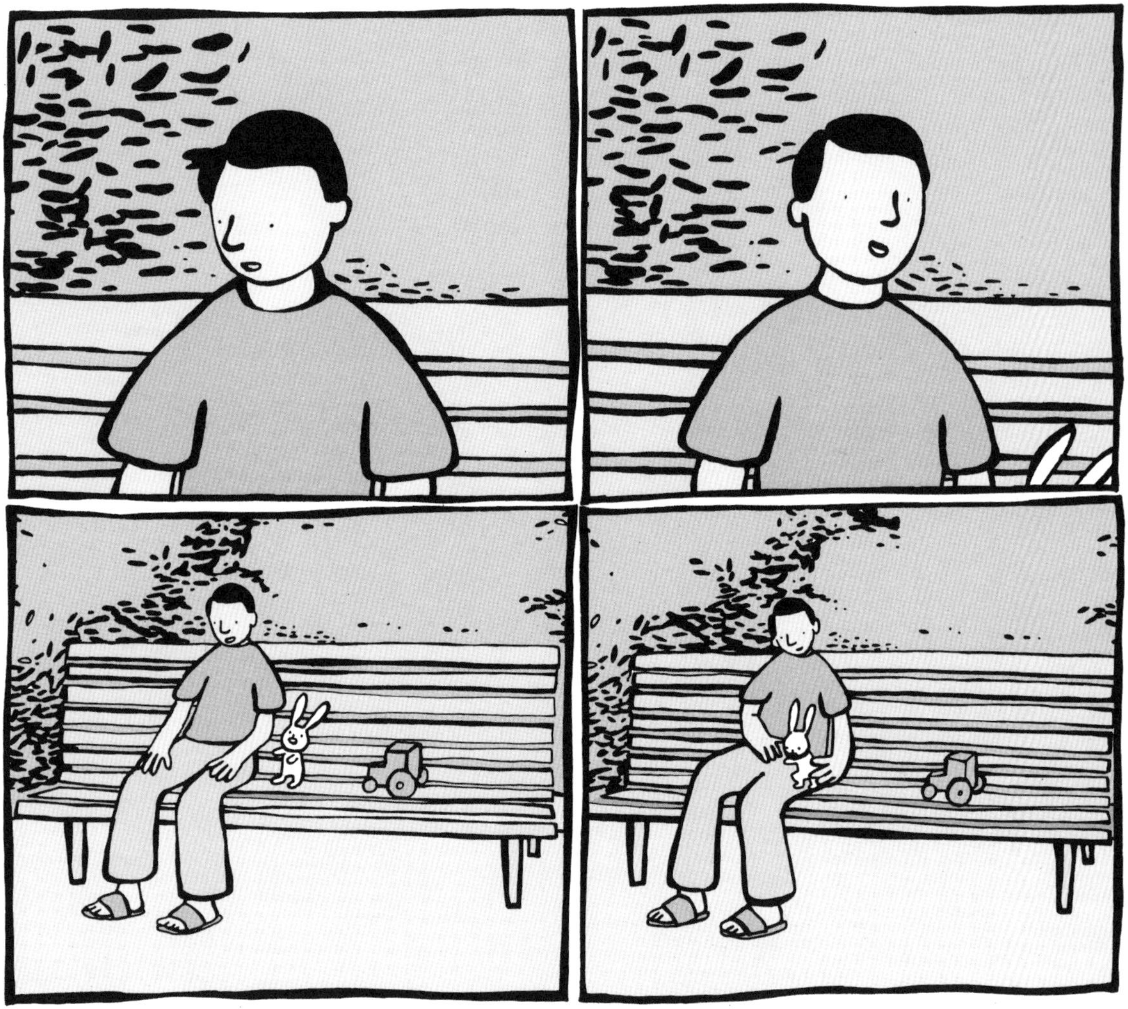

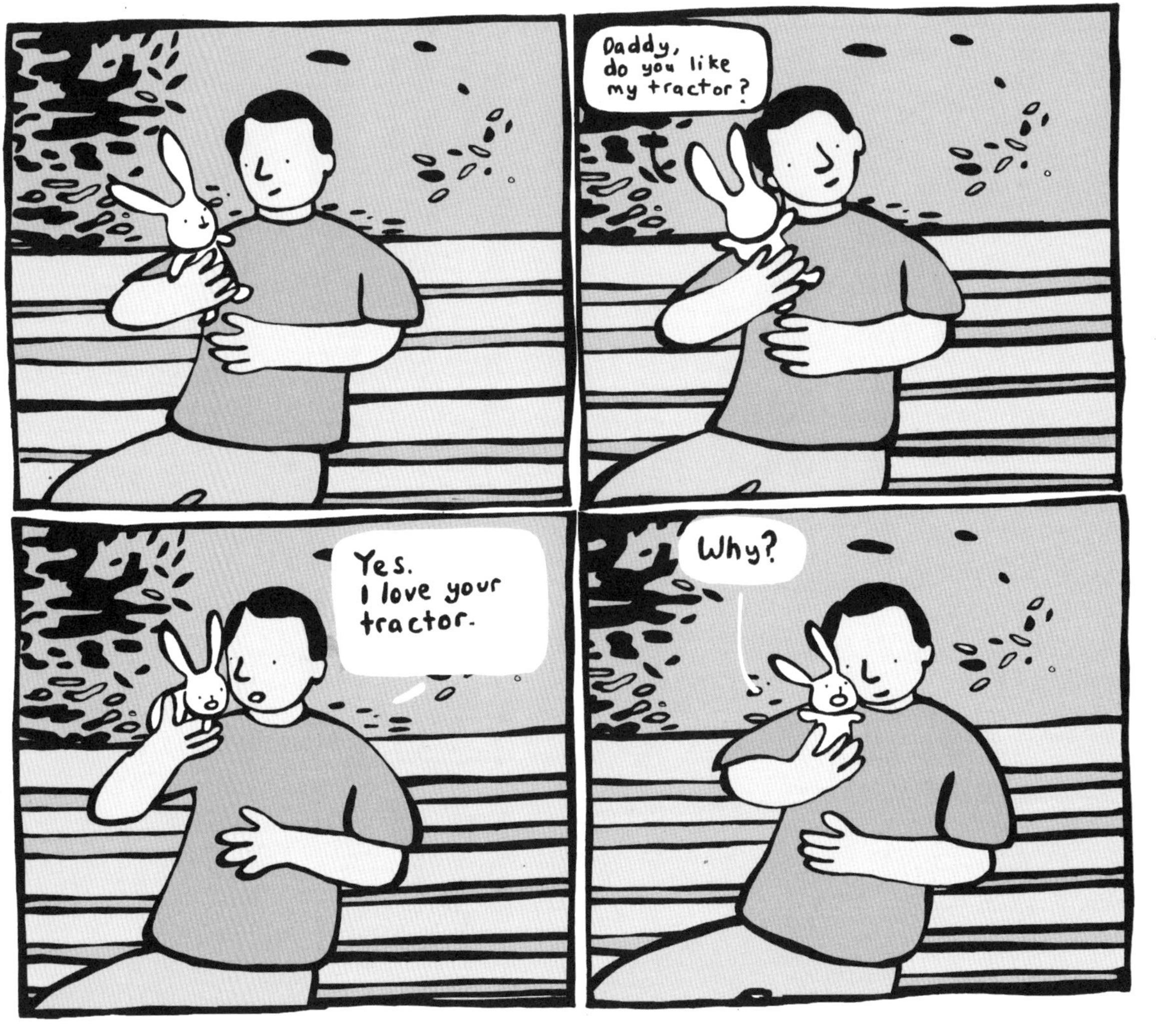
Daddy, do you like my tractor?
Yes. I love your tractor.
Why?

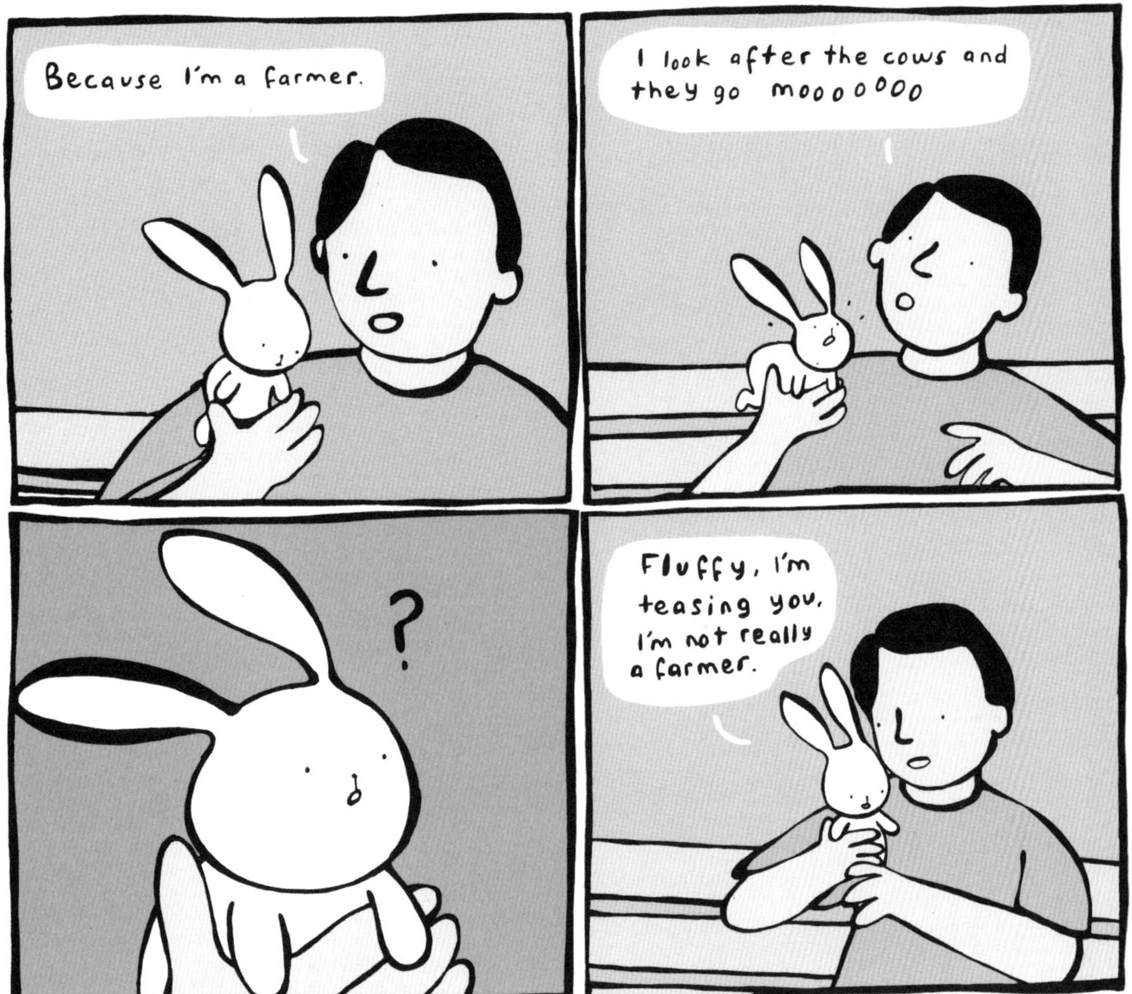
Because I'm a farmer.
I look after the cows and they go moooooOOo
?
Fluffy, I'm teasing you, I'm not really a farmer.

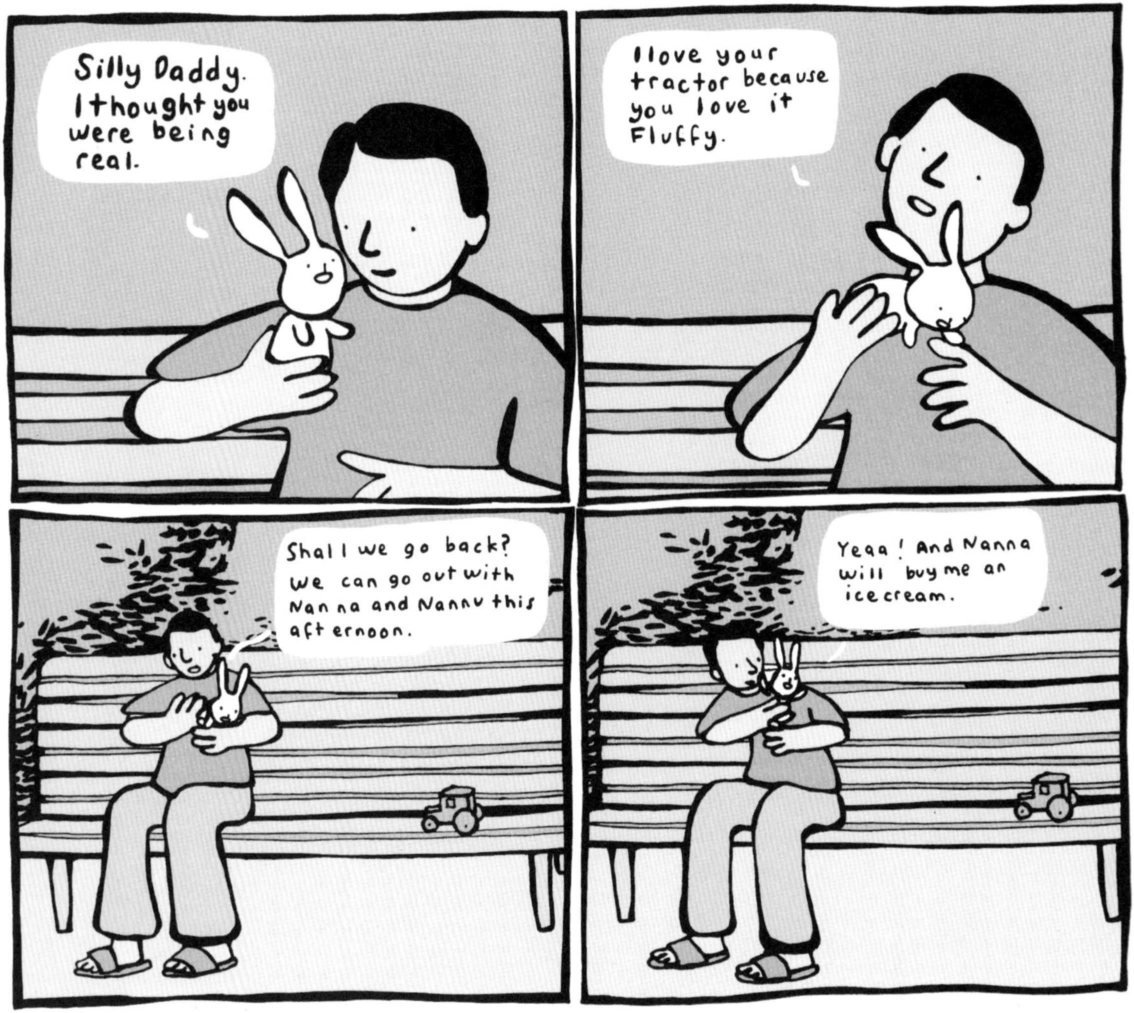
Silly Daddy. I thought you were being real.
I love your tractor because you love it Fluffy.
Shall we go back? We can go out with Nanna and Nannu this afternoon.
Yeaa! And Nanna will buy me an ice cream.

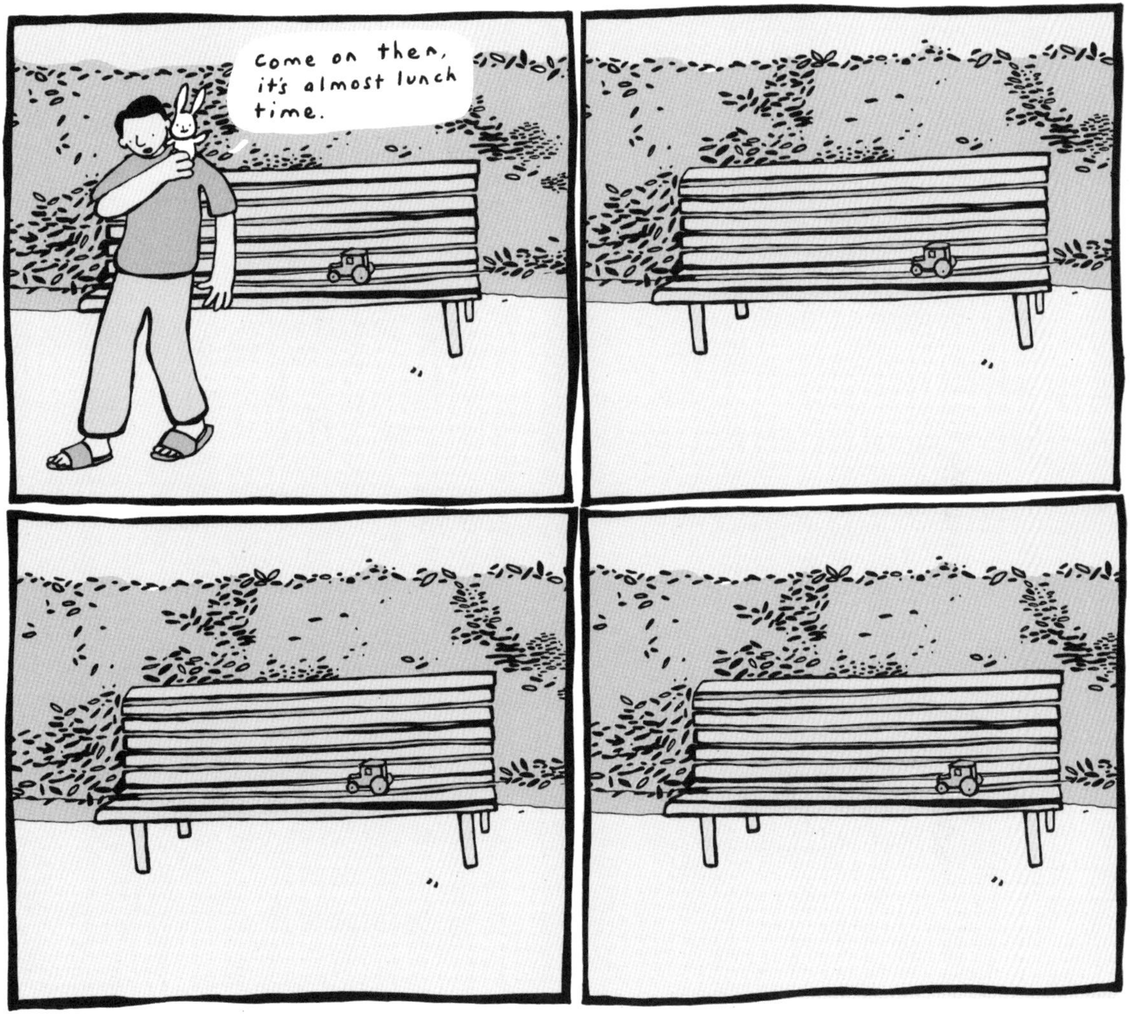
come on then, it's almost lunch time.

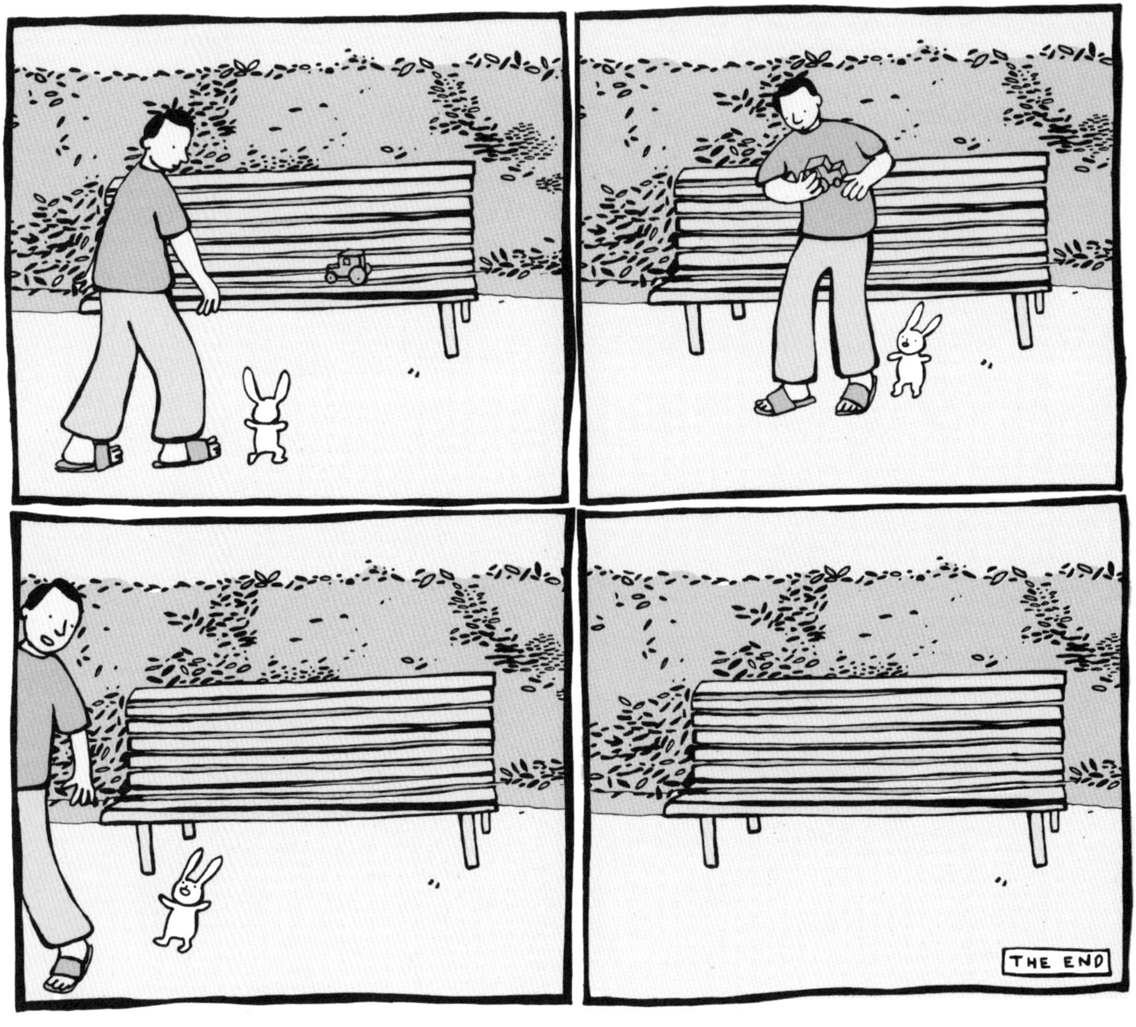
THE END

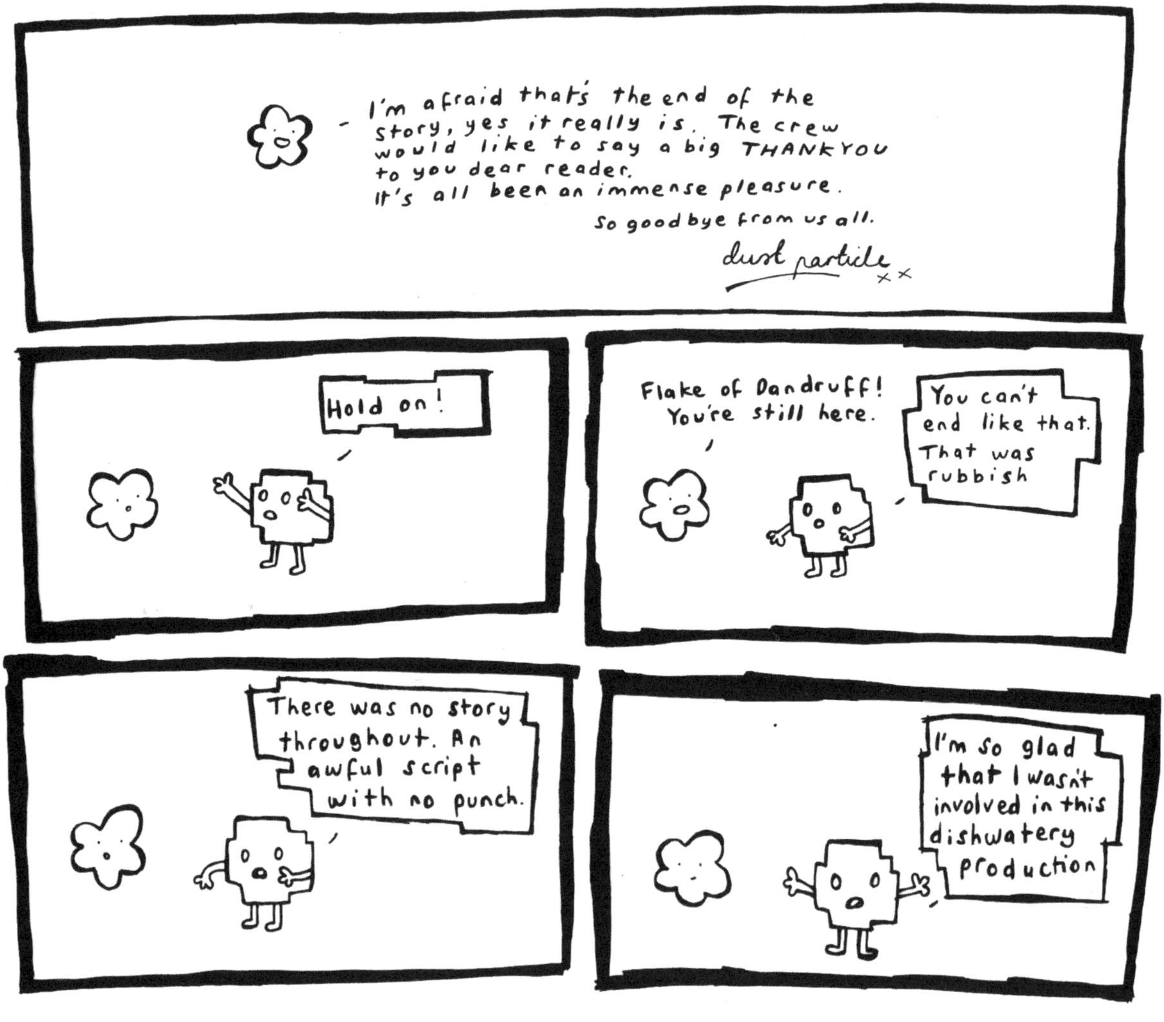
I'm afraid that's the end of the story, yes it really is. The crew would like to say a big THANKYOU to you dear reader.
It's all been an immense pleasure.
So goodbye from us all.
dust particle xx
Hold on!
Flake of Dandruff! You're still here.
You can't end like that. That was rubbish
There was no story throughout. An awful script with no punch.
I'm so glad that I wasn't involved in this dishwatery production

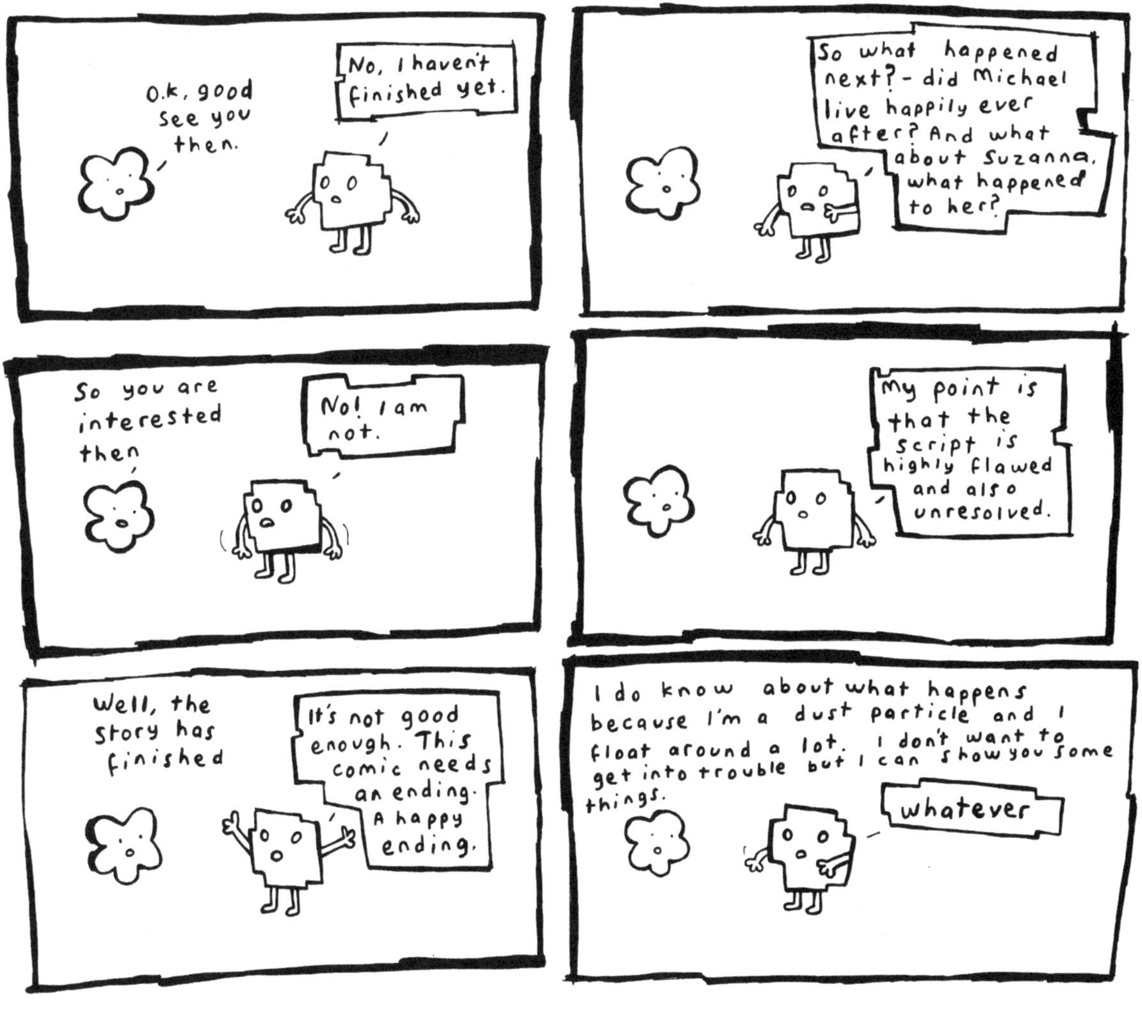
No, I haven't finished yet.
O.k, good see you then.
So what happened next? - did Michael live happily ever after? And what about Suzanna, what happened to her?
So you are interested then
No! I am not.
My point is that the script is highly flawed and also unresolved.
Well, the story has finished
It's not good enough. This comic needs an ending. A happy ending.
I do know about what happens because I'm a dust particle and I float around a lot. I don't want to get into trouble but I can show you some things.
whatever

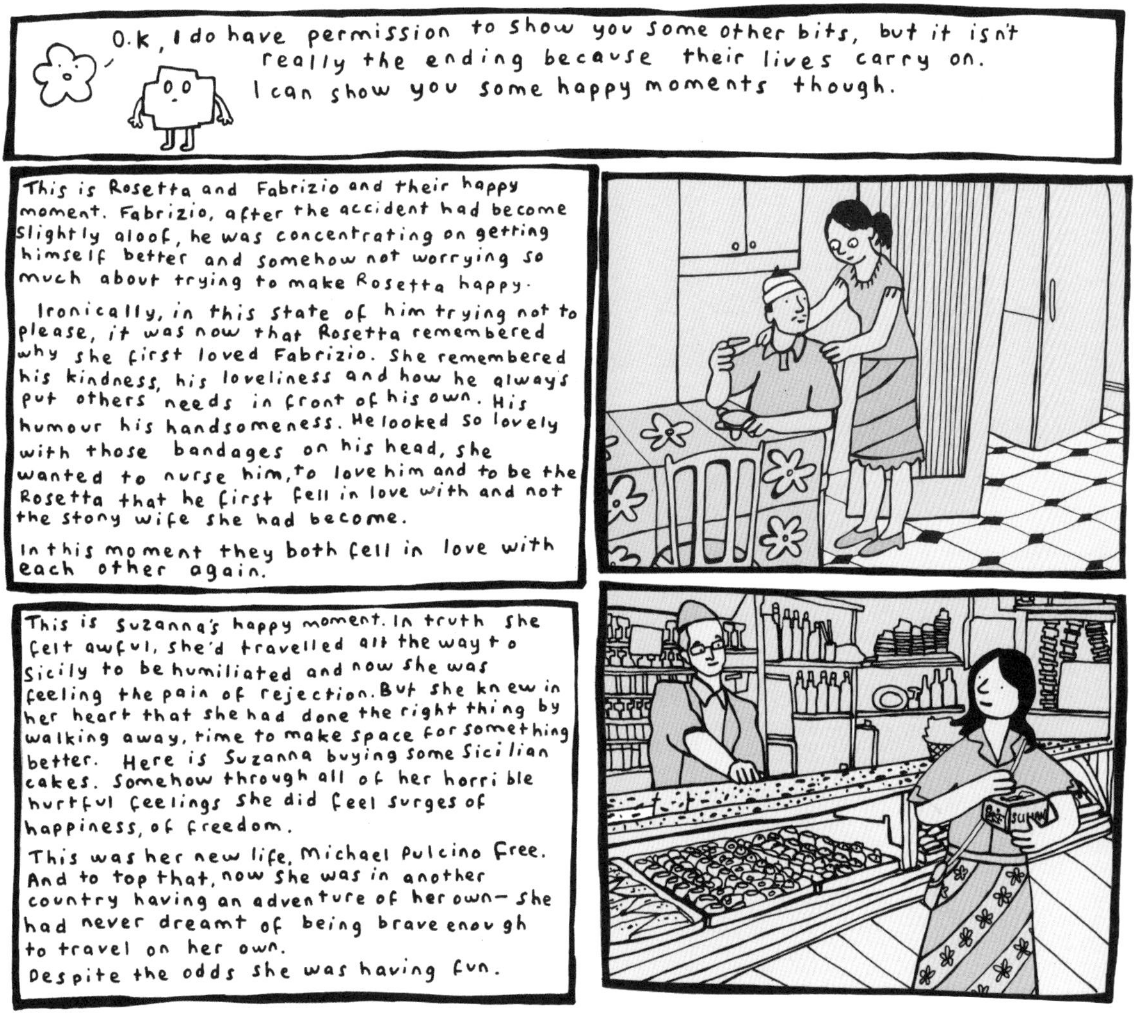
O.k, I do have permission to show you some other bits, but it isn't really the ending because their lives carry on. I can show you some happy moments though.
This is Rosetta and Fabrizio and their happy moment. Fabrizio, after the accident had become slightly aloof, he was concentrating on getting himself better and somehow not worrying so much about trying to make Rosetta happy.
Ironically, in this state of him trying not to please, it was now that Rosetta remembered why she first loved Fabrizio. She remembered his kindness, his loveliness and how he always put others' needs in front of his own. His humour his handsomeness. He looked so lovely with those bandages on his head, she wanted to nurse him, to love him and to be the Rosetta that he first fell in love with and not the stony wife she had become.
In this moment they both fell in love with each other again.
This is Suzanna's happy moment. In truth she felt awful, she'd travelled all the way to Sicily to be humiliated and now she was feeling the pain of rejection. But she knew in her heart that she had done the right thing by walking away, time to make space for something better. Here is Suzanna buying some Sicilian cakes. Somehow through all of her horrible hurtful feelings she did feel surges of happiness, of freedom.
This was her new life, Michael Pulcino free. And to top that, now she was in another country having an adventure of her own — she had never dreamt of being brave enough to travel on her own.
Despite the odds she was having fun.

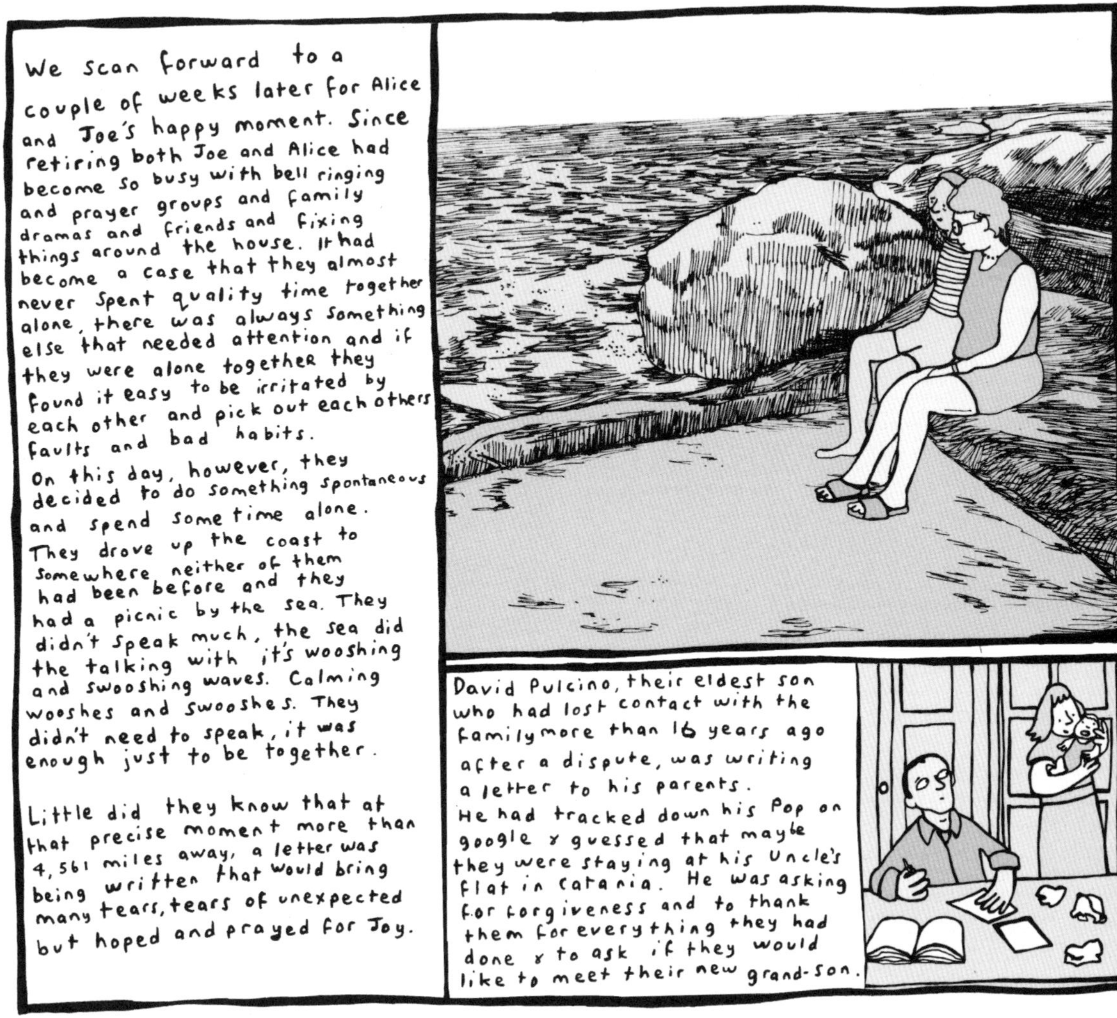

We scan forward to a couple of weeks later for Alice and Joe's happy moment. Since retiring both Joe and Alice had become so busy with bell ringing and prayer groups and family dramas and friends and fixing things around the house. It had become a case that they almost never spent quality time together alone, there was always something else that needed attention and if they were alone together they found it easy to be irritated by each other and pick out each others faults and bad habits.
On this day, however, they decided to do something spontaneous and spend some time alone. They drove up the coast to somewhere neither of them had been before and they had a picnic by the sea. They didn't speak much, the sea did the talking with it's wooshing and swooshing waves. Calming wooshes and swooshes. They didn't need to speak, it was enough just to be together.
Little did they know that at that precise moment more than 4,561 miles away, a letter was being written that would bring many tears, tears of unexpected but hoped and prayed for Joy.
David Pulcino, their eldest son who had lost contact with the family more than 16 years ago after a dispute, was writing a letter to his parents.
He had tracked down his Pop on google & guessed that maybe they were staying at his Uncle's flat in Catania. He was asking for forgiveness and to thank them for everything they had done & to ask if they would like to meet their new grand-son.

and then do you remember this little girl? Her name is Silvia, she met Fluffy on the train in chapter 2. She and her mother Angela were on holiday in Italy, going to Naples. Angela wanted to get away from it all, for them to experience something that might actually be fun. She had just been through a painful and messy divorce with Silvia's Dad. The trip didn't turn out to be that enjoyable though, everything seemed to remind Angela of her failed relationship especially and unfortunately for Silvia, her striking resemblance to her father. She got the brunt of her mother's hurt and anger, it was easier to stay out of her way and keep quiet. That was when the accident happened. Silvia already had a fractured arm from tripping over a ball just before the holiday but as she played quietly on her own stepping on and off a kerb, she somehow managed to lose balance and break both her arm and leg and fracture the other. It was hideous. They were flown home to Munich and Silvia had day care from a nurse whilst her mother was at work. You would imagine this to be miserable, but no, this was Silvia's happy moment, she didn't want those weeks to end or for her bandages to be taken off. The nurse who was looking after her was the most kind, warm, human being that Silvia had ever met. She told her gentle and funny stories about her youth and she listened to Silvia like no one had ever listened before. As the nurse took care of her broken limbs, they healed and so did the invisible hurts inside of Silvia.

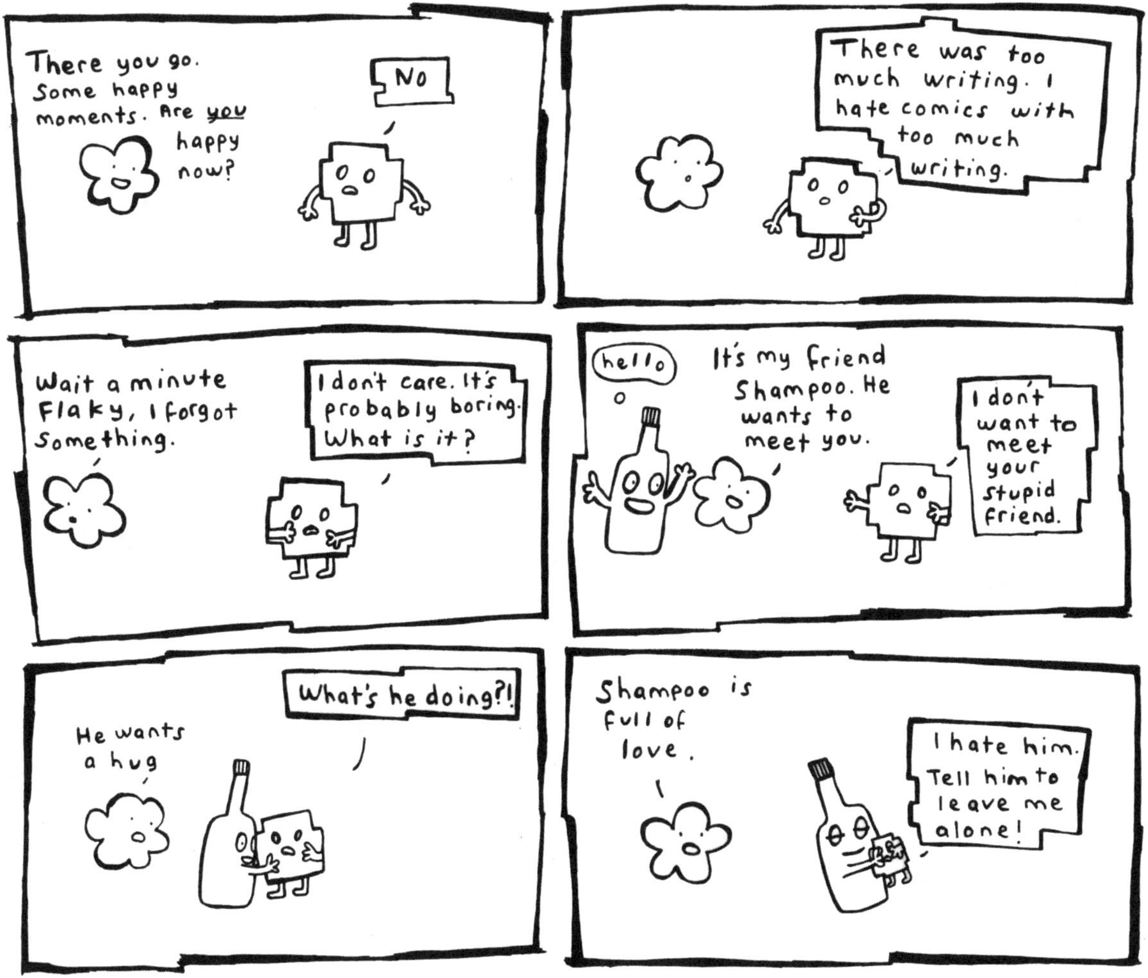
There you go. Some happy moments. Are you happy now?
No
There was too much writing. I hate comics with too much writing.
Wait a minute Flaky, I forgot something.
I don't care. It's probably boring. What is it?
hello
It's my friend Shampoo. He wants to meet you.
I don't want to meet your stupid friend.
What's he doing?!
He wants a hug
Shampoo is full of love.
I hate him. Tell him to leave me alone!

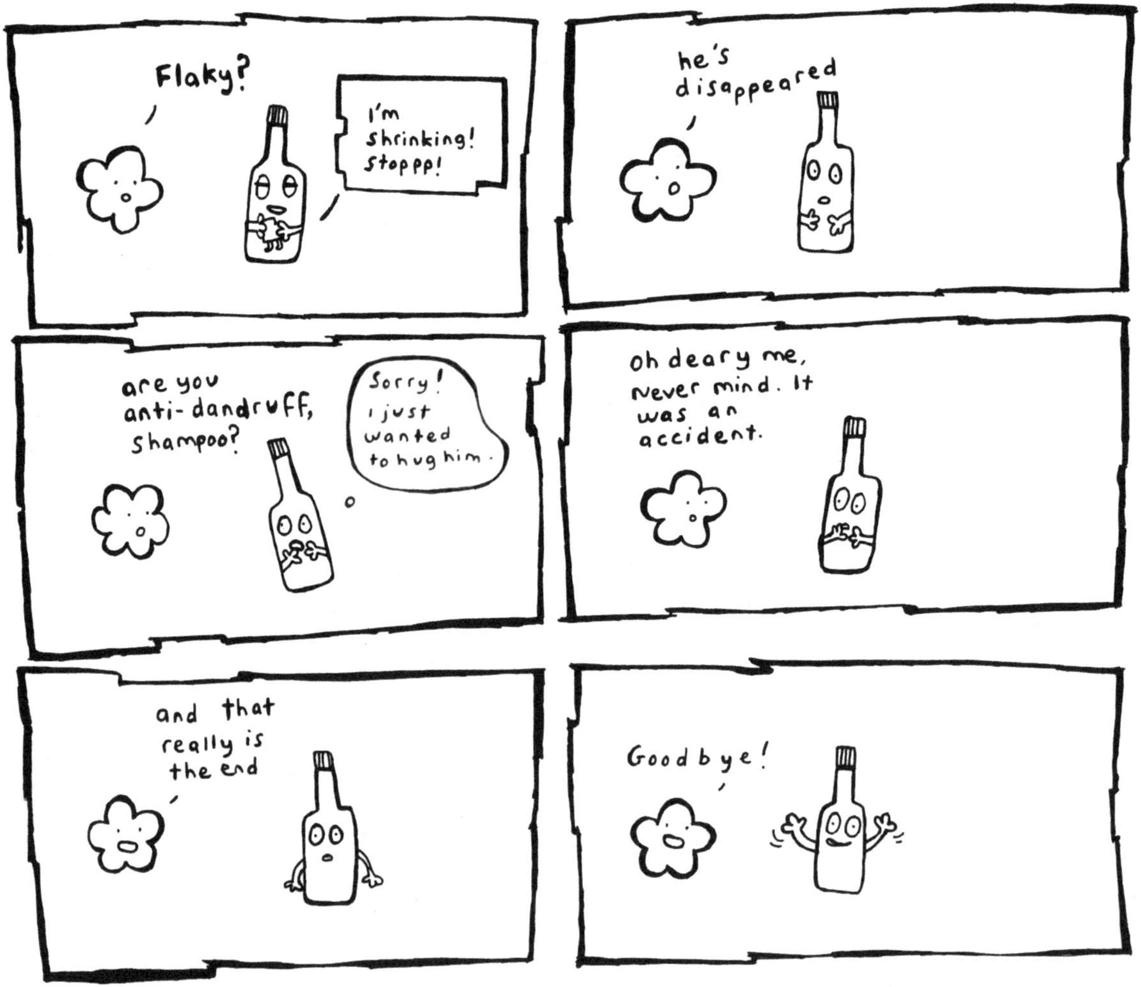
Flaky?
I'm shrinking! Stoppp!
he's disappeared
are you anti-dandruff, shampoo?
Sorry! I just wanted to hug him.
Oh deary me, Never mind. It was an accident.
and that really is the end
Goodbye!

. *the end*